# )F LEGAL WORDS AND PHRASES

WITH APPENDICES

NING ABBREVIATIONS AND REFERENCES TO REPORTS
) GIVING THE MEANING OF LATIN AND FRENCH
MAXIMS COMMONLY FOUND IN LAW BOOKS

BY
WILLIAM C. COCHRAN
Of the Cincinnati Bar

CINCINNATI
ROBERT CLARKE & CO
1888

ELECTROTYPED BY
CAMPBELL & CO.
CINCINNATI, OHIO.

TO THE HONORABLE

JACOB D. COX, A.M., LL.D.,

PRESIDENT OF THE UNIVERSITY OF CINCINNATI AND DEAN OF THE LAW SCHOOL OF THE CINCINNATI COLLEGE,

LAWYER, SOLDIER, STATESMAN, AND SCHOLAR,

**This Work is Dedicated,**

AS A TOKEN OF AFFECTIONATE REGARD,

BY

THE AUTHOR.

# PREFACE.

It is the aim of this book to give, in condensed form, the meaning and application of all such words, phrases, maxims, abbreviations and references to reports, as a student of the law will be likely to encounter in his reading, and which the ordinary knowledge of the English language might not enable him to understand. The long dissertations on the law, which appear in older and larger dictionaries, and which, useful as they are in works approaching the magnitude of an encyclopædia, are incompatible with the objects of this book, have been avoided; yet, where an example, or illustration of the use of a word could be stated in brief, so as to help the student to a fuller understanding of its meaning and application, it has been supplied.

To bring the work within the required compass, a large number of obsolete words and phrases, whose meaning is a matter of curiosity rather than importance, and many words of current English usage, which can not be said to have any special significance in connection with the law, have been omitted. Where one form of a word is used it has not been deemed necessary to introduce other forms; the given meaning of the *verb*, for instance, being quite sufficient to enable the student of ordinary intelligence to understand *nouns*, *adjectives*, or *participles*, derived from the same root.

Condensation and facility of reference have been further secured by arranging in one paragraph phrases beginning with the same word, and compound words having the same stem; by using **bold-faced type** to point out with distinctness the successive words or phrases defined; and by the frequent use of cross-references. While intended primarily for the student, it is hoped that the book may also prove a serviceable desk companion for the practicing lawyer; and, in this connection, special attention is called to the very full table of abbreviations and references to the reports, contained in Appendix A.

The author can not boast, as Jacob did in 1732, "that considerable above two Thirds of my Work, with some Hundreds of very material Words, are entirely New in a Performance of this Kind;" or that, "There is not any Thing in the following Dictionary directly the same as appears elsewhere;" or that, "I now have render'd my Useful Book so full and perfect as to admit of little or no further Improvement."

He is indebted to a great and learned body of lexicographers, digesters, and law writers, whose works he has consulted with much profit, and his acknowledgments are especially due to Wharton's Law Lexicon, and Bouvier's Law Dictionary.

While *perfection* is not claimed for it, he hopes that the book will be found to possess *utility*; and if it affords assistance to others, he will feel amply rewarded for the time and thought he has bestowed upon it.

W. C. COCHRAN.

CINCINNATI, *August* 1, 1888.

THE

# STUDENTS' LAW LEXICON.

---

## A.

**A, or ab,** *l.*, from; by; in; of; at. **Ab actis,** one who writes from words spoken; a notary, or reporter. **Ab ante,** in advance. **Ab antecedente,** beforehand. **Ab antiquo,** from ancient time. **A cancellis,** at the cancelli; the chancellor. **A consiliis,** of counsel; a counsellor. **Ab extra,** from without. **A fortiori,** by so much the stronger; all the more. **Ab inconvenienti,** from the inconvenience or hardship (of the case). **Ab initio,** from the beginning. **Ab intestato,** from one who died without making a will. **Ab invito,** unwillingly. **Ab irato,** by one who is angry. **A latere,** from the side of; collateral. **A me,** from me. **A mensa et thoro,** from bed and board; a kind of divorce (*q. v.*) **A posteriori, A priori,** see *Argument*. **A quo,** from which. **A retro,** from back; in arrears. **A vinculo matrimonii,** from the bond of marriage; a complete divorce (*q. v.*)

**A,** *fr.*, of; at; to; for; in; with. **A aver et tener,** to have and to hold. **A prendre,** to take, as from the soil. **A rendre,** to render, or yield, as services or rent.

**Abandonment,** desertion, by husband or wife. (2) Relinquishment, or surrender of property, or rights. (3) Leaving a vessel and giving it up as a total loss. (4) Surrendering to the underwriters all interest in the thing insured.

**Abactor,** one who steals and drives away cattle by herds.

**Abandum,** or **abandun,** any thing abandoned, forfeited, or confiscated.

**Abatement,** a making less, or destroying. A suspension or termination of an action for want of proper parties, or a de-

---

NOTE.—Abbreviations used in the text are: *l.*, Latin; *fr.*, French; *L. fr.*, Law French; Sc., Scotch; Rom., Roman or Civil Law; (*q. v.*), which see; *e. g.*, for example; *i. e.*, that is; *scil.*, being understood.

fect in the writ or its service. (2) A reduction of rent, interest, or an amount due. (3) A removal or cessation of a nuisance. (4) A diminution of a freehold by the entry of a stranger upon lands after the death of the former owner and before the heirs or devisees take possession. (5) The reduction of a legacy when an estate is insufficient to pay all debts and legacies. (6) A reduction of duties on account of damage to imported goods, or a decrease in the amount of taxes assessed upon a particular person or property. See *Rebate.*

**Abator,** or **Abater,** one who abates a nuisance. (2) One who enters into a house or land vacant by the death of the former possessor, and not yet taken possession of by his heir or devisee. See *Disseisin, Intrusion.*

**Abatuda,** or **Abatude,** any thing diminished. *Moneta abatuda* is money clipped and so diminished in value.

**Abavus** (Rom.), a great grandfather's father. See *Atavus.*

**Abbreviations.** See Appendix A.

**Abbreviatio Placitorum,** an abstract of ancient pleadings, prior to the year books.

**Abbroach,** to monopolize goods or forestall a market.

**Abdicate,** to renounce the throne or government. (2) (Rom.), to disinherit.

**Abduction,** forcibly taking away a man's wife, child, or maid.

**Abearance,** carriage or behavior.

**Abeched,** satisfied.

**Aberemurder,** deliberate murder, as distinguished from the less heinous crime of manslaughter, or killing in chance medley.

**Abet,** to aid, encourage, or incite another to commit a crime. An **abettor** is one who is present inciting the principal.

**Abeyance,** in expectation; the condition of an estate or right when there is no person presently entitled to it.

**Abide,** to perform, obey, or conform to an order of court, or an award of arbitrators.

**Abigeus,** same as *Abactor* (*q.v.*).

**Abjudicate,** to give away or transfer by judgment.

**Abjuration,** a renunciation of allegiance upon oath. An oath, formerly taken by a felon who had claimed sanctuary, to forsake the realm forever.

**Abortion,** a miscarriage, or premature expulsion of the foetus. To procure or produce an abortion was formerly a misdemeanor, and is now generally declared a felony.

**Abridgment,** an orderly abstract or digest of the law.

The principal are Brooke's, Fitzherbert's, Rolle's, Comyn's, Viner's, and Bacon's. The more recent ones are called Digests, *e.g.*, Fisher's.

**Abrogate,** to annul or repeal a former law by the passage of a new one. **Abrogation** may be by express words, or by necessary inplication.

**Abscond,** to leave one's usual residence, or to conceal one's self in order to avoid legal proceedings.

**Absence,** non-appearance; being away from one's domicile. When continued for seven years, without the person being heard from, a presumption of death arises. *Absence beyond seas, i.e.*, from the United Kingdom and the adjacent (including the Channel) islands, was a disability (*q.v.*,) and still in some cases entitles a person to an extension of time for pleading or appealing. The operation of statues of *Limitation* (*q. v.*) is generally suspended or modified as *against* a person who absents himself from the country or state in which a cause of action arises, though seldom, *in favor* of the absentee.

**Absolute,** complete; unconditional; not relative or qualified. A rule absolute is an order which can be forthwith enforced in contradistinction to a rule *nisi*, which commands the opposite party to appear on a day therein named, and *show cause* why he should not perform the act, or submit to the terms therein set forth. In default of his appearance or showing good cause, the rule is made absolute.

**Absolution,** the dismissal of a charge, declaration of a person's innocence, or remission of sins or penalties.

**Absque,** *l.*, without. **Absque aliquo inde reddendo,** without reserving any rent therefrom; used of a grant by the crown. **Absque hoc,** without this; technical words of exception formerly made use of in a special traverse. **Absque impetitione vasti,** without impeachment of waste; terms indicating the tenant's freedom from liability for waste. **Absque tali causa,** without such cause; formal words in the now obsolete replication *de injuria.*

**Abstention,** keeping an heir from possession. (2) The tacit renunciation of a succession by an heir.

**Abstract,** a summary, epitome, or brief statement of essential points. **Abstract of a fine,** an abstract of covenant and the concord, naming the parties, the parcel of land, and the agreement. **Abstract of title,** a summary of all the deeds, wills, and legal proceedings which show the nature of a person's right to a given estate, together with the mortgages, judgments, etc., which constitute liens or incumbrances thereon.

**Abuse,** ill-use; improper treatment of a thing. (2) Words or acts contrary to good order. (3) Rape. **Abuse of dis-**

**tress,** using an animal or chattel distrained, which makes the distrainer liable as for a conversion. **Abuse of process,** the improper use of some regular legal proceding to obtain an advantage over an opponent.

**Abuttals,** the boundaries of any piece of land. In old law the ends were said to *abut*; the sides, to *adjoin* contiguous tracts.

**Ac etiam,** *l.*, and also; the introduction to the statement of the *real* cause of action which followed the *fictitious* cause alleged to give the court jurisdiction in the old English practice.

**Accapitare,** to pay relief to lords of manors. *Capitali domino accapitare*, is to pay a relief or homage to the chief lord on becoming his vassal.

**Accapitum,**, money paid by a vassal upon his admission to a feud or holding; the relief due to the chief lord.

**Accedas,** *l.*, go you. **Accedas ad curiam,** go to the court; an original writ to the sheriff, issued out of Chancery for the purpose of removing a suit from a Hundred Court, or Court Baron, to one of the superior courts: **Accedas ad vicecomitem,** go to the sheriff; a writ to the coroner, commanding him to deliver a writ to the sheriff, requiring him to return a writ called *pone*, which he has suppressed.

**Acceptance,** the receipt of a thing, offered by another, with the intention of retaining it. (2) The agreeing to terms or proposals by which a bargain is concluded and the parties are bound. (3) An agreement by the person, on whom a draft, or bill of exchange is drawn, to pay the same according to its terms, generally expressed by writing the word "accepted" across the face and signing his name under it. Before acceptance he is called the *drawee*, after it, the *acceptor*. An acceptance may be *general* (absolute); or *qualified*, *i. e.*, conditional, or partial. An acceptance may be *implied* from acts of the drawee warranting the inference that he intends to pay, and it may be *expressed* in writing on another paper, or by giving previous written authority to draw the draft and agreeing to accept the same. If the drawee refuses to accept a bill drawn on him, it is *dishonored*, and the holder must look to the *drawer*. **Acceptance supra protest,** is the acceptance, by a person not named in the bill or liable thereon, of a bill which has been protested, for the honor of the drawer or a particular indorser.

**Acceptilation** (Sc.), the verbal extinction of a verbal contract, with a declaration that the debt has been paid when it has not; the acceptance of something merely imaginary in satisfaction of a verbal contract.

**Access,** approach, or the means of approaching. The presumption of a child's legitimacy is rebutted, if it be shown that the husband had not access to his wife within such a period of time before the birth, as admits of his having been the father.

**Accessary,** or **Accessory,** one who is not the actual perpetrator of a felony, but is in some way concerned therein. He may be an accessory (*a*) *before the fact*, *e. g.*, by inciting or counseling, or (*b*) *after the fact*, by relieving or assisting the felon.

**Accession,** the right to all which one's own property produces, as the fruit of trees or the young of animals, and to that which becomes added to or incorporated with it either naturally or artificially, as land formed by gradual deposit of soil (*see Alluvion*) and buildings erected on, or trees, vines, etc., planted in the ground of another. (2) The right, upon paying for the materials, to an article manufactured out of materials belonging to another, as bread made from flour, or wine made from grapes, where the conversion was effected innocently, the person believing the materials to be his own. (3) Coming into the enjoyment of an office or dignity.

**Accident,** such an unforeseen event, misfortune, act, or omission as is not the result of negligence or misconduct in the party. (2) Something which happens without any human agency. See *Act of God.* A recognized ground for equitable relief.

**Accite,** to summon.

**Accommodation paper,** a promissory note, or bill of exchange which a party makes, indorses, or accepts without consideration, for the benefit of another, who receives money on it and is to provide for its payment when due. The want of consideration is a valid defense to an action brought on such paper by the person accommodated, but is no defense to an action by a third person who is a *bona fide* holder for value.

**Accomplice,** one concerned with others in the commission of a crime.

**Accord,** an agreement between two (or more) persons, one of whom has a right of action against the other, that the latter should do or give, and the former accept, something in satisfaction of the right of action. When the agreement is executed, and satisfaction has been made, it is called *accord and satisfaction*, and operates as a bar to the right of action.

**Account,** or **Accompt,** a detailed statement of receipts and payments of money, or of trade transactions which have taken place between two or more persons. Accounts are either—(1) *open* or *current*, where the balance is not struck, or is not accepted by all the parties; (2) *stated*, where it has been expressly or impliedly acknowledged to be correct by all the parties; or

(3) *settled,* where it has been accepted and discharged. To make a *rest* in an account, or an *account with rests* is, at stated periods, to strike a balance, so that interest may thenceforward be computed on the sum actually due, not merely on the original principal or debt.

**Accountable receipt,** a written acknowledgment of the receipt of money or goods to be accounted for by the receiver, as distinguished from an ordinary receipt or acquittance for money paid in discharge of a debt.

**Accouple,** to marry.

**Accredit,** to acknowledge; to send a diplomatic agent with proper credentials.

**Accretion,** addition to property by operation of natural causes, (*e. g.*) gain of land by gradual deposition of soil washed up from the sea or a river. See *Alluvion.*

**Accroach,** to attempt to exercise royal power.

**Accrue,** to grow to; to be added to, as interest to principal. (2) To arise; to happen or come to pass, as a cause of action.

**Accrual, Accruer.** A right accrues when it vests in a person, especially when it arises without his active intervention, *e. g.*, by lapse of time, or determination of a previous right. For cases of *accruer* see *Accession, Alluvion, Survivorship.*

**Accumulative sentence,** one passed before the first has expired, to commence upon its expiration.

**Accusation,** the charge that one has been guilty of a crime or misdemeanor, made to a proper officr.

**Acknowledgment,** the act of going before a competent officer or court and declaring the execution of a deed or other instrument. The acknowledgment is certified by the officer, and his certificate is sometimes called the acknowledgment. Acknowledgment of deeds, mortgages, and instruments conveying an interest in real estate is required by the laws of most of the states to entitle them to be recorded, and to dispense with other proof of their execution.

**Acknowledgment money,** a sum formerly paid by tenants of copyhold in some parts of England, on the succession of a new landlord, as a recognition of his rights.

**Acquest,** or **Acquit,** property obtained by purchase or gift.

**Acquiescence,** silent assent, or neglect to speak when one wishing to object or stand on his rights would naturally speak or act. Conduct from which consent may be implied, as distinguished from express *consent* (*q.v.*).

**Acquittal,** a release or discharge, especially by verdict of a jury.

**Acquittance,** a release or written discharge of a sum of money due.

**Act,** something done or established. Laws passed by Congress and the legislatures of the several states are styled **Acts.** These may be (*a*) general or public, affecting the whole community; (*b*) private or special, affecting only particular persons and places and private concerns. **Act of bankruptcy,** an act fraudulent in its character, or indicative of insolvency, which makes a person liable to be proceeded against and adjudged a bankrupt. **Act of God,** an inevitable event, one which occurs without human intervention, and for which, therefore, no one is to be blamed, *e.g.*, death, flood, or tempest. On this ground carriers are released from liability for loss, and a person is in some cases discharged from his covenant or contract. **Act in pais,** a thing done out of court, and not a matter of record. **Act on petition,** a summary mode of proceeding to obtain an adjudication on questions in divorce, probate, and ecclesiastical matters. **Acts of Sederunt,** ordinances or rules of the Court of Sessions in Scotland, corresponding to the "General Rules" made under statutory authority by other courts. **Act of Settlement,** 12 and 13 Wm. III. c. 2, limiting the crown to the Princess Sophia, of Hanover, and to the heirs of her body being protestants. **Act of Supremacy,** 1 Eliz. c. 1, declaring the supremacy of the crown in matters ecclesiastical as well as civil. **Act of Uniformity,** 13 and 14 Car. II. c. 11, requiring the use of the Book of Common Prayer, then recently revised, in every parish church, and other places of public worship. **Acts of Union.** With *Wales*, 27 Hen. VIII. c. 27, confirmed by 34 & 35 Hen. VIII. c. 26. With *Scotland*, 5 Anne, c. 8, and see 6 Anne, cc. 6 and 23. With *Ireland*, 39 & 40 Geo. III. c. 67.

**Actio,** *l.*, an action. **Actio ad exhibendum** (Rom.), an action instituted for the purpose of compelling production of documents or testimony. **Actio bonae fidei** (Rom.), one which the judge decided according to equity, acting as *arbiter* with a wide discretion. **Actio commodati contraria** (Rom.), one by a borrower against a lender, to enforce the contract. **Actio condictio indebiti** (Rom.), one for the recovery of a sum of money paid by mistake. **Actio depositi contraria** (Rom.), one which a depositary has against a depositor, to compel him to fulfill his engagement. **Actio depositi directa** (Rom.), one brought by a depositor against a depositary, to get back the thing deposited. **Actio ex conducto** (Rom.), one by a bailor for hire against a bailee, to compel him to deliver the thing hired. **Actio exercitoria**

(Rom.), one brought against the owner of a ship (*Exercitor*) who employed his slave to navigate her, on contracts made by the slave in such capacity. **Actio institoria** (Rom.), a similar action against the owner of a shop served by his slave. In both cases the slave was held to contract only as representing the master. **Actio pro socio** (Rom.), an action by which a partner could compel his co-partners to perform the partnership contract. **Actio redhibitoria** (Rom.), one brought by a purchaser to recover the price, for breach of implied warranty on the sale. See *Action*.

**Action,** a proceeding taken in a court of law. Its chief classifications are these:—(1) (*a*) *civil*, to enforce a right; (*b*) *criminal*, to punish an offender. (2) (*a*) *in rem* (against a thing), to bind a thing; (*b*) *in personam* (against a person), to bind a person. (3) (*a*) *real*, to recover lands, tenements, or hereditaments; (*b*) *personal*, to recover money, damages, or specific personal property; (*c*) *mixed*, which partake of the nature of both real and personal actions, as actions of partition, actions to recover possession of property and damages, etc.; (4) *ex contractu*, those which arise out of contract; and *ex delicto*, those which arise out of tort or the fault of the defendant. In common law pleading actions *ex contractu* were classed as follows:—(*a*) *covenant*, being on a deed alone; (*b*) *assumpsit*, being on a simple contract only; (*c*) *debt*, being indifferently on a deed or simple contract; (*d*) *scire facias*, being on a judgment; (*e*) *account*, to compel an account and enforce the payment of the balance found due; (*f*) *annuity*, to enforce the payment of an annuity. Actions *ex delicto* were classed as follows:—(*a*) *trespass quare clausum fregit*, on real property, or *de bonis asportatis*, to personal property; (*b*) *case*, being for torts which had no special writ or remedy, prior to 13 Edw. I. c. 24, and for which, by that statute, special writs were to be framed, according to the circumstances of each case, on the lines of those already existing, such as torts committed without force, injuries resulting from negligence, abuse of legal process, etc., and injuries to reversionary, incorporeal and relative rights; (*c*) *trover*, to recover damages for the wrongful appropriation or conversion of property; (*d*) *detinue*, for the wrongful detention of property lawfully taken, and (*e*) *replevin*, to recover specific personal property, unlawfully taken. By the codes of civil practice adopted in many of the states, all common law forms are abolished, and but one form of action, known as civil action, is recognized.

**Actions ordinary** (Sc.), all actions not rescissory.

**Actions rescissory** (Sc.), are (1) actions *of proper improbation*, for declaring a writing false or forged; (2) actions *of re-*

*duction—improbation*, for the production of a writing in order to have it set aside or its effect ascertained, under the certification that the writing if not produced shall be declared false or forged; and (3) actions *of simple reduction*, for declaring a writing called for null until produced.

**Action of a writ,** a phrase formerly used when a defendant pleaded that the plaintiff had no right to the writ sued upon, although it might be that he was entitled to another writ or action for the same matter.

**Actionable,** for which an action will lie; used chiefly of words spoken or written which constitute slander or libel.

**Actiones nominatae,** *l.*, writs for which there were precedents, prior to 13 Edw. I. c. 24, as distinguished from *Actiones innominatae*, for which there were none. See *Trespass*.

**Acton Burnel,** a statute, enacted in 1283 by a Parliament held at the village of that name, for the benefit of merchants, by which a debtor's body and goods might be attached.

**Actor,** a manager, an advocate. (2) The plaintiff or active claimant in a case, as distinguished from *Reus*, the defendant. **Actor dominae,** manager of the home estate. **Actor ecclesiae,** the manager of church property; one who advocates or protects its interests.

**Actuary,** a registrar of a public body; a clerk. (2) One skilled in the business of insurance, the calculation of life interests, annuities, etc.

**Ad,** *l.*, at; by; for; near; on account of; to; until; upon. **Ad abundantiorem cautelam,** for greater caution. **Ad aliud examen,** to another tribunal. **Ad custagia, ad custum,** at the costs. **Ad damnum,** to the damage; that part of a pleading or writ which states the amount of the plaintiff's loss or injury. **Ad diem,** at the day. **Ad exhaeridationem,** to the disinheriting; a term used in the old writ of waste against a tenant. **Ad fidem,** in allegiance. **Ad filum aquae,** or **viae,** to the thread or center line of the stream, or road. **Ad finem,** at or near to the end. **Ad hominem,** to the man; argument adapted especially to the person spoken to. **Ad idem,** to the same point, essential agreement. **Ad infinitum,** without limit. **Ad inquirendum,** for inquiry; a judicial writ commanding inquiry to be made into matters related to the suit pending. **Ad interim,** in the meantime. **Ad jura regis,** for the king's rights; a writ which was brought by a clerk who had been presented to a royal living, against those who endeavored to eject him to the prejudice of the king's title. **Ad largum,** at large. **Ad litem,** for the suit. **Ad longum,** at length. **Ad nocumentum,** to the hurt or injury. **Ad ostium ecclesiae,** at the church door.

See *Dower*. **Ad quem,** to which; correlative to *a quo*, from which. **Ad quod damnum,** to what injury; (1) a writ by which the owner of land over which a highway passes may obtain leave to divert it. (2) A writ issued to the sheriff before the Crown granted new liberties, *e.g.*, fairs, markets, highways, etc., commanding him to inquire by a jury what damage would accrue to the king or any one else, on account of such grant. **Ad rationem ponere,** to cite a person to appear. **Ad respondendum,** for answering. **Ad sectam,** at the suit of. **Ad terminum annorum,** for a term of years. **Ad terminum qui preterit,** a writ of entry which lay for the owners of the reversion upon a lease, when the lease had expired. **Ad tunc et 'ibidem,** then and there; technical words in the old form of indictment. **Ad valorem,** according to the value, *e.g.*, a duty or tax. **Ad ventrem inspiciendum,** inspection of the womb; a writ issued for the purpose of ascertaining whether a woman condemned to death, or from whom an heir might be born, is really with child. **Ad vitam aut culpam,** for life, or until bad behavior.

**Addictio,** (Rom.), the giving up to a creditor of his debtor's person or goods.

**Addition,** the title or place of abode of a person.

**Ademption,** a revocation, or a taking away of a legacy. Where a testator having given a specific thing by his will, alters or parts with it before his death, he *adeems* the legacy. See *Satisfaction.*

**Aditus,** an approach; a public way.

**Adjacent,** next to, or near.

**Adjourn,** to put off the hearing to another day.

**Adjudication,** a judgment or decision, *e.g.*, on claims of creditors. (2) That part of a docket of enrolment of a decree in chancery under the old practice which set forth the order made by the court. (3) Of *bankruptcy*, the declaring a debtor bankrupt. See *Bankrupt.*

**Adjunction,** the attachment or permanent union of a thing belonging to one to that which belongs to another, by which the right of property passes to the person owning the principal; *e.g.*, the building of a house on another's ground, setting a diamond in another's ring, using the thread of one to make another's coat, etc.

**Adjuration,** a swearing or binding upon oath.

**Adjustment,** in the law of insurance is the settlement of the amount to be received by the insured, and to be contributed by the several underwriters to the policy.

**Admanuensis,** one who swears laying his hand on the Testament.

**Admeasurement, Writ of,** (1) *of dower*, lay where a widow took or had assigned to her a larger dower than rightly belonged to her; (2) *of pasture*, lay where any one having common of pasture surcharged the common—to correct the excess in either case. See *Surcharge*.

**Adminicular evidence,** explanatory, or in support.

**Administration,** the management and disposal, under legal authority, of the estate of a deceased person. If the deceased left a will and nominated a person to manage his estate, such person, when appointed by the court, is called an executor. If the deceased left no will, the court appoints a person who is termed an **administrator. Administration** is *general*, relating to the whole management and closing up of the estate; or, *special*, *e.g.*, **ad colligendum,** for collecting and preserving goods which are perishable or liable to loss, when for any reason regular probate and administration can not be granted at once: **ancillary,** subordinate to the principal administration, for collecting assets in a foreign country: **cum testamento annexo,** with the will annexed, when no executor is named in the will, or the person named is unable or unwilling to serve: **de bonis non,** concerning the goods not administered, when the first administrator dies without having fully administered: **durante minore aetate,** or **absentia,** where the sole executor is a minor or beyond seas: **pendente lite,** while a suit is pending respecting the will, to take care of the estate only till the suit is ended. The mode of appointing administrators, their duties and powers, and the judicial supervision of their acts and accounts, are regulated by the statutes of the several states.

**Admiralty,** the jurisdiction exercised by district courts of the United States over maritime contracts, torts, injuries, etc., including cases arising on the navigable lakes and rivers. In England, this jurisdiction is conferred by the Judicature Act of 1873, upon the Probate, Divorce and Admiralty Division of the High Court of Justice, and is confined to cases arising on the high seas and those portions of rivers and sounds in which the tides rise and fall.

**Admission,** the approval and institution of a clerk in his living in obedience to a writ *admittendo clerico*. (2) The act by which attorneys and counselors become officers of the court and are allowed to practice. The requirements for admission vary greatly in the different states. (3) A voluntary statement or acknowledgment, made by an interested party, which is admissible in evidence against said party. (4) An express or implied acknowledgment that an allegation in the pleading of the opposite party is true. In general, every thing that is stated in a petition or answer, and not specifically denied, is taken as admitted.

**Admittance,** *giving possession of a copyhold estate.* Formal admittance is usually made by the steward handing to the tenant a rod (see *Verge*), or other symbol, according to the custom. It may, however, be dispensed with.

**Admittendo clerico,** *l.*, a writ of execution, addressed to the bishop or his metropolitan, requiring him to *admit* and institute the clerk or presentee of the plaintiff.

**Admittendo in socium,** *l.*, a writ for associating certain persons with justices of assize on the circuit.

**Admonition,** the lightest form of ecclesiastical censure.

**Admortization,** the reduction of property in lands or tenements to mortmain, in the feudal custom.

**Adolescence,** the period commencing at 12 in females, and 14 in males, and ending at 21 years of age.

**Adoption,** the act by which a person takes the child of another into his family and makes him, for all legal purposes, his own. Its force and validity depend upon the statutes of the several states. (2) The affirmation or acceptance of a contract which one is at liberty otherwise to repudiate; *e.g.*, a contract made by an infant during his minority.

**Ad promissor,** (Rom.), a species of surety, or guarantor.

**Adrogatio,** (Rom.), the adoption of an *impubes, i.e.*, a male under 14, or a female under 12 years old.

**Adscripti,** joined to by writing; *e.g.*, **adscriptitii glebae,** a kind of slaves among the Romans, attached to and transferred along with the land which they cultivated.

**Adstipulator,** (Rom.), an accessory party to a promise, who received the same promise, in whole or in part, as his principal did, and could equally exact fulfilment even after death of the principal.

**Adult,** of full age. In civil law, a male who has reached the age of 14, a female who has reached the age of 12. In common law, one who has attained to the age of 21.

**Adulteration,** the offense of mixing cheap or inferior substances with another substance, with the intent that the compound may be sold as pure and genuine.

**Adulterine,** the issue of an adulterous intercourse.

**Adultery,** the voluntary sexual intercourse of a married person with a person other than his or her wife or husband. It was not an indictable offense at common law, but was left to the ecclesiastical courts for punishment. It is made punishable by fine and imprisonment by the statutes of most of the states, and is a generally recognized ground for an absolute divorce.

**Advancement,** a gift by a parent to a child with the intent to vest in him the whole or part of what he would otherwise inherit on the death of the parent, the amount of which is deducted from the distributive share of such child. The purchase of land by the parent in the name of the child, or the settlement of a portion on him, is presumed to be an advancement. Money paid out for the maintenance or education of a child is not.

**Advances,** payments made to the owner of goods by the factor or consignee who is to have possession of the goods for the purpose of selling them. An agent is entitled to a lien on the goods and the proceeds of their sale for the amount of such advances, and a right of action against the principal for the balance, if the proceeds are insufficient to cover the advances.

**Adventure,** the sending to sea of a ship or goods at the risk of the sender, to be sold by the supercargo for his benefit.

**Adversaria,** rough memoranda, common-place books.

**Adverse,** opposing; conflicting; contrary to. **Adverse enjoyment,** or **user,** the possession or exercise of an easement or privilege under a claim of right as against the owner of the land. **Adverse possession,** the actual holding and enjoyment of land under a claim of right which is opposed to or inconsistent with another's claims.

**Advocate,** one who conducts or pleads a cause for another.

**Advocate-General,** the adviser of the crown on questions of naval and military law. See *Judge Advocate.*

**Advocate, Lord,** the principal crown lawyer in Scotland.

**Advowson,** the right of presenting to a church or ecclesiastical benefice whenever it becomes vacant. It is either *appendant, i.e.,* annexed to some corporeal hereditament, *e.g.,* a manor, by the grant whereof it passes; or *in gross, i.e.,* belonging to an individual, and not so annexed. Advowsons are also divided into (1) *presentative,* where the patron presents to the bishop; (2) *donative,* one bestowed upon a private individual by the crown without presentation; (3) *collative,* where the right of patronage is in the bishop.

**Advowtry,** continuous living in adultery.

**Aestimatio capitis,** *l.,* the value of a head. A fine paid for taking human life, estimated according to the rank and quality of the person killed, ordained by King Athelstane.

**Aetas infantile** (or **infantiae**) **proxima,** *l.,* the age next to infancy.

**Affeer,** to assess amerciaments or fines by a jury in courts-leet.

**Affiance,** a plighting of troth, or agreement to marry.

**Affiant,** one who makes oath to a statement.

**Affidatus,** a tenant by fealty, a retainer.

**Affidavit,** a written statement sworn to before a person having authority to administer an oath, by a person called an *affiant*, or *deponent*.

**Affiliation,** the fixing any one with the paternity of a bastard child, and with the obligation to maintain it.

**Affinity,** relationship by marriage between the husband and the blood relations of the wife, and between the wife and the blood relations of the husband. See *Consanguinity*.

**Affirm,** to make firm; to establish. (1) To ratify or confirm the judgment of a lower court. (2) To ratify or confirm a voidable contract.

**Affirmation,** a solemn declaration without oath. The privilege of affirming in judicial proceedings is now generally extended to all persons who object to taking an oath.

**Afforce the assize,** to compel a verdict, either by adding to the jury until some twelve agree, or by confining them without meat and drink until they agree. The practice is now discontinued.

**Afforest,** to turn into a "forest" (*q.v.*)

**Affranchise,** to make free.

**Affray,** the fighting of persons in a public place to the terror of the people.

**Affreightment,** the contract by which a ship is hired to carry goods.

**Aforethought,** planned beforehand; premeditated.

**Aftermath,** the second crop of grass. (2) The right to have the last crop of grass or pasturage.

**Age,** the time of life; formerly used as equivalent to **full age,** or **majority;** that period of life at which infancy terminates and the law recognizes the full capacity of a man to make contracts, convey land, vote, etc. Males come to full age on the day preceding the twenty-first anniversary of birth. The time at which females come to full age varies somewhat in the different states, as also the time at which infants of both sexes attain to years of discretion, the power to marry to choose a guardian, etc. Unless otherwise regulated by statute, a male can legally marry (with the proper consents) at 14; a female at 12; a child under 7 can not be held criminally responsible; and between 7 and 14 there is a presumption of ignorance or incapacity.

**Agent,** one authorized by another (the *principal*), to do an act or transact business for him, and to bind his principal within the limits of that authority. An agent may be *general*, to do all business of a particular kind; or *special*, to do one particular act; and according to the scope of his authority is his power to bind his principal.

**Age prayer,** a plea of infancy and request that proceedings be stayed until the infant party becomes of age, formerly used in real actions.

**Aggravation,** that which adds to the enormity of a crime, or is ground for increasing the damages awarded for an injury. See *Exemplary damages.*

**Agiler,** an observer or informer.

**Agist, Agistment,** the feeding of other men's cattle on one's land for reward. (2) The profit of such feeding. (3) The charging of lands with a certain payment toward maintenance of sea banks.

**Agnation,** kinship by the father's side, as distinct from *cognation,* or kinship by the mother's side.

**Agnomen,** a name added to the Christian and surname as a mark of distinction; usually derived from some personal characteristic or achievement.

**Agreement,** the concurrence of two or more minds in any thing done or to be done. (2) A contract, especially one which is not under seal. If under seal it is called a deed. (3) The preliminary heads of a formal contract to be afterward drawn up. Agreements may be *executed, i.e,* complete, performed; or *executory,* where something remains to be done by one or both of the parties; *express,* where the terms are stated orally or in writing; and *implied,* which the law presumes the parties to have made from their acts and surrounding circumstances, though the terms were not expressed.

**Aids** (*Auxilia*), were originally free gifts from the tenant to his lord, but came afterward to be regarded as a right. They were—(*a*) to ransom the lord; (*b*) to make his eldest son a knight; (*c*) to portion his eldest daughter (2) Extraordinary grants to the crown. (3) *To aid* is to remedy a defect in pleading by some subsequent proceeding, *e.g.,* a verdict. (4) See *Writ in aid.*

**Air.** The right to a free access of air is the natural right of every one, interference with which by interruption or pollution, unless by virtue of an acquired easement (*q.v.*), is actionable. An easement of light and air coming over the land of another can not be acquired by prescription in the United States, though the rule is otherwise in England.

**Alba firma,** *l.,* white rents; rents payable in silver, as distinguishable from rents payable in work, grain, and the like.

**Alia enormia,** *l.,* other wrongs; words used in the conclusion of a declaration in trespass.

**Aliamenta,** a liberty of passage, open way, water-course, etc., for the tenant's accommodation.

**Alias,** *l.*, (*otherwise*), a second or further writ, which was issued after a former writ had expired without effect. (2) (Scil., *dictus*), a second name applied to a person where it is doubtful which of two or more names is his real name.

**Alibi,** *l.*, (*elsewhere*), a defense resorted to where the party accused, in order to prove that he could not have committed the crime with which he is charged, offers evidence that he was *in a different place* at the time the offense was committed.

**Alien,** a person of foreign birth who has not become a naturalized citizen. Formerly aliens were not capable of taking or holding real estate in England or the United States, but these common-law disabilities have been generally removed by statute. **Alien ami,** or **Amy** (*friend*), a subject of a nation which is at peace with this country. **Alien enemy,** a subject of a nation which is at war with this country.

**Alienage,** the state of an alien.

**Alienate,** or **Aliene,** to transfer property. (2) To cause the loss or transfer of a wife's or husband's affections. *Alienor* is one who transfers to an *alienee.*

**Alieni juris,** *l.*, under another's authority. See *Sui juris.*

**Alimenta,** things necessary to support life, as food, clothing, and shelter.

**Alimony,** the allowance made to a wife out of her husband's estate for her support, either during a matrimonial suit, which is called alimony *pendente lite*, or at its termination, when she proves herself entitled to a separate maintenance, the fact of marriage being established.

**Alio intuitu,** *l.*, with another intent than that alleged, *i.e.*, not *bona fide.*

**Aliter,** *l.*, otherwise; otherwise held or decided.

**Aliunde,** *l.*, from elsewhere, from another source, *e.g.*, *proof aliunde.*

**All fours.** A case is said to be on "all fours" with another, when it agrees with it in the material points.

**Allegation,** a statement of fact made in a legal proceeding. A plaintiff can only recover *secundum allegata et probata*, *i.e.*, according to the tenor of such of his allegations as he can duly prove.

**Allegiance,** obedience due from the citizen to the government. It may be (*a*) natural, by birth; (*b*) acquired by naturalization, etc.; or (*c*) local, during residence in a country.

**Aller san jour,** *fr.*, to go without day, *i.e.*, to be finally dismissed from the court, no further day being assigned for appearance. Said formerly of a successful defendant.

**Allocation,** an allowance made upon accounts in the exchequer.

**Allocatione facienda,** *l.*, a writ allowing to an accountant such sums of money as he has lawfully expended.

**Allocatur** (*it is allowed*), the certificate of the allowance of costs by the master on taxation.

**Allodium,** without vassalage. Land held by absolute ownership, and not under any lord or superior. All land in England is held, in theory, of the crown, and can not therefore be allodial.

**Allograph,** a document not written by any of the parties thereto; opposed to autograph.

**Allonge,** a piece of paper annexed to a bill of exchange or promissory note on which indorsements may be written, for which there is no room on the instrument itself.

**Allot,** to assign a share, *e.g.*, of land on partition or inclosure, or of stock in a company

**Allotment,** (1) the share of land or stock allotted. (2) The act of allotting; partition. (3) *Allotment note*, a document by which a seaman stipulates for payment of part of his wages, at stated intervals, to persons therein named.

**Alluvion,** or **Alluvio,** land gradually gained from the sea or a river by the washing up of sand and soil, so as to form *terra firma*. The new land belongs to the owner of that to which it is annexed and whereof it forms part. See *Avulsion; Derelict lands; Aqua cedit solo.*

**Alteration,** changing an instrument, by erasure or addition, so as to alter its sense or effect. A *material* alteration is one which affects the rights of parties under the instrument, or may do so, and avoids the instrument if made by one of the parties without the consent of the other

**Alternative writ,** one which commands the defendant to do the thing required, or show cause why he should not do it.

**Altius tollendi,** *l.*, (Rom.), the right to build one's house as high as he may think proper.

**Amalgamation,** the union of two incorporated companies or societies by one being merged in the other. (2) The marriage of people of different races, as of whites with blacks.

**Ambassador,** a representative sent by one sovereign or country to another, with authority to treat on affairs of state. His person is protected from civil arrest, and his goods from seizure. His is the highest rank among diplomatic officials.

**Ambidexter,** *l.*, (*one who uses both hands*), a juror who takes bribes from both parties to influence his verdict. See *Embraceror.*

**Ambiguity,** doubtfulness, obscurity. There are two species of ambiguity (*a*) *patent, i. e.*, apparent on the face of the instrument, which may not be supplied or explained by *extrinsic* evidence, *i.e.*, evidence not contained in the instrument itself; (*b*) *latent*, where the instrument being apparently free from obscurity, a doubt arises in carrying it into execution; *e.g.*, from a name used in it being applicable to two persons or things. In such case extrinsic evidence is admissible.

**Amendment,** a correction, or alteration of any pleading, or statement in a cause or matter. (2) An addition to, or modification of an existing constitution, or law duly adopted or enacted.

**Amentia,** insanity idiocy

**Amercement,** or **Amerciament,** a fine assessed by a jury, not, as is usually the case, fixed by the court or by statute.

**Amicus curiae,** *l.*, (*friend of the court*), a stander by, not being a party to, or interested in the cause, who informs the court of any decided case, statute, or other fact, of which it can take judicial notice.

**Amnesty** (*non-remembrance*), an act of pardon or oblivion, by which crimes against the government up to a date therein named are condoned, so that they can never thereafter be made the subject of a charge. An amnesty may be *general*, to all concerned in the offense, or *particular* to one or more.

**Amortization,** or **Amortisement,** an alienation of lands in mortmain (*q.v.*). (2) The payment off of bonds, stock, etc.

**Amotion, Amove,** to remove (1) from possession; (2) from a post or office.

**Ampliation,** an enlargement of time; a deferring of judgment till the cause be further examined.

**Amy,** or **Ami,** usually called *prochein amy*, the next friend (as distinguished from the guardian), suing on behalf of an infant, etc.

**An, jour, et waste,** *fr.*, (*year day, and waste*), a right of the crown to forfeit a felon's lands for a year and a day and to commit waste thereon. Now abolished.

**Ancestor,** a forefather; one from whom another has descended lineally. More strictly in law he from whom another inherits real estate.

**Ancient demesne,** a tenure existing only in those manors which belonged to the crown in the reigns of Edward the Confessor and William the Conqueror. The tenants are freeholders, and enjoy certain immunities, the chief of which is a right to sue and to be sued only in their lord's court.

**Ancient lights,** windows which have had uninterrupted access of light for twenty years and upward. The prescriptive right to light which they thereby acquire is called *ancienty* of light. In most of the United States this right can not be acquired except by express grant.

**Ancient messuage,** a house erected before the time of legal memory, *i.e.*, the reign of Richard the First In practice, any house is ancient which was built before the time of living memory, and the origin of which can not be proved to be modern. Such houses frequently have certain rights (*e.g.*, of common) attached to them, which extend to houses built on the same sites afterward. See *Prescription.*

**Ancient writings,** documents more than thirty years old, These are presumed to be genuine without express proof, when coming from the proper custody.

**Ancillary,** that which is subordinate to, or assists, some other thing, *e.g.*, ancillary administration.

**Angel,** an ancient English coin of the value of ten shillings.

**Aniens,** or **Anient,** void; of no force or effect.

**Animal,** any animate being endowed with the power of voluntary motion. Animals (excluding human beings) are either (*a*) *mansuetae*, tame or domesticated, or (*b*) *ferae naturae*, wild. The latter are the property of any one who catches and keeps them; but being by nature irreclaimable, they cease to be his as soon as they get their liberty again. In the case of certain animals (*e.g.*, pigeons), escape from the actual control of their owner does not affect his property in them, so long as they have the intention, or habit, of returning. At common law, only *ferae mansuetae* and *ferae naturae* which had been reclaimed or domesticated and were in the actual control of their owner were subjects of larceny.

**Animus,** mind; will; intention. **Animo cancellandi,** with intent to cancel. **Animo capiendi,** with intent to take. **Animo furandi,** with intent to steal. **Animo lucrendi,** with intent to profit. **Animo manendi,** with intent to remain. **Animo revertendi**, with intent to return. **Animo revocandi,** with intent to revoke. **Animo testandi,** with intent to make a will.

**Annats, Annates,** the first-fruits of a spiritual living, viz., one year's profits.

**Anni nubiles,** *l.*, the age at which a girl is, by law, fit for marriage; under the common law, the age of 12.

**Annuity,** a periodical payment of money, either bequeathed as a gift, or secured by the personal covenant or bond of the grantor. It is charged either upon personalty or realty, and may be either perpetual, for life, or for years. If perpetual, it may be limited to the heirs (*annuity in fee*), or to the executors of the grantee (*annuitant*).

**Annul,** to make void; to deprive of operation; *e.g.*, a decree, deed, contract, etc.

**Annus deliberandi,** *l.*, the year (now six months) allowed by the Scotch law for the heir to deliberate whether he will enter upon his ancestor's land and represent him.

**Annus luctus,** *l.*, the year of mourning; the year after her husband's death, during which a widow was not allowed to marry by Roman, Danish, and Saxon law.

**Annuus reditus,** *l.*, a yearly rent; annuity.

**Answer,** the defendant's statement of his case. (2) A statement under oath, in reply to interrogatories contained in a bill in equity, or annexed to a petition under modern code practice.

**Ante,** *l.*, (*before*), a word used to refer to a previous part of the same book or statement. **Antedate,** to date an instrument before the day of its execution. **Ante litem motam,** before suit brought. **Antenati,** those born before a certain period, *e.g.*, before the Declaration of Independence. **Ante nuptial,** before marriage. See *Settlement*.

**Antichresis,** (Rom.), an agreement by which the debtor gives the creditor the use and income from the land, or thing pledged, in lieu of interest on his debt. See *Welsh mortgage*.

**Anticipation,** doing a thing before its proper time; *e.g.*, dealing with or distributing property, income, etc., before the time fixed by the deed, or will conveying the same.

**Antigraphy,** a copy or counterpart of a deed.

**Antiqua statuta,** *l.*, ancient statutes. Specifically applied to the English statutes from Richard V. to Edward III.

**Apanage,** or **Appanage,** originally the lands assigned by kings of France for the maintenance of their younger sons; (2) a possession of the crown.

**Apertura testamenti,** (Rom.), a form of proving a will by acknowledgment of the witnesses before a magistrate.

**Apograph,** a copy, an inventory.

**Apparitor,** a messenger, who cites and arrests offenders and executes the decrees of the judges of the spiritual courts,

**Appeal,** an application by an *appellant* to a higher court to rectify the order of the court below. The opposite party is then called the *respondent*, or *appellee*. The manner of taking appeals, and the cases which may be appealed, are regulated by statutes. (2) *Of felony*, under the old law, was a criminal proceeding brought by one person against another, the ground for which was the particular injury done by the *appellee* to the *appellor: e.g.*, by a widow against the murderer of her husband. Abolished by 59 Geo. III. c. 46.

**Appearance,** a formal submission to the jurisdiction of the court by a party to a suit. It can be made in person; by an attorney duly authorized; or by a guardian or next friend, where the party is an infant or under some other disability.

**Appellate jurisdiction,** the power of a superior court to review the decision of an inferior court.

**Appendant,** a hereditament annexed to another, *e.g.*, an advowson is said to be appendant to a manor. See *Common.* Properly speaking, that only which is annexed by implication of law is appendant, all others being *appurtenant* (*q.v.*).

**Appointee,** a person selected for a particular purpose. (2) The person in whose favor a power of appointment is executed.

**Appointment.** (1) The designation of a person for a particular office. (2) *Under a power*, a gift or distribution of property made by a person (called the *donee of the power*, or *appointor*), under a power given him by some instrument. Such powers may be *general, i.e.*, authorizing the donee to appoint to any one he pleases, or *particular, i.e.*, limited to certain specified persons. An appointment is *exclusive* if limited to certain individuals out of the particular class specified by the power. Married women are often given a power of appointing by will, so as to avoid the necessity of obtaining their husband's consent.

**Apportionment,** a division of a rent, common, etc., according to the interest of the various parties therein. (2) The allowance to a party, who has performed part of a divisible contract, of a proportionate part of the stipulated compensation for the whole. (3) The determination of the amount which each of the parties interested in an estate must pay to clear off an incumbrance, satisfy an annuity, etc.

**Appraisement,** a valuation; generally required by law to be made of the goods of an intestate, or insolvent, or of goods attached or replevied.

**Apprentice,** one bound by indentures to serve a tradesman, or artificer, who covenants in turn to teach him his trade, art. or mystery.

**Appropriation,** the setting apart of money or goods to meet a particular demand. (2) The application of a payment made by a debtor to his creditor to the whole or partial discharge of a particular debt, as expressly or impliedly requested by the debtor at the time payment is made, or, in default of that, as the creditor may wish. (3) Statutory provision for the support of the government, or the payment of its various debts and obligations. (4) The annexing of an ecclesiastical benefice to the perpetual use of a religious body which thus becomes the patron. See *Impropriation.*

**Approve,** to approve, under the statute of Merton (20 Hen. III. c. 4), was to appropriate and inclose portions of the waste land of the manor.

**Approver,** or **Prover,** an accomplice in crime, who, while confessing himself guilty, accuses others of the same offense, and is admitted as a witness, at the discretion of the court, to give evidence against his companions in guilt. He is sometimes called "Queen's (or State's) evidence."

**Appurtenant,** pertaining or belonging to, by grant or prescription. See *Appendant; Common. Appurtenances,* in conveyancing, is a general term for that which passes with the principal subject of the grant, such as liberties and easements.

**Aqua,** *l.,* water. **Aquae ductus, Aquae haustus, Aquae immittendae,** (scil. *jus.*) are rights under Roman law (*a*) of carrying a water-course through another's land; (*b*) of drawing water from the fountain, pool, or spring of another; (*c*) of having the water from one's house run upon and over a neighbor's land.

**Arbitrary punishment** (Sc.), such as is left to the discretion of a judge, and not defined by statute.

**Arbitration,** the submitting of a matter in dispute to the judgment of one, two, or more disinterested persons, called arbitrators, whose decision, called an *award,* is binding upon the parties. In most of the states, arbitration is provided for by statute, and the award may be made a rule of court.

**Arbitrement and award,** the technical plea in an old common-law action, that the parties had submitted the matter to arbitration, and an award had been made.

**Arca cyrographica,** a chest wherein all the contracts, mortgages, and obligations belonging to the Jews were preserved to prevent fraud, by order of Richard I.

**Archaionomia,** a collection of Saxon laws, published during the reign of Queen Elizabeth, in the Saxon language, with a Latin version by Mr. Lambard.

**Archbishop,** the chief of the clergy in his province, where he is, under the queen, supreme in all ecclesiastical causes, and superintends the bishops. The Archbishops of Canterbury and Armagh are respectively called the Primate of all England and of all Ireland; those of York and Dublin the Primate of England and of Ireland, and are inferior in rank.

**Archdeacon,** a substitute for, and next in dignity and authority to, the bishop. He has an ecclesiastical jurisdiction and court.

**Arches Court,** a court of appeal belonging to the Archbishop of Canterbury, the judge of which is called the Dean of the Arches, because his court was anciently held in the church of Saint Mary-le-Bow (*Sancta Maria de arcubus*), so named from the steeple, which is raised upon pillars, built *archwise*.

**Archetype,** the original type, or copy.

**Archives,** a chamber or place where ancient records, charters, etc., are kept. (2) The records, etc., themselves.

**Argument,** the process of reasoning, or drawing inferences. (2) The discussion of a legal point by counsel. (3) The inference itself. There are several distinct kinds of argument to which different names have been assigned, *e.g.*: (*a*) *Ab auctoritate*, from authority; (*b*) *ab inconvenienti*, founded on the hardship of the case, of force only when the law is doubtful; (*c*) *ad hominem*, *i.e.*, founded on the individual circumstances or experience of the person to whom it is addressed; (*d*) *ad verecundiam*, *i.e.*, the appeal to respect for authority; (*e*) *ad ignorantiam*, founded on the inability (through ignorance) of the opposing party to reply; (*f*) *ad baculum*, the appeal to force; (*g*) *ad misericordiam*, the appeal to compassion. Argument is also divided into (*a*) *a priori*, from the antecedent or cause to the generally understood consequent or effect; and so in ordinary parlance *a priori* means "at first sight;" (*b*) *a posteriori*, from the consequent or effect to the antecedent, or cause.

**Argumentative,** the quality of a pleading or affidavit which states, not merely the facts, but the conclusions of law to be drawn from them; or which leaves that on which the pleader relies to be inferred instead of being expressly stated. Such pleading is improper.

**Armiger,** an armor bearer; esquire.

**Arms,** any thing carried for defense, or used to inflict injury on the person of another; including every thing with which one strikes, or which one may throw, as well as guns, pistols, swords, etc.

**Arraign,** to bring a prisoner to the bar of the court to answer the matter charged upon him in the indictment. It consists of three parts, (*a*) calling him by name, (*b*) reading him the indictment, (*c*) asking him if he be guilty or not guilty. He may then plead "guilty" or "not guilty," or stand mute, which is, in effect, the same as a plea of "not guilty."

**Array,** the whole body of jurors summoned to attend a court.

**Arrears, Arrearages,** money, *e.g.*, interest, rents, etc., overdue and unpaid.

**Arrest,** the seizing of a person and detaining him in custody by lawful authority. (2) The seizure and detention of personal chattels, especially of ships and vessels libeled in a Court of

Admirality. (3) **Arrest of judgment,** the refusal of a court to give judgment, notwithstanding a verdict, which may occur when there is some substantial error appearing on the face of the record which vitiates the proceeding, or when it appears on the face of the record that the plaintiff is not entitled to it.

**Arrestment** (Sc.), a process of attachment, corresponding to garnishment, or trustee process, in other countries. The judgment debtor is called the *arrestee;* the garnishee, the *common debtor;* and the judgment creditor, the *arrester* or *user of the arrestment.*

**Arretted,** charged, imputed, or laid unto.

**Arrha,** an earnest; evidence of the striking of a bargain.

**Arrogatio** (Rom.), adoption of a person of full age; *adoptio* being that of a person under age.

**Arson,** the malicious firing of a house or other building.

**Art and Part** (Sc.). One is "art and part guilty" who orders, incites, counsels, and assists a criminal in the execution of a crime. "To have neither art nor part" is to be neither contriver nor participator.

**Article,** a complaint exhibited in the Ecclesiastical Court by way of libel. (2) The different parts of a libel, or of a responsive or counter allegation in the Ecclesiastical Courts. (3) A clause or paragraph of a document or written instrument. **Articles of agreement,** a written memorandum of the terms of any agreement. **Articles of association,** the regulations of a company. **Articles of Faith,** or **Religion,** the thirty-nine articles agreed on by convocation in 1562, constituting the statement of the faith of the Church of England. **Articles of Confederation,** the compact of union adopted by the thirteen original states March 1st, 1781 superseded by the Constitution of the United States. **Articles of impeachment,** the written statement of the grounds for removing a person from office. **Articles of partnership,** the written terms on which two or more persons associate as partners. **Articles of the peace,** a complaint on oath made to a court that the applicant goes in fear of his life or of bodily harm from the threats of another person, from whom sureties of the peace are thereupon taken for such a length of time as the court shall think necessary. **Articles of war** the code of laws established for the government of the army.

**Articled clerk,** a pupil of a solicitor, who undertakes, by articles of clerkship containing covenants mutually binding, to instruct the pupil in the principles and practice of the profession.

**Artificial person,** a body corporation, or company, considered in law as an individual.

**Ascendants,** the progenitors of a person in a direct line.

**Ascriptitius** (Rom.), a naturalized foreigner.

**Asportation,** carrying away or removing goods. In all larcenies, there must be both a taking and a carrying away.

**Assault,** strictly speaking, is a threatening to strike or harm; if a blow be struck, it is *battery* (*q.v.*). Assaults are *common* or *aggravated*, the former being those for which no special punishment is prescribed by the law; the latter being made with an intent to commit some additional crime, as rape, murder, or robbery. An assault is in civil law a tort, for which damages are recoverable.

**Assay,** the testing of weights and measures and of coins.

**Assembly,** the meeting of a number of persons in the same place. **General Assembly,** the whole body of legislators, *i.e.*, the senate and house of representatives. **Unlawful assembly,** the meeting of three or more persons to do an unlawful act.

**Assent,** approval of something done. It may be *express*, *i.e.*, openly declared; *or implied, i.e.*, presumed by law, as when the thing done is for the person's benefit and he makes no express dissent.

**Assess,** to rate or ascertain the value of a man's property for taxation. (2) To charge a certain proportion of the cost of a public improvement on persons or property peculiarly benefited thereby. (3) To fix the amount to be paid on each share of stock of an incorporated company for the purposes of the corporation. (4) To fix the amount of damages to which the prevailing party in a suit is entitled.

**Assets,** property available for the payment of the debts of a person or corporation. The assets of a deceased person are: (1) *real*, which descend to the heir, and can be applied to the payment of debts only when the personal assets do not suffice; and *personal*, which go to the executor or administrator; (2) *legal*, *i.e.*, those which come to the hands of the executor by virtue of his office; or *equitable*, *i.e.*, those which can only be reached by help of a court of equity. See *Marshaling of Assets*.

**Assign,** to transfer property, especially rights in action. The person making the *assignment* is called the *assignor;* the person receiving it, the *assignee.* (2) To allot or set off, *e.g.*, a widow's *dower* (*q.v.*). (3) To point out or specify, *e.g.*, the *errors* complained of on the trial of a case in the court below.

**Assisa, assise,** or **assize,** an ordinance or statute, *e.g.*, **assisa armorum,** a statute ordering the keeping of arms. **Assisa de foresta,** a statute regulating conduct in and about the king's forests. **Assisa panis,** a law regulating the price of bread. (2) A sitting together; a session of the court; legal proceedings. (3) The jury, who sit together for the purpose of trying a cause. Hence the judicial assemblies held by the queen's commission in every county, as well to take indictments as to try causes at *nisi prius*, are commonly termed the assizes. There are two commissions: (I.) *General*, which is issued twice a year to the judges of the High Court of Justice; two judges being usually assigned to every circuit. The judges in this case have four several commissions: (*a*) Of *oyer and terminer*, directed to them and many other gentlemen of the county, by which they are empowered to try treasons, felonies, etc. This is the largest commission. (*b*) Of *gaol delivery*, directed to the judges and the clerk of assize associate, empowering them to try every prisoner in the gaol committed for any offense whatsoever, so as to clear the prisoners. (*c*) Of *nisi prius*, directed to the judges, the clerks of assize and others, by which civil causes, in which issue has been joined in one of the Divisions of the High Court of Justice, are tried on circuit by a jury of twelve men of the county in which the venue is laid. (*d*) A commission of the peace, by which all justices are bound to be present at their county assizes to give attendance to the judges, or else suffer a fine. (II.) The other division of commissions is *special*, granted to certain judges to try certain causes and crimes. **Assize of darrien presentment,** a real action which lay against any one who interfered with the plaintiff's right to present to a benefice. **Assize of mort d'ancestre,** a real action against an abator (*q.v.*). **Assize of novel disseisin,** a real action which lay when one had recently been disseised. **Assize of nuisance,** an action which lay, when something had been done which worked an injury to plaintiff's freehold, to abate the nuisance and recover damages. **Assize of utrum,** an action by a parson to recover lands which his predecessor had allowed the church to be deprived of improperly. **Assisa cadere** to be non-suited, as when there is such a plain legal insufficiency in an action that the plaintiff can not successfully proceed any further in it. **Assisa continuanda,** an ancient writ addressed to the justices of the assize for the continuation of a cause, when certain facts put in issue could not have been proved in time by the party alleging them. See *Grand Assize*

**Assistance, writ of,** a writ issued to the sheriff to carry out a decree of the court by putting the parties in possession; apparently first employed in the reign of James I.

**Assisus,** rented or farmed out for such an assize, or certain assessed rent in money or provisions.

**Associate,** was an officer in each of the Courts of Common

Law, his duties being to superintend the entry of causes, and to enter verdicts and draw up the certificates of judgments and orders at *Nisi Prius*. See *Postea*. Since the Judicature Act, *associates* are styled masters of the Supreme Court, of which they are now officers.

**Association,** a collection of persons for a certain purpose. (2) A writ or patent sent by the crown to the justices appointed to take assizes, to have others (sergeants at law, for instance) associated with them; it is usual where a judge becomes unable to attend to his circuit duties, or dies.

**Assoile,** to deliver from excommunication; to acquit.

**Assumpsit,** *l.*, (*he has undertaken*), the name of an action which lay for damage for breach of a *simple* contract, *i.e.*, one not under seal. It was a species of *action on the case* (*q.v.*).

**Assurance,** or **common assurance,** the legal evidence of the transfer of property. See *Conveyance*. (2) See *Insurance*.

**Assurer,** one who undertakes to indemnify another, called the *assured*, against risks or dangers; an underwriter. See *Insurance*.

**Assythment,** damages recoverable by the heirs or representatives of a person killed, from the person killing.

**At arms length.** One who stands toward another in such a position as to have an advantage of him, is bound, on a proposal for a contract between them, to divest himself entirely of that authority, influence, or advantage which he possesses, so as to place himself on an equality, and to let the negotiation proceed as between two independent persons. This is called putting *at arms length*. It is most frequently applicable to transactions between solicitor and client, trustee and cestui que trust.

**Atavus,** the great grandfather's or great grandmother's grandfather. The ascending line of lineal ancestry runs thus:—Pater, Avus, Proavus, Abavus, Atavus, Tritavus.

**Atheist,** one who does not believe in the existence of a God. At common law, such persons were incompetent as witnesses.

**Attachment,** the seizure and taking into custody of the law of the person or property of a party to the suit, either in an action already begun, *e.g.*, to punish for contempt of court, or at the beginning of an action to acquire jurisdiction, or to secure possession of property which the defendant is seeking to conceal or dispose of fraudulently. When debts are attached, the process is called *trustee process* (*q.v.*), or *garnishment* (*q.v.*). (2) The writ or order in pursuance of which the seizure is effected.

**Attachment of privilege.** When a person, by virtue of his privilege, calls another into that court to which he himself belongs, to answer some action. (2) A power to apprehend a person in a privileged place.

**Attainder,** the extinction of civil rights which resulted (until 1870, when it was finally abolished) from a sentence of death or outlawry for treason or felony. The chief consequences were forfeiture of the criminal's property, *corruption* of his blood, so that no title could be traced through him, and incapacity to sue in a court of justice.

**Attaint,** under attainder. (2) *writ of,* issued to inquire whether a jury gave a false (*i.e.*, corrupt) verdict, so that the judgment following thereupon might be reversed.

**Attempt,** an intent to commit a crime, combined with an act which falls short of the thing intended.

**Attendant term.** See *Term.*

**Attentat,** a proceeding wrongfully attempted by a judge in a suit, which has been removed from his court to a higher by appeal.

**Attermining,** granting time for payment of a debt.

**Attestation,** evidence by witnesses to the execution of any instrument.

**Attestation clause,** the sentence subscribed to a written instrument, signed by the witnesses to its execution, stating that they have witnessed it. They are then *attesting witnesses,* and can be called at any future time to identify the instrument and prove its due *execution.*

**Attested copy,** a verified transcript of a document.

**Attorney,** one appointed by another to act in his place. **Attorney at law,** an officer in a court of justice employed by a party to represent him and manage his case. **Attorney in fact,** one appointed to act for another in a private matter, or for a special purpose, designated in the instrument of appointment called a *Power of Attorney* (*q.v.*).

**Attorney-General,** the principal counsel of the crown, who conducts prosecutions on behalf of the crown if required (see *Public Prosecutor*), and represents the crown in matters connected with charities and patents. He also is responsible in the House of Commons for the Government of the day in all questions of law. The Prince of Wales and the Queen Consort have each an Attorney-General. (2) An officer appointed by the President, whose duties are to appear for the United States, in all suits in the Supreme Court to which the United States is a party, and to give his opinion on questions of law when requested by the President or the heads of departments. He is a member of the *cabinet* (*q.v.*), and the head of the Department of Justice. (3) An officer with similar duties, elected or appointed in each of the states.

**Attornment,** the acknowledgment of a new lord on the alienation of land. (2) The agreement of the owner of a particular estate in land to *attorn to*, or become the tenant of, a person who has acquired the estate next in reversion or remainder, or the right to the rent or other services by which the land is held.

**Auction,** a public sale of property to the highest bidder, usually conducted by a person licensed for that purpose, who is called the *auctioneer*, and who is regarded in law as the agent of both vendor and purchaser, for the purpose of binding them by his memorandum of sale.

**Audience Court,** a court of the Archbishop of Canterbury, having the same authority as the Court of Arches, but inferior in dignity.

**Audiendo et terminando,** *l.*, a writ or commission to certain persons to appease and punish any insurrection or great riot.

**Audita querela [defendentis],** *l.*, an equitable action whereby a person against whom judgment had been given might prevent execution, on the ground of some matter of defense which there was no opportunity of raising in the original action. Now generally abolished by statute, and superseded by proceedings on motion to set aside the judgment in the court which rendered it.

**Auditor,** one who examines accounts. The officer of the government charged with the duty of examining the accounts of officers who have received and disbursed public moneys. (2) An officer appointed by the court to take and state an account between parties to a suit.

**Aula,** *l.*, a hall, or palace. **Aula ecclesiae,** the nave of a church, where temporal courts were anciently held. **Aula Regis,** or **Regia,** a court established by William the Conqueror; it was composed of the great officers of state, and followed the king's household in all his expeditions. Out of this grew the *Court of King's Bench*, *Court of Common Pleas*, and *Court of Exchequer* (*q.v.*).

**Aurum Reginæ,** *l.*, (*Queen's gold*), anciently a revenue of the queen consort, due from every person who made a voluntary offering or fine to the king amounting to ten marks or upward, for some privilege conferred upon him by the king.

**Auter,** or **Autre,** *fr.*, another. **Autre action pendant,** a plea that another suit for the same cause is already pending. **Autre droit,** in right of another; *e.g.*, a trustee holds in the right of his *cestui que trust*. **Autre vie,** for or during the life of another; *e.g.*, an estate for the life of another, which is the lowest estate of freehold known to the law.

**Authentic act,** that which has been executed before a notary or other public officer, duly authorized, or which is attested by a public seal, or has been rendered public by the authority of a competent magistrate, or which is certified as being a copy of a public register.

**Authentication,** an attestation made by a proper officer, by which he certifies that a record is in due form of law, and that the person who certifies it is the officer appointed so to do.

**Authentics,** a collection of the Novellæ Constitutiones (*additions to the Code*) of Justinian, made by an anonymous author.

**Authority,** power or right conferred on a person; usually by another to act on his behalf, so that the person authorized may do such act without incurring liability. See *Agent*. (2) A public officer or body having certain powers or jurisdiction. (3) Decided cases, opinions of text writers, and the like, cited in arguments.

**Auto da fe** (*Act of faith*), public readings of trials and sentences of the Inquisition.

**Autrefois,** *fr.*, formerly. **Autrefois acquit, Autrefois attaint, Autrefois convict,** pleas in criminal cases that one has already been acquitted on the same charge; or attainted, so that he can not be prosecuted for another felony; or convicted on the same charge, not good if the former judgment was reversed for error.

**Auxilium,** *l.*, an aid. **Auxilium curiae,** an order of court summoning a person at the suit of another to appear and warrant something. **Auxilium regis,** the king's aid; money levied in former times, when the sovereign provided out of his privy purse for many departments of the public service. **Auxilium vicecomiti,** a duty formerly paid to sheriffs for the better support of their offices.

**Aval,** surety for payment.

**Avenage,** payment in oats made by a tenant to his landlord for rent, etc.

**Aver,** (1) a beast of the plow (see *Averium*). (2) The rent paid for plowed land, whether in corn, money, or services. (3) To prove to be true. (4) To allege as true (in pleadings), whence *Averment*.

**Average,** (1) A service which a tenant owes to his lord by doing work with his *avers* or beasts. (2) A contribution, or adjustment of loss, made by merchants when goods have been thrown overboard for the safety of a ship. It is either *general*, *i.e.*, where the loss having been incurred for the general benefit, the owners of the ship and all that have cargo on board contribute proportionately toward making good the loss; or *particular*, where the loss has been accidental, or not for the general benefit, and therefore there is no general contribution. An *average bond* is a deed executed by the several persons liable to contribute, empowering an arbitrator to assess the amount of their contributions. See *General Average*. (3) A small duty paid to masters of ships over and above the freight; known also as *primage and average*.

**Averiis captis in withernam,** a writ granted to one whose cattle were unlawfully distrained by another and driven out of the county in which they were taken, so that they could not be replevied by the sheriff.

**Averium,** the best live beast, due to the lord as a heriot on his tenant's death.

**Aversio,** a turning away; a sale in gross or in bulk.

**Aversio periculi,** a turning away of peril; used of a contract of insurance.

**Avitious,** left by a person s ancestors.

**Avoidance,** of a *benefice*, takes place when it is void of an incumbent, in which sense it is opposed to *plenarty*. (2) The making of a transaction or instrument void, or of no effect. (3) See *Confession*.

**Avoucher,** the calling upon a warrantor to fulfill his undertaking. Under the feudal system, when the tenant's title was impugned, he *avouched* (or vouched) his landlord to defend his right. See *Vouch*.

**Avowry,** a declaration. (2) A pleading in an action of replevin brought to recover property taken in distress, in which the defendant acknowledges the taking, and, setting forth the cause thereof, justifies his right to do so.

**Avowterer, Avouterer** (*Avowtry*), an adulterer.

**Avulsion,** land suddenly separated by an inundation or current from other land of which it originally formed part. See *Alluvion*.

**Avus,** a grandfather. See *Atavus*.

**Award,** (1) to adjudge, or assess, *e.g.*, damages. (2) The decision of an arbitration, which is binding on the parties, unless set aside on the ground of *mala fides* on the part of the arbitrator, or some palpable mistake in the award, or a misconception by him of his duty. When a submission to arbitration (*q.v.*) is made a rule of court under statutory authority, the award can be enforced like the judgment of a court of law.

**Away-going** (or *Way-going*) **crops,** those sown during the last year of a tenancy, but not ripe until after its expiration The right which an out-going tenant has to enter, cut, and take an away-going crop when ripe is sometimes given to him by the express terms of the contract; but, where that is not the case, he is generally entitled to do so by the custom of the country

**Awm,** a measure of wine containing forty gallons.

**Ayant cause,** a receiver; also, a successor, or one to whom a right has been assigned, either by will, gift, sale, or the like.

**Ayle,** a grandfather.

## B.

**Backberinde,** or **Backverinde** (*bearing upon the back*), used formerly of a thief apprehended with the things stolen in his possession.

**Back-bond** (Sc.), a deed, usually separate, attaching a qualification or condition to the terms of an absolute disposition, and thus constituting a trust.

**Backing,** indorsing. **Backing a warrant,** indorsing a warrant issued by a justice in another county, so as to authorize its service in the county to which it is sent, done by a justice of the latter county

**Backside,** a yard at the back part of or behind a house.

**Back water,** water checked or turned back in its flow by a dam or other obstruction. At common law, a riparian proprietor had no right to obstruct the flow of water, unless he acquired it by grant or prescription, and was liable to an action on the case for damages for flowing lands above his own, or diminishing the flow of water through lands below

**Bad,** the technical word for unsoundness in pleading.

**Badger,** a person who buys corn or victuals in one place, and carries them to another to sell and make profit by them.

**Baggage,** wearing apparel, and such other articles as are necessary to the comfort and convenience of a traveler, and carried with him in bags or trunks, as distinguished from merchandise. The distinction is important in the law of common carriers.

**Bail,** to set at liberty a person arrested or imprisoned, on security (or bail) being taken for his appearance on a day, and at a place named. The term is applied, as a noun, to the persons who become security for the defendant's appearance; to the act of delivering such defendant to his bondsmen; and also to the bond given by the sureties to secure his release. Between bail and mainpernors there is this marked distinction: *mainpernors* are merely a person's sureties, who can not imprison him themselves to secure his appearance, but *bail* may, for they are regarded as his jailers, to whose custody he is committed. The word "bail" is never used with a plural termination. See

*Bailable.* There are several kinds of bail at common law: (1) *Common bail*, or bail below, is given to the sheriff, after arresting a person, on a bail bond (*q.v.*) entered into by two or more sureties, on condition that the defendant appear at the day and in such place as the arresting process commands. (2) *Special bail*, or bail above, or bail to the action, are persons who undertake generally, after appearance of a defendant, that if he be condemned in the action, he shall satisfy the debt, costs, and damages, or render himself to the proper prison, or that they will do it for him. (3) *Bail on an attachment*, given when a defendant is arrested upon a writ of attachment, to secure his appearance in court whenever required to answer such matters as may be charged or objected against him. **Bail bond,** the bond taken with sureties at the time the defendant is released, conditioned for the due appearance of such defendant. **Bail Court,** sometimes called the Practice Court, was an auxiliary of the Court of Queen's Bench, wherein points connected with pleading and practice and common motions were determined. **Bail-piece,** a piece of parchment containing the names of special bail, with other particulars, which, being signed by a judge, is filed in the court in which the action is pending; whereupon notice of the bail having justified (*i.e.*, been approved) is then given to the opposite party

**Bailable,** an arresting process is said to be bailable when the person arrested may obtain his liberty on giving bail; *e.g.*, a *capias* on *mesne* process is bailable; a *capias ad satisfaciendum* is non-bailable. In criminal cases, the defendant may generally be admitted to bail, unless he is charged with a capital offense.

**Bailee,** a person to whom goods are intrusted for a specific purpose. See *Bailment.*

**Bailie** (Sc.), a magistrate.

**Bailiff,** an officer who puts in force an arresting process; a sheriff's officer. He usually gives security to the sheriff against liability for his actions, hence *bum-bailiff*, *i.e.*, bound-bailiff.

**Bailiwick,** (1) the jurisdiction of a bailiff. (2) A county, (3) A liberty exempted from a sheriff, over which a bailiff is appointed by the lord of the liberty or franchise, with such powers within his precinct as an under-sheriff exercises under a sheriff.

**Bailment,** a compendious expression to signify a contract resulting from the delivery of goods by a *bailor* to a *bailee*, on a promise by the latter to return them when the purpose is fulfilled, for which they were delivered. Bailments are divisible into three kinds: (1) Those in which the trust is exclusively for the benefit of the bailor, or of a third person, when the bailee is liable for gross negligence only (2) Those in which the trust is exclusively for the benefit of the bailee, who is then bound to the very strictest diligence; and (3) Those in which the trust is for the benefit of both parties, or of both or one of them and a third party, when the bailee must exercise an ordinary and average degree of diligence. (1) embraces deposits, and mandates ("*depositum*," "*mandatum*"); (2) gratuitous loans for use ("*commodatum*"); and (3) pledges or pawns, hiring, and letting to hire ("*locatio et conductio*"), and carriage. See *Carrier*.

**Bailor,** or **Bailer,** a person who commits goods to another person (the *bailee*) in trust for a specific purpose.

**Balance-order,** an order served on a contributory to a company to pay up the balance of a call due from him.

**Ballastage,** a toll paid for the privilege of taking up ballast from the bottom of a port or harbor.

**Ballivo amovendo,** *l.*, an ancient writ to remove a bailiff from office.

**Ban,** or **Bann,** a proclamation, or public notice, or summons, or edict, whereby a thing is commanded or forbidden. Hence *bannire*, to summon, and *banns*, in the plural, the publication of an intended marriage. (2) A denunciation or curse.

**Banc,** or **Bancus,** *fr.*, a bench; the seat of judgment. The sitting together of all the judges of a supreme or superior court, or a quorum thereof, is termed sitting in *banc*, as distinguished from their separate sittings at *nisi prius*, in chambers, or on circuit **Bancus Regis,** or **Reginae,** the Court of King's or Queen's Bench. **Bancus Communium Placitorum,** the Court of Common Pleas. **Bancus Superior,** the Upper Bench, or Superior Court.

**Bandit,** a man outlawed, put under the ban of the law.

**Baneret,** or **Banneret,** a knight made on the field of battle. He ranks next to a baron.

**Banishment,** a forsaking or quitting the realm, entailing civil death It is of two kinds:—one, voluntary and upon oath, called abjuration; the other upon compulsion, for some offense

**Bank,** an institution, generally incorporated, authorized to receive deposits of and to lend money, and to issue promissory notes, payable on demand, known as *bank notes*, or to perform some one or more of these functions. Since the National Bank Act, June 3, 1864 (v. 13, p. 100), none but banks duly incorporated under the laws of the United States, and complying with the terms and conditions of that act, can issue bank-notes.

**Bankrupt,** broken up; ruined; insolvent. A bankrupt is

one who has failed in business, is unable to pay his debts as they become due, or who does, or suffers to be done, certain acts calculated to defraud his creditors, or some of them, which are declared by law to be acts of bankruptcy. At present there is no bankruptcy law in force in the United States, and insolvents are dealt with under the laws of the several states. The principal bankrupt acts which have been in force in the United States are those of April 4, 1800, repealed December 19, 1803; August 19, 1841, repealed March 3, 1843; and March 2, 1867, repealed June 7, 1878. The principal bankrupt acts passed in England are those of 34 and 35 Henry VIII.; 6 Geo. IV. c. 1, b, and the consolidating acts of 1824, 1849, 1854, 1861, and 1869.

**Bannitus,** or **Banniatus,** an outlaw; a banished man.

**Bannum,** or **Banleuga,** a ban; the bounds of a manor or town.

**Bar,** a partition running across the courts of law, within which solicitors, being officers of the court, are admitted, as are also queen's counsel, barristers with patents of precedence, and sergeants, in virtue of their ranks. All other barristers and the public must remain outside it. Parties who appear in person are placed within the bar on the floor of the court. In the United States generally the distinction between attorneys and *counsellors, or barristers*, is abolished, and the whole body of the legal profession is called "the bar." A man is "called to" or "admitted to the bar" when he is authorized by a court to practice before it. The case on trial is frequently called the case *at bar*, but in England this expression applies only to cases tried before a full court of three or more judges of the Supreme Court, instead of a single judge at *nisi prius*. (2) A legal obstacle. To *bar* a debt or entail is to destroy it.

**Bar, plea in,** a pleading showing some ground for barring or defeating an action at common law.

**Bare,** or **dry, trustee,** one whose active duties have come to an end, so that he can be compelled by his *cestui que trust* to convey the property according to his direction.

**Bar-fee,** or **barr-fee,** a payment formerly taken by a sheriff or jailer from an acquitted prisoner.

**Bargain and sale,** an agreement for sale of goods which passes the property at once. (2) A form of conveyance of real property, (*a*) statutory (see *lease and release*); (*b*) at common law, which is used in the case of a sale by executors with a mere power to sell.

**Barleycorn,** the third of an inch. (2) In conveyancing, a nominal consideration or rent.

**Baron,** the lowest degree of nobility. He holds (*a*) by prescription; (*b*) by patent. (2) A judge of the Exchequer. (3) A husband. **Baron et feme,** husband and wife; seldom used. **Baron of the Cinque Ports,** a freeman (old charters); later, a member of Parliament from one of the *Cinque Ports* (*q.v*).

**Baronet,** a dignity descendible to issue male, originally created in 1611, and taking precedence of all knights.

**Barony of land,** a quantity of land amounting to 15 acres. In Ireland, a subdivision of a county.

**Barratry,** or **Barretry,** the offense of constantly stirring up quarrels and suits, either at law or otherwise. (2) Any illegal or fraudulent conduct by the master or crew of a ship by which the freighter or owner is injured. (3) In Scotland, the crime of a judge who is induced, by bribery, to pronounce a judgment. (4) The simony of clergymen, going abroad to purchase benefices from the see of Rome.

**Barrier,** the wall of coal left between two contiguous mines.

**Barrister,** one who has been admitted to plead at the bar.

**Barter,** a contract by which parties exchange goods for goods, differing from sale, in which they exchange goods for *money*.

**Base-estate,** land held by a tenant, who performed certain prescribed menial services for his lord.

**Base-fee,** otherwise called a fee *qualified* or *conditional*, is an estate of freehold conditioned to determine on the happening of a particular event, such as the failure of heirs male, the ceasing to be tenant of Blackacre, and the like. (2) The estate created by a tenant in tail who bars the entail without the consent of the Protector of the Settlement (*q.v.*); and thus, only the issue of the tenant in tail being barred, the estate determines on their failure.

**Basilica,** an abridgment of the Corpus Juris Civilis of Justinian, completed about A. D. 880.

**Bastard,** one born out of wedlock. (2) One born in wedlock who has been bastardized by legal sentence. He has, at common law, no claim to succeed to property of his parents, nor to the name of either.

**Bastard-eigne.** If a man have a natural son, and afterward marry the mother, and by her have a legitimate son, the latter is called *mulier puisné*, and the elder son *bastard eigné*.

**Bastardize,** to judicially declare one a bastard. (2) To give evidence in proof of bastardy.

**Battel, wager of,** a form of trial by combat anciently used in military, and certain criminal cases; abolished by statute, 59 George III. c. 46.

**Battery,** beating and wounding, including every touching

or laying hold, however trifling, of another's person or clothes, in an angry, insolent, or hostile manner.

**Batture,** *fr.*, shoals; shallows; an elevation of the bed of a river under the surface of the water.

**Bawd,** a person who keeps a house of prostitution, or *bawdy house*, and procures opportunities for illicit intercourse.

**Bear** (stock exchange), one who speculates for a fall in prices.

**Bearer,** one who bears or carries a thing. A check or draft drawn "*to bearer*" is payable to any one who may present it. (2) Such as bear down or oppress others. See *Maintainor.*

**Beasts** *of chase* [*feræ campestres*], are the buck, doe, fox, marten, and roe; *of the forest*, are the hart, hind, hare, boar, and wolf, which are also called beasts of venary; *of the warren*, are the hare and coney.

**Beau-pleader,** *L. fr.*, (*to plead fairly*), the name of an obsolete writ founded on the statute of Marlbridge (52 Hen. III. c. 11.).

**Bederepe,** or **Biderepe,** a service which certain tenants were anciently bound to perform; as to reap their landlord's corn.

**Bench,** a tribunal of justice. (2) The judges, as distinguished from the bar. See *Banc.*

**Benchers,** seniors in the inns of court, intrusted with their government or direction.

**Bench warrant,** an order issued by a court for the attachment or arrest of an individual for contempt, or where an indictment has been found.

**Benefice,** an ecclesiastical living, usually parochial.

**Beneficial interest,** profit, benefit, or advantage resulting from a contract or estate, as distinct from legal ownership or control.

**Beneficiary,** he that is in possession of a benefice; also a *cestui que trust* (*q.v.*).

**Beneficio primo ecclesiastico habendo,** *l.*, an ancient writ, which was addressed by the king to the lord chancellor, to bestow the benefice that should *first* fall in the royal gift, above or under a specified value, upon a person named therein.

**Beneficium,** an ecclesiastical living; (2) any favor or privilege. **Beneficium abstinendi,** the power of an heir to decline an inheritance. **Beneficium cedendarum actionum,** the right of the surety to demand from the creditor, before paying him, the *choses in action* of his principal. **Beneficium competentiae,** the privilege of retaining a competence, or the necessaries of life, granted to an obligor in a gratuitous obligation in Scotch law, and an insolvent debtor on making cession of his property for the benefit of his creditors, in Roman law. **Beneficium divisionis,** the right of a surety to contribute only ratably with his solvent co-sureties. **Beneficium inventarii,** the privilege which an heir had, by having an inventory taken of the testator's property before he entered into possession of it, to protect himself from liability beyond the amount of the property inventoried.

**Beneficium ordinis, excussionis** or **discussionis** (Rom.), a privilege by which a surety, called in Scotch law a *cautioner*, could call on the creditor to sue the principal debtor first, and only to sue the sureties for that which he could not recover from the principal.

**Beneficium separationis** (Rom.), the privilege, sometimes granted to creditors, of having the goods of an heir separated from those of the testator; *e.g.*, if the heir was insolvent.

**Benefit of clergy,** a privilege originally granted to the clergy, and subsequently extended to all persons who could read, whereby they were exempted from capital punishment and trial by the secular courts in criminal cases. Finally abolished by 7 and 8 Geo. IV. c. 28.

**Benevolence,** nominally a voluntary gratuity made by subjects to the sovereign, which came to be a forced loan or tax. By the Petition of Right, 3 Car. I., it was declared to be leviable for the future only with the consent of the House of Commons.

**Bequeath,** to make a *bequest*, or gift of personal property by will. See *Legacy*.

**Bercaria,** a sheep-fold, or other inclosure to keep sheep.

**Bestiality,** carnal intercourse with the lower animals.

**Betrothment,** a contract for future marriage.

**Betterments,** improvements made to an estate which render it better than mere repairs would do.

**Beyond seas,** meant originally out of the United Kingdom and Channel islands; out of the United States; out of the state. See *Absence*.

**Bid,** an offer of a price for any thing which is being sold by auction. It may be retracted before acceptance.

**Bigamy,** the offense of having two husbands or two wives at the same time.

**Bilateral contract,** a contract in which both the contracting parties are bound to fulfill obligations reciprocally toward each other.

**Bilboes,** a punishment at sea answering to the stocks.

**Bilinguis,** *l.*, speaking two languages. See *Jury de medietate linguæ*.

**Bill,** a written statement of one's claim or account against another. (2) A written order, drawn by one person upon another, to pay a certain sum of money to a third; *e.g.*, a *bill of exchange*, also called a draft. (3) A promissory note, or written obligation to pay, especially the note of a government or bank, designed to circulate as money. (4) The original draft of a law presented to a legislative body for enactment. It is a *bill* until passed, and then becomes an *act*, or *statute*. The term is applied to some special acts after their passage; *e.g.*, *bill of attainder*, *bill of indemnity*, etc. (5) A carrier's acknowledgment of the receipt of goods, to be transported from place to place—a *bill of lading*. (6) The written statement of an offense charged against a person, which is presented to a grand jury. If satisfied by the evidence that the charge is probably true, they indorse it "*a true bill*," and it is then called an *indictment*. (7) The written statement of his cause of complaint, made by a party to a suit in equity. **Bill of adventure,** a writing signed by a person who takes goods on board a vessel, wholly at the risk of the owner, and agreeing to account solely for the proceeds of the goods when sold. **Bill of attainder,** a bill declaring persons attainted and their property confiscated. See *Attainder*. **Bill of certiorari,** one praying for a writ of certiorari to remove a cause from an inferior court of equity to a superior one; rarely used in the United States. **Bill of conformity,** a bill filed by an executor or administrator, when the affairs of the deceased were so much involved that he could not safely administer the estate, except under the direction of the Court of Chancery. **Bill of costs,** a statement of the items which form the total amount of the taxable costs in a suit or action. **Bill of credit,** paper issued by the authority of the state, on the faith of the state, and designed to circulate as money. See *Letter of credit*. **Bill of debt,** or **Bill obligatory,** an acknowledgment in writing of debt, specifying the amount and the date and place of payment. **Bill of discovery,** one which prays for the discovery of facts resting within the knowledge of the person against whom the bill is exhibited, or of deeds, writings, or other things, in his custody or power, and material to enable the party filing the bill to prosecute or defend some action at law. **Bill of exceptions,** a written statement of objections to decisions of the trial court upon questions of law arising during the progress of the trial, so as to put the decision objected to on record for the information of the court having cognizance of the cause in error. Authorized by statute, Westm. 2 (13 Edw. I.), c. 31, and the laws of the several states. **Bill of exchange,** an unconditional order in writing, addressed by one person to another, signed by the person giving it, requiring the person to whom it is addressed to pay on demand, or at a fixed or determinable future time, a sum certain in money to, or to the order of, a specified person, or to bearer. See *Acceptance*. **Bill of health,** a certificate by the proper officer, usually a consul, that a vessel therein named comes from a place where no contagious diseases prevail, and that none of her crew were affected with any such disease at the time of her departure. **Bill of indemnity,** an act of Parliament, passed every session, until 1869, for the relief of those who had unwittingly or unavoidably neglected to take the necessary oaths, etc., required for the purpose of qualifying them to hold their respective offices. **Bill of interpleader,** one brought by a person who has money or property in his possession, or owes rents, etc., claimed by two or more persons, praying that they may be required to interplead and set up their claims, and that the court may adjudge to which of them he shall pay or deliver. **Bill of lading,** a memorandum, usually in duplicate or triplicate, signed by a carrier, showing the receipt of goods and the contract of transportation. While the goods are in transit, the bill of lading represents them, so that its indorsement and transfer operate as a delivery of the goods. **Bill of pains and penalties,** a special act of the legislature, whereby any punishment, less than death, may be inflicted upon persons supposed to be guilty of treason or felony, without any conviction in the ordinary course of judicial proceedings. **Bill of particulars,** a statement of a plaintiff's cause of action, or of a defendant's set-off. **Bills payable,** bills of exchange accepted, or promissory notes made, which one is obliged to pay. **Bill of peace,** one filed when a person has a right which may be controverted by various persons, to have his right established against them all in one suit, and thus prevent a multiplicity of suits. **Bill penal,** a written obligation, by which one acknowledges an indebtedness for a certain sum, and binds himself for the payment thereof in a larger sum. Bonds with conditions have superseded such bills in modern practice. **Bill to perpetuate testimony,** one brought to secure the testimony of witnesses with reference to some matter which is not in litigation, but may become so. **Bill quia timet,** one filed by a person entitled to property on the death of another, to prevent the apprehended destruction or injury of such property by the wilful acts or the neglect of another. **Bills receivable,** promissory notes, or bills of exchange, entitling the holder to receive the amount of money specified at maturity. **Bill of review,** one brought to have a decree of the court reviewed, modified, or reversed, on account of error in the proceedings or newly discovered testimony. **Bill of revivor,** one brought by the legal representatives of a deceased plaintiff, to continue a suit abated by the death of the plaintiff before judgment. **Bill of Rights,** a declaration delivered by the Lords and Commons to the Prince and Princess of Orange, 13th February, 1689, and afterward enacted in Parliament, when they became king and queen, declaring illegal certain acts of the late king, and setting forth the rights and privileges of the people. Such a statement of rights and privileges is prefixed to the constitutions of most of the states of the Union. **Bill of sale,** an agreement in writing, by which one transfers his right to or interest in goods and personal chattels to another. It is either absolute, in which case it must be accompanied by a transfer of possession to the grantee, where that is possible, or by way of mortgage, in which case it is provided by law, in most of the states, that the instrument must be filed with the county recorder or township clerk, or be recorded. The transfer of a ship is usually evidenced by a bill of sale. **Bill of sight,** an imperfect and preliminary *bill of entry* at the custom-house, describing goods to the best of the merchant's belief. **Bill to take testimony de bene esse,** one brought to take the testimony of witnesses to facts material to a case already pending, when there is cause to fear that, on account of the age, or infirmity, or intended absence of the witnesses, the testimony may otherwise be lost before the time of trial.

**Billa cassetur,** *l.*, that the bill may be quashed or made void; the conclusion of a plea in abatement, when proceedings were conducted in Latin.

**Bind,** to oblige, constrain, or hold, by legal obligation, or contract; *e.g.*, to *bind out* an apprentice to service; to *bind over* a party accused to appear before a grand jury or court having jurisdiction of the offense charged, or to keep the peace, by taking bail.

**Bipartite,** of two parts; used in conveyancing.

**Birds.** Domestic fowls, and tame pigeons and pheasants are subjects of larceny. Certain wild birds are protected by statute during their breeding season. See *Game.*

**Birretum,** the cap or coif of a judge or sergeant-at-law.

**Birth,** the act of coming into life; the whole body must be brought into the world alive, and have an independent circulation.

**Bishop,** an ecclesiastical dignitary nominated by the crown; chief of the clergy within his diocese. *Suffragan* bishop, one who acts for an absent bishop. See *Congé d'Elire.*

**Bishop's court,** an ecclesiastical court, held in the cathedral of each diocese, the judge whereof is the bishop's chancellor, who judges by the civil canon law; and if the diocese be large, he has his commissaries in remote parts, who hold *consistory courts*, for matters limited to them by their commission.

**Bissextile,** the day added every fourth year to the month of February. The extra day was by Julius Cæsar appointed to be the day before the 24th of February, which was the sixth before the Kalends, so that the intercalated day was called the double sextile, or *bis-sextilis*. It is now the 29th of February.

**Blackmail,** a species of rent formerly paid by inhabitants in the north of England and south of Scotland to men allied to robbers and marauders to be protected by them from theft and violence; hence, money extorted from anybody by threats of ill treatment, libelous accusations, or exposure of faults committed. **Black rents,** rents reserved payable in work, grain, etc., as distinguished from *white rents* (*alba firma*) payable in silver. **Black rod,** the usher who, during the session of Parliament, attends on the peers, and to whose custody all peers impeached for any crime or contempt are first committed; so-called from the black rod which he carries.

**Blanch-holding** (Sc.), an ancient tenure, the duty payable being nominal, as a penny, or a peppercorn, if required.

**Blank,** a space left in writing or printing, to be filled up with a word or words to complete the sense. (2) A paper without marks or writing; *e.g.*, a blank ballot. (3) A printed paper containing the formal parts of a deed, release, power of attorney, or like instrument, with vacant spaces left to be filled in with the names of the parties, consideration, description of the property or subject-matter to be affected by it, etc. (4) A small coin (value, 8*d.*), put in circulation by Henry V. in those parts of France then subject to England. **Blank acceptance,** one written on the paper before the bill is made, and delivered by the acceptor, which will bind him to the extent of any amount that may afterward be written in. **Blank bar,** common bar; a plea in bar, which, in an action of trespass, was resorted to to compel the plaintiff to *assign*, or name the place where the alleged trespass was committed. **Blank indorsement,** one written on the back of a note or other instrument, which does not mention the name of the person in whose favor it was made, and which makes such instrument transferable by delivery merely.

**Blasphemy,** in England, the offense of speaking against God, Jesus Christ, the Bible, or the Book of Common Prayer, with intent to excite contempt against the established religion, or to promote immorality. In most of the United States, the offense is defined and made penal by statute.

**Blockade,** the maintenance of vessels of war outside a port so as to prevent the ingress or egress of ships. Vessels attempting to pass it are liable to confiscation.

**Blood,** that quality or relationship which enables a person to succed to another by descent. See *Attainder*. Brothers and sisters are said to be of the *whole blood*, if they have the same father and mother; of the *half blood*, if they have only one parent in common.

**Board,** a body of men elected or appointed to take the care and management of a public trust or institution, or conduct the business of a municipal or private corporation; *e.g.*, a board of health, a board of trade, a board of directors, etc. (2) Food and lodging furnished under a contract, express or implied, for a stipulated compensation. The liability of a boarding-house keeper is much more limited than that of an inn-keeper.

**Boc,** a charter, or written evidence of title, used among the Saxons, corresponding to a modern deed. **Bock-hord,** or **Book-hoard,** a place where books, documentary evidence, or writings are kept. **Bock-land, Boc-land,** or **Book-land,** also called charter-land or deed-land, was, under the Saxon system, land held by deed under certain rents and services, and in effect differed in no respect from free-socage lands.

**Body,** a person; used of a natural body, or an artificial one created by law, as a *body corporate*, or corporation; a *body politic*, or state. (2) A mass, or collection of individual things in a general system; *e.g.*, a *body of laws; a body of divinity*. (3) The main part of any instrument; in *deeds*, it is spoken of as distinguished from the recitals and introductory parts, and from the signatures; in *affidavits*, from the title, and jurat.

**Bona,** *l.*, goods; personal property; in Roman law, all kinds of property, real, personal, and mixed. **Bona confiscata,** or **forisfacta,** goods confiscated or forfeited to the imperial *fisc* or treasury. **Bona fide,** in good faith; honestly; without fraud or unfair dealing. A *bona fide* purchaser, or holder, is one who bought a note or chattel, in good faith, for a valuable consideration, and without notice of any defect attaching to it, or adverse claims. **Bona gestura,** good behavior. **Bona gratia,** voluntarily. **Bona mobilia; immobilia,** goods movable; immovable. **Bona notabilia,** *notable goods, i.e.*, goods sufficient in amount to require, under the ecclesiastical law, probate or administration to be taken out. They were fixed by the 93rd canon (excepting in London, where the sum is 10*l.*), to be legal personal estate to the value of 5*l.* or upward. **Bona patria,** an assize of countrymen or good neighbors; sometimes called *assiza bonae patriae*. **Bona peritura,** perishable goods. **Bona vacantia,** goods to which no one claimed property, as shipwrecks, treasure trove, etc. **Bona waviata,** (1) (Rom.), property of an intestate. (2) Goods thrown away by a thief in his flight, for fear of being apprehended. They are given to the crown by the common law as a punishment upon the owner for not himself pursuing the felon and taking away his goods from him; but if the owner prosecutes the thief to conviction, the goods are restored. (3) Waifs (*q.v.*).

**Bond,** a written acknowledgment of a debt or contract to pay, under seal. If this be all, it is called a *simple* or *single* bond. If a condition be added that the bond shall be void when the *obligor*, or giver of it, shall have performed an act specified, it is called *double* or *conditional*. The person to whom the undertaking is given is the *obligee*. See *Bail; Bottomry; Post obit; Replevin.* (2) An instrument of indebtedness issued by governments and companies.

**Bondage,** the state of being bound, or under restraint; involuntary servitude; slavery. (2) An ancient tenure of land on condition of doing the meanest services for the owner.

**Bondsman,** a slave; one held to involuntary servitude. (2) A surety; one who is bound or gives security for another.

**Bonis asportatis,** (*Writ* **De**), a writ of trespass for the wrongful taking of chattels.

**Bonis non amovendis,** *l.*, (*that the goods be not removed*), a writ addressed to the sheriff, where error was brought, commanding that the person against whom judgment is obtained be not suffered to remove his goods till the error be tried and determined.

**Bono et malo,** *l.*, (*for good and bad*), a special writ of jail delivery, which issued for every prisoner Now abolished.

**Bonus,** premium or advantage. (2) An occasional extra dividend given by a company to its share-holders.

**Bookland.** See *Bockland.*

**Booty,** the personal property of an enemy captured by an army on land; it belongs by right to the sovereign or public.

**Bordage,** a species of tenure by which *bord lands, i.e.*, lands kept for the maintenance of the *bord* or table, were held. The rents were paid in eggs, poultry, and such small matters for the table.

**Borough,** a town; part of a township organized for municipal purposes; in England, a town that sends a burgess or burgesses to parliament. **Borough Courts,** local borough tribunals, held by prescription, charter, or act of parliament. They are Courts of Record, and usually the recorder of the borough is the judge. **Borough-English,** or **Postremogeniture,** a custom of Saxon origin, occasionally met with in burgage tenures, by which the youngest son of an intestate inherits all the realty which belonged to his father, situated within such borough.

**Bote,** an obsolete term, signifying necessaries for housekeeping, or husbandry; *e.g.*, *house bote*, firewood; *plough bote*, wood for repairing instruments of husbandry. (2) Reparation for injury; *e.g.*, *man bote*, for homicide. See *Estovers.*

**Bottom,** a valley; (2) a ship.

**Bottomry,** or **Bummaree,** a species of mortgage or hypothecation of a ship, by which she and her freight or cargo are pledged as a security for the repayment of a sum of money. If the ship be totally lost, the lender loses his money; but if she return safely, he recovers his principal, together with the interest agreed upon, which is at a high rate corresponding to the risk. The contract may be by deed-poll, which is called a *bottomry bill*, or by bond, called a *bottomry bond.* See *Respondentia.*

**Bought and sold notes,** documents delivered by a broker to his principals on the conclusion of a sale of stock, etc., containing particulars of the transaction.

**Bound,** or **Boundary,** the limit or dividing line of two pieces of land. Boundaries may be *natural*, as a stream, river, or sea shore, or *artificial*, as a highway, hedge, or imaginary line drawn from fixed stakes, stones (called monuments), or trees, to other like objects.

**Bounty,** a premium given by a government to manufacturers and others to encourage particular industries. (2) An extra sum paid to induce a person to enlist as a soldier.

**Brawling,** the offense of quarreling or creating a disturbance.

**Breach,** a breaking, is either the invasion of a right, or the violation of a duty. It may be *actual* or *constructive.* To *assign* breaches, in an action, is to specify them in the pleadings. **Breach of close,** an unwarrantable entry on another's land. See *Trespass.* **Breach of covenant,** a violation of an agreement contained in a deed, either to do or not to do some act; it is a civil injury. **Breach of Peace,** a violation of public order; an act calculated to disturb the public peace. It may be *actual*, *constructive*, *i.e.*, tending to make others break it, or *apprehended.* **Breach of pound,** the breaking any pound or place where cattle or goods distrained are deposited, to rescue such distress. **Breach of prison,** an escape by a prisoner lawfully in prison. **Breach of promise of marriage,** a violation of a promise to marry, which gives rise to an action of damages, unless the breach was justifiable, *e.g.*, on the ground of want of chastity. **Breach of trust,** the willful misappropriation, by a trustee, of a thing which has been committed to him in trust for certain purposes, and was lawfully in his possession.

**Breaking,** parting, or dividing by force; bursting through or removing an obstruction. **Breaking bulk,** opening a box, bale, or package, and removing part of the contents, or taking away a portion of the goods which constitute a wagon, boat, or car-load. **House breaking,** bursting or removing fastenings provided to secure doors or windows, with a view to entering the house. Obtaining entrance by fraud, threats, or conspiracy is a *constructive breaking.*

**Brehon law,** a traditional and customary law, formerly in force in Ireland. Abolished by 40 Edw. III.

**Bretoise,** the law of the Welsh Marches, observed by the Ancient Britons.

**Breve,** a writ; used more frequently in the plural *brevia.* **Brevia magistralia,** official writs framed by the clerks in chancery to meet new injuries, to which the old forms of action were inapplicable. See *Trespass on the case.* **Brevia testata,** short attested memoranda, originally introduced to obviate the uncertainty arising from parol feoffments; hence modern conveyances have gradually arisen.

**Brevet,** a commission conferring on an officer in the army a rank above that which he holds, without, however, giving him increased pay.

**Brevibus et rotulis liberandis,** *l.*, a writ to a sheriff to deliver to his successor the county and appointments, with the rolls, briefs, and all other things belonging to his office.

**Bribery,** the offense of giving or receiving a gift or reward intended to influence a person in the exercise of a judicial or public duty.

**Bridewell,** a house of correction.

**Brief,** an abbreviated statement of the pleadings, proofs, and affidavits in any legal proceeding, with a concise narrative of the facts and merits of the plaintiff's case, or the defendant's defense, for the instruction of counsel at the trial or hearing. (2) A written or printed argument of counsel submitted to the court. (3) A writ. (4) A letter. **Brief al'evesque,** a writ to the bishop by which, in *quare impedit,* an incumbent was removed unless he recovered judgment, or was presented *pendente lite.*

**Brocage,** or **Brokerage,** the wage or commission of a broker. The trade or occupation of a broker.

**Brocards,** law maxims.

**Broker,** an agent employed to make contracts in matters of trade, and to find persons who may be willing to enter into such contracts. He is paid by a commission, or *brokerage.* See *Ship*; *Stock*; *Insurance*; *Factor.*

**Brothel,** a house kept for purposes of prostitution; a common habitation of prostitutes.

**Brother,** a male born of the same parents as another. A *half-brother* is one who has but one parent in common with another. A *brother-in-law* is the brother of one's wife, or the husband of one's sister.

**Bull** (stock exchange), one who speculates for a rise in the market.

**Bum-bailiff,** or **Bound-bailiff.** See *Bailiff.*

**Burden of proof,** (*onus probandi*), the duty of proving facts disputed on the trial of a case. It commonly lies on the person who asserts the affirmative of an issue, and is said to be *shifted* when sufficient evidence is furnished to raise a presumption that what is alleged is true. See *Evidence; Proof.*

**Burgage-tenure,** one whereby houses and lands in ancient boroughs are held of the lord. Some of these boroughs have been disfranchised, and continue such only in name and by virtue of their ancient customs. See *Borough-English.*

**Burgess,** an inhabitant of a borough. (2) A representative of a borough in Parliament. (3) A magistrate of a borough, discharging duties similar to those of a mayor of a city.

**Burgh,** (Sc.), equivalent to the English "borough."

**Burglary,** a breaking and entering by night into a dwelling-house with intent to commit a felony. *Breaking,* in the eye of the law, includes entering a house by fraud, threats, or collusion.

**By-laws,** or **Bye-laws,** the laws, regulations, and constitutions made by companies, societies, corporations, etc., for the government of their members, the management of their business, and the like.

## C.

**Cabinet,** an advisory board, composed of the heads of the principal departments of state, to consult with and aid the chief executive in his administration. In the United States, the cabinet is composed of the secretaries of state, the treasury, the interior, war and the navy, the postmaster-general, and the attorney-general.

**Cachet, lettres de,** letters issued and signed by the kings of France, and countersigned by a secretary of state, authorizing the imprisonment of a person.

**Cadit actio; assisa; causa; quaestio;** *l.*, the action, assize, cause, or argument fails, or is at an end.

**Caduca** (Rom.), the lapse of a testamentary disposition.

**Call,** a demand for money by a company from its shareholders. (2) The election of students to the degree of barrister. (3) See *Option.* (4) The direction and length of a boundary line given in a deed, or survey, or the *monuments* between which it runs. (5) **Calling the plaintiff,** the formal action of the court crier preparatory to *non-suiting* a plaintiff.

**Calumnia,** (Rom.), malicious prosecution. **Calumniae jusjurandum,** an oath formerly taken by both parties to an action that the same was brought or defended in good faith, and that the facts alleged by them were true; used principally in divorce cases. The *verification* (*q.v.*) of pleadings, required by the codes of practice of many of the states, corresponds to this oath.

**Calvin's case** (7 Rep. 1), decided that persons born in Scotland after the accession of James I. to the crown of England were natural-born English subjects.

**Camera,** a chamber; the judge's private room behind the court. Cases are sometimes heard there by him, especially in divorce matters. **Camera Stellata,** the Star Chamber, a court originally created to prevent the obstruction of justice in the inferior courts by undue influence. It consisted of the Privy Council, the Common Law Judges, and Peers of Parliament. Its authority was enlarged and confirmed by *Rot. Parl.* 3 Hen. VII. n. 17, fell subsequently into abuse, and was abolished in the reign of Charles I.

**Cancellaria; Cancellarius;** *l.*, chancery; the Court of Chancery; the chancellor; derived from *cancelli*, the rails or lattice work inclosing the bar of a court of justice.

**Cancellation,** an invalidation or revocation of an instrument by lines drawn across it (*cancelli*). A deed is usually canceled by striking out the signatures and tearing off the seal.

**Candlemas day,** the 2d of February. It is the fourth of the four half or *cross* quarter-days of the year (used in Scotland as quarter-days), the others being Whitsunday (fixed on May 15), Lammas, and Martinmas.

**Canon,** in ecclesiastical law, a rule of the *jus canonicum* contained in the *Decretum Gratiani.* (2) A rule of ecclesiastical conduct promulgated by Convocation. (3) In civil law, a rule; *e.g.*, the canons of inheritance. (4) A member of a chapter.

**Canon law,** a body of Roman ecclesiastical law, first codified by Gratianus in 1139. This and five subsequent collections form the *Corpus Juris Canonici.* In England, the canon law (or *Canons' of the Church*) consists of certain ecclesiastical laws, or constitutions, which were ratified after the Reformation by 25 Hen. VIII., c. 19, so far as they are not repugnant to the law of the land. They were revised in 1603, and again in 1865.

**Capacity,** the power to alter one's legal position, *e.g.*, by alienating property, committing crime, etc. This a lunatic has not, and infants and married women only in a modified degree, defined by statute in the several states.

**Cape,** a judicial writ touching a plea of lands or tenements, divided into *cape magnum*, or the *grand cape*, which lay, before appearance, to summon the tenant to answer the default and also over to the demandment; the *cape ad valentiam*, which was a species of grand cape; and the *cape parvum*, or *petit cape*, after appearance or view granted, summoning the tenant to answer the default only

**Capias** (*that you take*), a generic name for writs (usually addressed to the sheriff), ordering the person to whom they are addressed to arrest a person therein named. See *Mesne process.* **Capias ad audiendum judicium,** a writ issued in case the defendant be found guilty of a misdemeanor, to bring him up to the court *to receive sentence.* **Capias ad computandum,** a writ issued in the action of account, to compel the defendant to come before the auditors and enter into his account. **Capias ad respondendum,** a writ issued for the arrest of a person against whom an indictment for misdemeanor has been found, in order that he may be arraigned. (2) Under the old practice, it issued against an absconding debtor, who was then made to give special bail. **Capias ad satisfaciendum,** or *ca. sa.*, a writ whereby a defendant in a civil action, when judgment has been recovered against him for a sum of money is arrested and held in prison until payment is made. Imprisonment for debt is now generally abolished. **Capias extendi facias.** See *Extent.* **Capias in withernam,** a writ directing the sheriff to take other goods of the distrainor equal in value to those he has taken in distress and *elcigned*, *i e.*, removed or concealed, so that the sheriff could not take them when directed to do so in an action of *replevin* (*q.v.*); now obsolete. **Capias pro fine,** a writ which formerly issued against a defendant who had been fined and had not discharged the judgment, used in cases of torts *vi et armis*, of falsely denying one's deed, etc.; now abolished. **Capias utlagatum,** a writ directing the arrest of an outlaw. It was either *general*, against the person only; or *special*, against the person, lands, and goods. Outlawry having been abolished in civil cases, this writ is rarely issued.

**Capita,** *l.*, heads. Distribution of personalty *per capita* happens when all the claimants claim in their own right, as kindred in the same degree; this being opposed to a claim *per stirpes* (*q.v.*), as representing another person whose right or share they claim. (2) Boundaries.

**Capital felonies,** those crimes upon conviction of which the offender is condemned to be hanged. The crimes now punishable with death, in England, are high treason and murder. Capital punishment has been abolished in several states.

**Capital stock,** the sum, divided into shares, which is raised by mutual subscription of the members of a corporation, and upon which calls and dividends are based.

**Capitation tax, grant, etc.,** is one raised or made according to the *heads*, *i.e.*, from or for each one of a community, school, etc.

**Capite, tenure in,** the holding of land direct from the sovereign, or *head* of the nation.

**Caption,** that part of a legal instrument or record, *e.g.*, a commission or indictment, which shows where, when, and by what authority it is taken, found or executed.

**Capture,** seizure of the property of an enemy. See *Booty*; *Prize*; *Reprisals*. Capture at sea can only be lawfully made by persons holding a commission from their government. See *Piracy*. *Actual captors* are the crew of the ship to which the prize strikes its flag; *constructive*, those belonging to ships that assisted, or were at hand.

**Carcel-age,** prison fees.

**Cargo,** the entire load of a ship, steamboat, or other vessel, usually applied to *goods* only and not to passengers.

**Carnal knowledge,** sexual intercourse. The technical expression in an indictment for rape is that the man "carnally knew," etc.

**Carrier,** one who receives goods for hire to convey from one place to another. If he does so as his regular business, he is a *common carrier*; if by special contract, a bailee. See *Bailment*. A *common carrier* is bound to carry the goods of any one who offers to pay his hire, and is liable for loss or injury to them. The common-law liability has been much restricted by statutes in England and the several states.

**Cartel,** or **Chartel,** an agreement to exchange prisoners. *Cartel-ship*, one in which they are conveyed to be exchanged.

**Carucate,** or **Carve of land,** a plough-land of 60 to 100 acres, being as much as a man could cultivate in a year and a day, with a single plow (*caruca*).

**Case,** an abbreviation for *Trespass on the case* (*q. v.*). (2) A statement of facts for counsel's opinion. (3) An action or suit at law, or in equity. (4) A written statement of the facts by an inferior court, for the opinion of the superior court. (5) An agreed statement of the facts made by the parties to a dispute for the purpose of obtaining the opinion of the court thereon.

**Cash,** that which circulates as money, including bank bills, but not mere bills receivable. A **cash sale** is one of goods to be paid for at the time of purchase or delivery.

**Cassetur billa,** *l.*, (*let the bill be quashed*), an entry on the record that the plaintiff withdraws his bill. So in the old common law practice, *cassetur breve*, which was equivalent to the modern notice of *discontinuance* (*q. v.*).

**Cast,** defeated at law, condemned in costs or damages.

**Casu consimili, Casu proviso,** *l.*, writs of entry, now abolished, which lay for the benefit of a reversioner, when a tenant by courtesy, or in dower, had aliened in fee, or for life.

**Casual ejector,** the fictitious *Richard Roe*, the nominal defendant in the old action of ejectment (*q. v.*).

**Casualty,** inevitable accident. An unforeseen circumstance occasioning loss or damage without human agency.

**Casus,** *l.*, a case; cause; event; occurrence. **Casus belli,** an act giving rise to or justifying war. **Casus foederis,** a case stipulated by treaty, or which comes within the terms of a compact. **Casus fortuitus,** an accidental occurrence not foreseen and provided against. **Casus omissus,** a case not provided for by contract, or statutes intended to govern like cases.

**Catalla, Catals,** chattels. **Catalla otiosa,** dead animals, other than beasts of the plow and sheep.

**Catching bargain,** one made with an expectant heir (*q. v.*) or reversioner, for inadequate consideration.

**Catchland,** land in Norfolk, so called because it is uncertain to what parish it belongs, and the minister who first seizes the tithes enjoys them for that year.

**Catchpole,** a sheriff's officer, or constable.

**Cattle-gate,** common for one beast.

**Causa,** *l.*, a cause; a reason; a writ or action pending. **Causa causans,** the immediate or operating cause. **Causa mortis,** by reason of, or in view of, death. **Causa proxima,** the direct, as distinguished from **causa remota,** the remote cause.

**Cause of action.** a right to sue.

**Cautio; Caution,** a species of bail or security given for the performance of an obligation. The surety is termed the *cautioner.* (2) A notice not to deal concerning land described in the notice without informing the person giving the notice; provided for by a recent English statute.

**Caveat,** *l.*, (*let him take heed*), notice entered on the books of a registry of court to prevent a certain step being taken, *e.g.*, probate of a will without informing the *caveator.* (2) A legal notice, filed in the patent office, that the *caveator* has invented a certain thing, describing it, the effect of which is to prevent the granting of a patent to another for the same thing, without giving him an opportunity to establish his priority of invention. **Caveat emptor** (*let the buyer beware*), a principle of law which imposes on the purchaser of property the risk of defects in title or quality of the thing purchased, unless there is an express or implied warranty, or some fraud or misrepresentation on the part of the seller. **Caveat viator** (*let the traveler beware*), a notice to persons who have gratuitous permission to pass over private land, that they must take the risk of accident arising from negligence of the owner.

**Cede,** to assign or transfer.

**Cedent,** (Sc.), an assignor.

**Census,** a numbering of the population, now taken in England and the United States every ten years. The first English census was taken in 1801. The census papers now require (*inter alia*) particulars as to name, sex, age, birthplace, occupation, ability to read and write, and whether married or single.

**Central Criminal Court,** created in 1834 for the trial of offenses committed in the city of London, and certain parts adjoining.

**Cepi corpus,** *l.*, I have taken the body. Formerly used by a sheriff in making a return upon an attachment, *capias*, etc., when he had taken the person against whom the writ was issued. If he had dischaged him on bail bond, he added **et B. B.** If the person was in custody, he added **et paratum habeo,** or **et est in custodia.** If the person was sick, and unable to appear, he added **et est languidus.**

**Cepit in alio loco,** *l.*, a plea in replevin, when the defendant *took* the goods *in another place* than that mentioned in the declaration.

**Certainty,** clearness and definiteness of statement, which may be (*a*) *to a certain extent in every particular*, as in criminal pleadings, where the court presumes the negative of every thing not affirmed, and *vice versa;* (*b*) *to a common intent,* where the presumption is in favor of the pleader; (*c*) *to a certain intent in general,* where the meaning is to be gathered from a fair and reasonable construction of the words used.

**Certificate,** a statement, usually in writing, given by a person having some official status, relative to some matter within his official knowledge or authority.

**Certified check,** one that has been presented to the bank on which it is drawn and marked good by the proper officer. Such *certification* is a warranty that the signature is genuine, and that the drawer has funds in the bank to meet it, and obligates the bank to pay it on presentation.

**Certified copy,** one signed and certified as true by the official in whose custody the original is.

**Certiorari** (*to be more fully informed*), an original writ or action whereby a cause is removed from an inferior to a superior court for trial. The record of the proceedings is then transmitted to the superior court.

**Cert-money,** *quasi* certain money. Head-money paid yearly by the residents of several manors to the lords thereof, for the certain keeping of the leet. See *Court leet.*

**Cessavit,** an action which lay when a man cessed or ceased, for two years together, to pay rent or perform services due. Now abolished.

**Cesser,** the coming to an end; *e.g.*, of a term or annuity. (2) *Proviso for cesser.* Where terms for years are created by settlement, it is usual to introduce a proviso that they shall cease in case of—(*a*) the trusts never arising; (*b*) their becoming unnecessary or incapable of taking effect; (*c*) the completed performance of them.

**Cesset-executio,** a stay of execution in trials of co-defendants, where the entire damages have been assessed against the first defendant found guilty, *e.g.*, in actions of trespass.

**Cesset processus,** a stay of proceedings entered on the record.

**Cessio bonorum,** (Rom.), (*a surrender of goods*), was the foundation of the modern law of bankruptcy. It operated only as a discharge *pro tanto* of a man's debts, but exempted him from imprisonment. The Scotch and French laws conform in this matter to the leading outlines of the Roman law.

**Cession,** a yielding up; *e.g.*, of a benefice (ecclesiastical law), or of territory, by one nation to another.

**Cessionary,** (Sc.), an assignee.

**Cessor,** a yielding up, ceasing, or departing from. (2) One who ceases or neglects so long to perform a duty that he thereby incurs the danger of the law.

**Cestui que trust,** the person who possesses the equitable or beneficial right to property, the legal estate of which is vested in a trustee. Also called a *beneficiary.*

**Cestui que use,** (orig. *cestut à que use*) previous to 27 Hen.

VIII c. 10, was equivalent to a *cestui que trust* (*q.v*). That statute converted his equitable estate in land into a legal one. See *Statute of Uses*.

**Cestui que vie,** the person for whose life any lands, tenements, or hereditaments are held by another who is beneficially entitled to them.

**Challenge,** an exception or objection. Challenge of jurors may be (i) *to the array, i.e.*, to the whole jury on account of partiality in the officer who arrayed the *panel*, or some error in forming the same; or (ii) *to the polls, i e.*, to individual jurymen. Challenges may be (*a*) *principal, i.e.*, for a *cause* which manifestly disqualifies the jury, or jurymen, from sitting; (*b*) *for favor, i. e.*, where there is some reason to suspect bias or prejudice on the part of a juror, decided at common law by *triers* (*q.v.*), and not by the court; and (*c*) *peremptory*, those made without assigning any reason, and which the court must allow. The number of peremptory challenges allowed at common law in trials for felonies was thirty-five, but the number has been greatly reduced by statutes in England and most of the states. (2) A request by one person to another to fight a duel. At common law, sending or carrying a challenge was an indictable offense, and it is severely punished by the laws of most of the states.

**Chambers,** *quasi*-private rooms, in which the judges dispose of points of practice and other matters not sufficiently important to be heard and argued in court. (2) **Chambers of the king** [*Regiae camerae*], bays or portions of the sea cut off by lines drawn from one promontory to another.

**Champerty,** a bargain, by the terms of which a person, having otherwise no interest in the subject-matter of an action, undertakes to carry on the suit at his own expense, in consideration of receiving, in the event of success, some share of the lands or property recovered, or deriving some benefit therefrom. (2) The purchase of a right of action. Champerty is illegal at common law, and a champertous contract can not be enforced in England and most of the states. See *Maintenance*.

**Chancellor,** a judge who presides over a court of chancery. (2) A minister of state, in most countries of Europe, having high rank and extensive authority, corresponding somewhat to that of our secretary of state. **Chancellor of the Exchequer,** an officer in England who presides in the exchequer, and, in addition to his duties in connection with the treasury, used to sit as one of the judges in the equity court. **Lord Chancellor,** the highest judicial functionary in the kingdom, and superior in order of precedence to every temporal lord; (2) *of a diocese*, a law officer, who holds the bishop's court.

**Chance-medley,** a sudden affray, not prearranged or intended. The term is sometimes applied to a homicide committed in such an affray, or in self-defense.

**Chancery,** equity. (2) A court exercising equitable jurisdiction. The terms equity and chancery are used as synonymous in the United States, yet in England the common-law jurisdiction of the court of chancery was more ancient than the equitable, which was thus called its extraordinary jurisdiction. The High Court of Chancery was the highest court of judicature next to the Parliament and was of very ancient institution. The jurisdiction was formerly of two kinds—*ordinary*, in which the proceedings and judgment were according to the common law; and *extraordinary*, in which they were according to the rules of equity and conscience, the plaintiff being unable to invoke this latter unless his case was one for which he could not obtain relief at the common law. The court consisted of six tribunals, viz.: the Court of the Lord High Chancellor of Great Britain; the Court of the Master of the Rolls; the Court of Appeal in Chancery; and the three separate Courts of the Vice-Chancellors. By the Judicature Act of 1873, the Court of Chancery was merged in the Supreme Court as the Chancery Division of the High Court of Justice. It retains all its extraordinary jurisdiction, but apparently no part of its ordinary jurisdiction, which is transferred to other divisions of the High Court of Justice. Separate courts of chancery or equity exist in a few of the states, but in others the same court exercises jurisdiction in both law and equity cases. All distinctions in form between actions at law and suits in equity have been abolished in many states which have adopted the code of practice.

**Chapter,** a community or corporation composed of the prebends and other clergymen belonging to a cathedral or collegiate church, and presided over by the dean. It is an advisory body, having power to rule or govern the diocese in the vacation of the bishopric. (2) The room in which the members of the community meet to treat of their common affairs.

**Charge,** a duty or obligation imposed upon some person; or a lien, incumbrance, or claim to be satisfied out of a particular estate. (2) An accusation. (3) The instructions given by the court to a grand jury before they enter upon their investigations, or to a petit jury at the close of a trial as to the principles of law which should guide them in arriving at a verdict.

**Charitable uses, charities,** gifts to general public uses; *e.g.*, the establishment of colleges, schools, and hospitals, the carrying on of religious and missionary enterprises and the like.

**Charta,** *l.*, a charter, deed, or writing under seal. **Charta chirographata,** or, **communis,** an indenture, the two parts of which were written on the same sheet with the word *chirograph* between, so that it was divided when the two parts were separated. See *Magna Charta*.

**Charter,** an evidence by deed of things done between man and man. (2) A grant of lands and privileges by a sovereign. (3) The act creating a corporation and defining its powers.

**Charter-land,** that which is held by deed; cf. *Bock-land.*

**Charter-party,** the written contract by which the owner of a ship or other vessel hired her out to another person for a particular period or voyage.

**Chase,** a privileged place for the preservation of wild beasts of chase, intermediate between a forest and a park.

**Chattels,** goods movable and immovable, except such as are in the nature of freehold or parcel of it. Chattels are (*a*) *personal, i.e.,* tangible, or appertaining to the person; (*b*) *real,* pertaining to land, such as leases and interests in land which do not amount to a freehold.

**Cheat,** the generic term for the fraudulent obtaining of another's property by any deceitful practice not amounting to felony.

**Check,** or **Cheque,** an order addressed by a person to his banker, directing him to pay on demand a certain sum to the person therein mentioned. The former is called the *drawer,* the latter the *payee.*

**Chevage,** money formerly paid by tenants in villainage to their lord in acknowledgment of his headship.

**Chevisance,** or **Chievance,** a usurious contract.

**Chief,** principal; one put over others; the best of a number of things. **Chief Baron,** the presiding judge in the Court of Exchequer. **Chief clerk,** the principal clerk in a department of the government, who supervises the correspondence and all matters of routine, and carries out the orders of the head of the department. **Chief Justice,** the presiding judge of the Supreme Court. **Chief-rents,** the annual payments of freeholders of manors; also called *quit-rents.* **Declaration in chief,** a statement of the principal cause of action. **Examination in chief,** the first examination of a witness by the party who calls him. **Tenant in chief,** one who held lands direct from the king.

**Chivalry, Court of,** an ancient court of honor held before the Lord High Constable and Earl Marshal; important while England held possessions in France, but latterly fallen into disuse.

**Chose,** *fr.,* a thing; personal property. **Chose in action,** a right to demand by action a debt or sum of money. **Chose**

**in possession,** personal property of which one has the actual possession and enjoyment.

**Church-rates,** those by which the expenses of a church are defrayed. Compulsory church-rates were abolished in England in 1868.

**Cinque ports,** the five ports of England which lie toward France, Dover, Sandwich, Romney, Hastings, and Hythe. On account of their importance as defenses to the kingdom they early had certain privileges, were bound to certain services upon the king's summons, and were placed under the jurisdic- of a lord-warden, which was abolished in 1855.

**Circuits,** judicial divisions of a county or state for the convenient administration of justice; so called from the custom of the judges to go around and visit each in turn. In England and Wales there are at present seven circuits. The United States is divided into nine circuits. Many of the states are divided into circuits, each containing several counties.

**Circuit courts,** courts of the United States, next in rank to the Supreme Court, held at stated intervals in each judicial district composing the *circuit* (*q.v.*). They may be held by the "circuit justice" (a justice of the Supreme Court allotted to that circuit), a circuit judge appointed for the circuit, or a district judge, sitting alone, or by two or more of them sitting together. The jurisdiction of the circuit courts is *original* in suits in which there is a controversy between citizens of different states, or citizens of a state and a foreign state or its citizens or subjects, and the value of the matter in dispute exceeds two thousand dollars; in civil causes in which the United States are plaintiffs or petitioners; and in various other causes arising under the constitution, laws, or treaties of the United States. It has *appellate* jurisdiction in certain cases, over which the district court has original jurisdiction. (2) Courts created by the laws of many of the states, whose jurisdiction extends to several counties, in which terms of court are held in turn. They are courts of original and general jurisdiction in some of the states. In others, their jurisdiction is chiefly appellate.

**Circuity of action,** the bringing of more than one action to effect what one action would suffice for, if properly brought. To prevent this is one of the grounds for the exercise of equity jurisdiction, and the object of many statutes.

**Circumstantial evidence,** evidence from which the fact in question is not directly proved, but is to be inferred; circumstances being proved which either necessarily or usually attend such facts.

**Circumstantibus,** *l.*, bystanders. See *Tales*.

**Citation,** a summons to appear, applied particularly to process in probate courts. (2) *Citation viis et modis,* one posted up in a public place. (3) A reference to authorities in support of an argument.

**Citizen,** of the United States, any person born in the United States, except an Indian; or born out of the United States, if his parents were citizens; or one of foreign birth and parentage who has became naturalized. A citizen of the United States residing in any of the states is a citizen of that state.

**City,** in England, a town corporate, which usually has or has had a bishop and cathedral church. In the United States, a municipal corporation organized under the laws of the state, which prescribe the number of inhabitants and other conditions necessary to the enjoyment of that dignity.

**Civil,** pertaining to a city or state, and man in his relations to his fellow citizens. Thus we speak of civil life, civil government, etc., as opposed to savage or barbarous; civil rights and relations, as opposed to domestic; civil law and actions, as opposed to criminal, or ecclesiastical; civil officer, as opposed to military; civil death, when a person is attainted or outlawed, as opposed to natural; civil war, between citizens of the same state, as opposed to foreign; civil remedy, one that may be enforced by a private person for a tort, as opposed to indictment and public prosecution, etc. **Civil law,** Roman law; more particularly, the law compiled by the Roman jurists under the auspices of the Emperor Justinian, still in force in many of the states of modern Europe, and of high authority. **Civil list,** the revenue settled on the sovereign, out of which are defrayed his personal and household expenses, as well as those for secret or special services.

**Claim,** the assertion of a right; a demand. (2) The possession of a settler, or miner, of the tract of wild or mineral land which he intends to acquire from the government. (3) The tract of wild or mineral land staked out and held by such settler or miner.

**Claimant,** one who makes a claim. (2) The plaintiff in the old action of ejectment. (3) In admiralty practice, the person admitted to defend a libel *in rem.*; so called because he claimed the property seized.

**Clarendon, constitutions of,** were enacted by Henry II., in 1164, to limit the pretensions of the clergy within the realm.

**Clausum,** close; an inclosure. Writs were either *clausum* (close), or *apertum* (open). Grants were by *literae patentae* (open grant or patent), or *literae clausae* (close grant). **Clausum fregit,** see *Trespass.*

**Clayton's case,** decided that in cases of current accounts, *e.g.*, a banker's, in the absence of an express appropriation by a creditor, the first payment is to be set off against the first charge.

**Clean hands,** an expression, meaning free from the taint of fraud; applied to a suitor in equity

**Clearance,** a certificate given by the collector of a port to the master of a vessel, that his vessel has been entered and cleared according to law. A permission to sail. The act of clearing.

**Clear days,** days reckoned exclusively of the first day and the day on which a thing must be done.

**Clearing-house,** an office in large cities where banks exchange checks and drafts drawn on each other and settle their balances.

**Clergy,** ecclesiastical ministers as a class, as distinguished from the *laity* (*q.v.*).

**Clergyable,** allowing of, or entitled to, the *benefit of clergy* (*q.v.*); used of crimes or persons.

**Clerical error,** one made by a clerk in transcribing, or otherwise, and which is readily corrected by the court.

**Clericus,** *l.*; **clerk,** a clergyman; one who has taken orders in the church. (2) One who is devoted to the pursuit of letters and learned therein, hence an amanuensis. (3) An officer of a court, who files pleadings, etc., issues writs, and keeps the records of legal proceedings. (4) A person employed to sell goods or attend to business in the store or office of another.

**Client,** one who employs an attorney or counselor to manage his case in court, or to advise him about legal matters.

**Close,** a piece of land. See *Clausum*. **Close Rolls,** rolls containing the record of *close writs* (*literae clausae*), and royal grants not intended for public inspection.

**Code,** a collection or system of laws. The collection of laws and constitutions, made by order of the Emperor Justinian in 528, is distinguished by the appellation of "The Code." The *Code Napoleon*, or Civil Code of France, is the most celebrated modern code. Many of the states, following the lead of New York, have adopted a code of civil procedure, intended to do away with the forms and fictions of the common law, and to simplify the practice of law. By lawyers such states are frequently called "code states."

**Codicil,** a supplement to a will, containing any thing which the testator wishes to add or alter. It must be executed with the same formalities as a will.

**Co-emptio,** (Rom.), the sale of a wife to a husband.

**Coercion,** constraint; compulsion; compelling a person by physical force, or by threats and the wrongful exercise of authority, to do what he would otherwise not do. Coercion is implied in many cases, as in the commission of crime by a wife in the presence of her husband.

**Cognati,** relations by the mother's side.

**Cognizance,** or **conusance,** acknowledgment; recognition; jurisdiction; hearing a matter judicially. A judge is bound to take judicial cognizance of certain matters without having them proved in evidence, *e.g.*, the statutes of the state in which he holds court, the extent of his jurdisdiction geographically and otherwise, etc. In pleading, the acknowledgment of a fine; or in the action of replevin, the acknowledgment by a bailiff or servant of taking the goods, and the plea that they were taken in distress by the command of another who was entitled.

**Cognovit (actionem),** *l.*, a defendant's written *confession* of an action brought against him; *i.e.*, his admission that he has no available defense, and consents to judgment being entered against him.

**Cohabit,** to live together in the same house as man and wife.

**Co-heir,** one of several to whom an inheritance descends.

**Coif,** a white silk cap, the badge of sergeants-at-law.

**Collateral,** by the side of; indirect. **Collateral facts,** those not directly connected with the issue or matter in dispute. **Collateral issue,** an issue raised which is foreign to the general issue in the case. **Collateral limitation,** one which makes the enjoyment of an estate depend upon the happening of some event not related to or depending upon the parties. **Collateral relationship,** as opposed to lineal, is that of persons descended from a common ancester, *e.g.*, cousins. **Collateral security,** property or other contracts transferred to secure the performance of the principal obligation.

**Collatio bonorum,** *l.*, a bringing into *hotchpot* (*q.v.*).

**Collation,** the comparison of a copy with its original, to ascertain its correctness. (2) The act of bestowing a benefice upon an incumbent where the bishop and patron are one and the same person, thus dispensing with presentation and institution **Collative advowson.** See *Advowson.*

**Collegatory,** a person who has a legacy left to him in common with other persons.

**Colligenda bona.** See *Administration.*

**Collision,** the act of ships or other vessels striking together, or of one vessel running into or foul of another. The vessel in fault must suffer its own loss and pay for the damage occasioned to the other. Where both are at fault each pays to the other one-half the damage sustained.

**Colloquium,** (*a talking together*), the statement in a declaration for libel or slander that the libelous or slanderous imputation had reference to the plaintiff.

**Collusion,** a secret compact between persons apparently hostile, to do some act in order to defraud or prejudice a third person, or for some improper purpose. Judgment obtained by collusion is a nullity.

**Color,** a *prima facie* right or title. Pleadings in *confession and avoidance* (*q.v.*) had to give color, *i.e.*, to admit some apparent right in the opposite party so as to justify the allegation of new matter. Color was either express or implied. Obsolete. (2) Color of right means semblance of right.

**Colorable,** that which is not what it purports or professes to be; deceptive; *e.g.*, an alteration made only for the purpose of evading a patent or the law of copyright, which leaves the thing substantially as much an infringement as before.

**Comes,** an earl, or count. **Comitatus,** or county, is dederived from *comes*, the earl to whom its government was intrusted. His authority was exercised usually through the *vice-comes*, or *shire-reeve* (whence our sheriff).

**Comitatu commisso,** *l.*, a writ or commission whereby a sheriff is authorized to enter upon the charge of a county.

**Comity of nations,** the obligation granted by courtesy to the laws of one nation within the territories of another, when they do not conflict with the laws of the latter.

**Commandite,** or **In commendam,** a form of partnership in France (*Société en Commandite*) in which certain of the partners (*commandataires*) take no active share in the business, but merely lend money to it, and are only liable to the extent of such money.

**Commendam,** (*Ecclesia commendata*), a living committed to the care of a clergyman until a proper pastor can be provided.

**Commendatus,** one who by commendation, *i.e.*, voluntary homage, puts himself under the protection of a superior lord.

**Commercial,** relating to trade or commerce. **Commercial law,** that branch of the law which grew out of and applies to the relations of men engaged in business. **Commercial paper,** notes, bills of exchange, etc., which pass from hand to hand by indorsement. The term is applied specially to *bills receivable* (*q.v.*), which a merchant discounts, or transfers by indorsement.

**Commissary,** a delegate of the bishop, who exercises spiritual jurisdiction in distant parts of the diocese. (2) An officer of the army, whose principal duty is to supply it with food.

**Commission,** an authority or order to do some act; *e.g.*, to take depositions; to hold an inquest of lunacy, etc. (2) The evidence of an officer's appointment and authority to discharge the duties of his office. (3) A body of persons appointed with necessary powers to do certain things. (4) The act of perpetrating an offense. (5) The compensation of a factor employed to sell goods consigned to him, usually a percentage on the amount realized from the sale. Hence the term commission merchant.

**Commissioner,** the title given by law to the heads of bureaus in certain departments of government, *e.g.*, Commissioner of Patents, Commissionsr of the General Land Office, Commissioner of Pensions, etc. Also to state officials charged with special duties, *e.g.*, railroad and insurance commissioners, county commissioners, etc.

**Commissoria lex,** *l.*, (Rom.), a clause by which a vendor reserved to himself the privilege of rescinding the sale, if the purchaser did not pay his purchase-money at the time agreed on.

**Commitment,** the sending a person to prison by warrant or order, either for a crime, contempt, or contumacy.

**Committee,** one or more members of a legislative body, or association of individuals for business, political, religious or social purposes, appointed to consider and report upon certain matters which were before the larger body, or to carry out the resolutions of that body.

**Committitur piece,** an instrument in writing on parchment, which charges a person, already in prison, in execution at the suit of the person who arrested him.

**Commodatum,** (Rom.), a thing lent for a definite time, to be enjoyed and used under certain conditions, without any pay or reward.

**Common,** a use which a man has of the land of another, in common with him and others. Except in the case of copyholders it can not be claimed by custom, but by grant or prescription only. It is of four principal kinds: (*a*) of *pasture*; (*b*) of *turbary*, *i.e.*, taking peat or turf; (*c*) of *estovers*, *i.e.*, taking wood for necessary repairs and house purposes; (*d*) of *piscary*, *i.e.*, fishing. Commons may be *appendant*, *i.e.*, enjoyed by all the freehold tenants of a manor; *appurtenant*, *i.e.*, attached to the ownership of a particular land or house; *in gross*, *i.e.*, not connected with tenure, but belonging to individuals; or *because of vicinage*, *i.e.*, belonging to tenants of adjoining townships or manors. (2) *Common* also signifies land subject to rights of common. See *Tenancy*.

**Common bench,** a name of the court of common pleas.

**Common carrier.** See *Carrier.*

**Common council,** the inferior branch of the municipal legislative body in most American cities.

**Common counts,** general counts, not founded on any special contract, introduced in a declaration for the purpose of preventing a defeat of justice by a variance of the evidence, such as *indebitatus assumpsit, quantum meruit, quantum valebant, etc.*

**Common informer,** one who, without special authority, or being required to do so by virtue of any office, gives information which leads to the prosecution of offenders against the law.

**Common law,** that system of law which does not rest for its authority upon any express statutes, but derives its force and authority from universal consent and immemorial usage, and which is evidenced by the decisions of the courts of law, technically so called, in contradistinction to those of *equity* and the ecclesiastical courts. It prevails in England and most of the United States except when abrogated or modified by statute.

**Common nuisance,** one which affects the public generally and not merely some particular person.

**Common pleas** *(communia placita)*, such pleas or actions as are brought by man against man, or by the government when the cause of action is of a civil nature. (2) The court in which such pleas or actions are heard. See *Court of Common Pleas.*

**Common seal,** the seal used by a corporation.

**Commorancy,** residence within a certain district.

**Commorientes,** *l.*, those who perish at the same time and by a common calamity, *e.g.*, shipwreck, so that no presumption of survivorship can reasonably arise as to any.

**Commutation,** the modification of a sentence so as to make the punishment to which a person has been condemned less severe. (2) The conversion of a right to receive a variable, or periodical, into a fixed, or gross payment. See *Tithe.*

**Company,** an association of individuals for the purpose of carrying on some joint business, or enterprise, whether incorporated or not. (2) A term used to represent those partners whose names do not appear in the firm name.

**Competency,** the legal fitness or capacity of a witness to testify on the trial of a case; also, the quality of evidence offered which makes it proper to be received.

**Complainant,** one who makes a complaint; the plaintiff in suit in equity.

**Complaint,** the charge, made before a proper officer, that an offense has been committed by a person named or described.

**Compos mentis,** *l.*, sound of mind; capable of transacting business.

**Composition,** an agreement between a debtor and his creditors, by which the latter agree to accept a certain proportion of their debts in satisfaction of the whole.

**Compound interest,** interest upon interest, *i.e.*, when the simple interest on a sum of money is added as it becomes due to the principal, and then bears interest, becoming a sort of secondary principal. See *Account with rests*

**Compounding,** a *debt*, making a *composition* (*q.v.*). (2) A *felony*, is to enter into an agreement for valuable consideration not to prosecute a felon.

**Comprint,** printing in violation of copyright.

**Compromise,** settlement of an action, or matters in dispute between two or more parties, by agreement.

**Comptroller,** an officer of the treasury department, appointed to examine accounts settled by the auditors, and to perform other duties defined by law.

**Compulsion,** force brought to bear to make a person do what he would otherwise not do. See *Coercion; Duress.*

**Compurgator,** one who, on oath, asserts another's innocence. Under the early Saxons a person accused of a crime was acquitted, if a certain number (twelve or more) of *compurgatores* (*juratores* or *justificatores*) came forward, and swore to a *veredictum* (or true statement) that they believed him innocent. This was also called *wager of law;* it was abolished, after long disuse, by 3 & 4 Wm. IV, c. 42.

**Computo,** an ancient writ to compel a bailiff, receiver, or accountant, to yield up his accounts.

**Concealers,** persons who were used to find out lands which had been privily appropriated from the Crown.

**Concealment,** the improper suppression of any fact or circumstance, by which one of the parties to a contract is induced to enter into the same. When fraudulent, and of such facts as the party is bound to disclose, it renders the contract voidable, especially where confidence is reposed, and the party deceived is dependent upon the others. (2) The fraudulent hiding of one's property, or the evidence of a crime.

**Concessi,** *l.*, I have granted; a term formerly used in deeds, equivalent to grant, lease, release, and the like.

**Concilium,** or **Consilium,** *l.*, consultation; determination; applied to the rule, setting a case down for argument on demurrer, or in proceedings on a writ of error.

**Conclude,** to end; close up; determine. To close a petition with the formal words, "to the damage of the plaintiff," etc.; or a plea, tendering an issue to the country, with the words, "and of this the said C. D. puts himself upon the country." (2) To make the last argument to the court or jury, a privilege generally accorded to the party on whom rests the *onus probandi* (*q.v.*) (3) To bar; estop; to prevent a man from denying what he has before asserted, or alleging what he has before denied, when the effect would be to defraud another.

**Conclusive,** that which can not be gainsaid or doubted.

**Conclusive presumption,** one which the law will not allow to be overthrown by the introduction of evidence to the contrary, *e.g.*, the presumption of a grant arising from the occupancy of land or the enjoyment of an easement under a claim of title for twenty-one years.

**Concord,** an agreement between parties, who intend to levy a fine of lands one to the other, how and in what manner the lands shall pass. (2) A compromise.

**Concurrent,** running along together. Two courts are said to have *concurrent jurisdiction* when either may entertain a suit relating to the same subject-matter at the choice of the plaintiff. (2) **Concurrent writ,** a writ of summons of the same tenor as the original writ, and remaining in force for the same time; used where there are several defendants, or it is advisable to try to serve the same defendant in different places.

**Condemnation,** adjudging a captured vessel to be lawful prize. The declaration of a competent tribunal that a vessel is unfit for use, or that a building is in a dangerous condition. (2) The judgment or decree by which property seized for a violation of the revenue or navigation laws is forfeited to the government. (3) The subjection of private property to public, or *quasi* public uses by legal proceedings; *e.g.*, the appropriation of a strip of land for a street or railroad. See *Conviction*.

**Condition,** a qualification, restriction, or limitation annexed to a grant or agreement, by which it is deprived of its absolute character, and may be defeated, suspended, or revoked on the happening of a certain event, or the performance, on the part of the grantee, of certain things; *e.g.*, the provision in a bond that it shall be void if the principal does certain things, or pays over certain moneys; the provision in a mortgage that the deed, absolute in form, shall be void if the mortgagor pays certain specified notes at maturity. Conditions may be *express*, or *implied* by law; *possible*, or *impossible*; *precedent*, or *subsequent* (*q.v.*).

**Conditional fee.** See *Base fee*.

**Conditional limitations,** partake of the nature both of a condition and a remainder; of a condition, so far as they abridge or defeat the estates previously limited; of a limitation, so far as, upon the contingency taking effect, they pass the estate to a stranger. They thus differ from a contingent remainder, which waits for the regular determination of the previous estate.

**Condonation,** a pardoning of a conjugal offense, which prevents it from being made at any future time the subject of legal proceedings.

**Conductio,** *l.*, (Rom.), a hiring (*q.v.*).

**Conduct-money,** money paid to a witness for his traveling expenses.

**Confederacy,** a combination of two or more persons to do some damage or injury to another, or to commit some unlawful act. See *Conspiracy.* (2) A union of two or more states or nations for mutual protection and advancement.

**Conference,** an interview between counsel and the solicitor who instructs him (with or without his client). (2) A meeting of committees appointed by the two houses of Congress, or a state legislature, to reconcile differences about proposed legislation.

**Confession,** an admission by a person accused of crime that he has committed the offense charged. It may be *judicial, i.e.,* made before a court or examining magistrate, or *extra-judicial, i.e.,* made outside of court. Voluntary confessions, not made in pursuance of threats or the hope of favor, are admissible in evidence against the persons making them.

**Confession and avoidance,** a plea *admitting* certain facts alleged by the opponent's preceding pleading, but *avoiding* their legal effect by alleging new matter. These pleas were distinguished as pleas in justification or excuse, which go to show that the plaintiff never had a right of action, and pleas in discharge which go to show that his right has been released by some matter subsequent. See *Color.*

**Confession, judgment by.** See *Cognovit.*

**Confidential communications,** statements made by one person to another, when there is a necessary relation of trust and confidence between them, and which the person receiving them can not, upon grounds of public policy, be compelled to disclose; *e.g.,* the statements made by a husband to his wife, a client to his attorney, and, in some states, by a penitent to his confessor.

**Confirmatio Chartarum,** *l.*, the statute 25 Edw. I., A. D. 1297, which re-enacted Magna Charta with some additions.

**Confirmation,** a species of conveyance by which a voidable estate is made valid and unavoidable, or by which a particular estate is increased. Estates which are void can not be confirmed, but only those which are voidable. (2) The ratification of a bishop's election by the archbishop.

**Confiscation,** the appropriation of property taken from an enemy, or seized for a violation of law, to the use of the state.

**Conflict of laws** the variance between the laws of two countries or states relating to the subject-matter of a suit brought in one of them, when the parties to the suit, or some of them, or the subject-matter belong to the other. See *Lex loci contractus; Lex rei sitae.*

**Confrontation,** in matrimonial suits, is the bringing of the respondent into court for identification by the witnesses. In criminal cases, bringing the witnesses face to face with the accused.

**Confusion,** a mixing together of the goods of two or more persons, so that the several portions can be no longer distinguished. If by consent, the owners have an interest in the mixture proportioned to their respective shares. If by the willful act of one, without the consent of the others, he must separate at his peril, or lose his own.

**Conge,** *fr.*, leave; permission; license. **Conge d'accorder,** leave to accord or agree. An expression used in levying a fine. **Conge d'emparler,** leave to imparl or talk together with the opposite party. **Conge d'elire,** or **d'eslire,** a license from the crown to a dean and chapter to proceed to the election of a bishop when a see becomes vacant. It is accompanied by a *letter missive*, giving the name of the person to be elected.

**Congeable,** lawful; done with permission.

**Congress,** the name of the legislative body of the United States, composed of the *Senate* and *House of Representatives* (*q.v.*).

**Conjoints,** persons married to each other

**Conjugal rights,** the rights arising from the relation of husband and wife. See *Restitution.*

**Conjuration,** a compact made by persons combining by oath to do any public harm. (2) The attempt to have conference with evil spirits.

**Connivance,** guilty knowledge of, or assistance in, a crime. (2) Consent, express or implied, by one spouse to the adultery of the other.

**Consanguineus frater** (Rom.), a brother who has the same father.

**Consanguinity, or kindred,** the connection or relationship of persons descended from some common ancestor. It is either lineal, as that of father and son, or collateral, as that of brothers or cousins.

**Consent,** agreement; the meeting of minds. It presupposes mental capacity to act. It may be *express*, by word of mouth, or in writing; or *implied*, from acts, inaction, or silence, which are consistent only with assent. If obtained by fraud or duress, it is not binding.

**Consequential damages,** those losses or injuries which follow an act, but are not direct and immediate upon it.

**Conservators of the peace,** officers appointed to preserve the public peace. Some are so by virtue of their office; *e.g.*, judges and coroners: those specially appointed are now called *justices of the peace*.

**Consideration,** the price, motive, or matter of inducement of a contract, which must be lawful in itself. A simple contract, *i.e.*, one not under seal, derives its binding force from the existence of a valuable consideration between the parties; but a deed imports a consideration and so is binding though *voluntary*, *i.e.*, without consideration. Consideration may be *executed*, past, or performed; *executory*, to be performed; or *continuing*, partly both. *Good* or *meritorious* consideration is that originating in relationship and natural affection; *valuable*, that which has a money value. The former was never binding in the eye of the law, except in the case of a covenant to stand seized to uses, which is now disused: and "good" consideration now usually means "valuable." See *Turpis causa; Nudum pactum.*

**Consideratum est per curiam,** *l.*, (*it is considered by the court*), the formal commencement of a judgment.

**Consign,** to send goods to a purchaser, or to a factor or agent to sell. The person sending the goods is called the *consignor*, the person to whom they are sent, the *consignee*, and the goods themselves the *consignment*.

**Consignation,** (Rom.), the deposit of a thing owed with a third person, under the authority of the court.

**Consistory court,** the ecclesiastical court of a diocese.

**Consolato del mare, Il,** a code of sea-laws compiled by order of the ancient kings of Arragon.

**Consolidated fund,** in England, the public revenue, which is derived from customs, excise, stamps, and other taxes, and out of which provision is made for the payment of interest on the public debt. Hence the term "*consols*" applied to government securities.

**Consolidation,** (Rom.), the uniting of the possession, use, or profits of land with the title, by the same person's acquiring both. (2) (Ecclesiastical law), the union of two or more benefices in one by the consent of the ordinary, patron, and incumbent. (3) The fusing of many acts of a legislative body into one. (4) The joining in one of several suits between the same parties, for causes of action which may properly be tried together; provided for by statute in many of the states.

**Conspiracy,** an unlawful combination or agreement between two or more persons to carry into effect a purpose hurtful to some individual, or class, or to the public at large.

**Constables,** inferior officers appointed to keep the peace, and to serve writs, levy executions, etc., issued by a justice of the peace.

**Constablewick,** the jurisdiction of a constable.

**Constat,** *l.*, (*it appears*), a certificate of that which *appears* on the record.

**Constituent,** one who appoints an agent or attorney. (2) One who helps by his vote to elect a member of Congress, or of some other legislative body

**Constitution,** the fundamental law of a state or nation, establishing the form and limitations of government, securing the rights of the citizen, etc. The Constitution of the United States was adopted in a convention of representatives of the people, at Philadelphia, September 17 1787, and became the law of the land on the first Wednesday in March, 1789. Each of the states composing the United States has a constitution of its own. Constitutions usually prescribe the manner in which they may be amended.

**Constitutional,** in accordance with the constitution. Laws which are unconstitutional are null and void.

**Construction,** the interpretation of a statute, or written instrument.

**Constructive,** implied by law though not actual in fact; *e.g.*, *delivery*, *notice*, *total loss*, *trust*. See those titles.

**Consuetudinibus et servitiis,** *l.*, a writ to recover arrears of rent.

**Consul,** an official appointed by government to reside in a foreign country, and there to look after the interests of the subjects of the country which appoints him; *e.g.*, by giving them assistance or advice, or by making due representations to the proper authorities, taking charge of the effects of a deceased citizen, settling disputes between the master and seamen of a vessel of his country, etc.

**Consultation,** a writ whereby a cause, having been wrongfully removed by prohibition from an ecclesiastical to a temporal court, is returned thither again. (2) A meeting of two or more counsel, with the solicitors instructing them, for the purpose of deliberation.

**Consummation,** the due completion of a thing; *e.g.*, of marriage. (2) *Of tenancy by the curtesy*, is when a husband, upon his wife's death, becomes entitled to hold her lands by curtesy (*q.v.*). His estate becomes *inittate* upon birth of a child.

**Contemner,** one who has committed contempt of court.

**Contempt,** a willful disregard or disobedience of public authority. Each house of Congress, and of a state legislature, has power to punish contempts on the part of members or persons properly brought before it, by imprisonment, reprimand, or expulsion. Courts may punish one who disobeys the rules, orders, or process, or willfully offends against the dignity and good order of the court, by fine or imprisonment. A person is said to *purge* or *clear* his contempt, when he expresses contrition and submits himself to the court.

**Contentious jurisdiction,** jurisdiction to hear and determine any matter between party and party in an action or other judicial proceeding, as opposed to jurisdiction in voluntary and *ex-parte* actions, taking probate of wills, granting letters of administration and the like, when there is no opposition.

**Contentment,** a man's countenance or credit, which he has together with, and by reason of, his freehold. (2) That which is necessary for the support and maintenance of men, agreeably to their several qualities or states of life.

**Contestatio litis,** *l.*, (Rom.), the statement of the plaintiff, and answer or plea of the defendant, by which a case is brought before the judge. (2) The joinder of issue in the ecclesiastical courts.

**Context,** that which is interwoven; those parts of a writing which precede and follow a phrase or passage in question, and which may be looked at to explain its meaning.

**Contingency with a double aspect,** one which arises when two events are expressly named, or evidently implied, upon the happening of either of which an estate will vest.

**Contingent,** conditional; doubtful; dependent upon the happening of an uncertain event; *e.g.*, a contingent *estate, legacy, remainder, use.* See those titles.

**Continuance,** the adjournment of a cause from one day to another of the same or a subsequent term.

**Continuando.** Under the old action of trespass, to *lay the action with a continuando*, was to allege that the defendant's trespass was a *continuing* one, whereby multiplicity of actions was avoided.

**Contra,** *l.*, against; contrary to. **Contra bonos mores,** against good morals. **Contra formam collationis** (*against the form of the gift*), a writ that issued, where lands given in perpetuity for religious or charitable purposes were alienated, in a suit by the donor or his heirs to recover the lands.

**Contra formam feoffamenti** (*against the form of the feoffment*), a writ that lay for the heir of a tenant distrained for more services than his ancestor was required to perform by the charter of feoffment. **Contra formam statuti** (*contrary to the form of the statute*), the formal conclusion of every indictment for an offense forbidden by statute. **Contra pacem** (*against the peace*), the formal conclusion in an action of trespass, or ejectment, after stating the facts constituting the cause or complaint. **Contra proferentem,** against the one putting it forth; a rule of construction.

**Contraband,** goods exported or imported in violation of law. (2) In international law, those goods which a neutral may not carry to a belligerent, *e.g.*, munitions of war.

**Contract,** an agreement between competent parties, upon a legal consideration, to do, or to abstain from doing, some act. In its widest use the term includes agreements of record, judgments, and contracts under seal, or *specialties*. It is, however, usually applied to *simple* or *parol* contracts, not under seal, including written as well as verbal contracts. Contracts may be *express*, in which the terms are stated in words; or *implied*, *i.e.*, presumed by law to have been made from the relations of the parties; *mutual* and *dependent*, in which the performance by one is dependent upon the performance by the other; *independent*, when either promise may be performed without reference to the other; *entire*, in which the complete performance by one is a condition precedent to demanding performance of the other; *severable*, in which the things to be performed are capable of separation, so that on performance of part the party performing may demand a proportionate part of the consideration from the other; *executed*, in which the things each agrees to perform are done at the time the contract is made; *executory*, in which some act remains to be done by one or both of the parties; *personal*, *i.e.*, depending on the skill or qualities of one of the parties; *contracts of beneficence*, by which only one of the contracting parties is to be benefited; as loans, deposit, and mandate. See also *Agreement; Consideration.*

**Contravention,** an act done in violation of a legal obligation. (2) (Sc.) the action founded on a breach of *law-burrows* (*q.v*).

**Contribution,** the payment by each of two or more persons, *e.g.*, sureties, jointly liable by contract or otherwise, of his share of the liability, (2) The satisfaction by a devisee, or legatee, of his share of the debts, or liabilities imposed, by the will of the testator, or by law, upon the estate devised or bequeathed to him. (3) In maritime law *average contribution* is the amount to be contributed by each person toward making good a loss at sea, and is proportioned to the value of goods he may have shipped. See *Average.*

**Contributione facienda,** *l.*, a writ where tenants in common were equally bound to do some act, and one of them was put to the whole burden, to compel the rest to make contribution.

**Contributory,** a person liable to contribute to the assets of a joint-stock company in the event of the same being wound up. Those who are members at the time of winding up are primarily liable.

**Contubernium,** (Rom.), the marriage of persons, one or both of whom were slaves, with the master's consent.

**Contumace capiendo,** *l.*, a writ issued out of the court of chancery for the commitment of a person pronounced by an ecclesiastical court to be guilty of contempt.

**Contumacy,** a refusal to appear in court when legally summoned; disobedience to the rules and orders of a court.

**Conusance.** See *Cognizance.*

**Conusant,** knowing, or aware of.

**Conventio in unum,** *l.*, agreement between two parties upon the sense of the contract proposed.

**Convention,** a coming together, or assembly of delegates chosen by the people for the purpose of framing or amending a constitution, making a political platform and nominating candidates, or any other purpose, except legislation, for which a representative body may be called. (2) An agreement with a foreign state, *e.g.*, as to the extradition of fugitive offenders.

**Conventional estates,** those which are created by the express acts of the parties, in contradistinction to those which are legal and arise from the operation of law.

**Conversion,** the wrongful appropriation of the goods of another. See *Trover.* (2) *Equitable* conversion is the changing of the nature of property, which may be (*a*) *actual*, *e.g.*, by converting land into money by selling it, or *vice versa;* or (*b*) *constructive*, where such an operation is assumed to have, though it has not actually, taken place, as, for example, when an owner has agreed to sell land, and dies before executing the conveyance, the executors are entitled to the money, and not the heirs. The property constructively converted immediately assumes the same qualities as if the operation had been actually carried out.

**Conveyance,** the transfer of the title of land from one to another. (2) The instrument for effecting such transfer. (3) The transfer of the title of vessels. The person drawing the instrument is called a *conveyancer.*

**Conveyancing,** the science and art of the alienation of property by means of appropriate instruments. It includes the examination of title, and preparation of an abstract, as well as the instruments of transfer.

**Convict,** to prove or find guilty of a crime or misdemeanor. (2) A person found guilty of a crime or misdemeanor, and sentenced to death or imprisonment. *Conviction* may be by trial and the verdict of a jury; or *summary*, by magistrates or justices, under statutory powers, without the intervention of a jury.

**Convocation,** in ecclesiastical law, the general assembly of the clergy to consult upon ecclesiastical matters.

**Convoy,** ships of war which accompany merchantmen, in time of war, to protect them from the enemy.

**Coparcenary,** a tenancy which arises when an inheritable estate descends from the ancestor to several persons possessing an equal title to it, who are called *coparceners* or *parceners; e.g.*, to daughters by the common law, or to sons by the custom in gavelkind.

**Copy,** a transcript of an original document. *Office copy,* one made by an officer appointed for the purpose, and officially sealed.

**Copyhold,** a base tenure founded upon immemorial custom. *Copyhold estate,* one held by *copy* of the court rolls, and originally by the will of the lord, though this is no longer so. The freehold of copyhold estate is in the lord; but in most respects, the ownership of a copyholder is as absolute as that of a freeholder. The method of alienation is by *surrender* and *admittance* of the surrenderee. See *Heriot; Fine; Customary freehold.* The doctrine of copyhold has no application to the United States.

**Copyright,** an incorporeal right, being the exclusive privilege of printing, reprinting, selling, and publishing his own original work, which the law allows an author. In England, it lasts for life and seven years longer, or for forty-two years, whichever is the longer period. In the United States, it lasts for twenty-eight years, with a privilege of renewal for fourteen more under certain conditions. It extends (*inter alia*) to maps, prints, engravings, and musical compositions. The right may be assigned by a written instrument duly attested and recorded.

**Coram,** *l.*, before; in the presence of. **Coram ipso rege,** before the king himself; applied to proceedings in the Court of King's Bench. **Coram nobis,** before us; applied to writs of error on a judgment in king's bench. **Coram non judice,** before one not the (proper) judge; applied to the acts of a court which has no jurisdiction either over the person, the subject-matter, or the process. Such acts are wholly void. **Coram paribus,** before his peers. **Coram vobis,** before you; a writ of error directed to the court which tried the cause; to correct an error in fact.

**Co-respondent,** the man charged by a husband with adultery, and made a party to a suit for dissolution of marriage.

**Cornage,** a form of tenure in grand sergeantry, by which the tenant was bound to blow a *horn* to give warning on the approach of an enemy.

**Corody,** an allowance of meat, drink, etc., made by an abbey, or religious foundation, to a person nominated by the king. Obsolete.

**Coroner,** a person possessing judicial and ministerial functions. In the former capacity, his chief duty is to hold inquests, in doing which he may commit for trial any person against whom the jury find a verdict of murder or manslaughter. In the latter, he acts as sheriff's substitute, when there is a vacancy in the office of sheriff, or when the sheriff is incapacitated by interest or otherwise.

**Coronatore eligendo,** or **exonerando,** *l.*, the writ issued to the sheriff commanding him to elect or remove a coroner.

**Corporal oath,** so called because the party taking it lays his hand on the New Testament.

**Corporation,** an artificial person or body of persons, established under a corporate name, for preserving in succession certain rights differing from those of the individuals or *corporators* who constitute the corporation from time to time. It is either *aggregate*, consisting of many members, or *sole*, consisting of one person at a time. Corporations may be further subdivided into *public*, or *municipal*, created wholly for public interests; *ecclesiastical*, for religious purposes; and *lay*, subdivided into *civil*, or *private*, for purposes of private gain, and *eleemosynary*, for charitable purposes, schools, hospitals, and the like.

**Corporeal,** having a body; material; tangible. **Corporeal hereditaments,** such property as is tangible and capable of being inherited, *e.g.*, houses and lands, embraced under the term *things real*.

**Corpus,** the body; the person; the whole. **Corpus comitatus,** the whole county. **Corpus cum causa,** see *Habeas corpus*. **Corpus delicti,** the body of the offense; that, the commission of which must be established, before the accused can be legally convicted. **Corpus juris canonici,** the collection of the decrees and canons of the Roman church. **Corpus juris civilis,** the body of the civil law; the Institutes, Pandects, Code, and Novels of Justinian. See those titles.

**Correction,** punishment by one having authority over

another; *e.g.*, a parent over a child, a teacher over a scholar, a master over an apprentice, for the purpose of bringing the latter to obedience. **House of correction,** one designed for the imprisonment and discipline of those guilty of petty offenses and misdemeanors.

**Corruption,** influencing a judge, juror, or public officer, by improper means, to do wrong, or to disregard his duty. **Corruption of blood,** see *Attainder*.

**Cosening,** cheating.

**Cosinage,** or **Cousinage,** consanguinity. (2) A writ that lay for the heir whose great grandfather was seized of lands and tenements in fee at his death, against a stranger who entered upon the land and abated. Obsolete.

**Costs,** the expenses incurred by the parties in the prosecution or defense of an action at law. They were not recoverable at common law; but court costs, and in some cases counsel fees are taxed against the losing party, or the fund which becomes the subject of litigation, by statutory authority.

**Co-surety,** a fellow-surety.

**Couchant,** lying down; used of cattle trespassing. See *Levant*.

**Council,** the legislative body of a municipal corporation. Its acts are usually termed *ordinances* (*q.v.*). See *Privy Council*.

**Counsel,** one who gives advice, especially legal; one who manages a cause in court. More often used as a collective noun, applied to all who are united in the management of a cause, or in advising with reference to a particular matter requiring legal knowledge.

**Counselor-at-law,** an officer of the court employed by a party to a cause to conduct the same on its trial, in his behalf; a barrister. The distinction which formerly existed between *counselors* and *attorneys-at-law* (*q.v.*) has gradually been abolished.

**Count,** the statement of a cause of action. A declaration has as many *counts* as there are causes of action, or different statements of the same cause of action. (2) In criminal law, each part of an indictment which charges a distinct offense. See *Common count*.

**Counter,** contrary; opposed to. **Counter affidavit,** one made in opposition to another already made. **Counter bond,** a bond given to indemnify a security for going on one's bond. **Counterclaim,** the defendant's claim against the plaintiff, which the laws of most states permit him to set up in his answer or cross-petition, and to have adjudicated at the same time with the plaintiff's claim, to avoid a multiplicity of actions. It must not require different parties, and in general must be founded on contract, and if unliquidated damages are claimed, they must grow out of or be connected in some way with the plaintiff's cause of action. **Counter deed,** a secret writing, either before a notary or under a private seal, which invalidates or alters another. **Counterfeit,** an imitation made without lawful authority, and with a view to defraud. **Countermand,** to revoke or recall an order. **Counterpart,** the corresponding part or duplicate. Where a deed is executed in several *parts* or copies by the different parties, that signed by the grantor is the *original*, the others the *counterparts*. (2) The key of a cipher. **Counter-security,** a security given to one who has entered into a bond or become surety for another. **Countersign,** the signature of a secretary, agent, or other subordinate officer to any writing signed by the principal or superior, to vouch for the authenticity of it.

**Countor,** in England, a sergeant-at-law; an advocate.

**County,** a shire, or civil division of a country or state for judicial or political purposes. Etymologically, that portion of a country under the immediate authority of a count. Most of the United States are divided into counties. **County courts,** inferior courts of record, whose jurisdiction is limited to the county in which they are established. **Counties Palatine,** counties in which earls formerly had peculiar privileges, and exercised some royal powers, such as issuing writs, pardoning crimes, etc. They were Lancaster, Durham, and Chester. **County rate,** one levied on the occupiers of lands in a county for local purposes. **County sessions,** the general quarter sessions of the peace for each county, held four times a year. They have both civil and criminal jurisdiction.

**Court,** a place where justice is administered. (2) The judge or judges when sitting to administer justice. Courts may be classified in general as *courts of record*, those in which a final record of the proceedings is made, which imports verity and can not be collaterally impeached, and *courts not of record*, in which no final record is made, though it may keep a docket and enter in it notes of the various proceedings; *courts of original jurisdiction*, in which suits are brought, and which have power to hear and determine causes in the first instance, and *appellate courts*, which take cognizance of causes removed from other courts by appeal or writ of error; *courts of equity* or *chancery*, which administer justice according to the principles of equity, and *courts of law*, which administer justice according to the principles of the common law; *civil courts*, which give remedies for private wrongs; *criminal courts*, in which public offenders are tried, convicted, and sentenced;

*ecclesiastical courts*, which formerly had jurisdiction over testamentary and matrimonial causes, but which are now limited to causes which grow out of the rules and discipline of the church; *courts of admiralty*, which have jurisdiction over maritime causes, civil and criminal; *courts-martial*, composed of a number of commissioned officers, especially assigned to such duty, which have jurisdiction of offenses against the military or naval laws, committed by persons in that service. For particular courts, see their respective titles.

**Court of Ancient Demesne,** one formerly held by a bailiff appointed by the king, in which alone the tenants of the king's demesne could be impleaded.

**Court of Appeals,** the name of the court of last resort in New York, Maryland, Virginia, Kentucky, and a few other states. (2) A division of the *Supreme Court of Judicature* (*q.v.*), in England, for the correcting of errors in the *High Court of Justice* (*q.v.*) It is composed of the lord high chancellor, the lord chief justice, the master of the rolls, the chief justice of the common pleas, and the chief baron of the exchequer, and such other judges as the queen may appoint.

**Court of Arches; Audience.** See *Arches* and *Audience court.*

**Courts of assize and nisi prius,** courts composed of two or more judges of assize, sent twice a year to the various circuits to try by a jury of the respective counties such matters of fact as were then under dispute in the courts of Westminster Hall. An action was originally triable only in the Superior Court of Westminster, where it was brought, but tho commission of *nisi prius* secured the trial of the case before a jury of the county where the venire was laid, and the verdict was returned to the court above, where judgment was rendered upon it, unless before (*nisi prius*) the fifth day after, one of the parties moves for a new trial. Three other commissions were issued to the judges of assize, viz.: of *the peace;* of *oyer and terminer*, to hear and determine treasons, felonies, robberies, murders, and criminal offenses in general; of *jail delivery*, to try prisoners confined, and clear the jails.

**Court-Baron,** in England, a court which, although not one of record, is incident to every manor, and may be held at any place within the same, on giving due notice. It generally assembles but once in the year. See *Presentment; Manor.*

**Court of Claims,** a court of the United States established for the purpose of hearing and determining all claims founded upon any law of Congress, or upon any regulation of an executive department, or upon any contract, express or implied, with the Government of the United States, and all claims which may be referred to it by either House of Congress, and all set-offs, counter-claims, and demands whatsoever on the part of the government against any person making claim against the government in said court; also all claims which may be referred to it by any executive department where the amount in controversy exceeds $3,000, or where the decision will affect a class of cases and furnish a precedent for future action, or where any authority, right, privilege, or exemption is claimed or denied under the Constitution of the United States. The court is composed of one chief justice and four judges, who hold their office during good behavior, and their sessions are held in Washington, D. C. An appeal, only on questions of law, lies to the Supreme Court on the part of the United States in all cases, and on the part of the claimants when the amount in controversy exceeds $3,000; but the findings of fact of the Court of Claims are conclusive.

**Court of Common Pleas,** in England, one of the three Superior Courts of Common Law at Westminster, a branch of the *aula regis*, and formerly ambulatory, but fixed at Westminster by virtue of the 11th clause of *Magna Charta*. It derived its name from the fact that the causes of the *common people* were heard there. It had exclusive jurisdiction of all *real actions*, and, for a long time, exclusive jurisdiction of all personal actions between subject and subject; but the *courts of King's Bench* and *Exchequer* gradually encroached upon this jurisdiction. It consists of one chief and four puisne or associate justices. By the Judicature Act of 1873, it was made a division of the High Court of Justice (*q.v.*). In many of the United States, courts of original and general jurisdiction, hearing also criminal and divorce cases.

**Courts of Conscience.** See *Courts of Request.*

**Court for Crown Cases Reserved,** in England, created by 11 & 12 Vict. c. 78, for the decision of points of law arising in criminal trials, and specially reserved by the judge or justices.

**Court for Divorce and Matrimonial Causes,** in England, a court established by 20 and 21 Vict. c. 85, to take exclusive jurisdiction over such causes. To it was transferred the jurisdiction of the ecclesiastical courts in such matters, and that exercised by Parliament in granting divorces.

**Court of Exchequer,** in England, a superior court of record which formerly had jurisdiction only of revenue cases, and then, by a fiction that the plaintiff was a debtor to the King (see *Quo minus*), took jurisdiction of all actions between man and man, except real actions. It consisted of one chief and four puisne judges or barons. By the Judicature Act, 1873, it was made the Exchequer Division of the High Court of of Justice, and by order in council it was, in 1881, merged in the Queen's Bench Division.

**Court of Exchequer Chamber,** in England, a court for the correction and prevention of errors of law in the three superior common-law courts. It consisted of the judges of two of the courts sitting together to decide questions appealed from the other. Questions of unusual difficulty and importance were reserved for the decision of the full court, consisting of all the judges of the three courts, and sometimes the lord chancellor. By the Judicature Act, this court was abolished, and its jurisdiction transferred to the *Court of Appeal* (*q.v.*).

**Court of Hustings,** a court in the city of London, analogous to the sheriffs' county court.

**Court of Inquiry,** a court consisting of one or more officers, not exceeding three, and a judge-advocate, invested with power to examine into the nature of any accusation or imputation against any military officer or soldier, and decide whether ulterior proceedings should be resorted to.

**Court of King's** or **Queen's Bench,** the supreme court of common law in England; the principal branch of the *aula regis* (*q.v.*), so-called, because the King formerly sat in it in person. Its jurisdiction was formerly confined to the trials of crimes and misdemeanors which amounted to a breach of the peace, and trespasses committed *vi et armis*, but by a fiction of the law was gradually extended to all actions of case, actions where fraud was alleged, and finally to all personal actions and the action of ejectment. Its chief judge was and is still called the Lord Chief Justice of England, and there were four puisne judges. By the Judicature Act, 1873, its jurisdiction was transferred to the High Court of Justice (*q.v.*).

**Court-Leet,** in England, a court of record, held once a year within a particular hundred or manor, before the steward of the leet. At it petty offenses are *presented* and punished.

**Court of Passage,** in England, has jurisdiction over causes of action arising within the borough of Liverpool; and also in admiralty matters.

**Court of Peculiars,** in England, a branch of the Arches Court (*q.v*).

**Court of Probate,** in England, took the place of the ecclesiastical and other probate courts in 1857. It is now the Probate, Divorce, and Admiralty Division of the *High Court of Justice* (*q.v*)

**Courts of Request,** or *courts of conscience*, are courts which were established by act of Parliament in London and other cities for the recovery of debts not exceeding forty shillings. They were courts *not of record* and proceeded in a summary way to examine upon oath the parties and other witnesses without a jury, and make such order as was consonant with equity and good conscience. They were abolished in 1846, and their jurisdiction transferred to the *county courts* (*q.v*).

**Court of Session,** the supreme civil court of Scotland, consisting of the Lord President, the Lord Justice-Clerk and eleven ordinary lords.

**Courts of Survey,** in England, hear appeals by masters or owners from orders for the detention of their ships.

**Courts of the Universities** of Oxford and Cambridge, have civil and criminal jurisdiction in matters affecting their own members.

**Cousin-german,** a first cousin, or child of one's uncle or aunt; the child (grandchild, etc.) of a first cousin is a cousin once (twice, etc.) removed.

**Covenant,** an agreement or unilateral contract under seal, *i,e.*, by deed. See *Agreement; Contract.* The principal covenants in a deed conveying land are *seisin, right to convey, for quiet enjoyment, against incumbrances,* and *for further assurances.* A covenant is said to *run with the land* (or *the reversion*) when the benefit or burden of it passes to the assignee of the land, etc. See *Title.*

**Covenant to stand seized to uses,** a "voluntary" assurance, operating under the Statute of Uses, and without transfer of possession. Now almost disused.

**Coverture,** the condition of a woman during marriage. (2) The continuance of the married state.

**Covin,** fraud, collusion.

**Creditor,** one who trusts or gives credit, correlative to debtor. A secured creditor is one who holds property of the debtor in pledge or mortgage, in addition to his promise to pay, express or implied.

**Creditors' bill,** a bill in equity filed by one or more creditors, by and on behalf of himself or themselves, and all other creditors who shall come in under the decree, for an account of the assets and a due administration of the estate.

**Cretio,** (Rom.), the period fixed by a testator within which the heir had to formally declare his intention to accept the inheritance.

**Crime,** any violation of public law. When the act is of an inferior degree of guilt, it is called a misdemeanor.

**Crimen,** *l.*, a crime. **Crimen falsi,** (Rom.), forgery, perjury, counterfeiting, alteration of instruments, and other frauds. **Crimen laesae majestatis,** (Rom.), treason. **Crimen repetundarum,** (Rom.), bribery.

**Criminal,** one guilty of committing a crime. (2) *Adj.*, involving an offense against law; relating to crime. **Criminal conversation,** unlawful intercourse with a married woman; adultery. **Criminal information,** a proceeding brought against a criminal, by the proper officer without a previous indictment or presentment to the grand jury. **Criminal law,** relates to crimes and their punishment.

**Criminal letters,** (Sc.), one form of criminal process before the High Court of Justiciary the other being indictment (*q.v.*). They resemble in form a summons in a civil action.

**Cross-action, claim,** or **petition,** is one brought, made, or filed by a defendant against a person who is claiming relief as plaintiff in an action against him. See *Counterclaim.*

**Cross-examination,** the examination of a witness by the side which did not call him; generally after examination in chief.

**Cross-remainders.** See *Remainder.*

**Crown, The,** the sovereign. (2) *Adj.*, relating to or connected with the sovereign. **Crown lands,** the demesne lands of the crown, which are now usually surrendered by each sovereign on coming to the throne, in return for the *Civil list* (*q.v*). **Crown law,** criminal law, the crown being the prosecutor. **Crown office,** a department formerly belonging to the Court of Queen's Bench, and amalgamated by the Judicature Act, 1879, with the central office of the Supreme Court. Its chief official is the queen's coroner and attorney. **Crown Office in Chancery,** now transferred to the High Court. Its chief official, the clerk of the crown, issues the writ of summons and election for both Houses of Parliament, and performs the duties of the old Hanaper Office (*q.v.*). **Crown side,** the criminal side of the court of King's bench. **Crown solicitor,** the solicitor to the treasury, who acted, prior to 1879, in state prosecutions as solicitor for the crown in preparing the prosecution. See *Public prosecutor.*

**Cruelty,** acts which give pain, and affect the life, health, or physical comfort of another. Cruelty to a husband or wife is a generally recognized ground for judicial separation, if not absolute divorce. Cruelty to animals is made an indictable offense by the laws of most of the states.

**Cry de pais,** or **Cri de pais,** hue and cry.

**Cryer,** an officer of a court, whose duty it is to make proclamations.

**Cucking-stool,** a chair on which females, for certain offenses, *e.g.*, that of being a "common scold," were fastened and ducked in a pond.

**Cui ante divortium,** *l.*, (*cui in vita*), an old writ for a woman divorced from her husband, to recover her lands from him, to whom her husband alienated them during the marriage, against her will.

**Culpa,** (Rom.), fault; neglect. *Culpa levis,* slight or excusable neglect; *culpa lata* or *magna,* gross neglect, also called *crassa negligentia.*

**Cum,** *l.,* with. **Cum grano salis,** with a grain of salt, *i.e.,* with due allowance for exaggeration. **Cum onere,** with the burden; subject to the incumbrance. A purchaser of land, with knowledge of an incumbrance, takes it *cum onere.* **Cum testamento annexo,** with the will annexed. See *Administration.*

**Cumulative,** additional, as distinct from substitutional or alternative, *e.g.,* legacies, sentences, remedies. **Cumulative evidence,** that which goes to prove what has already been proved by other evidence.

**Curate,** one who has the cure of souls; the lowest ecclesiastical degree. He may be (*a*) *temporary,* or *stipendiary,* or (*b*) *perpetual,* in which case he resembles a vicar.

**Curator,** a guardian. He may be (*a*) of a minor; (*b*) of a person *non compos mentis;* (*c*) of property *ad interim,* called *curator bonis;* (*d*) for the purpose of conducting a suit for a minor, called *curator ad litem.* See *Guardian; Tutor.*

**Curia,** *l.,* the court. **Curia advisari vult,** the court wishes to consider the matter; an entry reserving judgment until some subsequent day. **Curia claudenda,** an old writ to compel the defendant to erect a wall between his land and the plaintiff's. **Curia regis,** the king's court. Applied to the *aula regis, communis bancus,* and *iter,* or *eyre,* as courts of the king, but especially to the *aula regis* (*q.v.*).

**Cursitors,** clerks of the Court of Chancery, who drew up writs that were "of course" (*de cursu*).

**Curtesy,** the estate which a husband has for his life in his wife's fee-simple or fee-tail estates, general or special, after her death. Three things are necessary to this estate: A legal marriage, seizin of the wife and birth of issue, capable of inheriting, alive and during the mother's life.

**Curtilage,** a yard, piece of ground, or garden which adjoins a dwelling-house.

**Custodian lease,** a grant from the crown under the exchequer seal, by which lands, etc., of the king were demised or committed to some person as custodee or lessee thereof.

**Custody,** care; in criminal law, detention. (2) See *Infant.*

**Custom,** unwritten law established by long usage. It may be (*a*) *general,* which is the common law; or (*b*) *particular* or local, which is custom proper; (*c*) *personal, e.g.,* the custom of merchants, or "law-merchant," as distinguished from "customs of trade," which apply only to one particular trade. Customs must be immemorial, continuous, peaceable, reasonable, certain (*i.e.*, definite), compulsory (*i.e.*, not optional), and consistent.

**Custom-house,** the office where goods are entered for import or export.

**Customary court,** a court which should be kept within the manor for which it is held, for the benefit of the copyholders of the manor (*q.v.*).

**Customary freehold,** is one held by privilege of *frank tenure*, *i.e.*, by custom, and not by the will of the lord, wherein it differs from copyholds. Otherwise, it resembles them.

**Customs,** duties levied on commodities, imported or exported.

**Custos rotulorum** (*the keeper of the rolls or records*), the principal justice of the peace within the county.

**Cy-pres,** *fr.*, (*as near as*), a doctrine of the courts, whereby if a person expresses a general intention with regard to his property, and also directs a particular mode of carrying out the same which is contrary to law, they, in some cases, give effect to his general intention *as near as possible; e.g.*, in the case of charitable legacies.

## D.

**Damage,** an injury to person, property, or reputation, occasioned by the wrongful act or negligence of another, or by accident. **Damage feasant,** or **faisant,** (*doing damage*), a term applied to the act of animals going upon another's land and feeding, tramping down grass, corn, etc.

**Damages,** the amount claimed, or allowed, as compensation for injuries sustained through the wrongful act or negligence of another. They may be *general*, such as necessarily and by implication of law arise from the act complained of; or *special*, such as under the peculiar circumstances of the case arise from the act complained of, but are not implied by law; *compensatory*, sufficient in amount to cover the loss actually sustained; *exemplary*, *punitive*, or *vindictive*, when in excess of the loss sustained and allowed as a punishment for torts committed with fraud, actual malice, or violence; *nominal*, when the act was wrong, but the loss sustained was trifling; *substantial*, when the loss was serious; *liquidated*, *i.e.*, fixed by agreement of the parties, as when it is agreed beforehand what amount one shall receive in case of a breach of contract by the other.

**Dame,** the legal title of the wife of a knight or baronet.

**Damnify,** to damage, to injure, to cause loss to any person.

**Damnosa haereditas,** (Rom.), a disadvantageous or unprofitable inheritance.

**Damnum absque injuria,** *l.*, loss or damage occasioned without wrong, and for which there is no legal remedy.

**Darraign,** to clear a legal account; to answer an accusation.

**Darrein,** last. **Darrein continuance,** last continuance. **Darrein seisin,** a plea which lay in some cases for a tenant in a writ of right. See *Puis darrein.*

**Date,** from *l.*, *datum*, given. The designation of the time when an instrument was executed.

**Datum, data,** facts or principles given or allowed.

**Day,** The space of time which elapses between two successive midnights. That portion of such time during which the sun is shining. The law, as a rule, takes no account of fractions of a day, except in cases of registration, where priority decides rights. *Days of grace*, see *Grace.*

**Daysman,** an arbitrator; an elected judge.

**De,** *l.*, of; for; about; concerning; from; out of. For the various writs beginning with this word, see generally the second word of the title of the writ, *admittendo, bonis*, etc. **De annuo reditu,** a writ to recover an annuity. **De averiis replegiandis,** a writ to replevy cattle. **De bene esse,** a technical phrase applied to a thing done provisionally, and out of due course, *e.g.*, evidence taken in advance of a trial, where there is danger that it may be lost, owing to the age, infirmity, or intended absence of the witness. **De bonis non,** see *Administration.* **De bonis propriis,** a judgment against an administrator or executor, to be satisfied out of his own property, when he has been guilty of a *devastavit*, or has falsely pleaded *plene administravit* in a suit brought by a creditor of the estate. **De die in diem,** from day to day, continuously. **De Donis, statute of,** see *Donis*, *Tail.* **De dote unde nihil habet,** a writ of dower which lay for a widow when no part of her dower had been assigned to her. **De estoveriis habendis,** a writ which lay for a woman divorced *a mensa et thoro*, to recover her alimony. **De facto, de jure,** in fact; by right. These are mutually opposed terms. **De homine replegiando,** a writ to take a man out of prison, or out of the custody of a private person, upon giving security that the man shall appear to answer any charge against him. **De injuria,** the replication by which the plaintiff in an action of tort denies the sufficiency of the excuse or justification set up by the defendant. **De la plus belle,** see *Dower.* **De lunatico inquirendo,** a writ for ascertaining whether a party charged is a lunatic or not. **De manucaptiare,** a writ commanding the sheriff to take sureties for a prisoner's appearance, and to set him free.

**De medietate linguae,** see *Jury*. **De melioribus damnis,** the liberty granted to a plaintiff, who has sued several defendants and had damages assessed severally against each, of electing which he will take. **De mercatoribus,** see *Acton Burnel*. **De non decimando,** a claim to exemption from the payment of tithes. **De novo,** anew; afresh. **De odio et atia,** a writ commanding the sheriff to inquire whether a person charged with murder was committed upon just cause of suspicion, or merely on account of some one's hatred and ill will, and in the latter case to admit him to bail. **De partitione facienda,** the ancient writ for the partition of lands held by tenants in common. **De perambulatione facienda,** a writ commanding the sheriff, in case of a boundary dispute between two towns, to take with him twelve knights and walk the bounds, establishing them to a certainty. **De plegiis acquietandis,** a writ which lay in behalf of a surety who had been compelled to pay, against his principal. **De reparatione facienda,** a writ which lies for one tenant in common, to compel another to aid in repairing the common property. **De son tort, executor,** one who, not being appointed an executor, takes upon himself to act in that capacity at his own risk (lit. *of his own wrong*). **De tallagio non concedendo,** the statute 34 Edw. I., restricting the power of the king to grant *talliage* (*q.v.*). **De una parte,** of one part, applied to a deed in which only one party gives, grants, or binds himself to do a thing, as opposed to a deed *inter partes*. **De ventre inspiciendo,** a writ to inspect the body, where a woman claims to be pregnant, to see whether she is with child.

**Dead freight,** money paid by a person who has chartered a ship and only partly loaded her, in respect of the part left empty.

**Dead man's part,** that part of an intestate's personalty which, prior to 1 Jac. II. c. 17, was not divided between his wife and children, but became the administrator's.

**Dean,** an ecclesiastical officer, who derives his name from the fact that he presides over *ten* canons or prebendaries at least. **Dean and chapter,** the council of a bishop, who assist him with their advice in regard to the temporal and religious affairs of his see. **Dean of the Arches,** the presiding judge of the *Arches Court* (*q.v.*).

**Death,** the ceasing to live. *Civil death,* is the state of a man who has lost all his civil rights, and, as to them, is considered as dead. Death is presumed from an absence of seven years or more, when the person has not been heard of in that time. There is not in English law any presumption as to which died first of two persons killed by the same accident, *e.g.*, by a shipwreck.

**Debenture,** an instrument under seal issued by a company, or public body, as security for a loan. (2) A certificate issued by the collector of a port to an importer for drawback of duties imported and then exported by him.

**Debet et detinet,** *l.*, an action brought by the original creditor against the original debtor. One by a person representing a creditor, *e.g.*, an executor, was in the *detinet* only.

**Debitum fundi,** *l.*, (Sc.), a real debt, or charge on land.

**Debt,** a sum certain due from one person (the *debtor*) to another (the *creditor*). Debts are (*a*) of *record*, being those proved by the records of a court, *e.g.*, judgment debts; (*b*) *specialty*, those under seal; (*c*) *simple contract*, those not under seal. (2) The common-law form of action which lies to recover a sum certain.

**Debtee-executor,** a creditor made executor by the will of his debtor.

**Decedent,** a deceased person.

**Deceit,** a fraudulent misrepresentation or contrivance, by which a person is misled to his injury. (2) A common-law action to recover damages for loss caused by misrepresentation or fraud. *Trespass on the case* (*q.v.*) was, however, more employed for this purpose.

**Declarant,** a person who makes a declaration.

**Declaration,** a public proclamation, *e.g.*, the Declaration of Independence; a declaration of war. (2) The statement by a plaintiff of his cause of action. (3) A statement made by one of the parties to a transaction, frequently admissible in evidence; *e.g.*, when it is against the pecuniary interest of the party making it, when it is part of the *res gestae* (*q.v.*), or when made by a dying person, in cases of homicide.

**Declaration of intention,** the formal statement by an alien that he renounces his allegiance to the sovereign of the country of which he is then a citizen, and will become a citizen of the United States, made before the proper court, with a view to *naturalization* (*q.v*). **Declaration of trust,** an acknowledgment, generally in writing, by a person having the possession of and legal title to property, that he holds it for the use of another.

**Declaratory,** that which explains or fixes the meaning of something which was before doubtful or uncertain, *e.g.*, a declaratory statute. **Declaratory decree,** one declaring the rights of the parties without ordering any thing to be done.

**Decree**; (Sc.), **decreet.** an order made by the court in a suit in equity, or libel in admiralty. It is *interlocutory*, if it does not finally dispose of the case, *e.g.*, an order directing an accounting, or a sale, appointing a receiver, etc.; or *final*, when it does dispose of the case. A **Decree nisi,** is one which is at first conditional, but becomes *absolute*, unless within a given time the party against whom it is rendered shows good cause why it should not be.

**Decreet arbitral,** (Sc.), the award of an arbitrator.

**Decretal order,** a chancery order in the nature of a decree, but not made at the hearing

**Decretals,** a volume of the canon law, so called as containing the decrees of sundry popes. (2) A digest of the canons.

**Dedi,** *l.*, I have given. The aptest words to denote a feoffment when deeds were written in Latin. It formerly carried with it a warranty in law. **Dedi et concessi,** I have given and granted.

**Dedicate,** to devote land to some public use; *e.g.*, to make a private way public; to set apart ground for a public park, etc. **Dedication** may be *express*, *i.e.*, made by deed, or declaration; or *implied*, *i.e.*, to be presumed from acts of the owner, such as acquiescence in the public use. A dedication is not complete until accepted by the public authorities.

**Dedimus potestatem,** *l.*, (*we have given the power*), a writ or commission empowering the persons to whom it is directed to do a certain act, such as to administer the oath to a newly appointed justice, to take testimony, and the like. (2) A writ formerly issued, appointing an attorney to appear for the defendant.

**Dedition,** the act of yielding up any thing; surrendry.

**Deed,** an instrument written on paper or parchment, duly signed, sealed, and delivered, used chiefly to convey an estate in land not less than a freehold. In many states a mere scroll suffices for a seal. **Deed poll,** is one which is made by one party only, as opposed to an *indenture* (*q.v.*).

**Deemster,** or **Dempster,** a judge in the Isle of Man, who is chosen by the people, and decides all disputes without process or pleadings.

**Defamation,** scandalous words written or spoken concerning another, tending to the injury of his reputation, for which an action on the case for damages would lie. See *Libel; Slander.*

**Default,** omission of that which a man ought to do. (2) The non-appearance, or failure to plead, of a party to a suit.

**Defeasance,** a condition, especially one contained in a collateral deed or document accompanying another, providing that upon the performance or occurrence of certain matters, an estate or interest created by such other deed shall be defeated and determined.

**Defeasible,** that which may be defeated, determined, or divested.

**Defectus sanguinis,** *l.*, failure of issue.

**Defendant,** the person against whom an action is brought, or an indictment found.

**Defendemus,** *l.*, (*we will defend*), a word used in old grants and donations, which binds the donor and his heirs to indemnify the donee against any incumbrance other than what is mentioned therein.

**Defense,** a forcible resistance of an attempt to injure one's self, one's family, or property, or to commit a felony. (2) In pleading, the denial by the defendant of the truth of plaintiff's complaint. (3) The conduct of the trial, on behalf of the defendant, whether he be sued in a civil action or be prosecuted criminally.

**Definitive,** that which terminates a suit. **Definitive sentence,** the final judgment of a court, in opposition to provisional or interlocutory judgment.

**Deforcement,** the holding of lands or tenements to which another person has a right; so that this includes as well an abatement, an intrusion, or a disseisin, as any other species of wrong, by which he that has a right to a freehold is kept out of possession; but it is used especially of keeping out of possession one who has never had possession. Hence, *deforceor*, one who withholds possession wrongfully and *deforciant*, the person against whom the fictitious action used to be brought in levying a fine.

**Degradation,** an ecclesiastical censure; whereby a clergyman is divested of holy orders.

**Degree,** a step, from generation to generation, in the distance between kindred.

**Dehors,** *fr.*, out of; without; foreign to.

**Del credere commission,** one for which the agent or factor guarantees prompt payment on the part of the persons to whom he sells his principal's goods.

**Delegate,** one authorized to act for another (2) A person elected to represent others in a deliberative assembly, such as a nominating convention. (3) A person elected to represent a territory of the United States in Congress. He has a seat, and the right of debate, but not the right to vote.

**Delegation,** (Rom.), the substitution, by means of novation, of a new debtor for the original one, with the latter's consent. See *Expromissio.* (2) Appointment of a delegate. (3) The whole body of delegates representing a particular state, district, or county, in a legislative or other assembly, or at the court of a foreign power.

**Deletion,** (Sc.), erasure.

**Delictum,** *l.*, a crime, tort, or wrong. See *Action; Ex delicto; Flagrante delicto.*

**Delivery,** the act of transferring possession. It may be *actual;* or *constructive, i.e.*, implied by law from the acts of the parties; *e.g.*, handing to the buyer the key of the warehouse where his goods are stored; separating and marking them with his name; transferring to him a warehouse receipt; or giving him an order on the person with whom the goods are stored, which operates as a delivery as soon as accepted by the latter, and the like (2) In conveyancing, the transfer of a deed from the grantor to the grantee, or some one acting in his behalf, which is *absolute*, when the deed is intended to take effect immediately; or *conditional*, when the deed is handed by the grantor to a third person, to be by him handed to the grantee when certain specified conditions shall be performed. Until the conditions are performed, the instrument is called an *escrow* (*q.v.*)

**Demand,** the widest word for a claim, including any right of action. (2) A request to pay money, or to do something, made under a claim of right to have it paid or done. **Demand note,** a note payable on demand. Payment must be demanded, before suit can be brought, or the statute of limitations begins to run.

**Demandant,** the old term for a plaintiff in a *real action* (*q.v.*).

**Demesne,** own; private. *Demesne land* or *manor*, that which is in the owner's or lord's own occupation, by himself or his tenants for years. See *Ancient demesne; Crown lands.*

**Demise,** a transfer of a right or dignity; *e.g., demise of the crown*, which usually occurs on the death of the sovereign; hence the word "demise" is sometimes wrongly used for "decease." (2) A conveyance either in fee, for life, or for years, especially the latter. **Demise and redemise,** mutual leases or grants of the same land, or something out of it; *e.g.*, a rent-charge.

**Demur,** to stay, or abide. To object formally to a pleading, that, admitting the facts to be true as stated, no cause is shown why the party *demurring* should go further. It imports that the party demurring will stay, and not proceed until the court decides whether he is bound to do so. *Demurrers* are either *general*, where no particular cause is assigned, and the insufficiency of the pleading is stated in general terms, or *special*, where some particular defects are pointed out. *Demurrers* may be to the whole or to any part of a pleading.

**Demurrage,** in commercial navigation, an allowance made to the owners of a ship by the freighter, for detaining her in port longer than the period agreed upon. (2) The detention itself.

**Denizen,** in English law, an alien born, who has obtained from the crown letters patent, called *letters of denization*, to make him (either permanently, or for a time) an English subject.

**Deodand,** a personal chattel which has been the immediate occasion of the death of any human being who had reached years of discretion. Previous to 1846 it was forfeited to the crown, to be *given to God*, *i.e.*, applied to charitable uses.

**Department,** a civil or military division of a country. (2) One of the principal offices established by law for the administration of public affairs, whose chief officer is a member of the cabinet. There are seven, viz., the Department of State, the Treasury Department, the Interior Department, the Post-office Department, the Department of War the Department of the Navy, and the Department of Justice.

**Departure,** in maritime law, a deviation from the course prescribed in the policy of insurance. (2) In pleading, a statement of matter in a subsequent pleading which is inconsistent with, or not pursuant to, the ground taken by the same party in his previous pleading.

**Depasture,** to put cattle out to graze.

**Deponent,** a person who makes an affidavit, or gives testimony under oath, which is reduced to writing for use on the trial of a cause, called a *deposition*.

**Deposit,** money, deeds, etc., lodged by one person with another as a pledge or security, *e.g.*, that he will complete a purchase, or repay a loan. (2) A bailment of goods to be kept for the *depositor* without reward, and to be returned when he shall require it. The term is popularly applied to money placed in bank for safe-keeping, the bank undertaking to return not the specific money, but other money equal in amount.

**Deposition,** depriving a person of a dignity; used especially of ecclesiastical censure. (2) See *Deponent*.

**Deprivation,** taking away a benefice from a clergyman on account of some offense.

**Deputy,** one who acts for, or instead of, another in some office or dignity. In general, he has power to do any act which his principal might do, and should always act in the name of his principal.

**Deraign,** to degrade. (2) To prove; make good.

**Derelict,** abandoned; especially used of a vessel forsaken at sea; also of land left permanently uncovered by the receding of water from its former bed. See *Alluvion.*

**Derivative conveyances,** secondary deeds, which presuppose and confirm or alter some other.

**Derogate,** to lessen; impair. *A grantor may not derogate from his own grant; i.e.,* prejudice the right thereby created ,by any subsequent act of his own.

**Descent,** one of the two chief methods of acquiring an estate in lands. It is the passing of landed property of an intestate to another person by the operation of law, *i.e.,* by his right of representation as heir-at-law of the intestate. See *Heir.*

**Desertion,** the criminal offense of leaving the army or navy without license. (2) Abandoning wife or children. Continued desertion for a number of years is a valid ground for divorce in most states.

**Detainer, Unlawful,** the wrongful keeping of a person's goods, although the original taking may have been lawful. (2) *Writ of,* an obsolete form of process for commencing a personal action against one already in prison. See *Forcible entry and detainer*

**Determinable,** liable to come to an end on the happening of some contingency, *e.g.,* an estate devised to a widow during life or until she marry again.

**Detinet.** See *Debet.*

**Detinue,** a personal action at law arising *ex delicto* for the recovery of goods or their value. No longer in use.

**Devastavit,** (*he has wasted*), a misapplication or waste of the property of a deceased person by an executor or administrator, for which he is liable.

**Deviation,** by a ship, is departure from her proper course. This, when without necessity or just cause, invalidates her insurance policies.

**Devisavit vel non,** *l.*, an issue formerly sent from the Court of Chancery to be tried in a court of law, whether lands alleged to pass by a certain will did so pass or not.

**Devise,** a gift by will, properly applicable to realty; but it is also used sometimes of personalty. See *Legacy.*

**Dictum,** or *obiter dictum,* the expression by a judge of an opinion on a point of law arising during the hearing of a case, which, however, is not necessary for the decision of that case. A dictum is not, therefore, binding on other judges.

**Diem clausit extremum,** *l.*, (*he has died*), in England, a writ of extent, directing the sheriff, on the death of a crown debtor, to inquire by a jury when and where he died, and what chattels, debts, and lands he had at the time of his decease, and to seize them into the crown's hands. See *Extent.*

**Dies,** *l.*, a day. **Dies a quo,** the day from which; opposed to **Dies ad quem,** the day to which. **Dies amoris,** a day of favor; if obtained after default by the defendant it amounts to a waiver of the default. **Dies communes in banco,** regular days for appearance in court; common return days. **Dies datus,** a day given to the defendant in a suit; a continuance **Dies fasti, nefasti, et intercisi,** (Rom.), business days, holidays, and half-holidays. **Dies gratiae,** days of grace. **Dies non,** (Scil. **juridicus**), one on which no legal business can be transacted; *e.g.*, Sunday, Christmas-day. **Dies utiles,** available days.

**Digamy,** second marriage, after death of the first wife.

**Digest,** an abridged and methodically arranged compilation of decisions, or statutes, intended to aid one in finding out what the law is on a given subject. The principal digests now in use are the United States Digest, Jacob's Fisher's Digest, and the digests of the various state and United States reports. By "*The Digest,*" is commonly understood the Pandects of Justinian.

**Dignitary,** an ecclesiastic who holds a *dignity* (*q.v.*) which gives him pre-eminence over mere priests and canons, *e.g.*, a bishop, archbishop, etc.

**Dignity,** in England, the right to bear a title denoting rank or office. If inheritable it is a species of incorporeal hereditament.

**Dilapidation,** the ecclesiastical term for waste, as applied to the buildings of the benefice. See *Waste.*

**Dilatory plea,** one whose object is to defeat the particular action brought, without coming to a trial on the merits, *e.g.*, a plea to the jurisdiction, or a plea in abatement.

**Diligence,** care. See *Negligence; Culpa; Bailment.* (2) In Scotch law (*a*) a warrant to enforce attendance of witnesses or production of writings; (*b*) a writ of execution.

**Diminution,** making less; incompleteness, *e.g.*, of a record.

**Diocese,** a district subject to a bishop's authority.

**Direct,** straightforward; not collateral or indirect. **Direct evidence,** is opposed to circumstantial evidence (*q.v.*). **Direct examination,** the first examination of the witness by the party who calls him.

**Direction,** the explanation of the law given to a jury by the judge in a case where their verdict depends partly on the law. Erroneous or *mis-direction* is ground for a new trial.

**Director,** one elected or appointed to manage or superintend the affairs of a company, or a public institution.

**Directory statute,** is opposed (1) to *declaratory, i.e.*, a statute which merely declares what the law is; and (2) to *imperative.* When a statute directs that an act should be done in a specific manner, or authorizes it upon certain conditions, if a strict compliance with its provisions is not essential to the validity of the act, it is said to be *directory*, although the performance may be enforced by mandamus; but if such compliance is essential, it is said to be *imperative.*

**Dirimant impediments,** absolute bars to marriage, which would make it null *ab initio.*

**Disability,** incapacity to do any legal act, *e.g.*, to sue or contract. It may be (*a*) *absolute* or perpetual, as in the case of felons; or (*b*) *partial* or personal, as in the case of infants, lunatics, etc.

**Disabling statutes,** those which restrict the exercise of a right, or the power of alienation.

**Disafforest,** to throw open; to reduce from the privileges of a for[illegible] to the state of common ground.

**Disagreement,** of a jury is a failure to unite upon a verdict. In criminal law, this does not prevent a second trial of the accused for the same offense.

**Disbar,** to expel a barrister or counselor from the bar for misconduct

**Discharge,** the act by which a person held to answer a charge of felony or misdemeanor is set at liberty (2) The decree by which a bankrupt is released from all liability for debts incurred prior to the adjudication of bankruptcy. (3) A rule *nisi* is *discharged*, when the court decides that it shall not be made absolute. (4) The act by which a jury is relieved from further consideration of a case, *e.g.*, the finding of a verdict; the death of one of the jurymen, although by agreement of the parties the case may still go on before the survivors. A jury may be discharged, when the judge is satisfied that they are and will be unable to agree on a verdict, or when the trial is unable to proceed on account of the sickness of the judge.

**Disclaimer,** a disavowal or formal renunciation, *e.g.*, *by a trustee*, of the trust (which is usually evidenced by a deed); or *by a patentee*, of part of his patent. (2) A refusal to accept, *e.g.*, an office, by an *executor* who declines to prove a will; or an estate, by one to whom it was conveyed or devised. (3) A denial by a tenant of his landlord's title. (4) In equity, a renunciation by defendants of all claim to the thing demanded by the plaintiff.

**Discontinuance,** an interruption or breaking of the right of entry. This formerly happened where a person aliened a larger estate than he had, so that on his death the next owner had to bring an action. (2) A failure to proceed in, or the voluntary dismissal of, a case by the plaintiff.

**Discovert,** a widow; a woman unmarried.

**Discovery.** It is the right, as a general rule, of a party to an action, to exact from any other party thereto discovery, or information upon oath, as to (*a*) matters of fact (see *Interrogatories*), and (*b*) documents in defendant's past or present possession or power. See *Production; Inspection.* The right of a plaintiff to this benefit, as against a defendant, is limited to a discovery of such material facts as relate to the *plaintiff's* case, and does not extend to a discovery of the manner in which the *defendant's* case is to be established, or to evidence which relates exclusively to his case.

**Discredit,** to throw doubt on a witness's evidence by assailing his character, or otherwise. A party may not, as a rule, discredit his own witness.

**Discretion,** the use of private and independent judgment. Such matters as are left to the discretion of the trial judge, *e.g.*, the order in which the parties shall introduce evidence, the proportion of costs which each shall bear, etc., can not be reviewed by the court to which the case is taken on error. (2) Ability to distinguish between good and evil. This is presumed to exist at the age of fourteen, and may be proved to exist between the ages of seven and fourteen.

**Discussion,** (Sc.), the sureties' right to defer paying the debt for which they become bound until the creditor has *discussed,* (*i.e.*, brought process of execution against) the principal debtor, and he has failed to pay,

**Disentailing deed,** in England, an enrolled assurance by which a tenant in tail may bar the entail, *i.e.*, convert it into an estate in fee. See *Protector; Base fee.*

**Disfranchisement,** the act of depriving of a franchise, such as the right to vote or the right to act as a member of a corporation.

**Disgavel,** to exempt from the rules of *gavelkind* (*q.v.*).

**Disherison,** the act of debarring from inheritance.

**Disheritor,** one who puts another out of his inheritance.

**Dishonor,** to refuse to accept or pay a bill of exchange, or draft, or to pay a promissory note when duly presented. See *Acceptance; Bill of exchange.*

**Disme,** a tenth or tithe; whence our word *dime.*

**Dismiss,** to send out of court, as a defendant, or an action. *Dismissal,* may be *final, i.e.*, made after a full hearing on the merits; or *without prejudice,* before the case has been heard on its merits, when the plaintiff is at liberty to bring another action for the same cause.

**Disparagement,** in England, matching an heir in marriage beneath his degree or against decency; used of a marriage proposed by a guardian and injurious to his ward.

**Dispauper,** to prevent a person suing any longer in *forma pauperis* (*q.v*), if it appear during the action that he has property.

**Dispensation,** an exemption from some law. (2) A license. (Ecclesiastical term.)

**Dispone,** (Sc.), to grant. An essential word to convey an inheritable estate. **Disponer,** a grantor.

**Disseisee,** a person turned out of possession, or *disseised.*

**Disseisin,** a wrongful putting out of him that is seized of the freehold; as distinct from *abatement* or *intrusion.*

**Dissolution,** a legal severance or breaking up. This may take place in cases of (1) *partnership*, by death of a partner, by agreement, or by order of a court; (2) *companies*, by winding up, or cessation of working; (3) *marriage*, by decree of divorce; (4) an *attachment*, by an order of court releasing the goods taken, on giving bond, or proving that the writ was improperly issued.

**Distrain,** to make seizure of goods or chattels by way of distress.

**Distress,** a taking without legal process of a personal chattel from the possession of a wrong-doer, to enforce payment (*e.g.*, of rent), performance of duty, or satisfaction for an injury. The right to distrain arises (*a*) by common-law, *e.g.*, where beasts of a stranger are found damage feasant; (*b*) by statute; or (*c*) by power reserved in an agreement. It can not be exercised at night, and must be made, in the case of rent, upon the land whence the rent issues, and for the whole at one time. See *Replevin.* (2) The thing distrained or taken. Some goods and animals are exempt, *e.g.*, those necessary for carrying on the debtor's trade. **Distress infinite,** one that has no bounds with regard to its quantity, and may be repeated from time to time, until the stubbornness of the party is conquered. Such are distresses for fealty or suit of court, and for compelling jurors to attend. The right to distrain for rent does not exist in many states.

**Distribution,** the division, according to law, among the heirs of an intestate of the residue of the personal estate remaining after paying the debts and costs of administration.

**District,** a division of the United States, or each of the several states for political or judicial purposes. Each state is divided into congressional districts, corresponding in number to the number of representatives it is entitled to send to the House, in each of which a congressman is elected by the qualified voters thereof. In a similar manner the states are divided into districts for the election of members of the legislature. See *District Courts.*

**District attorney,** an officer appointed for each judicial district of the United States, whose duty it is to prosecute in such district, all persons charged with violating the laws of the United States, and to represent the United States in all civil actions pending in such district to which the United States is a party.

**District Courts,** United States Courts of Record of the lowest rank established and sitting in the respective judicial districts into which the whole United States is divided. Some states constitute a single district each, but the larger states are divided into two or more. One judge, called the district judge, is appointed by the President, by and with the advice of the senate, for each district, and holds his office during good behavior. District Courts have original jurisdiction in admiralty, bankruptcy and revenue cases, but none in common-law or equity cases, except such as grow out of the revenue laws and a few other statutory matters. (2) Courts of some of the states established for the purpose of hearing and deciding causes in limited districts to which their jurisdiction is confined. In some of the states their jurisdiction is chiefly appellate, in others it is original and inferior.

**Distringas** (*that you distrain*), anciently called *constringas*, a writ addressed to the sheriff, directing him to distrain on a person therein named, in order to compel the performance of a duty or the delivery of a chattel. See *Fieri.* (2) An order forbidding the transfer of stock on a company's books; or the payment of dividends, without notice to the person who has put on the *distringas.*

**Disturbance,** the infringement of an incorporeal right, easement, etc. (2) *Of tenure,* is wrongfully to cause a person to quit his tenancy.

**Dittay,** (Sc.), the matter of charge against a person accused.

**Diversity,** a plea by a prisoner, alleging that his identity is mistaken.

**Divest,** or **Devest,** to take away from a person an estate or interest which has already vested.

**Dividenda,** an indenture; one part of an indenture.

**Divisa,** an award, or decree. (2) A devise. (3) Boundaries of a parish, farm, etc. (4) A boundary court.

**Division of opinion,** such a disagreement between the judges constituting a court as prevents any judgment being rendered in a matter before them. When it occurs in a Circuit

Court of the United States the case may be certified to the Supreme Court for decision.

**Divisional Courts,** in England, are courts consisting of two or more judges of the High Court, which transact certain business which can not be disposed of by a single judge, *e.g.*, appeals from county courts.

**Divisions,** of the High Court of Justice, in England, are now three, viz.: Chancery; Probate, Divorce and Admiralty; and Queen's Bench; the Common Pleas and Exchequer Divisions having in 1881 been consolidated with the latter.

**Divorce,** a judicial severance of the tie of matrimony. It may be (*a*) by a decree of dissolution (*a vinculo matrimonii*), or nullity of marriage, which is complete; or (*b*) by a decree of judicial separation (*a mensâ et thoro*), which, being only partial, does not enable the parties to marry again. See *Adultery; Judicial separation.*

**Dock,** the place in court where a prisoner is put during his trial. (2) The space for vessels between two wharves.

**Dock warrant,** a document issued by a dock owner stating that the goods mentioned in it are deliverable to a person therein named, or to his assigns by indorsement.

**Docket,** an abstract or brief entry in writing. (2) A book in which brief entries of all important acts done in court in each case are made.

**Doctor's Commons,** the buildings in which the Ecclesiastical and Admiralty Courts were held, near St. Paul's Cathedral.

**Document,** a deed, agreement, letter, receipt, or other instrument in writing used to prove a fact (2) In civil law, evidence delivered in due form, of whatever nature such evidence may be.

**Doe, John,** the nominal plaintiff, fictitious lessee of the real plaintiff, in the old action of ejectment, which was abolished in England by the Common Law Procedure Act, 1852.

**Dole,** a share allotted, *e.g.*, of common land, which is also called *dole-meadow.*

**Doli capax,** or **Incapax,** *l.*, capable, or incapable, of distinguishing between right and wrong. See *Discretion.*

**Dolus,** *l.*, an act which deceives another to his harm, or violates the just confidence reposed by him. Used generally in the sense of **Dolus malus,** willful deceit; fraud. See *Misrepresentation.*

**Domain,** dominion; possession; the right to dispose of a thing at pleasure. (2) Land about the manor-house of a lord.

**Domboc,** or **Dome-book,** a collection of local customs compiled by the order of King Alfred.

**Domesday,** or **Doomsday-book,** a record of surveys of the greater part of England, made in the time of William the Conqueror.

**Domestic,** relating to the household, including those who live with and serve the family, as well as the family itself.

**Domicile,** the place where a person has his legal home or place of permanent residence. It depends (*a*) on the fact of residing; (*b*) on the intention of remaining. Domicile is acquired (1) *by birth;* (2) *by choice;* (3) *by operation of law; e.g.*, the domicile of an infant is the same as that of his parents, though they are temporarily absent from it at the time of his birth.

**Dominant tenement,** one to which a servitude or easement is due, or for the benefit of which the service is constituted. See *Easement.*

**Dominium directum,** *l.*, in the feudal law, the ownership left in the superior lord, as distinguished from *dominium utile*, the possessory right granted to the vassal. See *Feud.*

**Dominus litis,** *l.*, the controller of a suit or litigation; generally the client, as distinguished from an attorney.

**Domo reparanda,** *l.*, a writ that lay for one against his neighbor, by the anticipated fall of whose house he feared a damage.

**Donatio,** *l.*, a gift. A voluntary transfer of the title and possession of property to another without consideration. It may be *inter vivos*, between living persons, and is completed at once by delivery and acceptance; or *mortis causa*, made in prospect of death, which can be recalled at any time during the donor's life, but is consummated by his dying of the illness then existing, and which must be accompanied by delivery; or *propter nuptias*, made by a husband as a security for the marriage portion.

**Donative advowson.** See *Advowson.*

**Donee,** one to whom a gift is made, or a power of appointment is given; *donor*, the giver.

**Donis conditionalibus, Statute de,** 13 Edward I. c. 1, otherwise called *Statute of Westminster the 2d*, restrained the barring or alienation of estates tail by the tenant in tail, until its effect was evaded by the system of *common recoveries.* See *Tail; Recovery.*

**Dormant,** sleeping; silent; not acting. **Dormant claim,** a claim in abeyance; not enforced. **Dormant judgment,** one on which execution has not been issued for so long a time that it can not be enforced without further proceedings to *revive* it. **Dormant partners,** those who do not appear or take any active part as partners, but who, nevertheless, share in the profits and losses of the business, and thereby incur the responsibility of partners.

**Dos,** in English law, the portion which a husband bestows upon a wife at her marriage, or which she takes by law after his death. In Roman law, it signified what was received *by*, or promised *to*, the husband from the wife, or some one in her interest, at the time of marriage. See *Dot.*

**Dot,** *fr.*, the fortune, portion, or dowry which a wife brings *to* her husband.

**Dotal,** in English law, relating to the portion or dowry of a woman. (2) In the civil law relating to the property which a wife brings *to* her husband.

**Dotation,** the act of giving a dowry or portion. (2) Endowment in general.

**Double,** twice as much. **Double or treble damages,** an increase of the damages found by the jury, made by the court in giving judgment in some cases, in pursuance of legal authority, *e.g.*, in case of a malicious infringement of a patentee's rights. **Double entry**, a term used by merchants to designate books of account so kept that they show the debit and credit of every transaction. **Double insurance,** insurance effected in two or more companies upon the same property or interest and in excess of its value. In England, the insured in such case may recover against either but the underwriter who pays him is entitled to contribution from the others. In the United States the subject is usually provided for by express stipulations in the policy of insurance. **Double pleading,** alleging for one purpose two or more distinct grounds of action or defense, when one would be as effectual in law as both or all. **Double waste.** When a tenant, bound to repair suffers a house to be wasted, and then unlawfully fells timber to repair it, he is said to commit double waste.

**Dowable,** entitled to dower.

**Dowager,** a widow endowed.

**Dower,** by common-law, the life estate which a widow has in one-third of all the lands of which her husband was seised in fee-simple, or fee tail, at any time during coverture. Dower is regulated by statute in the several states, but is substantially the same as that by common-law, except in some states where it is abolished. Ancient forms of dower, long since extinguished, were *ad ostium ecclesiae*, bestowed by the husband on coming to the church door to be married; *ex assensu patris*, made out of the lands of the husband's father, and with his assent; and *de la plus belle*, where the widow was required to endow herself out of the best lands she held as guardian in socage and to release from dower the lands her husband held in chivalry.

**Dowress,** a widow entitled to dower.

**Dowry,** otherwise called *dos* or *maritagium*, the portion which the wife brings the husband in marriage.

**Draft,** an order in writing to pay money, addressed by one person to another, on whom it is said to be *drawn*. (2) A preliminary or rough copy of a legal document. Hence *Draftsman*, one who draws up legal documents.

**Drawer,** the person who draws a bill of exchange on the *drawee* for his acceptance. See *Bill*.

**Drift-land, Drofland,** or **Dryfland,** a yearly rent paid by some tenants for driving cattle through the manor.

**Droit,** *fr.*, law; a right. **Droit d'accession.** See *Accession*. **Droits of admiralty,** rights claimed by a government over the property of an enemy found in her ports at the breaking out of hostilities. **Droit d'aubaine,** the right of the French crown to an alien's property at his death. Now extinct.

**Drunkenness,** the condition of a man whose mind is directly affected by the use of intoxicating drinks. It is a ground for avoiding a contract entered into by a party while under its influence, if the other party knew at the time that he was incapable of understanding its terms. It is not an excuse for the commission of a crime, but is sometimes taken into account in fixing the degree of a man's guilt or the extent of his punishment. When *habitual*, the laws commonly provide for the appointment of a guardian to take charge of the person and property, or property alone, of the drunkard.

**Dry-rent,** a rent reserved without clause of distress. See *Rent-seck*.

**Duces tecum.** See *Subpoena*.

**Dum,** *l.*, while. **Dum bene se gesserit,** while he conducts himself well: during good behavior; a limitation of appointments. **Dum fuit in prisona; infra aetatem,** an old writ to recover land aliened while the plaintiff was under duress in prison; during his infancy. **Dum non fuit compos mentis,** a writ which the heirs of an insane person, who aliened his lands, might have sued out to restore him to his rights. **Dum sola,** whilst single or unmarried.

**Dumb bidding,** in sales at auctions, a reserve price secretly fixed.

**Dunnage,** wood or other material placed in the hold of a ship, under or between the cargo.

**Duplex querela** (*a double plaint*), a process ecclesiastical, in the nature of an appeal from the refusal of an ordinary to institute, brought by the clerk in holy orders, who desires to be instituted. He is called the *promovent.*

**Duplicate,** one of two documents which are essentially the same; an executed copy. Leases, contracts, etc., are usually executed in duplicate, so that each party to one may have in his possession evidence of it. **Tax duplicate,** the copy of the auditor's book, showing the names of the tax-payers, the value of the taxable property owned by each, etc., made for the use of the treasurer in collecting taxes. **Duplicate will,** where a testator executes two copies of his will, one to keep himself, and the other to be deposited with another person.

**Duplicatio,** (Rom.), the defendant's second answer; *i.e.*, the rejoinder to the replication.

**Duplicity,** in pleading, the union of more than one cause of action, or defense, in one pleading. Such pleadings were called *multifarious*, and were formerly not allowed at common law; but the rule is modified by the statutes of the several states.

**Durante,** *l.*, during. **Durante absentia; minore aetate.** See *Administration.* **Durante bene placito,** during good pleasure; the ancient tenure of English judges.

**Duress,** imprisonment; compulsion; sometimes called *duress proper.* (2) Threats of injury or imprisonment (*duress per minas*). A contract made under duress is voidable at the option of the person forced into it.

**Dutch auction,** the setting up of property for sale by auction above its value, and gradually lowering the price till some person takes it.

**Duty,** an obligation; the correlative to a right. (2) A tax. See *Excise; Customs.* *Dutiable,* liable to pay duty.

**Dying declarations.** See *Declaration.*

## E.

**E,** or **Ex,** *l.*, from; out of. **Ex abundanti cautela,** out of abundant caution. **Ex aequo et bono,** in justice and fair dealing. **Ex assensu patris.** See *Dower.* **Ex cathedra,** from the chair, *i.e.*, with authority; originally applied to decisions of the popes. **E converso,** on the other hand. **Ex contractu; Ex delicto.** See *Action.* **Ex debito justitiae,** from a debt of justice; as a matter of legal right. **Ex gratia,** as a matter of favor. **Ex gravi querela,** a devisee's writ to recover lands held by the heirs. **Ex industria**, from fixed purpose. **Ex jurae naturae**, by the law of nature. **Ex maleficio**, out of misconduct. **Ex mero motu**, of his own accord. **Ex mora**, from delay, or default. **Ex more**, according to custom. **Ex natura rei**, from the nature of the thing. **Ex necessitate legis; rei**, from the necessity of the law; the thing. **Ex officio**, by virtue of his office. **Ex parte**, of the one part. An action is *ex parte* when it is not an adverse proceeding against any one else. **Ex parte materna; paterna**, from the mother's, father's side. **Ex post facto**, made after the occurrence; *e.g.*, legislation, which has, or would have if passed, a retrospective application. **Ex proprio moto**, of his own motion. **Ex proprio vigore**, of its own force. **Ex provisione viri.** See *Tail.* **Ex relatione**, on the relation or information. **Ex tempore**, from the time; without forethought. **Ex vi termini**, from the force of the term. **Ex visitatione dei**, from the visitation of God.

**Earl**, in England, a title of nobility next below a marquis and above a viscount. They formerly had the civil government of a shire or county, and were styled *comites* or *counts*. **Earl Marshal of England**, a high officer of state, who formerly had under his jurisdiction the Courts of Chivalry, Honor, etc. Under him is the Herald's office.

**Earmark**, a mark for identification; applied to the common indications of fraud.

**Earnest**, the sum paid by the buyer of goods in order to bind the seller to the terms of the agreement.

**Ear-witness**, one who attests any thing as heard by himself.

**Easement**, an incorporeal hereditament relating to user, and not to the taking of profit, and created by grant, express or implied. A privilege which the owner of one neighboring tenement, called the *dominant* tenement, has as against another person, the owner of what is called the *servient* tenement, whereby the latter is obliged to suffer or not to do something on his own land for the advantage of the owner of the other. The principal easements are rights of (1) *light*, (2) *air*, (3) *way*, (4) *water*, and (5) *support*. See those titles. (1), (2), and (5) are instances of *negative* easements; *i.e.*, where the *servient tenant* is restrained from exercising an ordinary right of property to the prejudice of the *dominant owner*. (3) and (4) are *affirmative* easements. A continuous easement is one which continues to be enjoyed without any act on the part of the person entitled to it, *e.g.*, the access of light; whereas a right of way is *discontinuous*. An apparent easement is one which is evident from inspection of the tenement; *e.g.*, a right of way.

**Eat inde sine die,** *l.*, words used on the acquittal of a defendant, *that he may go thence without a day, i.e.*, be dismissed.

**Ecclesiastical,** connected with, or set apart for, the church, as distinguished from *lay* or *civil. Eccles. corporations* are *sole, e.g.*, a bishop, or *aggregate, e.g.*, a chapter. *Eccles. Courts* are the Archdeacons', the Consistory, the Arches, the Prerogative or Archbishops', the Faculty, the Court of Peculiars, and the Privy Council. See those titles.

**Ecumenical,** general, universal; *e.g.*, an ecumenical council.

**Edict,** (lat. *Edictum*), a law ordained by a sovereign. **Edicts of Justinian,** thirteen constitutions or laws of this emperor, found in most editions of the *Corpus Juris Civilis*, after the novels. They are comparatively of little importance. **Edictum perpetuum,** a compilation of all the edicts, in fifty books, made by Salvius Julianus under the Emperor Adrian, parts of which are cited in the *Digest.* **Edictum Theodorici,** the first collection of law made after the downfall of the Roman power in Italy It was promulgated by Theodoric, king of the Ostrogoths, at Rome, A. D. 500.

**Effects,** property of all sorts, except real.

**Eigne.** See *Bastard.*

**Eire,** or **Eyre,** a journey. **Justices in Eyre,** the old name for *judges of assize and nisi prius* (*q.v.*), when they went on the *circuit* (*q.v.*).

**Ejectione custodiae,** *l.*, a writ that lay against him who ejected a guardian during the minority of the heir.

**Ejectione firmae,** a writ which lay to eject a tenant.

**Ejectment,** was the only *mixed* action at common law, and depended on fictions invented in order to escape from the inconveniences which were found to attend the ancient forms of real actions. It was a "mixed" action, as seeking to recover both possession of land (a *real* claim), and also damages (a *personal* claim). In this action the plaintiff was called John Doe; the defendant, or *casual ejector* (*i.e.*, some person, other than the prior tenant, who usually acted by arrangement), Richard Roe. Doe declared that he was in possession under a demise from a third person, who claimed to be entitled to the land (who was the real plaintiff). This action was abolished in England by the Common Law Procedure Act, 1852, and statutory proceedings for the recovery of land have taken its place in most of the states.

**Ejuration,** renouncing or resigning one's place.

**Ejusdem generis,** *l.*, of the same kind or nature.

**Election,** the act of choosing between two alternative or inconsistent rights, in cases where there is a clear intention on the part of the donor of one that the donee should not take both; the condition is therefore implied that the donee shall carry out the donor's intention if he chooses to accept his gift. (2) Choice of a representative, officer, etc.

**Elector,** in general, one who has the right to vote. **Presidential electors,** persons elected by the people of the several states, whose duty it is to meet in their respective states and vote by ballot for President and Vice-President of the United States, one of whom, at least, shall not be a resident of the same state with themselves. Distinct lists of the persons thus voted for for President and Vice-President, duly certified, are then forwarded to the president of the Senate, to be by him opened and counted in the presence of both houses of Congress.

**Eleemosyna,** alms, possessions belonging to the church.

**Eleemosynary corporations,** corporate bodies, constituted for the perpetual distribution of the free alms or bounty of the founder of them. Such are hospitals, colleges in the universities, etc. They are, however, *lay* corporations.

**Elegit** (*he has chosen*, so called because the creditor could choose between this writ and a writ of *fieri facias*), a judicial writ of execution founded on the statute of Westminster II. (13 Edw. I. c. 18) issuing out of the court where the record or other proceeding is upon which it is grounded, and addressed to the sheriff, who, by virtue of it, gives to the judgment-creditor possession of the lands and tenements of the judgment-debtor, to be held by him until the money due on such judgment is fully paid. During the time the creditor holds them, he is called tenant by *elegit*.

**Elisors,** two persons appointed to choose a jury when the sheriff and coroner have been challenged for interest or partiality. Their return is final.

**Eloign,** to remove; to take to a distance.

**Elongata,** a return made by a sheriff in replevin, that cattle, etc., are not to be found, or are removed to a place unknown to him. **Elongatus,** a return to a writ *de homine replegiando*, that the man was out of the sheriff's jurisdiction, whereupon a process was issued, called a *capias in withernam*, to imprison the defendant himself without bail until he produces the missing party.

**Emancipatio,** (Rom.), a solemn act by which a *pater-*

*familias* divested himself of his power over his *filius-familias*, so that the *filius-familias* might become *sui juris*.

**Embargo,** a detention of vessels in port by order of the government prohibiting their departure, usually issued in time of war or threatened hostilities.

**Embezzlement,** the appropriation to his own use, by an agent or employe, of money or chattels received by him for and on account of his employer. It differs from larceny in this, that property embezzled is not at the time in the actual or legal possession of the owner. It was not an offense punishable at common law, but is made so by the statutes of the United States, and the several states.

**Emblements,** growing crops. The *right to emblements* is the right which an outgoing tenant (or the representatives of a deceased one) has, in certain cases, to enter on the land (see *Ingress*) and cut and take away the crop when mature, after the expiration of his tenancy. It does not apply to crops which do not represent labor expended by the tenant; *e.g.*, orchard fruit.

**Embracery,** an attempt to influence a jury corruptly in favor of one party in a trial. The person making the attempt is called an *embraceor*.

**Emergent year,** the epoch or date whence any people begin to compute their time.

**Eminent domain,** the right which a government retains over the estates of individuals to resume them for public use.

**Empanel.** See *Impanel; Panel.*

**Emparl.** See *Imparl.*

**Emphyteusis,** (Rom.), the right of enjoying all the fruits, and disposing at pleasure of the property of another, subject to the payment of a yearly rent (*pensio* or *canon*), analogous to the modern "ground rent," to the owner. The payer of the rent was called *emphyteuta*.

**Empiric,** a practitioner who proceeds on experience only, without scientific knowledge; one not properly qualified; a quack.

**Emption,** the act of buying; *emptor*, a purchaser.

**En,** *fr.*, in. **En autre droit,** in the right of another. **En demeure,** in default. **En owel main,** in equal hand. **En ventre sa mere,** in its mother's womb.

**Enabling statute,** one which removes a restriction or disability. By *the enabling statute*, is commonly understood the act of 32 Henry VIII. c. 28, giving tenants in tail and others power to make leases for life, or for twenty-one years, which they could not do before.

**Enact,** to establish by law; to decree.

**Enciente,** pregnant; with child.

**Enclosure.** See *Inclosure.*

**Encroachment,** an unlawful extension of a right to the prejudice of another's property; *e.g.*, by taking in adjoining land.

**Encumbrance.** See *Incumbrance.*

**Endorsement.** See *Indorsement.*

**Enfeoffment,** the act of investing with any estate or possession. See *Feoffment.*

**Enfranchise,** to make free, or incorporate a person into a privileged society. (2) To invest with the elective franchise. (3) To turn copyhold into freehold land, which is done by the lord (*a*) conveying the fee to the copyholder; (*b*) releasing him from his *services* (*q.v.*).

**Engross,** to copy in a clerkly hand; to prepare a deed for execution. (2) To *regrate,* or buy large quantities of a commodity, with the object of selling it again in the same place at a higher price; also called *forestalling the market.* This was a criminal offense, until 7 & 8 Vict. c. 24.

**Enitia pars,** the part of the eldest. See *Esnecy.*

**Enjoin,** to command; to require. See *Injunction.*

**Enlarge,** to extend; *e.g.*, to enlarge a rule is to extend the time within which it is returnable.

**Enlarger l'estate,** or **Enlargement,** a species of release which consists of a conveyance of the ulterior interest of a remainderman or reversioner to the particular tenant.

**Enormia,** *l.* See *Alia enormia.*

**Enquiry.** See *Inquiry.*

**Enroll,** to record; to register; to enter on the rolls of chancery, or other court, any lawful act, as a recognizance, a deed of bargain and sale, and the like.

**Entail,** land, or money directed to be invested in realty, which is settled on a man and the heirs of his body. See *Tail.*

**Enter,** to enroll; to inscribe upon the records. (2) See *Entry.*

**Entire contract,** a contract wherein every thing to be done on the one side must be performed before the consideration is due from the other. This is opposed to an apportionable or *severable* contract. See *Apportionment.*

**Entirety,** the whole, as distinguished from *moiety*, the half. Where an estate is conveyed or devised to a man and his wife, *during coverture,* they are said to be tenants by entireties, *per* *tout et non per my;* that is, each is seized of the *whole estate,* and neither can aliene alone; so that in default of joint alienation, the estate goes to the survivor.

**Entry,** enrollment, inscription. See *Enter.* (2) A memorandum in an account book of the particulars of a sale or other transaction. (3) A listing of imported goods for the payment of duties at the custom house. (4) The written order of a court in proceedings pending before it. (5) The going on land for the purpose of asserting or acquiring a right therein. This is called *actual* entry, which is necessary in certain cases; *e.g.*, to constitute a seisin in deed, and to perfect a common-law lease for years. Entry *in law* may be made constructively. Since the introduction of modern conveyances, which do not require livery of *seisin* (*q.v.*), entry is seldom made, except to retake possession, in which case it must be peaceable. See *Writ of Entry.*

**Enumerators,** persons appointed to take the census.

**Enure,** to take effect or be available; *e.g.*, the discharge of the principal enures to the benefit of the surety.

**Equality,** the condition of parties when one has no unfair advantage over another. Money paid on a partition or exchange to equalize the shares is said to be paid for equality or *owelty.*

**Equitable,** that which exists, or can be reached, only by virtue of, or through a court of, *equity* (*q.v*). Thus an equitable or beneficial, is opposed to a legal, estate. See *Trustee; Assets.* An *equitable mortgage,* is (*a*) where the property mortgaged is an equitable interest only *e.g.*, that of a *cestui que trust,* or owner of an equity of redemption; (*b*) where, though the mortgagor has the legal estate, he does not convey it, but effects the security by giving a written agreement to convey it, or by depositing his title deeds with the mortgagee, either with or without a written agreement or *memorandum of deposit.* In such case, the deposit is deemed evidence of an executed agreement for a legal mortgage. See *Lien; Waste.*

**Equity,** fairness. That system of jurisprudence which grew up in and was first administered by the English Courts of Chancery. See *Chancery.* As the courts of equity had in early times, a power of framing and adapting new remedies to particular cases, which the common-law courts did not possess, and in doing so allowed themselves a certain latitude of construction, and assumed in certain matters, such as trusts, a power of enforcing moral obligations which the courts of law did not admit or recognize, there grew up by degrees a characteristic distinction between the rules of equity and common law, which has only been lately abolished, in England, by the

Judicature Acts, 1873, and 1875, whereby those rules have in certain points been assimilated, and it has been enacted that in all others where there is a conflict, the rules of equity shall prevail. Equity, however, did not assume the right to control or supersede the common law, as is shown by the maxims, *Equity follows the law,* and *Where the equities are equal the law must prevail.* (2) The right or obligation attaching to a property or contract. In this sense, a person is said to have a *better equity* than another. *Collateral equities,* in the law of bills of exchange, are those (such as *set-off*) which arise without special agreement between the parties. **Equity of redemption,** the right which the mortgagee of an estate has of redeeming it, after it has been forfeited at law by the non-payment of the money it was given to secure, on paying principal, interest and costs. See *Foreclosure.* **Equity of a statute,** the spirit and intent of a statute, as opposed to the strict letter. A case may fall within the former which is apparently excluded by the latter. **Equity to a settlement,** is the claim of a wife to have some portion (usually one-half) of property coming to her husband in her right during the coverture settled on herself. This claim is enforced by a court of equity, whenever the husband has to invoke its assistance for the purpose of getting possession of the property. The laws of most of the states recognizing and protecting a married woman's *separate estate* (*q.v.*), render the equity to a settlement obsolete.

**Erasure,** or **Rasure,** rubbing out or obliteration; if a material erasure be made, it invalidates the instrument. In a deed, an erasure or interlineation is presumed to have been made *on or before* its execution; in a will, *after.*

**Errant,** wandering; a term applied to justices on circuit. See *Eyre.*

**Error,** a mistake in judgment. An incorrect ruling or charge on the trial of a cause. Contracts and settlements made under error of fact will in some cases be avoided; those made under error of law will not, as a matter of public policy. See *Courts of error; Writ of error.* **Errors excepted,** a phrase appended to an account stated, in order to excuse slight mistakes or oversights.

**Escape,** the departure of a prisoner from custody before he is released by lawful authority. It is distinguished from prison-breach, which is committed with force, and rescue, through the intervention of third parties. It is punishable, generally, as a misdemeanor; and assisting one to escape is a felony. (2) Sometimes applied to the act of the officer who negligently allows the prisoner to get away. **Escape-war-**

**rant,** in England, a process addressed to all sheriffs, etc., to retake an escaped prisoner

**Escheat,** a species of reversion of any estate of inheritance which is the subject of tenure, to the crown or the lord of the fee from whom, or from whose ancestor, the estate was originally derived, upon the determination of the estate. This may arise (*a*) *propter defectum sanguinis*, for want of an heir; or, (*b*) *propter delictum tenentis*, by the felony of the tenant. Outlawry is the only cause that now exists for escheat under the latter head. In most of the states, the right of the government to such estate is declared by statute. (2) The estate itself, which reverts to the lord of the fee.

**Escrow** (scroll or writing), a writing under seal delivered to a third person, to be delivered by him to the person whom it purports to benefit, when certain specified conditions shall have been performed or satisfied; until which time, it does not acquire the force of a deed. If, however, it be delivered to the *grantee*, the delivery is absolute, and the deed takes immediate effect.

**Escuage** (*scutum*, a shield), tenure by, was where the tenant was obliged to accompany the lord to war or to pay a certain sum instead.

**Esnecy,** the right of first choice, allowed to the eldest coparcener, after the inheritance is divided into shares.

**Esquires,** in England, are, strictly speaking, only (*a*) the younger sons of peers, and their eldest sons; (*b*) the eldest sons of knights, and their eldest sons; (*c*) by creation; (*d*) by office; and (*e*) foreign peers. In the United States, the title *esquire* is given to members of the bar and others, as a matter of courtesy.

**Essence,** that which is essential to or a necessary element of a thing. Thus, *time* is said to be of the *essence of a contract*, when it is understood that compliance with the conditions respecting it is necessary, and that a breach of such conditions invalidates the contract.

**Essoin, Essoign,** an excuse for non-appearance in court when summoned.

**Estate,** the condition and circumstance in which a person stands with regard to (1) those around him; (2) his property. Hence, estate means (3) the quantum or quality of the interest which a person has in property. Estates may be (*a*) legal or equitable; (*b*) real or personal; (*c*) vested or contingent; (*d*) in possession or in expectancy; (*e*) absolute, determinable, or conditional; (*f*) sole, joint, or in common; (*g*) of freehold or less than freehold.

**Estates of the Realm,** in England, the three branches

of the legislature—the Lords Spiritual, the Lords Temporal, and the Commons.

**Estoppel,** an admission or declaration, by which a person is concluded or prevented from bringing evidence to controvert it, or prove the contrary. It may be: (1) By matter of record, which imports such absolute and incontrovertible verity that no person against whom it is produced is permitted to deny it. (2) By deed. No person can dispute his own solemn deed, which is, therefore, conclusive against him, and those claiming under him, even as to facts recited in it. (3) By matter in *pais; e.g.*, a tenant can not dispute his landlord's title. This includes estoppel by misrepresentation or negligence.

**Estovers,** or botes (*q.v.*), a right to take wood in reasonable quantities for house purposes or repairs. This a tenant for life or years may do on his holding, and some commoners on their lord's waste.

**Estrays,** valuable animals found wandering at large, whose owner is unknown.

**Estreat,** to enforce a recognizance which has been forfeited. This is done by sending an extract (*estreat*), or copy, to the proper authority, to be enforced.

**Estrepe,** to commit waste in lands, to the damage of another.

**Et,** *l.*, and. **Et cetera,** and others; and so forth.

**Eviction,** dispossession of land. See *Ejectment.*

**Evidence,** proof, either written or unwritten, of allegations in issue between parties. It may be (*a*) direct; or indirect, which latter includes *circumstantial evidence, i.e.*, that which seeks to establish a conclusion by inference from proved facts; (*b*) substantive, *i.e.*, directed to proof of a distinct fact; or corroborative, *i.e.*, in support of previous evidence; (*c*) intrinsic, *i.e.*, internal; or extrinsic (sometimes called parol), *i.e.*, not derived from any thing to be found in the document itself; (*d*) original (see *Primary*); or derivative, *i.e.*, which passes through some channel, *e.g.*, hearsay, parol, and reported evidence, as opposed to original documents, or evidence as to matters of certain knowledge. See *Relevancy*, and *Hearsay*, for the chief rules as to evidence. See also *Ambiguity*.

**Exaction,** a wrong done by an officer, or one in pretended authority, by taking a reward or fee contrary to law.

**Examination,** the preliminary investigation of the grounds for an accusation against a person arrested for crime, made by an authorized magistrate, with a view to discharging the person so arrested, or securing his commitment and appearance before the proper court for trial. (2) Of witnesses, is an interrogation on oath. It may be *viva voce*, or by written interrogatories (*q.v.*); by a court, an officer called an *examiner*, or a commission. *Examination in chief* is made by the party calling the witness; *cross-examination*, by the opposite party, which again may be followed by a *re-examination* by the former party.

**Examined copy,** a copy of a record, public book, or register, which has been compared with the original.

**Examiner,** an officer appointed by a court of equity to take the testimony of witnesses, under oath, and reduce it to writing.

**Excambion,** (Sc.), exchange of land.

**Exceptio,** *l.*, an exception; a plea; an objection. **Exceptio non numeratae pecuniae,** (Rom.), the defense that the *money* had *never been advanced*. **Exceptio rei judicatae,** a defense that the matter has been *already decided* in another cause between the same parties.

**Exception,** the express exclusion of something from the operation of a deed or contract. (2) An objection; *e.g.*, to the sufficiency of bail. See *Bill of exceptions*.

**Excerpta,** or **Excerpts,** extracts.

**Excess,** that which goes beyond what is right, proper, or necessary; *e. g.*, undue violence in ejecting a trespasser from one's land, or a non-paying passenger from a railroad car.

**Exchange,** the transfer by one person to another of funds which he has at another place, by means of a *bill of exchange* (*q.v.*). (2) The transfer of goods and chattels for other goods and chattels of like value, commonly called *barter* (*q.v*). (3) The place where merchants and persons engaged in trade meet to transact business. (4) An obsolete mode of conveyancing, by which mutual grants of interests in land were made, the one in consideration for the other.

**Exchequer,** in England, a public office which manages the revenues, and to the credit of which at the Bank of England the receipts from customs, etc., are paid. See. *Court of Exchequer*. **Exchequer bills,** bills of credit issued by order of parliament, on which the bank advances money to the government. These constitute the chief part of the unfunded public debt.

**Excise,** the duty or tax on certain articles produced and consumed within the country, *e.g.*, spirits, or on licenses.

**Excommunication,** an ecclesiastical interdict or censure. By the *greater excommunication* a person was rendered incapable of any legal act; by the *lesser*, he was merely debarred from participation in the sacraments.

**Excommunicato deliberando,** *l.*, a writ to the sheriff for delivery of an excommunicated person out of prison, upon certificate of his conformity to the ecclesiastical jurisdiction.

**Excusable homicide,** the killing of a human being, either by misadventure or in self-defense. See *Homicide.*

**Excuss,** to seize and detain by law.

**Execute,** to accomplish, perform, complete. To *execute a deed* is to complete it by signing, sealing, and delivery. (2) The Statute of Uses, 27 Hen. VIII. c. 10, is said to *execute a use* when it converts a use or trust estate into a legal one. (3) To exercise, *e.g.*, a power of appointment. (4) To enforce, *e.g.*, a judgment. (5) To put to death a criminal according to law, in pursuance of his sentence.

**Executed,** done; completed; performed; vested. **Executed consideration,** one which is wholly past; and, to be valid, must have been done or paid upon a request, express or implied. **Executed contract,** one which has been wholly performed, as opposed to an *executory* one (*q.v*). **Executed estate,** a vested estate, whether possession and enjoyment be present or postponed. **Executed remainder.** See *Vested Remainder.* **Executed trust,** one in which the disposition (or "limitations") of the beneficial estate is complete and final. **Executed use,** one with which the legal title and possession have been united by virtue of the *Statute of Uses* (*q.v.*).

**Execution,** signing, sealing, acknowledging, and delivering, with proper formalities, and in the presence of a proper number of witnesses, or before a proper officer, of a deed, will, or other instrument. A *defective execution* is one which has not duly complied with the prescribed formalities. (2) The writ, or final process, issued to the sheriff to carry out the judgment of a court; *e.g.*, to make the money due on the judgment out of the property of the defendant. See *Execute.*

**Executive,** that branch of the government which puts the laws into execution, as distinguished from the *legislative* and *judicial* branches.

**Executor,** a person appointed by a testator in his will, or any codicil thereto, to carry out the directions and requests therein contained, with reference to his estate. His duties are, in general, the same as those of an administrator, except as to matters specifically mentioned in the will. See *Administration.* **Executor de son tort,** is one who, without lawful authority, undertakes to act as the executor of a deceased person.

**Executory,** that which is not completed; which requires something to be done, or to happen, before it is perfect or assured—opposed to *executed* (*q.v.*). **Executory considera-**

**tion,** something to be paid or done at a future time, in return for a promise presently made. **Executory contract,** one in which some future act is to be done. **Executory devise,** or **bequest,** an estate in lands, or chattels, which vests only on the happening of a future contingency. It differs from reversions, in that these, though deferred, have a present existence; and from remainders, in that these must be "supported" by an existing (or "particular") legal estate. An executory devise will, where it is possible, be construed as a contingent remainder. **Executory trust,** one in which the limitations are incomplete and in the form of general directions to be carried out in detail by a future deed or declaration of trust. **Executory use,** sometimes called a *shifting* or *springing* use, one which is to come into operation at a future date, or to pass from one person to another on the happening of a certain event, or the non-performance of a condition.

**Executrix,** a female executor.

**Exemplary,** or **vindictive, damages,** are those given for torts committed through malice or with circumstances of aggravation; and include, besides compensation for the injury inflicted, an additional fine by way of punishment.

**Exempli gratia,** for the sake of example; for instance.

**Exemplification,** a certified transcript, or copy, under the great seal, or under the seal of a particular court or public office.

**Exempts,** persons privileged, or not bound by law.

**Exequatur,** the permission given by a government to a foreign consul to enter on his appointment.

**Exercise,** to make use of; (2) to execute, *e.g.*, a power.

**Exercitor maris,** *l.*, the managing owner of a vessel, or ship's husband.

**Exercitor navis,** *l.*, (Rom.), the temporary owner or charterer of a ship. See *Actio Exercitoria.*

**Exercitual,** consisting of military accouterments, *e.g.*, a heriot.

**Exheredatio,** (Rom.), the act of disinheriting.

**Exhibit,** a document or other thing shown to a witness when giving evidence, and referred to by him in his evidence; usually a document referred to in a pleading or an affidavit, and therein identified by a letter or number.

**Exigent,** or **Exigi facias,** in England, a writ commanding the sheriff to *exact,* or call on the defendant at five successive county courts (or hustings, if in London): if he fail to appear he is outlawed (*q.v.*).

**Exigenter,** an officer who makes exigents, proclamations, etc.

**Exilium,** spoiling; exile; it is applied especially to the turning of enfranchised tenants out of their holdings.

**Exitus,** children; offspring. (2) The *issues*, *i.e.*, the rents and profits of lands. (3) The conclusion of the pleadings.

**Exlegalitus, Exlex,** an outlaw.

**Exoneration,** relieving a person or estate, or some part thereof, from liability or burden by placing it on another. Thus a testator is said to exonerate his personality from payment of his debts if he charges them on other part of his estate which is not primarily liable.

**Exoneretur,** an entry of *discharge* of the bail, made on the recognizance or bail-piece, when the condition is fulfilled.

**Exordium,** the introductory part of a speech.

**Expatriation,** the forsaking one's own country, and renouncing allegiance, with the intention of becoming a permanent resident and citizen in another country. See *Naturalization.*

**Expectant** or **in expectancy,** estates or interests which are to come into possession and be enjoyed *in futuro; e.g.*, reversions. (2) *Expectant heir*, one who has a prospect of coming into property on the death of another person.

**Expert,** one who has acquired by special study, practice, and experience, peculiar skill and knowledge in relation to some particular science, art, or trade. (2) A witness who, because of such special knowledge, is called to testify in cases depending on questions peculiar to such science, art, or trade.

**Expilation,** robbery—especially, of an heir.

**Express,** that which is stated in direct words, and not left to implication; *e.g.*, an express promise, express trust.

**Expromissio,** (Rom.), a species of novation; a creditor's acceptance of a new debtor (*expromissor*) who took the place of the old debtor, who was discharged.

**Extend,** to value property. See *Extent.*

**Extension,** of time, further time allowed by way of indulgence to pay a debt, put in a pleading, or the like.

**Extent,** or **Extendi facias,** (*that you cause to be extended* or *appraised at their full value*), the peculiar writ issued from the exchequer, to recover debts of record due to the crown; it differs from an ordinary writ of execution at the suit of a subject, because under it the lands and goods of the debtor may all be taken at once in order to compel the payment of the debt. An *extent in chief* is made by the crown to recover its own debt. An *extent in aid* is made to recover a debt due to a crown debtor from a third person. Writs in the nature of extent were formerly issued by private persons in certain cases.

**Extinguishment,** the destruction or cessation of a right, either by satisfaction, or by the acquisition of one which is greater. Thus a debt is extinguished by payment, or by the creditor's acceptance of a security higher in the estimation of law, *e.g.*, a bond instead of a simple contract; an easement, by release, or by acquiring the tenement over which the easement existed. See *Merger*.

**Extortion,** the unlawful taking, by color of office or of right, of money or anything of value which is not due.

**Extra,** *l.*, out of; beyond. **Extra viam,** out of the way. **Extra vires.** See *Ultra vires.*

**Extradition,** the surrender by one nation or state to another, of a person accused of crime committed in the latter, so that he may be tried there, pursuant to treaty stipulations, or the constitution and laws of the United States.

**Extrajudicial,** out of the regular course of legal procedure; *e.g.*, a remedy, or dictum.

**Extra-territoriality,** that quality of laws which gives them operative force, beyond the territory of the power which enacted them, upon certain persons (*e.g.*, ambassadors), or rights.

**Extrinsic.** See *Evidence.*

**Eye-witness,** one who gives evidence as to facts seen by himself.

**Eyre.** See *Eire.*

## F.

**F,** a mark formerly sranded on the cheek of fighters (who had no ears to cut off) and those convicted of falsehood.

**Fabric-lands,** those given for repair of a church, etc.

**Facias,** *l.*, that you do, or cause. **Facio ut des,** I do that you may give; a species of contract in which one agrees to do something for wages or an agreed sum of money. **Facio ut facias,** I do that you may do; a species of contract in which one agrees to do or forbear doing something in consideration of the other's doing or forbearing to do something, *e.g.*, a marriage contract.

**Fac simile** (*make it like*), an exact copy.

**Fact,** a thing done, or existing. Whether a thing was done or does exist, is a question of *fact* for the jury. What are the rights and liabilities of the parties, the facts being proven, is a matter of *law* for the court.

**Factor,** an agent employed to sell goods or merchandise consigned or delivered to him by or for his principal, for a compensation commonly called *factorage* or commission. See *Broker*. (2) (Sc.). A land agent.

**Factory,** a place where traders reside in a foreign country to carry on their trade. (2) A building in which goods are manufactured.

**Failure,** want; neglect; non success. **Failure of issue,** dying without children. **Failure of record,** the neglect or inability of a defendant, who has pleaded matter of record in bar to an action, to which plaintiff has replied *nul tiel record* (there is no such record), to produce such record on the day assigned. On such failure, plaintiff is entitled to judgment.

**Faint action,** or **pleader;** a feigned action, or false plea.

**Fair,** a large concourse of persons having goods and chattels to exhibit and sell, held at stated intervals, or on special appointment, and attracting large numbers of spectators and buyers.

**Fair-play-men,** three men elected annually by the early inhabitants of that part of Pennsylvania which lies between Lycoming and Pine Creek, and was supposed to be outside of the lands ceded by the Indians, and therefore out of the jurisdiction of the colonial authorities, to settle disputes.

**Fait enrolle,** a deed enrolled.

**Faitours,** evil-doers; vagabonds.

**Faldage.** See *Foldage*.

**Fallow,** land plowed and left unsown.

**False,** not true or just. **False imprisonment,** restraint imposed on a man's liberty without proper legal authority. **False judgment,** in England, a process that lay by way of appeal to the superior courts from inferior courts not of record, to amend errors in their proceedings. **False pretenses,** untrue statements made with a view to obtaining money, goods, etc., and to defraud the owner. **False return,** a return made by a sheriff, constable, or other ministerial officer in which statements are made contrary to fact.

**Falsify,** in taking accounts, is to prove a debit charged to be incorrect. See *Surcharge*. (2) To defeat; reverse; *e.g.*, a judgment. (3) To make incorrect; to alter fraudulently; *e.g.*, a pedigree or record.

**Farm,** originally land let on lease under a rent, generally payable annually. *To farm let*, are operative words in a lease. It has come to mean in the United States any large tract of land used for agricultural purposes or stock raising, whether leased or not.

**Farmer,** originally the lessee of a tract of land. Now, one who cultivates a farm, whether he owns it, leases it, or not.

**Fasti,** (Rom.). The epithet *fastus* is properly applied to any thing in accordance with divine law, and hence those days upon which legal business might, without impiety, be transacted, were technically denominated *fasti dies, i.e.*, lawful days, as opposed to *dies nefasti.* (2) The sacred books in which the *dies fasti* were marked.

**Fauces terrae,** projecting headlands inclosing an arm of the sea.

**Favor,** bias; partiality; prejudice. See *Challenge.*

**Fealty,** the oath of fidelity which used formerly to be taken by every free and copyhold tenant to his lord. See *Homage*

**Fee,** a recompense for official or professional services. (2) An estate of inheritance, *i.e.*, which goes to the heir of the owner, if he dies without disposing of it. It is divided into three species: (*a*) **Fee-simple,** a freehold estate of inheritance, absolute and unqualified. This is the highest and most ample estate known to the law, out of which all others are taken or "carved." An owner in fee has absolute power of disposition. This estate is created in a deed by the limitation to A. *and his heirs;* but in a will, the intention to give a fee is sufficient without these words. (*b*) **Qualified,** or *base fee* (*q.v.*). (*c*) **Fee tail,** a freehold estate of inheritance, limited to a person and particular heirs of his body, male or female. **Fee-farm,** land held of another in perpetuity by the tenant and his heirs at a yearly rent. A perpetual leasehold estate. The rent reserved on such a lease is called *fee-farm rent*

**Feigned issue,** a proceeding whereby an important point may, by consent of the parties, be determined by a jury, without the formality of bringing an action, or raising it in the pleadings, where an action is in progress By recent legislation, power has generally been given to the courts to refer issues to a jury for trial; the resort to feigned issues is now obsolete.

**Fellow-servant,** one employed in the same general service with another, so that both are subjected to common risks, and each is liable to suffer by the other's negligence.

**Felo de se** (*a felon with respect to himself*), a suicide.

**Felonious homicide,** killing a human creature without justification or excuse. See *Homicide*

**Felony,** at common law, was every offense which caused a forfeiture of lands or goods, besides being punishable by death, imprisonment, or other severe penalty. Forfeiture has, however, been abolished, like attainder and escheat; and now felony signifies any indictable offense which is greater than a misdemeanor.

**Feme-covert,** a married woman. See *Baron.*

**Feme-sole,** an unmarried woman.

**Fence,** or **Defense-months,** otherwise called *close time,* in England, the time during which wild beasts, birds, or fishes are occupied in bringing forth their young, incubating, or spawning, and the law consequently forbids them to be taken or destroyed.

**Feod; Feodal; Feodum.** See *Feud.*

**Feoffee,** one enfeoffed. See *Feoffment.*

**Feoffee to uses,** the person in whom, before the Statute of Uses, the legal seisin of the land was vested, the beneficial ownership or use being in the *cestui que use.* See *Use.*

**Feoffment,** the transfer of possession of a freehold estate by a ceremony technically called livery of seisin, which consisted of a public delivery of the land by the owner (or *feoffor*) to the *feoffee.* This was usually recorded in an instrument called a deed of feoffment. Except in the case of an infant tenant in gavelkind, who can thus transfer his estate at the age of fifteen, feoffment is now disused in England. It never came into practical use in the United States, the statutes relating to the execution and recording of deeds having supplanted it.

**Ferae,** beasts; animals. **Ferae mansuaetae,** tame or domesticated animals. **Ferae naturae,** wild animals. See *Animal.*

**Feriae,** (Rom.), holidays, public or private.

**Ferme,** a farm; rent; a lease.

**Ferry,** the right to carry persons or goods across a river for a toll. It is a franchise (*q.v.*).

**Feu,** (Sc.), vassal tenure, as distinguished from *ward holding* or military tenure, the service being commuted for a return in money, called *feu-duty,* analogous to rent. *To feu* is to lease.

**Feud,** was a grant of land made by a feudal superior or lord to a tenant or *feudatory* in return for fealty and certain services. The lord in return was bound to protect the tenant. This was called the *feudal system,* which prevailed over the greater part of Europe in the middle ages, and was perfected by William the Conqueror in England, thereby displacing the Saxon laws of property. See *Dominium.* (2) The land itself granted by a lord to a tenant on condition of fealty, military service, and the like

**Fiar,** (Sc.), the person in whom is the ownership of property, real or personal, subject to the estate of a *life-renter* (*q.v.*).

**Fiat** (*let it be done*), a decree; an order or warrant by a judge or other constituted authority.

**Fidei-commissum,** (Rom.), a trust imposed on a person by will. If it related to the inheritance, it was called *fidei-commissaria haereditas.*

**Fide-jussor,** (Rom.), a surety whose heirs were bound.

**Fidepromissor,** (Rom.), a surety who was not a Roman citizen, and could not therefore bind himself by the word *spondeo.* His heirs were not bound. See *Sponsor.*

**Fiducia,** (Rom.). If a man transferred his property to another, on condition that it should be restored to him, this contract was called *fiducia,* and the person to whom the property was so transferred was said, *fiduciam accipere,* and to be a *fiduciary.*

**Fief,** a fee; a manor; a possession held of a superior.

**Fieri facias** (*that you cause to be made*), a writ whereby one who has recovered judgment for any debt or damages may obtain execution of the personal property of the judgment debtor. **Fieri feci** (*I have caused to be made*), a return made by a sheriff when he has executed a writ of *fi. fa.,* and levied the debt or part of it.

**Filacer,** an officer who filed original writs, etc., at Westminster.

**File,** literally a thread or wire on which writs, etc., were fastened when deposited with the proper officer. A paper is said to be *filed* when delivered to the proper officer, and by him kept with other papers of a similar character in suitable boxes, pigeon-holes, or bundles.

**Filiation,** the relation of a son to his father. See *Affiliation.*

**Filum,** *l.,* a thread; a line. **Altum filum,** high water line. **Filum aquae,** a thread of water, used generally to denote the middle line of a stream. **Filum forestae,** the border of a forest. **Filum viae,** the middle line of a road.

**Final,** last; that which ends or concludes. See *Judgment; Interlocutory.*

**Finding,** the conclusion of a court or jury as to a question of fact or law at issue. (2) The discovery and possession of that which belongs to, and was lost by another. The *finder's* rights are superior to those of all others, except the owner. He should restore lost property to the true owner when he can be found, and is entitled to reasonable compensation for his services and expenses, and any reward that may be offered.

**Fine,** a money penalty, or mulct. (2) A sum paid by a feudal tenant to his lord, usually on a change of estate, *e.g.,* in copyholds, on death or alienation. Such fines may be (*a*) fixed or certain, or (*b*) arbitrary, or at the will of the lord, provided it be reasonable. (3) Before the Fines and Recoveries

Act, 3 and 4 Wm. IV. c. 74, a fine was a fictitious judicial method of transferring property, so called because a fine was paid on compromising the suit. It consisted of five parts: (*a*) the *praecipe*, (*b*) the *licentia concordandi*, or leave to compromise, (*c*) the agreement between the parties, whereby one acknowledged a supposed right in the other, (*d*) the note of the proceedings, and (*e*) the *chirograph*, which recited the whole proceedings. Fines were also used prior to the above-named act, by tenants in tail to bar the entail, and by a married woman conveying her estate jointly with her husband. See *Cognizance; Deforciant; Recovery*.

**Fine-force,** compulsion; absolute necessity; or inevitable constraint.

**Firm,** the persons composing a partnership, taken collectively. (2) The name or title under which a partnership transacts business.

**First impression,** *A case of*, is one raising a new point of law.

**First instance, Court of,** that before which an action is first brought for trial, as contrasted with a court of appeal.

**Fiscal,** belonging to the public treasury (*Fisc*), or revenue.

**Fishery,** the right of catching fish, which may be (*a*) public or common, as the right to catch fish in the sea and navigable rivers; (*b*) private, *e.g.*, the right to fish in streams not navigable, which belong to riparian owners.

**Fish-royal,** whale, porpoise, and sturgeon, so called because they belonged to the king when thrown ashore on the coast of England.

**Fisk** (Sc.), the right of the crown to the movable estate of a person pronounced rebel.

**Fixture,** an article which was a personal chattel, but which, by being physically annexed to a building or land, becomes accessory to it, and part and parcel of it. Formerly it was treated as belonging to the owner of the freehold, and passed with it to a vendee; and, though annexed by a tenant for his own convenience in the occupation of the premises, could not be removed by him. The rule has been modified by statute in England and many of the states, and is much relaxed in practice, especially as between landlord and tenant, so that trade fixtures and ornamental fixtures may generally be removed at the end of his term by the tenant, provided he does thereby no material injury to the freehold.

**Flagrante delicto,** *l.*, in the very act of committing the crime.

**Floating,** current; changing; not fixed. **Floating cap-**

**ital,** that retained to meet current expenses. **Floating indebtedness,** that which grows out of current operations, and is not funded or fixed.

**Flotsam,** or **floatsam,** goods cast overboard, or lost from a vessel, when floating upon the sea, as distinguished from *jetsam* and *ligan* (*q.v.*).

**Foenus nauticum,** *l.*, marine interest, not limited by law, because the lender runs so great a risk of losing his principal. See *Bottomry.*

**Foetus,** a babe in the womb. *Foeticide,* abortion (*q.v.*).

**Folc,** or **Folk,** the people. **Folkland,** under the Saxon system, was the public or common land of the community as opposed to *boc-land* (*q.v.*), which was the property of private individuals. A single person, however, could have a life estate in folkland. **Folk-mote,** or *gemote,* a general assembly or court to consider matters concerning the commonwealth. **Folk-right,** the common law.

**Foldage,** the lord's right to have his tenant's sheep graze on his land so as to manure it.

**Fold-course,** the lord's right to graze his sheep on his tenant's land, or *vice versa.* (2) Land subject to this right.

**Folio,** a certain number of words in a writing, *e.g.*, in England, seventy-two in conveyancing, and ninety in chancery and parliamentary proceedings; in the United States, generally one hundred. (2) The number of a page. (3) The largest size of a book.

**Force,** unlawful violence. It may be (*a*) *simple;* (*b*) *compound, i.e.*, when some other crime is committed at the same time, (*c*) *implied,* as in every trespass. "With force and arms" (*vi et armis*), words usually inserted in a declaration of trespass or indictment, though not absolutely necessary.

**Forcible entry,** or **detainer,** a *taking* possession of lands, tenements, etc., with force, threats, or actual violence (*vi et armis*), whether done by the actual owner or a stranger; the forcible *keeping* of possession of lands and tenements by one not the owner and not entitled to the possession.

**Foreclosure,** a proceeding in equity, by which a mortgagor's right to redeem the mortgaged premises at any time, on payment of the debt secured, with interest, is barred or *closed forever,* after a day certain named by the court.

**Foregift,** a premium for a lease.

**Fore-hand rent,** rent payable in advance.

**Foreign,** that which belongs to another country, or subject-matter. Every nation is foreign to all the rest, and the several states are foreign to each other, with respect to their municipal laws, though all are domestic in relation to the United States government and laws. **Foreign attachment,** a process by which the property of a debtor residing in a foreign state or country may be seized for the purpose of compelling an appearance, or subjecting it to the payment of a debt. **Foreign bill of exchange,** one drawn on a drawee residing in a different state or country from the drawer. **Foreign judgment,** one rendered by a court of another state, or country, than the one in which it is sought to enforce the judgment. The records and judicial proceedings of the courts of any of the states, when properly authenticated, are entitled to the same faith and credit in the courts of any other state as they have in the courts from whence the records are taken. **Foreign laws,** those enacted and in force in a foreign state, or country. Courts do not take judicial cognizance of such laws, and they must be proved as facts. **Foreign plea,** one objecting to the court's jurisdiction.

**Forejudger,** a judgment whereby a person is deprived of a thing or right. A solicitor was said to be *forejudged by the court* when he was expelled.

**Forensic,** belonging to or applied in courts of justice, *e.g.*, *forensic medicine*, otherwise called medical jurisprudence.

**Forest,** a wooded tract reserved for beasts and fowls of forest, chase and warren, as a hunting-ground. **Forest courts,** courts instituted for the government of the king's forests and the punishment of trespassers and poachers; now obsolete.

**Forestall,** to head off, or obstruct, *e.g.*, a traveler on the highway; a tenant coming to take possession of his premises; a dear trying to regain the forest, etc.

**Forestalling the market,** buying merchandise or provisions on their way to market in such quantities as to destroy competition, and enhance the price, with the intent to sell again at the higher price.

**Forfeiture,** the loss of some right or property as a penalty for some illegal act, or some negligence or breach of contract. In England, prior to 1870, forfeiture of lands and goods resulted from conviction for felony; now it is only caused by outlawry. Forfeiture for crimes is almost unknown in the United States. **Forfeiture of a bond,** failure to perform the condition on which the obligee was to be excused from the penalty in the bond. **Forfeiture of a lease,** putting an end to the term, for the non-payment of rent, or non-performance of other conditions at the stipulated time. Courts of equity grant relief against such forfeitures in many cases. **Forfeiture of marriage,** the liability incurred by a ward in chivalry, who refuses an equal marriage tendered by his guardian, to pay the guardian as much as he had been offered for it, or as much as a jury would assess.

**Forgavel,** a quit-rent; a small reserved rent in money.

**Forgery** (the *crimen falsi* of the Roman law), the false making or alteration of an instrument, which purports on the face of it to be good and valid for the purposes for which it was created, or the false or unauthorized signature of a document, with a design to defraud.

**Forinsecus,** *l.*, outward; foreign; without.

**Forisfactus,** *l.*, outlawed.

**Forisfamiliation,** (Rom.). A son was forisfamiliated, or *put out of the family*, if his father assigned him part of his land, and the son expressed himself satisfied with such portion. (2) By Scotch law, a child is forisfamiliated who has expressly discharged his claim to *legitim* (*q.v.*).

**Form,** the manner, *e.g.*, of a pleading, as opposed to the matter. (2) A model to aid one in drawing up an instrument, pleading, entry, or other legal document.

**Formedon,** an ancient writ provided by statute, 13 Edw. I. c. 1, for a person claiming a right to lands or tenements by virtue of a gift in tail (*per formam doni*), when out of possession; now abolished.

**Formulary,** a form; a precedent.

**Fornication,** sexual intercourse by an unmarried person with another, whether married or not.

**Forprise,** an exception, or reservation; also an exaction.

**Forschel,** a strip of land lying next to the highway.

**Forswear,** to swear to a falsehood; to reject or renounce upon oath.

**Forthcoming,** (Sc.), a proceeding in attachment to subject the goods to the payment of the debt. **Forthcoming bond,** one taken by a sheriff to secure the production of goods levied upon, when required.

**Forthwith,** immediately; as soon as the nature of the case will permit.

**Fortuitous,** accidental; happening by chance; unexpected; inevitable.

**Forum,** *l.*, an open space in Roman cities, where the people assembled on solemn occasions, where markets were held, and where the magistrates sat to transact their business. Hence, a court of justice; the place where justice must be sought. Used also in the sense of *jurisdiction*. **Forum competens,** the court having jurisdiction. **Forum contractus,** the place of making a contract. **Forum domicilii,** the court of a man's domicile. **Forum originis,** the court of that place of which, at the time of his birth, a person's father was a citizen. **Forum rei gestae,** or **sitae,** the court of the place where a thing was done; or where the thing (*e.g.*, real estate), which is the subject of the action, is situated.

**Four corners.** That which is apparent on the face of a deed, will, or contract, without aid from extrinsic testimony, is said to be within its four corners.

**Four seas,** the seas surrounding England. Within the four seas, means the jurisdiction of England.

**Franchise,** a special privilege or liberty, conferred by government, and vested in particular individuals. In the United States, franchises are generally exercised by corporations created for the purpose, and deriving their powers under general or special laws. **Elective franchise,** the privilege of voting at an election of public officers, members of Congress, etc.

**Frank;** free; the privilege of sending letters and other matters by the public mails without paying postage, formerly possessed by members of Parliament, members of Congress, etc. (2) The signature placed on the envelope or wrapper by one having the franking privilege, to indicate that it goes free. **Frank-almoign** (*free alms*), the tenure by which religious corporations hold land, so called because it was free of service, except the *trinoda necessitas* (*q.v.*). **Frank-bank.** See *Free-bench*. **Frank-fee,** lands held by a man to himself and his heirs, free of such service as was required in *ancient demesne* (*q.v.*). A fine had in the king's court might convert demesne lands into frank-fee. **Frank-marriage,** land given by way of dowry to a woman and her husband, *free of services*. **Frank-pledge,** the bond or pledge which the inhabitants of a tithing entered into, under early Norman reigns, by which they became mutually responsible for each other's good behavior, and bound themselves that any transgressor should be forthcoming to answer for his offense. **Frank-tenement,** a freehold estate.

**Fraud,** the gain of an advantage to another's detriment by deceitful or unfair means. It may be (*a*) *actual*, where there is deliberate misrepresentation, concealment, or fraudulent intent; or (*b*) *constructive*, where the court implies it, either from the nature of the contract, or from the relation of the parties, as in the case of a trustee and his *cestui que trust*. *Fraudulent* dealings with property in particular cases, *e.g.*, by a debtor to defraud his creditors, are often dealt with by statute. *Fraud on a power* is where it is so exercised as to violate the intention of the person who created it. Fraud is a ground for setting aside a transaction, at the option of the person prejudiced by it, or for recovery of damages. See *Deceit; Mistake; Suppressio veri; Suggestio falsi.*

**Frauds, Statute of,** 29 Car. II. c. 3. The main object of this statute was to take away the facilities for fraud and the temptation to perjury which arose in verbal obligations, the proof of which depended upon unwritten evidence. Its most important provisions are these: (*a*) all leases of lands, etc. (excepting those for less than three years), shall have the force of leases at will only, unless they are in writing and signed by the parties or their agents; (*b*) assignments and surrenders of leases and interests in land must be in writing; (*c*) all declarations and assignments of trusts must be in writing, signed by the party (trusts arising by implication of law are, however, excepted); (*d*) no action shall be brought upon a guarantee, or upon any contract for sale of lands, or any interest in or concerning them, or upon any agreement which is not to be performed within a year, unless the agreement is in writing and signed by the party to be charged or his agent; (*e*) no contract for the sale of goods for the price of £10 or upward shall be good, unless the buyer accept part, or give something in part payment, or some memorandum thereof be signed by the parties to be charged or their agents. The substance of this statute has been enacted in almost all states of the Union, together with other provisions of the same general character, designed to prevent frauds and perjuries.

**Frater consanguineus,** *l.*, a brother by the father's side, opposed to *frater uterinus*, a brother by the mother's side.

**Free,** not bound; unrestricted; at liberty to act as one pleases. **Free-bench,** a widow's dower out of her husband's copyholds, to which she is entitled by the custom of some manors. Unlike dower, it does not attach, even in right, until the death of the husband. See *Dower*. **Free-board,** land claimed beyond or without the fence; said to be two feet and a half. **Free entry, egress, and regress,** the right to go on and off land at will; *e.g.*, to take emblements. **Freefold.** See *Fold-course*, **Freehold,** one of the two chief tenures, known in ancient times by the phrase "tenure in free socage," as opposed to land held in villenage or copyholds. (2) An estate either in fee simple or tail, or for a man's life, whether his own or another man's. See *Autre vie.* The owner of such an estate is called a *freeholder*, which term is also used specially as opposed to *leaseholder*. **Free ships,** neutral ships. "Free ships make free goods," is a phrase often used to denote that goods on board of a free ship shall be free from confiscation, even though belonging to an enemy. **Free-**

**warren,** in England, a franchise, granted by the crown to a subject. for the preservation of beasts and fowls of warren.

**Freight,** the sum paid for the carriage of goods by sea. See *Dead freight; Charter-party; Affreightment*. It is now applied to the sum paid for the carriage of goods by land, and also to the goods themselves in process of transportation

**Fresh,** recent; not old, or stale. **Fresh disseisin,** such a disseisin as formerly a man might seek to defeat by his own action, and without the aid of the courts; said, in one case, to be one committed within fifteen days; in another to be one committed within a year. **Fresh-fine,** a fine that has been levied within a year. **Fresh force,** an act committed by force within forty days. **Fresh-suit,** the immediate pursuit and apprehension of a robber by the person robbed

**Fructus,** *l.*, fruit; increase; that which results or springs from a thing. **Fructus civiles,** all revenues which, though not strictly *fruits*, are recognized as such by law. **Fructus industriales,** products obtained by the labor and cultivation of the occupant *Emblements* (*q.v.*). **Fructus naturales,** products resulting from the powers of nature alone, as wool, milk, etc **Fructus pendentes,** fruits united with the thing which produced them.

**Fugitive from justice,** one who, having committed a crime, flees from the jurisdiction within which it was committed to escape punishment. See *Extradition*.

**Full age.** See *Age*.

**Functus officio,** *l.*, is used of one who, *having discharged his duty*, has terminated his authority or appointment; also, of an instrument, which once had life and power, but is no longer of value, the power conferred by it having been exercised

**Fund,** money or securities devoted to a certain purpose; *e.g.*, a fund for payment of debts. (2) Capital; hence, *to fund* is to capitalize. (3) The *funds* are the public funded debt of the government; originally, the taxes, customs, etc., appropriated by the government for the payment of its debts.

**Fungibiles res,** *l.*, a term applied in the civil and Scotch law to things that can be replaced by equal quantities and qualities of the like kind; *e.g.*, a bushel of wheat. See *Mutuum*.

**Fur,** *l.*, a thief. One who steals without using force, as distinguished from a robber.

**Further assurance,** a covenant entered into by a vendor, to the effect that he will execute any additional conveyance or instrument that may be required to perfect the vendee's title.

**Future estate,** one which is to commence in possession at same future time. It includes remainders, reversions, and estates limited to commence *in futuro*, without any particular estate to support, which last were not good at common law, except in the case of terms for years.

## G.

**Gabel,** a rent, duty, or service yielded or done to the king or any other lord. A tax.

**Gage,** (*l.*, *vadium*), a pawn or pledge. See *Mortgage.*

**Gager,** to find security; to wage. **Gager deliverance,** to put in sureties, or a pledge, to deliver cattle distrained. **Gager ley,** to wage law.

**Gale.** See *Gabel.*

**Game,** birds and beasts of a wild nature that may be taken or killed by fowling and hunting. **Game laws,** laws relating to the preservation of game from useless and unreasonable destruction, and restricting their capture or killing to certain seasons of the year when it will interfere least with their propagation.

**Gaming**, or **Gambling,** playing at cards, dice, billiards, or other game for money, the winner taking the money of the loser. Gaming with certain devices is prohibited by the laws of nearly every state as demoralizing to the individual and contrary to public policy.

**Ganancial,** a species of community in property enjoyed by husband and wife, the property being divisible between them equally on a dissolution of the marriage.

**Gaol,** or **Jail,** a prison; a place for confining criminals and those detained for trial. **Gaol delivery,** in England, a commission to the judges, etc., to try prisoners at the assizes (*q.v.*), and deliver them out of jail.

**Garnish,** money paid by a prisoner on going into prison. Abolished, 4 Geo. IV. c. 43.

**Garnishee,** a person in whose hands a debt is attached, *i.e.*, who is warned not to pay money which he owes to another person, when the latter is indebted to the person warning or giving notice. See *Attachment.*

**Garth,** a close; a dam or weir.

**Gavel; Gavelgeld.** See *Gabel.*

**Gavelkind,** (*land that yields rent, i. e.*, not held by knight service), descends to all the sons equally, and in default of sons to the daughters in the ordinary manner. It was retained in Kent only, when the Normans introduced the law of primogeniture into the rest of the kingdom. The widow or widower of a deceased tenant takes *half*, and only till marrying again,

An infant tenant may alien by feoffment (*q.v.*) at fifteen. All land in Kent is presumed to be of this tenure unless the contrary is proved.

**Gemot,** a moot; meeting; public assembly. See *Folk.*

**General,** common to many or all; extensive; not restricted; not special. **General average.** See *Average.* **General demurrer.** See *Demur.* **General issue,** a plea simply traversing *modo et forma,* the allegations in the declaration without offering any special matter to evade it; *e g.,* the pleas of "not guilty" in torts and criminal proceedings, *nil debet,* in an action of debt, or *non assumpsit,* to an action on a simple contract. **General lien,** a right to detain a chattel, etc., until payment be made, not only of any debt due in respect of the particular chattel, but of any balance that may be due on general account in the same line of business. **General ship,** one which is not chartered to a particular person, but which undertakes to carry for freight the goods of any one wishing to send them to any of the ports it is bound for. The contract with each freighter is usually made by bill of lading. **General verdict,** the decision of the jury, when they find in general terms for the plaintiff or defendant.

**German,** whole as respects blood or descent. Thus, brothers-german, are those who had the same father and mother; cousins-german are those in the first and nearest degree, *i.e.,* children of brothers or sisters.

**Gestation,** the carrying of a child in the womb for the period which elapses between its conception and birth; usually nine months of thirty days, or thereabouts. This period is added, where gestation exists, to that which is allowed by the rule against perpetuities.

**Gestio pro haerede,** *l.,* (*behavior as heir,* Sc.), conduct by which the heir renders himself liable for his ancestor's debts, as by taking possession of title-deeds, receiving rents, etc.

**Gewrite,** writings, deeds, or charters.

**Gift,** a voluntary transfer of property, made without a binding consideration. (2) The right or power to give; hence to *lie in gift.* (3) A grant of land in tail. To *give* was the proper word of grant in feoffments. See *Donatio.*

**Gild,** or **Guild,** a society. (2) A contribution or tax.

**Gist,** the main point in question; the pith of a matter. **Gist of action,** the cause for which an action lies; the essential ground and foundation of a suit.

**Glebae ascriptitii,** *l.,* (*assigned to the land*), villein-socmen who could not be removed from the land while they did the service due.

**Glebe,** the land possessed as a part of the revenue of an ecclesiastical benefice.

**God-penny,** earnest money given to a servant on hiring.

**God's acre,** a church-yard.

**Good,** not bad; adequate; sufficient; valid. **Good behavior,** conduct in conformity with law. When a person is suspected, on reasonable grounds, of an intent to commit a crime or misdemeanor, he may be required to give security for his good behavior for a stated time. **Good consideration,** as distinguished from *valuable* consideration, is one founded on motives of generosity, prudence, and natural duty, such as "natural love and affection." **Good will,** the advantage or benefit which is acquired by a business, beyond the mere value of the capital or stock employed therein, in consequence of its having a body of regular customers and a general reputation.

**Goods and chattels,** the general denomination of things personal, as distinguished from things real, lands, tenements, and hereditaments. See *Chattel.*

**Grace, Days of,** time of indulgence, usually three days, granted to an acceptor or maker for the payment of his bill of exchange or note. It was originally a gratuitous favor (hence the name), but custom has rendered it a legal right.

**Graffer,** a notary, or scrivener.

**Grand assize,** a peculiar kind of trial by jury introduced in the time of Henry II., giving the alternative of trial by battle.

**Grand cape.** See *Cape.*

**Grand jury,** a body of men not less than twelve nor more than twenty-four freeholders of a county, returned by the sheriff to every session of the peace, oyer and terminer, and general jail delivery, whose duty it is, on hearing the evidence for the prosecution only in each bill of indictment, to decide whether a sufficient case is made out on which to hold the accused for trial by the common jury. See *Ignoramus; True bill.*

**Grand larceny,** in English law, consisted, prior to 1827, when the distinction between *grand* and *petit* larceny was abolished by statute, of the stealing of goods or money of the value of twelve dollars and upward. The distinction between *grand* and *petit* larceny, depending on the value of the goods stolen, is still maintained in many of the United States, and defined by statute.

**Grand serjeanty,** a tenure by personal services of an honorable nature.

**Grant,** a generic term applicable to all transfers of real property, and proper to be used in all conveyances of freeholds. The *grantor* is he who transfers to the *grantee.* See

*Uses.* (2) A license, right, or authority conferred; *e.g.*, grant of a patent, of probate, of administration. See those titles.

**Gratuitous,** made without consideration.

**Great charter.** See *Magna Charta.*

**Great seal,** the emblem of sovereignty introduced by Edward the Confessor; used for all public acts of state.

**Great tithes.** See *Tithe.*

**Gree,** satisfaction for an offense committed or injury done.

**Gross,** great; excessive; entire. A thing or right is said to exist *in gross* when it is not appendant or appurtenant. See those titles, *Collateral.* **Gross average,** that which falls on ship, cargo, and freight, as distinguished from particular average. **Gross negligence,** such want of care as not even inattentive and thoughtless men are guilty of with respect to their own property.

**Ground-annual,** (Sc.), ground-rent; feu-duty.

**Ground-rent,** that which is paid by a person for land which he has taken on lease and covenanted to build on.

**Growing crops.** See *Away-going; Emblements.*

**Guarantee,** he to whom a guaranty is made by a *guarantor.*

**Guaranty,** or **Guarantee,** a promise to a person to be answerable for the payment of a debt, or the performance of a duty by another, in case he should fail to perform his engagement. It may be for a single act, or be a *continuing* guaranty, covering all transactions of like kind and to a like amount, until revoked by the guarantor.

**Guardian,** one who has the control or management of the person, or property or both, of another, who is incapable of acting on his own behalf; *e.g.*, an infant, or a lunatic. (2) Guardians *ad litem* are appointed by the court to represent infants or lunatics in an action.

**Guest,** a person who is received and entertained at a house or inn. An innkeeper who furnishes lodgings and refreshment for a consideration is liable for all goods belonging to a guest brought within the inn, but not for goods left by a person not stopping at the inn, and not giving any consideration for the care of such goods.

**Guilty,** criminal. The state of one who has committed a crime, misdemeanor, or offense.

## H.

**Habeas corpus,** *l.*, (*that you have the body*), words used in various writs, commanding one who detains another to "have," or bring, him before the court issuing the same.

**Habeas corpus ad faciendum et recipiendum,** or **cum causa,** issues when a person is sued in some inferior jurisdiction, and is desirous to remove the action into the superior court. It commands the inferior judge to *produce the body* of the defendant, together with the day and cause of his caption and detainer, *to do and receive* whatever the superior court shall think fit. **Habeas corpus ad prosequendum,** issued to remove a prisoner, in order that he might be tried in the proper jurisdiction. **Habeas corpus ad respondendum,** issued in civil causes, to remove a person out of the custody of one court into that of another, so that he may be sued and answer in the latter. **Habeas corpus ad satisfaciendum,** issued to remove a prisoner from one court to another, in order to charge him in execution upon a judgment of the last court. **Habeas corpus ad subjiciendum.** This, the most celebrated prerogative writ in the English law, is the usual remedy for a person deprived of his liberty. It is addressed to him who detains another in custody, and commands him to *produce the body* of the person in custody, with the day and cause of his caption and detention, and to do, submit to, and receive whatever the judge or court shall think fit. **Habeas corpus ad testificandum,** issued to bring a witness into court, when he was in custody at the time of a trial. **Habeas corpus act,** the name given to the statute, 31 Car. II. c. 2, which established the right to this writ in all cases of illegal detention. The right appears to have existed and been exercised before, but its efficiency had been much impaired, and this act gave it renewed force.

**Habendum,** *l.*, the clause following the granting part of a deed, and beginning with the words "to have and to hold," which defines the extent of the interest conveyed.

**Habere facias,** *l.*, (*that you cause to have*), words used in various writs of execution, or in aid of execution. **Habere facias possessionem,** issued for a successful plaintiff in ejectment, to put him in possession of the premises recovered. See *Writ.* **Habere facias seisinam,** an older writ, to the same effect as the last. **Habere facias visum,** a writ that lay in divers real actions, where a view was required to be taken of the lands in controversy.

**Habitatio,** *l.*, (Rom.), the right of using a house as a dwelling-house only. It differed from a *jus utendi*, as it could not be extinguished by non-user.

**Haerede abducto, rapto, deliberando,** *l.*, writs which formerly lay for the lord, or other person having by right the wardship of a tenant under age, to recover the person of the ward.

**Haeredes proximi,** *l.*, (Rom.), heirs begotten by the person from whom they inherit; children.

**Haeredes remotiores,** *l.*, (Rom.), heirs not begotten by him from whom they inherit, as grandchildren, etc., descending in a direct line *in infinitum.*

**Haereditas jacens,** *l.*, an estate in abeyance; *i.e.*, after the ancestor's death, and before the heir assumes possession.

**Haeres,** *l.*, an heir. **Haeres factus** (Rom.), an heir appointed by will. **Haeres natus** (Rom.), an heir by descent.

**Haeretico comburendo,** *l.*, a writ (abolished, 29 Car. II.) against a heretic who, after abjuring his heresy, relapsed into it again; for which the punishment was burning at the stake.

**Half-blood,** one born of the same mother or father as another, but not having both parents in common.

**Hallmote,** or **Hallimote,** a court among the Saxons, answering to our court-baron. (2) An old name for the court held by each of the city companies in London.

**Ham, Hame,** a house; hence, *hamesoken, hamfare*, breach of peace in a house.

**Hanaper-office,** an office belonging to the common-law jurisdiction of the Court of Chancery, so called because all writs relating to the business of a subject, and their returns, were formerly kept there in a hamper, *in hanaperio.* The business of this office, which included the taking of an account of all patents, grants, etc., which passed the great seal, was transferred, in 1652, to the clerk of the crown. See *Crown Office in Chancery.*

**Hand-borrow,** a surety, a pledge *by taking the hand.* **Hand-habend,** a thief caught in the very act, having the thing stolen in his hand. **Hand-sale,** a sale confirmed by shaking hands, by which act the parties became bound. The custom was formerly common among all northern nations.

**Handsel,** earnest-money.

**Hand-writing,** any thing written by a person. Proof of, may be made by one who saw him write, one who has seen him write other documents, or is familiar with his hand-writing by correspondence, or by an expert, judging from comparison with documents admitted to be in his hand-writing.

**Harriot.** See *Heriot.*

**Hat-money,** primage; a small duty paid to the master and seamen of a ship.

**Hearing,** the trial of a suit. (2) The examination of a person charged with a crime or misdemeanor and of the witnesses for the accused.

**Hearsay evidence,** statements made by a witness on the authority of another, and not from personal knowledge or observation. As a general rule, such evidence is inadmissible; but exceptions are made (*inter alia*) in questions of pedigree, custom, general reputation, dying declarations, and those made against the interest of the declarant.

**Heir,** a person who succeeds by descent to an estate of inheritance in land, or would have succeeded, if his ancestor had died intestate. There can be no heir to a person who is living; but one whose right of inheritance is indefeasible, provided he outlive the ancestor, is styled an *heir apparent;* and one who would be the heir if the ancestor should die immediately, but whose right of inheritance may be defeated by the birth of some one nearer to him, is styled an *heir presumptive.* Heirs may be further classified as *heirs general, i.e.*, heirs at common law; *customary* heirs, *i.e.*, those who inherit by virtue of some custom peculiar to the place where they live (see *Gavelkind, Borough English*); *heirs, special, i.e.*, those who inherit by virtue of limitations in the deed to the ancestor, as in the case of tail male (*q.v.*); heirs by will (*haeres factus*), more commonly known as devisees; and *ultimate heirs* (*ultimus haeres*), either the lord of the manor or the crown, to whom the land comes by escheat, or forfeiture, for want of proper heirs, or on account of treason or felony. See *Forfeiture.*

**Heirdom,** succession by inheritance.

**Heirloom,** personal chattels which go by special custom to the heir or devisee, together with the inheritance, instead of going to the executor. Such are pictures, plate, and jewels.

**Heirship moveables** (Sc.), those things which the law withholds from the executors and next of kin, and gives to the heir, that he may not succeed to a house and lands completely dismantled. They consist of the best of certain things; *e.g.*, furniture and farming stock; but do not include fungibles. See *Fungibiles.*

**Heralds' college,** an ancient royal corporation, established in 1483, which is empowered to make grants of arms and to permit change of names. See *Kings-at-arms.*

**Herbage,** the right to pasture cattle in another's ground.

**Hereditaments,** every kind of property that can be inhertied. They are (*a*) *corporeal,* which "lie in livery," *e.g.*, lands and houses; (*b*) *incorporeal,* which lie only "in grant," *e.g.*, reversions, advowsons, and tithes. They are also (*a*) *real, i.e.*, lands; (*b*) *personal, i.e.*, which are not connected with lands; *e.g.*, an annuity to a man and his heirs; or (*c*) *mixed.*

**Heriot** (Sc., *Herezeld*), originally a tribute to the lord, consisting of the horse or habiliments of a deceased tenant. This was, in later times, commuted for a money payment, or the tenant's best beast (*averium*). **Heriot service,** is due by virtue of an express reservation in the grant or lease of lands, and therefore amounts to little more than rent. **Heriot Custom,** a tribute to the lord due by virtue of immemorial usage of a manor, generally upon the death of the tenant, but sometimes on alienation. **Heriot suit,** the right to some chattels (not a beast only) of a deceased tenant, reserved on a modern grant or lease of freehold.

**Heritable** (Sc.), that which goes to the heir, as distinct from *movables,* which go to the executor; generally all rights connected with land.

**Heritor,** an owner in fee of corporeal heritable property.

**Hermaphrodite,** one who partakes of the physical peculiarities of both sexes. The legal status of such an one is usually decided by the circumstance of which sex predominates.

**Hide of land,** or *plow land,* that amount which can be plowed in a year by one plow, varying, according to locality, from sixty to one hundred and twenty acres; that which can maintain a family. *Hidage,* a tax formerly paid on every hide.

**High Court of Admiralty,** in England, was a court of maritime jurisdiction, also called the Court of the Lord High Admiral. Its jurisdiction was by the Judicature Act, 1873, conferred on the Probate, Divorce, and Admiralty Division of the High Court of Justice (*q.v.*). See *Admiralty.* **High Court of Justice,** in England, a court established by the Judicature Act, 1873, as a substitute for the superior courts of law and equity—Exchequer, King's Bench, Common Pleas, etc.—which were then abolished. It has three divisions, *Chancery, Queen's Bench* (into which Exchequer and Common Pleas have been merged), and *Probate, Divorce and Admiralty.*

**High seas,** in English law, that part of the sea which is more than three miles distant from the coast of a country; within the three miles the territorial jurisdiction extends, but no further. By this term, in the United States, is understood all of the uninclosed waters of the ocean beyond low-water mark.

**High Steward, Court of the Lord,** in England, a tribunal instituted for the trial of peers indicted for treason or felony, or for misprision of either. The lord high steward is always a peer; he is appointed by commission under the great seal, and *pro hac vice* only.

**High treason.** See *Treason.*

**High-water-mark,** that part of the sea-shore to which the water ordinarily reaches when the tide is highest.

**Highways,** public ways, either on land or water, which every citizen has a right to use.

**Hilary,** in English law, a term of court formerly held, beginning on the 11th and ending on the 31st of January each year.

**Hiring** (Rom., *locatio-conductio*), a bailment for reward. It may be (*a*) of a thing for use (*rei*); (*b*) of work and labor (*operis faciendi*); (2) of services for taking care of a thing (*custodiae*); (3) of carriage of goods (*operis mercium vehendarum*). See *Bailment.*

**Hold,** to possess; as a tenant or grantee. (2) To bind under a contract; as an obligor is *held* and firmly bound. (3) To decide, adjudge, or decree; as a judge in disposing of a case.

**Holder,** a payee or indorsee in possession of a bill of exchange, check, or promissory note. *Holder for value* is one who has given valuable consideration.

**Holding,** a term used to signify the tenure or nature of the right given by a superior to the grantee or tenant. (2) A farm. **Holding over** keeping possession of premises by a lessee after the expiration of his term.

**Holiday,** or **Holy day,** formerly a day set apart for religious festivals; now a day of exemption from common labor. Legal holidays, generally established in the United States, are Sundays, Christmas, New Year's, Washington's birthday, the Fourth of July and a day of National Thanksgiving, appointed by the President and the governors of the several states.

**Holograph,** a deed, will, or instrument written entirely by the grantor himself, which, on account of the difficulty with which the forgery of such a document can be accomplished, is in some countries and states held as valid without witnesses.

**Homage,** the free tenants of a manor assembled in Court Baron (*q.v.*). (2) *Fealty,* the undertaking of a tenant in fee to his feudal lord to become his man "of life and limb." The tenant thereby promised to assist the lord when required, and the lord to protect the tenant. *Liege homage,* was that to the sovereign, or lord paramount; *simple homage,* that to the mesne lord. See *Lord. Homage ancestral,* was where the tenant and his ancestors had always held of the same lord or his ancestors. Homage was abolished by 12 Car. II. c. 24.

**Homager,** one who is bound to do homage.

**Homicide,** destroying the life of a human-being. It may be (*a*) *excusable,* as when committed by accident, and without any intent to injure; (*b*) *justifiable,* if committed with full intent, but under such circumstances as to render it proper and necessary, as where the proper officer executes a criminal in strict conformity with his sentence, or kills a man when forcibly resisting an arrest, or the discharge of a particular duty by the officer, or where one kills another in defense of himself or his family, or to prevent him from committing an atrocious crime attempted with violence, such as rape, highway robbery, burglary, and the like; (c) *felonious*, when committed willfully and without sufficient justification. The latter includes (1) self-murder; (2) manslaughter, where one kills another in a sudden quarrel, and without premeditation, or by accident while engaged in doing some unlawful act not amounting to felony; (3) murder, *i.e.*, willful and premeditated killing, "with malice aforethought," as it is often expressed. This last offense is frequently divided by statute into first, second, and even third degrees, according to the atrociousness of the motives with which, or the circumstances under which, the crime is committed.

**Homologation** (Sc.), the express or implied ratification of a deed that is null or voidable, or in some way defective. (2) In Roman law, approbation or confirmation by a court of justice of some finding, or award, and ordering execution to carry out the same.

**Honor,** a seigniory of several manors or lordships under a lord paramount. (2) The land or district included therein. (3) To accept a bill of exchange, or to pay an accepted bill, check, or promissory note at maturity.

**Honorarium,** a recompense; a voluntary fee to one exercising a liberal profession, *e.g.*, a barrister or physician.

**Honorary feuds,** titles of nobility descendible to the eldest son, in exclusion of all the rest.

**Honorary services.** Those without emolument. (2) Those by which lands in grand-serjeantry were held such as to hold the king's banner, or to perform like offices of distinction.

**Horngeld,** or **Hornagium,** payment for pasturing horned cattle.

**Horning, letters of,** (Sc.), a warrant for charging persons to pay or perform certain debts or duties; so called because they were originally proclaimed by horn or trumpet.

**Hostels,** the Inns of Court (*q.v.*).

**Hotchpot, Hotchpotch,** or **Hodge podge** (*collatio bonorum*), the blending of property belonging to different persons, in order to divide it equally among them. The taking into account *advances* (*q.v.*) made to children, in distributing the personal estate of a deceased person, so as to equalize the shares received by each.

**House,** a dwelling; an institution; a family; a mercantile firm; a collection of persons. **House of correction,** a place for the imprisonment of those convicted of petty crimes. **House of ill-fame,** a house resorted to for purposes of lewdness and prostitution. **Houses of Parliament,** are (*a*) the House of Lords, consisting, in 1883, of 26 spiritual and 491 temporal peers, the former including the 2 English archbishops and 24 English bishops; (*b*) the House of Commons, 656 in number, of whom 493 are English, 60 Scotch, and 103 Irish. **House of Representatives,** the more numerous branch of the federal congress, and of the several state legislatures. **House-bote,** the right of a tenant to take timber from his landlord's woods for necessary fuel and repairs. **Household,** those who dwell in the same house and constitute a family. **Household furniture; goods; stuff,** words frequently used in wills to pass all such personal property as was acquired by the testator for the furnishing and ornamentation of his house, and the use and convenience of his family in occupying it.

**Hue and cry,** "the old common law process of pursuing, with horn and voice, felons and such as have dangerously wounded another."

**Hundred,** a subdivision of a county, originally composed of a hundred freeholders' families. **Hundred court,** a larger court-baron (*q.v.*), being held for all the inhabitants of a particular hundred, instead of a manor.

**Hundredors,** men of a hundred; persons serving on juries, or fit to be impaneled thereon for trials, dwelling within the hundred where the cause of action arose.

**Hurdle,** a sledge used to draw traitors to execution.

**Husband,** a man who has a wife. Husband and wife were by the common law considered one person. He was bound to support the wife, and furnish her with necessaries and conveniences suited to her station and his means, and was liable for her debts incurred before coverture, and for torts committed by her. He could fix his domicile where he pleased, and change it at will. Could buy and sell all kinds of property without her control, subject only to her right of dower in real estate which he might purchase during coverture. All her personal property, choses in action, and chattels real belonged to him so far as he reduced the same to possession during her life. He had a life estate in all her real property, and if a child was born to them, an estate by *courtesy* (*q.v.*) in the same, after her death. Neither could convey real estate to the other direct, though it could be effected through the medium of a use or trust, or by will. A wife committing a felony in the presence of her husband was, in general, excused, as she was presumed to act under compulsion; but this presumption might be rebutted. Neither was competent as a witness for or against the other, except in the case of personal injuries. All these common-law rights, liabilities, relations, and restrictions have been greatly modified by legislation in England and the various states of the Union.

**Hush-money,** a bribe to hinder information being given.

**Hustings,** a local or county court, *e.g.*, in London, York, etc. The London Court of Hustings was an ancient court of the king. Its judicial functions no longer exist, having passed to the mayor's court and sheriffs' court; but it continues to elect the mayor and sheriffs. (2) A platform from which parliamentary candidates address the electors.

**Hypothecation,** in a strict sense, a species of pledge in which the pledger retained possession of the thing pledged, as distinguished from *pignus*, where the possession was transferred to the pledgee. The term is, however, generally applied to the deposit of stocks, bonds, and negotiable securities with another to secure the repayment of a loan, and with power to sell the same in case the debt is not paid, and to reimburse himself out of the proceeds. See *Bottomry; Respondentia.*

## I.

**Ibidem,** *l.*, the same; *e.g.*, the same volume, case or place.

**Idem,** *l.*, the same. **Idem per Idem,** the same by the same; an argument or illustration that adds nothing to the force of the proposition. **Idem sonans,** sounding the same; used of names misspelled which yet would not mislead, because the variance is trifling, or because they would be pronounced the same as if spelled aright.

**Identification,** is the proof of the identity of a person or thing; *i.e.*, that he or it is *the* person or thing alleged. See *Personation.*

**Ides,** *l.*, days in the months from which other days are reckoned; in the Roman calendar, the ides of March, May, July and October, were on the 15th of the month: of the remaining months on the 13th. This method of reckoning is still retained in the chancery of Rome, and in the calendar of the breviary.

**Idiocy,** mental deficiency; a species of insanity, differing from it chiefly in being congenital, *i.e.*, commencing at birth. See *Lunatic.*

**Ignoramus** (*we are ignorant*), the word formerly written on a bill of indictment by a grand jury when they rejected it, on the ground that a sufficient *prima facie* case was not made out: the indorsement now used is "not a true bill," or "not found," and the jury are said to "ignore" the bill.

**Ignore,** to throw out a bill of indictment. See *Ignoramus.*

**Illegal,** forbidden by law. (2) Unlawful. **Illegal conditions,** those that are contrary to law, immoral, or repugnant to the nature of the transaction.

**Illegitimate,** not regular, or authorized by law; usually applied to children born out of lawful wedlock.

**Illicit,** unlawful.

**Illusory,** deceptive; having a false appearance. **Illusory appointment,** one which in form carries out the wishes of the donor, but does not in spirit or reality; *e.g.*, where the donee of a power of appointment who could not appoint exclusively to one or more of a class does so practically by appointing a merely nominal sum to those he wishes to include.

**Immaterial,** unimportant; without weight or significance. **Immaterial averment;** or **evidence,** that which has no legal bearing on the point at issue. **Immaterial issue,** one taken upon some collateral matter the decision of which will not settle the dispute between the parties in action.

**Immemorial,** beyond the memory of man. By statute of 3 Edw. I. A. D. 1276, this was limited to the reign of Richard I. **Immemorial usage,** or **custom,** one that existed prior to the reign of Richard I.

**Immoral contracts,** those founded on an immoral consideration (*contra bonos mores*); *e.g.*, illicit cohabitation. They are void (cf., *ex turpi contractu non oritur actio*), and can not be enforced by any party thereto.

**Impanel,** originally to enter the names of a jury in a a parchment schedule, or panel (*q.v.*), by the sheriff; hence to draw a jury and enroll their names.

**Imparl,** to discuss a case apart with the opposite party or his counsel, with a view to an adjustment of differences and an amicable settlement. *Leave to imparl,* when granted by the court, amounts to a continuance of the case. In the obsolete process of barring an estate tail by suffering a common recovery (*q.v.*), the tenant in tail, on being vouched to warranty, craved leave to imparl or confer with the common vouchee, and, having thus got out of court, did not re-appear, and suffered judgment by default. See *Vouchee.*

**Impeach,** to charge with crime, or misdemeanor, or with misconduct in office; especially a judge, or high public official. (2) To prove that a witness has a bad reputation for truth and veracity, and is therefore unworthy of belief.

**Impeachment of waste,** a restraint from committing waste upon lands and tenements; a demand for compensation for waste done by a tenant.

**Impediment,** a legal hindrance, or bar, *e.g.*, to making a contract; such as infancy, coverture, want of reason, and the like.

**Impedimentum dirimens,** such an impediment to marriage as is not removed by the solemnization of the rite, but continues in force, and makes the marriage null and void.

**Imperative,** obligatory. See *Directory*.

**Imperfect obligations,** moral duties, such as charity, or gratitude, which can not be enforced by law. **Imperfect trust,** an executory trust. See *Executory*.

**Impertinence,** the statement in pleading of matter which is immaterial, prolix, or scandalous. Impertinent matter may be struck out at the cost of the offending party.

**Implead,** to sue; to prosecute.

**Implication,** a necessary, or possible, inference of something not directly declared.

**Impotence,** or **Impotency,** physical inability of a man or woman to perform the act of sexual intercourse. It is ground for a decree of nullity of marriage, if permanent and existing in either party at the time of the solemnization.

**Impound,** to put cattle in a pound (*q.v.*). (2) To place a suspected document, etc., in the custody of the law, when produced at a trial, until a question affecting it is decided.

**Imprescriptible rights,** those which can not be lost or gained by prescription (*q.v.*).

**Imprimatur,** *l.*, let it be printed; a license to print or publish.

**Imprisonment,** confinement in a prison; restraint of a man's liberty. It may be for the purpose of detaining in custody one accused of crime, or for punishing one convicted of crime. Imprisonment for debt, not fraudulently contracted, is generally abolished.

**Improbation,** (Sc.), the setting aside of deeds on the ground of falsehood or forgery.

**Impropriation,** applying the revenues of a church living to one's own use. (2) A parsonage or ecclesiastical living in the hands of a layman called an *impropriator*, to whom the revenues belong.

**Improvement,** a building erected on land, or other change for the better of its condition, effected by the expenditure of labor and money. (2) A new and useful addition to, or modification of, an existing machine, article of manufacture, process, or composition of matter.

**In,** *l.*, in; within; at; upon; for; against. **In action,** not in possession; applied to things which can only be recovered by an action, unless voluntarily paid or delivered. **In adversum,** against an adverse party. **In aequali jure,** in equal right. **In alio loco,** in another place. **In articulo mortis,** at the point of death. **In autre droit,** in another's right **In blank,** without restriction. See *Indorsement.* **In capite,** in chief. See *Capite, Tenure in.* **In casu consimili,** in a similar case. **In chief,** at first; direct. See *Examination.* **In commendam,** in care of. See *Commendam* **In communi,** in common. **In curia,** in court. **In custodia legis,** in the custody of the law. Goods are so called which have been seized by the sheriff, and are exempt from distress for rent. **In delicto,** in fault; guilty. **In esse,** in being; actually existing. **In extenso,** in its full extent; omitting nothing. **In extremis,** at the very end; at the last gasp. **In facto,** in fact. **In favorem libertatis,** or **vitae,** in favor of liberty, or life. **In feodo,** in fee. **In fieri,** in process of completion; still being done. **In flagrante delicto,** in the very act of committing the crime. **In forma pauperis,** in the character of a poor man; applied to persons asking to have process and subpoenas issued gratis and counsel assigned at the state's expense on account of poverty. **In foro conscientiae,** at the tribunal of conscience; applied to moral obligation as distinct from legal. **In fraudem legis,** in fraud of the law. **In futuro,** in the future. **In genere,** in kind; of the same kind. **In gremio legis,** in the bosom of the law; in abeyance. **In gross,** at large; not appurtenant or appendant. **In haec verba,** in these words. **In hunc modum,** after this manner. **In initialibus,** in the preliminaries. See *Initialia testimonii.* **In invidiam,** for ill-will. **In invitum,** against one unwilling. **In itinere,** on a journey; on the way. **In judicio,** in a judicial proceeding. **In jure,** in law; by right. **In limine,** at the outset. **In litem,** for a suit. **In loco parentis,** in the place of a parent. **In medias res,** to the heart of the matter. **In misericordia,** at the mercy. **In mitiori sensu,** in the milder sense. **In mora,** in delay. **In mortua manu,** in the dead hand; in mortmain (*q.v.*). **In notis,** in the notes. **In nubibus,** in the clouds; in abeyance. **In nullo est erratum,** in nothing is there error; an old plea to errors assigned in proceedings in error. **In odium spoliatoris,** in hatred of a despoiler, or wrong-doer. **In pais,** in the country; in the open; applied to simple words or acts as opposed to deeds or records in court. **In pari causa; delicto; materia,** in an equal case; in equal fault; upon the same matter or subject. **In perpetuam rei memoriam,** for the perpetual remembrance of a thing. **In personam,** against the person. **In posse,** possible; opposed to, *in esse,* actual. **In praesenti,** at the present time; opposed to *in futuro,* **In principio,** at the beginning. **In propria persona,** in his own person; not by attorney. **In re,** in the matter of; used in entitling matters in court other than actions between adverse parties. **In rem,** against the thing. **In render,** to be given, as rent; opposed to *in prender* to be taken. **In rerum natura,** in the nature of things. **In solido,** in the whole; entirely. **In specie,** in the same form. **In statu quo,** in the same situation as. **In terrorem,** for a threat, or by way of intimidation. **In totidem verbis,** in just so many words. **In toto,** in the whole; altogether. **In transitu,** in transit, or removal from one place to another. **In vadio,** in pledge. **In ventre sa mere,** in his mother's womb; applied to a child, begotten but not born, who is, for many purposes, *e.g.,* acquiring vested rights in property, considered by the law as already born.

**Inadequate,** insufficient; not equal to full value. An inadequate price, or consideration, is one which is less than would ordinarily be given or exacted; and, if gross and accompanied by fraud or deception, will sometimes operate to avoid a contract.

**Inadmissible,** what can not be received; *e.g.,* parol evidence is inadmissible to vary the terms of a written contract.

**Inalienable,** not transferable.

**Incapacity,** want of legal power to do a thing.

**Incendiary,** one who maliciously sets fire to a building. See *Arson.*

**Incest,** carnal knowledge of persons so related to each other that their marriage is prohibited by law; *e.g.,* of brother and sister, father and daughter, uncle and niece.

**Incident,** something which depends upon or appertains to another more important thing, termed the *principal.*

**Incipitur** (*it is begun*). This was the technical commencement of a declaration, demurrer-book, judgment, etc.

**Incite,** to stimulate or induce a person to commit a crime. This is a misdemeanor, whether the crime be committed or not.

**Inclosure,** is the act of freeing land from rights of common (*q.v.*), by vesting it in some person as absolute owner.

**Income,** the profits realized from property, labor, business, or the loaning of money. **Income tax,** an annual tax on the income, or profits derived by a person from his property, profession, trade, or office; not favored in the United States, as giving too much publicity to a man's private affairs.

**Incompetent,** unable, or unfit. A judge, or juror, is incompetent, when from interest in the subject-matter he is an unfit person to decide a controversy. Testimony is incompetent when it is not such as by law ought to be admitted. A witness is incompetent when by law he may not testify, either on account of relationship, interest, or infamous character.

**Incontinency,** unlawful indulgence of the sexual passion.

**Incorporeal,** not having a material body; intangible; invisible existing only in contemplatien of law. **Incorporeal hereditaments,** rights issuing out of, or connected with, things corporate; *e.g.*, easements of light and air.

**Incumbent,** a clergyman in possession of an ecclesiastical benefice. See *Induction.*

**Incumbrance,** a claim, lien, or liability attached to property; as a mortgage or a judgment.

**Indebitatus assumpsit,** one of the common counts (*q.v.*), in actions for debt, whereby the plaintiff alleged a debt, and a subsequent promise (*assumpsit*) on the part of the debtor to pay, founded on the consideration of the debt.

**Indecency,** conduct which offends against modesty; actions and language unfit to be seen or heard; *e.g.*, the exposure of one's person in a public place, or in view of others. Generally punishable as a misdemeanor.

**Indecimable,** not titheable.

**Indefeasible,** that can not be made void. See *Defeasible.*

**Indefinite payment,** one which is not appropriated by the debtor on making it. See *Appropriation.*

**Indemnify (Indemnification),** to make good another's loss caused by an act or omission of a nature specified.

**Indemnity,** that which is given, or granted, to a person to prevent his suffering damage. (2) A legislative act for the relief of officers who have exceeded their official powers, in cases of emergency, those who have lost public moneys through no fault of their own, etc.

**Indenture,** a deed between two or more parties; called *indented,* because duplicates of every deed *inter partes* were once written on one skin, which was cut in half with a jagged edge; so when the duplicates were produced in court they were seen to belong to one another by fitting into one another.

**Indicavit** (*he has proclaimed*), in England, a writ of prohibition that lies for a patron of a church, whose clerk is sued in the spiritual court by another clerk for tithes of a certain value, to bring the action into a court of common law.

**Indicia,** signs; marks.

**Indictment,** a written accusation against one or more persons, of a crime of a public nature, preferred to and presented upon oath by a grand jury. The person against whom the indictment is found is said to be *indicted.*

**Indirect evidence,** proof of collateral circumstances, from which a fact in controversy, not directly attested by witnesses or documents, may be inferred. See *Evidence.*

**Indivisum,** that which is held in common; not partitioned.

**Indorsement,** any thing written or printed on the back of an instrument in writing, and having relation to it. Used especially of the writing put on the back of a bill, or promissory note and signed, by which the party signing, called the *indorser*, transfers the property in the bill or note to another, called the *indorsee.* Indorsement may, however, be *in blank*, *i.e.*, not specifying the name of the indorsee, in which case it may be transferred from hand to hand without further indorsement, and is payable to bearer. Indorsement may also be made "*without recourse*," by which the indorser relieves himself from liability in case the note is not paid.

**Inducement,** that which constitutes the motive for doing a thing. (2) The introductory part of a pleading

**Induction,** in ecclesiastical law, is the giving a parson possession of a benefice to which he has been instituted; upon which he acquires a vested right to the profits of the living, and becomes complete incumbent.

**Indulgence,** a favor granted, such as forbearance to sue or to insist on payment of a debt at maturity.

**Inevitable,** that which can not be foreseen or prevented, as an *accident* (*q.v.*).

**Infamy,** that loss of character which is produced by conviction of any infamous crime, treason, felony, and the like, and which, under the common law rendered the person incompetent as a witness. Even where such conviction does not render a person incompetent, it may be shown as affecting his credibility as a witness

**Infant,** at common law, a person under twenty-one years of age, without regard to sex. By the statutes of many states, however, a woman ceases to be an infant at the age of eighteen. Infants are subjected by the law to various disabilities for their protection; thus, they can not bind themselves by contract, except for necessaries (*q.v.*); they can not aliene land (but see *Gavelkind*). Contracts, however, which are for their benefit, though voidable by them, bind the other party. Contracts of apprenticeship, executed marriage contracts, and contracts made by an infant in his representative capacity as executor or trustee, are commonly made binding by statute. An infant is conclusively presumed to be incapable of felony before he is seven years old. He is deemed *prima facie* incapable of felony from seven to fourteen, but this presumption may be overthrown by proof of malice and the possession of a good understanding as to right and wrong, and the consequences of his act. After fourteen, the presumption is the same as in the case of adults.

**Infanticide,** the killing of a child after it is born. The felonious destruction of the *foetus in utero* is more properly called foeticide, or criminal abortion.

**Infeoffment,** (Sc.), the act or instrument of feoffment (*q.v.*). or investiture, synonymous with *sasine,* the instrument of possession.

**Inferior courts,** in England, are the court-baron, the hundred-court, the borough civil court, and the county-court; and also all courts of a special jurisdiction. In the United States, all courts except the supreme court are so termed, but especially courts of limited jurisdiction

**Infeudation,** the placing in possession of a freehold estate. (2) The granting of tithes to laymen.

**Infidel,** one who does not accept the Christian religion, or believe in the existence of a God who will punish or reward according to desert.

**Infirmity,** of a bill, note, etc.; invalidity

**Informal,** deficient in legal form.

**Information,** communicated knowledge. (2) A formal accusation or complaint, filed by the attorney-general, or other law officer of the government, charging a person or corporation with some crime or violation of law. In certain classes of criminal cases, it is a statutory substitute for an indictment or presentment by a grand jury. It is used, chiefly, however, in civil cases, to exact penalties and forfeitures for violations of revenue and other laws, and in proceedings in *quo warranto,* to deprive a corporation of its franchise. The knowledge upon which the information is based is usually obtained from some other person, called the *relator,* and the information is in such cases brought *ex relatione*

**Informer,** a person who prosecutes those who break any law or penal statute; usually for the purpose of obtaining part, or the whole, of the penalty recoverable under the statute. A *common informer* is so called to distinguish him from persons specially damaged by the act complained of.

**Infra,** *l.,* below; under; within; occurring by itself in a book, it refers the reader to a subsequent part of the book, like *post.* **Infra aetatem,** within or under age. **Infra annum**

**luctus,** within the year of mourning. **Infra corpus comitatus,** within the body of the county. **Infra dignitatem curiae,** beneath the dignity of the court. **Infra hospitium,** within the inn, *i.e.*, in charge of the innkeeper. **Infra praesidia,** within the walls, *i.e.*, completely within the power of the captors.

**Infringement,** breach or violation; applied to the breach of a law, or violation of a right, as of copyright or patent right.

**Ingenuus,** *l.*, (Rom.), a freeman who was born free.

**Ingress, Egress,** and **Regress,** words frequently used in leases to express the right of the lessee to enter, go upon, and return from the lands in question. See *Free entry; Emblements.*

**Ingressu,** an abolished writ of entry. It was also called *praecipe quod reddat.*

**Ingrossing,** writing the fair copy of an instrument for the formal execution of it by the parties thereto. See *Engross.*

**Inheritance,** a perpetual or continuing right to an estate, vested in a person and his heirs. (2) A hereditament. (3) That which descends to the heir on death of the owner intestate. See *Descent; Heir.*

**Inhibition.** See *Prohibition.* (2) In Scotch law (*a*) a writ whereby a person is *inhibited* from contracting any debt which may become a burden on his heritable property; (*b*) a writ prohibiting all persons from giving credit to a man's wife.

**Initialia testimonii,** (Sc.), the obsolete practice of examining a witness, previous to taking his evidence, as to his disposition toward the parties, whether he has received a bribe, etc. See *Voir dire.*

**Initiate,** commenced; inchoate. A husband was in feudal law said to be tenant by the *curtesy initiate,* when a child who might inherit was born to his wife. See *Curtesy.*

**Injunction.** This was originally the court of chancery's discretionary process of preventive and remedial justice. Injunctions are (*a*) *preventive,* restraining a person from doing something, or *mandatory,* commanding something to be done; (*b*) *preliminary, provisional, interlocutory,* granted on the filing of a bill, or while the suit is pending, to restrain the party enjoined from doing or continuing to do the acts complained of, until final hearing or the further order of the court; or *final, perpetual,* awarded after full hearing on the merits, and as a final determination of the rights of the parties.

**Injuria, Injury,** a wrong, or tort; an infringement of a right. It is *injuria absque* (or *sine*) *damno,* where no damage ensues from the infringement, as when a stream already foul is still further polluted by the wrongful act of any one.

**Inlagary,** or **Inlagation,** a restitution of an outlaw to the protection and benefit of the law.

**Inland,** within the same state or territory. **Inland bill of exchange,** a bill drawn and payable within the same state or country. Any other is a *foreign bill* (*q.v.*).

**Inmate,** one who dwells in a part of another's house, or in a public institution.

**Inn,** a public house of entertainment, where all who choose to call may obtain food, lodging, and other accommodations necessary to a traveler.

**Innings,** lands recovered from the sea; when rendered profitable, they are termed *gainage* lands.

**Innkeeper,** one who keeps a house where travelers are furnished, for profit, with what they require, board, lodging, etc. He is bound to receive and entertain every traveler who presents himself for that purpose, and offers to pay; provided he conducts himself properly and there is room in the house. An innkeeper has a lien on the goods of his guests for his charges, but may not detain their persons, or seize their clothing in actual wear. He is liable for the safe-keeping of the goods, or baggage, brought by the guest to the inn.

**Innocent,** not guilty. Every man is presumed to be innocent until he is proved to be guilty. **Innocent conveyances,** such as may be made by a tenant of his leasehold, without occasioning a forfeiture; *e.g.*, lease and release, bargain and sale, and a covenant to stand seized for life.

**Innominate,** or **unnamed contracts,** (Rom.), were those which failed to satisfy the definitions of the *named contracts; e.g.*, sale (venditio), or letting (locatio), but which were enforced whenever there had been performance by one party. Such were exchange (*permutatio*) and compromise (*transactio*).

**Innotescimus,** an exemplification or copy of a charter of feoffment granted by the crown.

**Innovation,** (Sc.), an exchange of one obligation for another, so as to make the second come in place of the first. See *Novation*.

**Inns of Chancery,** were formerly institutions at which students prepared themselves to be admitted to the Inns of Court. There were nine: Clement's, Clifford's, Lyon's, Furnival's, Thavies', Symond's, New, Barnard's, and Staples' Inn. They now consist chiefly of solicitors, and possess corporate property, but no public functions. **Inns of Court,** colleges for students of the common law. There are four of them, exercising the right of admitting persons to practice at the bar: the

Inner Temple, the Middle Temple, Lincoln's Inn, and Gray's Inn.

**Innuendo** (*by hinting*), that part of the indictment or pleading in an action for libel which goes to explain a connection between what is said in the alleged libel, and certain persons or things not named or explicitly stated therein; whereby it is made to appear that the actual statement is libelous.

**Inofficious testament,** a will not in accordance with the testator's natural and moral duties. See *Officious.*

**Inops consilii,** *l.*, destitute of counsel. In the construction of wills greater latitude is given, because the testator is supposed to have been *inops consilii.*

**Inquest,** judicial inquiry. (2) An inquiry made by a coroner (*q.v.*) and jury as to the death of the person who has been killed, or has died suddenly, or under suspicious circumstances, or in prison. It is held *super visum corporis, i.e.*, after the jury has viewed the dead body, and the evidence is given on oath. (3) A jury. (4) The finding of a jury upon such inquiry.

**Inquest of office,** an inquiry made by a jury, before the sheriff, coroner, escheater, or other officer of the crown under writ sent to them for that purpose, or by commissioners specially appointed, concerning any matter that entitles the crown to the possession of lands or chattels.

**Inquiry, writ of,** is a judicial process addressed to the sheriff of the county in which the venue is laid, stating the former proceedings in the action, and directing him to make inquiry, with the assistance of a jury, as to the damages suffered by the plaintiff, and to return the inquisition into court. It is used in cases where judgment is allowed to be taken by default, and the damages are unliquidated, and not to be ascertained by mere calculation.

**Inquisition,** an inquiry by a jury. (See *Inquest of Office.*) (2) The document which records the result of the inquiry. A lunatic, "so found by inquisition," is one formally so declared, after inquiry by a master of the court, with or without a jury.

**Insanity,** mental unsoundness, aberration, or impairment. It implies disease or congenital defect in the brain, and, as a general term, embraces both *idiocy* and *lunacy* (*q.v.*).

**Inscriptio,** a written instrument of grant.

**Insimul computassent,** *l.*, they had accounted together; an obsolete action of account.

**Insinuatio,** (Rom.), registration among the public records.

**Insolvency,** the state of one who has not property sufficient for the full payment of his debts, or who is unable to pay his debts as they fall due in the usual course of business.

The statutes of most of the states provide for the proper administration and distribution of an insolvent's estate among his creditors, but do not exempt him from his liability to pay the unsatisfied balance remaining due; differing in this respect from *bankrupt* laws, which provide for the absolute discharge of a debtor, who has not been guilty of fraud, upon the surrender of all his property to the receiver or assignee in bankruptcy.

**Inspection,** examination by proper officers, called *inspectors,* of articles, to see whether they conform to the standard required by law, and to rate them according to their true character and quality. (2) Of *documents,* the right which a party to an action has to examine and take copies of documents admitted by any other party thereto to be in his possession. See *Production; Discovery.*

**Inspeximus,** *l.,* (*we have seen*), an exemplification or copy of the enrollment of a charter or of letters patent. See *Constat.*

**Installation,** the ceremony of inducting into, or investing with, any office or dignity.

**Installment,** a portion of a debt, annuity, etc.

**Instance court,** in England, one of the two divisions of the Admiraly branch of the Probate, Divorce and Admiralty Division of the High Court (*q.v.*). It has jurisdiction in cases of injuries to private rights committed at sea, or intimately connected with maritime subjects. See *Prize Court.*

**Instanter,** immediately; at once.

**Institor,** *l.,* (Rom.), a clerk in charge of a shop or store. His authority is called *institorial power.*

**Institute,** a commentary or treatise; *e.g.,* Coke's Institutes, four volumes of commentaries upon English law; the Institutes of Gaius and Justinian, treatises on the civil law, and Bouvier's Institutes of American Law. (2) In Scotch law, the person, *e.g.,* heir of entail, to whom an estate is first given in order of destination or limitation. (3) See *Institution.*

**Institution,** the ceremony of committing to a parson the care of souls in a parish. See *Presentation; Induction.* (2) A society for promoting any charitable or benevolent object. (3) In Roman law, the appointment of an heir.

**Instruct,** to convey information, as a client does to a solicitor, or a solicitor to a counsel. (2) To authorize one to appear as advocate. (3) To give orders or directions, as a principal does to his agent.

**Instrument,** a formal legal writing.

**Insufficiency,** the fault of an answer, or an affidavit in answer to interrogatories, which does not reply specifically to the charges made in the bill or the questions asked.

**Insurance,** (*a*) *by way of indemnity*, is the act of providing against a possible loss, by entering into a contract with one who is willing to bind himself to make good such loss, should it occur. The instrument by which the contract is made is called a *policy;* the consideration paid to the *insurer*, who is frequently called an *underwriter*, and which is relatively small, as compared with the sum insured, a *premium*. Fire and marine insurances are usually by way of indemnity; *i.e.*, only such sum is paid by the insurer as is actually lost, and, on making such payment, he is entitled to stand in the place of the assured. See *Loss.* (*b*) *Not by way of indemnity*, as in the case of life or accident insurance, is where the insurer undertakes, in consideration of a premium, to pay a certain sum to the assured, or his legal representatives, on his death or suffering injury by an accident. **Insurance broker,** one who effects insurance for others.

**Intake,** a temporary inclosure of the waste, made under a custom by a tenant of a manor.

**Intendment,** the true meaning. (2) *Of law*, a presumption.

**Intent; Intention,** design; resolve; determination of the mind. To render an act criminal, a wrongful *intent* must exist; but the wrongful intent may be presumed if the necessary or probable consequences of the act were wrongful or harmful, and the act was deliberately committed.

**Intentio,** *l.*, (Rom.), a count or charge.

**Inter,** *l.*, among; between. **Inter alia; alios,** among other things; persons. **Inter apices juris,** between the subtleties of the law **Inter canem et lupum,** between dog and wolf; an expression for twilight, because then the dog seeks his rest and the wolf his prey. **Inter partes,** between the parties. **Inter sese,** among themselves. **Inter vivos,** between living persons. A gift *inter vivos* is a gift by one living person to another.

**Interdict,** an injunction. (2) an ecclesiastical censure, by which divine services are prohibited to particular persons or in particular places. (3) (Rom.), a judicial decree, depriving a person, who has lost his reason or become incapable of understanding and transacting business, of all power to manage his own affairs.

**Interesse termini,** *l.*, the right which a lessee acquires in land, before entry, by virtue of a demise at common law.

**Interest,** an estate or right in property. (2) Money paid for the loan or use of another sum called the principal (*q.v.*). See *Compound interest; Bottomry.*

**Interference,** the state of things which exists when one applicant for a patent claims to be the first inventor of something claimed by another applicant, or granted to a prior patentee. (2) The case or proceedings in the patent office when opposing claimants are required to furnish proofs of their respective rights, and the commissioner of patents has to decide which is the prior inventor.

**Interim,** *l.*, in the meantime; meanwhile. **Interim order,** one made in the meantime, and until something is done. See *Injunction.*

**Interlineation,** writing between lines; the insertion of any matter in a written instrument after it is engrossed, and before or after its execution. If before, a memorandum thereof should be made at the time of the execution or attestation. An interlineation after execution, by one of the parties without the consent of the other, if material, will invalidate the instrument.

**Interlocutory,** an application, order, or judgment which is made during the course of an action, and has not the intention of finally determining it. See *Injunction.*

**International law,** is either public or private. The former regulates the conduct of independent states toward each other; the latter decides the tribunal before which, and the law by which, private rights shall be determined; this being a question of domicile of the parties, locality of the property at stake, and so on. See *Conflict of laws.*

**Interpleader,** a proceeding by which the defendant states that the money or thing in his hands, for which he is sued, is claimed by a third person, avers his readiness to deliver to either, as the court may direct, and prays that they may be compelled to interplead and have their rights determined.

**Interpolate,** to insert words in a complete document.

**Interpretation,** the discovery and declaration of the meaning of words or signs employed in a statute or instrument. See *Construction.*

**Interrogatories,** questions in writing *exhibited* or addressed on behalf of one party to an action to the other, before the trial thereof. The person interrogated must give his answers in writing, and upon oath. (2) Verbal questions put to a witness before an examiner, and answered on oath. (3) Framed questions in writing, annexed to a commission to take the deposition of a witness, to be put to and answered by the witness under oath, whose answers are to be reduced to writing by the commissioner.

**Interruption,** the stopping, or breaking in upon, the running of a prescription, or of limitations, or the exercise of a right, by which the prescription or limitation is defeated, or the right lost. It may be voluntary, or the adverse act of the person, against whom the right is claimed, or the statute runs.

**Intervention,** the act by which a third person, not originally a party to the suit, but claiming an interest in the subject-matter, comes into the case, in order to protect his right or interpose his claim. He is called the *intervener.*

**Intestate,** one who has left no will. A person dies intestate who either has made no will at all, or has made one not legally valid; or, has made one, but revoked or canceled it; or, if there is no one who can take under it.

**Intra vires,** *l.*, (*within its powers*), the opposite to *ultra vires* (*q.v.*).

**Intromission,** (Sc.), the assuming possession and management of property belonging to another; if without legal authority, it is called *vicious.*

**Intrusion,** the entry of a stranger on land on the determination of a particular estate, before the heir, or person entitled in reversion or remainder, can enter. (2) Taking possession, without authority, of a benefice which is not vacant.

**Inure,** or **Enure,** to take effect.

**Invalid,** not valid; of no binding force.

**Invention,** the finding out, or contriving of something new. (2) The thing itself which has been invented, and which is the subject-matter of a *patent* (*q.v.*).

**Inventory,** an itemized list, or schedule, in writing, of the goods and chattels belonging to the estate of an insolvent or deceased person.

**Investiture,** the open delivery of seisin or possession under the feudal law. See *Livery.* (2) One of the formalities by which the election of a bishop is confirmed by the archbishop.

**Investment,** the employment of moneys in such a way as to produce an income; *e.g.*, loaning them on notes secured by mortgage, purchasing interest bearing bonds, etc.

**Invito domino,** *l.*, without the consent of the owner—a necessary element in the taking of goods or money, in order to constitute a larceny.

**Invoice,** a written account of the particulars of goods sent or shipped to a purchaser, factor, etc., with the prices and other charges annexed.

**Ipse,** *l.*, a demonstrative pronoun, used for the sake of emphasis; myself; himself; itself, etc.; the very. **Ipse dixit** (*he himself said it*), a bare assertion, resting on the authority of an individual. **Ipso facto** (*by the very act itself*), *i.e.*, as the necessary consequence of the act. (2) A censure of excommunication in the ecclesiastical court, resulting immediately on condemnation. **Ipso jure,** by the law itself; *i.e.*, by the mere operation of law.

**Ipsissimis verbis,** *l.*, in the identical words, as opposed to *substantially.*

**Ire ad largum,** *l.*, to go at large; to be set at liberty.

**Irrebuttable,** that can not be rebutted. Presumptions of law are so called when it is not permitted to bring evidence to disprove them.

**Irregular,** done in the wrong manner, or without the proper formalities; as distinguished from *illegal.*

**Irrelevant,** not pertinent; not tending to aid or support, as evidence which does not tend to prove the fact at issue.

**Irrepleviable,** or **Irreplevisable,** that which can not be replevied. See *Replevin.*

**Irrevocable,** incapable of being revoked; powers of appointment may be exercised so as to be irrevocable; no will is ever irrevocable. A power of attorney, in which the attorney has an interest for which he has given a valuable consideration, is irrevocable

**Irritancy,** (Sc.), the becoming void; forfeiture; as of a deed or contract, on the happening of an event, or commission of an act which, by the terms of a restrictive clause, called the *irritant clause*, worked a forfeiture.

**Issint** (modern French, *ainsi*), thus; so; used to introduce a statement that special matter already pleaded amounts to a denial; *e.g.*, a married woman, instead of pleading *non est factum* to an action founded on a deed, might state that at the time of making the writing, she was a feme covert, *and so*, it is not her act

**Issuable,** that which raises an issue. (2) That which is put in issue. (3) *Issuable terms*, Hilary and Trinity, because in them issues were made up for the assizes. Obsolete.

**Issue,** offspring; lineal descendants. (2) (In the plural), the profits arising from lands, tenements, etc. (3) The point or points in question, at the conclusion of the pleadings which one side affirms, and the other denies Issues may be of fact or of law. *To join issue, i.e.*, to accept the issues appearing on the pleadings, is the technical phrase for closing the pleadings. *To plead the general issue*, was formerly to deny in general terms the opponent's allegations; in criminal practice it now means to plead "not guilty," without more. *To issue a writ*, is for the proper officer to deliver it, when properly sealed, etc., to the party suing it out.

**Item** (*also*), a word used when an article is added to the list.

**Iter** (Rom.), a foot-way; a right of passage.

**Itinerant,** wandering; traveling. See *Eyre, justices in.*

## J.

**Jactitation,** a false pretension to marriage. If a person falsely asserts that he or she is married to another, the latter may sue in the Probate, Divorce and Admiralty division for a decree enjoining silence on the *jactitator*.

**Jail.** See *Gaol.*

**Jedburgh justice,** also called **Lydford law,** a parody on justice, punishment coming first and trial afterward; lynch law.

**Jeofail** (corrupted from *j'ai failli*, Fr., I have failed), an expression used in the days of oral pleading to avow an oversight in pleading or other law proceedings. Statutes of *amendments and jeofails* were those passed from time to time to enable a pleader upon the discovery and avowal of an error in the form of his pleading to amend it.

**Jeopardy,** peril; danger. The situation of a prisoner who has been regularly tried upon a valid indictment. The constitution of the United States provides that "no person . . . shall be subject for the same offense to be twice put in jeopardy of life or limb."

**Jetsam,** (Rom., *jactus mercium*), things which having been cast overboard and sunk are thrown upon the shore. If the things float ashore they are called *flotsam*; if they are marked by a buoy attached to them, *ligan*.

**Jettison,** throwing overboard to lighten a ship. (2) The things cast overboard to save the vessel. See *General average.*

**Jobber,** one who buys and sells for others.

**Joinder,** *of causes of action*, coupling two or more matters in the same suit or proceeding. By statutes in England, and many of the states, the joinder of different causes of action, where the parties are the same and appear in the same capacity, is allowed to a much greater extent than at common law. **Joinder of parties,** uniting all as plaintiffs or defendants, who have the same right, or against whom the same rights are claimed or relief is demanded. See *Issue.*

**Joint,** united; coupled together in interest or liability; opposed to *several*. **Joint action,** one brought by two or more as plaintiffs, or against two or more as defendants. **Joint bond,** one executed by two or more obligors who must be united in any action on the same; as opposed to a *joint and several* bond, on which any or all of the obligors may be sued at the option of the obligee. **Joint contract,** one which two or more are jointly bound to perform, or the benefits of which two or more must jointly demand. **Joint executors** or **trustees,** two or more persons united in the execution of a will or trust. **Joint stock company,** a species of partnership, invested by the laws of England and of some states with some of the privileges of a corporation. **Joint tenants,** two or more persons, to whom, and their survivors, or survivor, is given by the same conveyance, or devise, the same estate in lands and tenements. The right of survivorship distinguishes *joint tenancy* from *tenancy in common.*

**Jointress,** or **Jointuress,** one entitled to jointure.

**Jointure,** (originally, a joint estate limited to husband and wife), a provision made by a husband for his widow.

**Judge,** one invested with authority to determine any cause or question in a court of justice.

**Judge advocate,** a legal adviser appointed to assist in the trial of offenders before a court-martial.

**Judgment,** the decision of a court; the expression by a judge of the reasons for his decision. Judgments may be *final,* putting an end to the case; *interlocutory,* given in the progress of a case upon some matter which does not finally determine the case. They may be rendered *on confession* by the defendant; *on default,* when the defendant fails to appear to answer or demur within the allotted time; or *on the merits,* after a full trial on the pleadings and evidence. The term judgment is also applied to the *decree* of a court of chancery in England and some states. **Judgment-debtor,** one against whom a judgment ordering him to pay a sum of money stands unsatisfied. **Judgment nisi,** one rendered on the verdict returned in a court of assize, to become absolute, *unless before* the fifth day of the following term the court shall otherwise order, for good cause shown. **Judgment note,** a promissory note, otherwise in the usual form, which contains a power of attorney to appear and confess judgment for the sum therein named, with interest, etc., if not paid at maturity. **Judgment record,** a formal transcript of the pleadings and proceedings in a court up to and including the judgment, made and kept by the clerk.

**Judicature acts,** the titles of the statutes passed in England in 1873 and 1875 (36 and 37 Vict. c. 66, and 38 and 39 Vict. c. 77), which regulated the organization and powers of the courts, and the procedure therein. They resemble somewhat the Codes of Civil Procedure enacted in New York, Ohio,

Kansas and other states. One chief alteration introduced by them is that common law and equity are for the future to be concurrently administered, and that in every court equitable estates, rights, duties, and liabilities are to be recognized and enforced.

**Judices pedanei,** *l.*, (Rom.), judges chosen by the litigants.

**Judicial,** relating to proceedings before a judge or in court. **Judicial admission,** or **confession,** one made in court in due course of legal proceedings, and which becomes a matter of record, or the ground of conviction. **Judicial mortgage,** the lien resulting from a judgment in favor of the person obtaining it. **Judicial sale,** a sale made under the authority of some competent court which conveys all the rights of the defendant to the purchaser, without any warranty, express or implied, as to title, or incumbrances, other than those of parties to the suit. **Judicial separation,** the proceeding in the divorce court, which has taken the place of a divorce *a mensâ et thoro* (*q.v.*). **Judicial writs,** all writs subsequent to the *original* writ which issued out of chancery. See *Writs.*

**Judicium dei,** *l.*, (*judgment of God*), a term applied to the obsolete forms of trial by ordeal.

**Jurat,** the memorandum of the time, place, and person before whom an affidavit is sworn. (2) An officer similar to an alderman, sworn for the government of some corporations, in England.

**Jurata,** the jury clause, formerly in the *nisi prius* record.

**Juration,** the act of swearing; the administration of an oath.

**Juridical,** relating to the administration of justice. Juridical days, those on which courts are held and justice is administered.

**Juris,** *l.*, of law; of right. **Juris et de jure** (*of law and from law*). A conclusive presumption, which can not be rebutted, is so called. **Juris et seisinae conjunctis,** the union of seisin, or possession, and the right of possession, constituting a complete title. **Juris utrum,** was an action by an incumbent to recover possession of land belonging to his living, which his predecessor had aliened.

**Jurisconsulti,** or **Jurisprudentes,** (Rom.), men who studied and expounded the forms and principles of law.

**Jurisdiction,** the power of a court to entertain and decide any action or matter. (2) The district over which the power of the court extends. Jurisdiction is *limited* when the court has power to act only in certain specified cases; *general*, when it may act in most cases in which the parties are before it; *concurrent*, when the same cause may be entertained by one court or another, at the option of the party bringing the suit; *original*, when the court has power to try the case in the first instance; *appellate*, when the court hears cases only on appeal, or writ of error from another court; *exclusive*, when no other court has power to hear and decide the same matter.

**Jurisinceptor,** (Rom.), a student of the law.

**Jurisprudence,** the science of law. (2) A body of law.

**Jurist,** a civilian; one versed in Roman law.

**Jury,** a body of men (see also *Jury of matrons*) sworn to consider and deliver a true verdict upon evidence submitted to them in a judicial proceeding. They are called *jury-men* or *jurors*. A *grand jury* is one summoned to consider whether the evidence, presented by the state against a person accused of crime, warrants his indictment. A *petty* or *petit* jury is the common or ordinary jury, drawn in the usual way, for the trial of causes, either civil or criminal. It usually consists of twelve men; but, by statutes in England and many of the states, six, or even a less number, may constitute a jury, before a justice of the peace or other inferior court. A *special* or *struck* jury is one selected especially for the trial of a given cause, generally by the assistance of the parties. See *Panel; Challenge; Tales*. **Jury-box,** the place in court where the jury sit. **Jury of matrons.** Women are impaneled as a jury in two cases only: (1) upon a writ *de ventre inspiciendo* (see *Ventre*); (2) where a female prisoner is condemned to be executed, and pleads pregnancy, as a ground for postponing execution until after her confinement. **Jury process,** the writ for the summoning of a jury.

**Jus,** *l.*, law; right; equity; authority. All law (*jus*) is distributed into two parts—*Jus Gentium* (*q.v.*), the law of nations, and *Jus Civile*, the civil law, *i.e.*, the whole body of law peculiar to any state. The Jus Civile of the Romans was divided into two parts—Jus Civile in the narrower sense, and Jus Pontificum, or the law of religion. This opposition was expressed by the words *Jus* and *Fas*. The terms *Jus Scriptum* and *Jus non Scriptum*, *i.e.*, the written and unwritten law, which corresponded roughly with our "statute" and "case" law, comprehended the whole of the Jus Civile. **Jus abutendi,** the right of abusing; *i.e.*, complete ownership. **Jus accrescendi,** the right of survivorship. See *Joint tenant*. **Jus ad rem,** an inchoate and imperfect right; such as a parson promoted to a living acquires, by nomination and institution without induction. **Jus aquaeductus,** the right to bring water from or through the land of another **Jus civitatis,** the right of citizenship. (2) The laws of the state, as opposed to *jus gentium*. **Jus deliberandi,** the right which an heir has, in Scotch law, of deliberating for a certain time whether he will take up representation to his predecessor. See *Annus deliberandi.* **Jus disponendi,** the right of disposing of property. **Jus duplicatum,** a double right, such as a man has when he has both title and possession. **Jus imaginis,** (Rom.), the right of using statues, etc., of ancestors; resembling somewhat the modern right of bearing a coat of arms. **Jus in personam,** a right against another person, to oblige him to do or not to do something. **Jus in re,** a complete and full right to a thing, to the exclusion of all other men. **Jus legitimum,** a legal right; one that may be enforced by due course of law. **Jus mariti,** the right to his wife's personal estate which a husband had at common law. **Jus merum,** a bare right, unaccompanied by possession. **Jus naturae,** the law of nature. **Jus patronatus,** a right of advowson. (2) A commission to inquire who is the rightful patron of a church. **Jus postliminii,** the right, in virtue of which persons and things taken by an enemy are restored to their former state, on their coming again into the power of the nation to which they belong; persons being re-established in their former rights, and things being restored to the original owner. **Jus precarium,** a right *depending on request,* and which can not be enforced at law. **Jus privatum,** the civil or municipal law of Rome. **Jus proprietatus,** the right of property. **Jus relictae,** the right of a widow in her deceased husband's personalty. **Jus rerum,** the law of things. **Jus tertii,** the right of a third person. A person is said to set up the *jus tertii* when, being *prima facie* liable to restore certain property to A., he alleges a paramount title in B. **Jus utendi,** the right to use property without destroying its substance.

**Justice,** just treatment; the rendering to every one his due, right, or desert; conformity to law and obligation; merited reward or punishment. (2) The title given, in England, to all the judges of the High Court of Judicature, except the lord chief-justice, the lord chancellor, and the master of the rolls; in the United States, to the judges of the Supreme Court. **Justice of the peace,** an officer having certain judicial powers for the purpose of preventing breaches of the peace, and causing the arrest and commitment of persons violating the law. They also have a limited jurisdiction in the trial of civil causes, varying somewhat in extent in the different states.

**Justiciars,** law officers instituted by William the Conqueror to assist the sovereign in administering the law. The *chief justiciar* was formerly the head of the justiciars and the principal minister of state. He was *ex officio* regent in the sovereign's absence. The last was Philip Basset, in the time of Hen. III.

**Justiciary, Court of,** the supreme criminal court in Scotland, which can revise the sentences of all the inferior criminal courts.

**Justicies,** an obsolete writ, directed to the sheriff, whereby he was enabled to hold plea of debt in his county court for sums exceeding the ordinary limit of 40*s*.

**Justifiable,** lawful. See *Justification*. **Justifiable homicide.** See *Homicide*.

**Justification,** is showing a sufficient reason in court why the defendant did what he is called upon to answer; thus, in an action of libel, a defense of justification is a defense showing the libel to be true; in an action of assault, showing the violence to have been necessary.

**Justificator.** See *Compurgator*.

**Justify.** Bail, or sureties, are said to *justify* when they swear that they are, after the payment of their debts, worth a sum specified, usually double the sum claimed in the action, and that they are householders or freeholders; thus satisfying the court that the security offered is good and sufficient.

**Juxta formam statuti,** *l.*, according to the form of the statute.

## K.

**Kain,** (Sc.), poultry given in part payment of rent.

**Keelage,** money paid by ships remaining in a harbor.

**Keeper of the great seal, Lord,** a judicial officer through whose hands pass all charters, commissions, and grants of the crown to be sealed with the great seal which is in his keeping. By 5 Eliz. c. 13, this office was consolidated with that of lord chancellor. **Keeper of the privy seal,** now called *lord privy seal*, a high officer of state, usually a cabinet minister. Through his hands all charters, etc., pass before they reach the great seal.

**Kenning to a terce,** (Sc.), the act of the sheriff in assigning dower to a widow.

**Kentlage,** ballast of a permanent kind; usually pigs of iron.

**Kidnapping,** the forcible abduction or stealing away of a man, woman, or child from his, or her domicile, parents, or legal protector.

**Kin,** or **Kindred,** relations by blood or consanguinity. They may be either (*a*) *lineal*, *i.e.*, in a direct line, either ascending; *e.g.*, a father or grandfather; or descending; *e.g.*, a son or grandson: or (*b*) *collateral*, *i. e.*, descended from a common ancestor; *e.g.*, a brother or cousin. In reckoning the degrees of kindred, the rule of the Roman law is followed, and each generation is reckoned as a degree, both up to the common ancestor and downward to the person whose relationship is to be traced. The *next of kin* of a man is the person (or persons, if there are more than one of the same degree) most nearly related to him.

**King.** See *Sovereign*.

**King's Bench.** See *Court of King's* or *Queen's Bench.*

**King's Chambers,** in England, that portion of the sea which is inclosed by an imaginary line from one headland to another. It is part of the territorial waters of the crown. **King's** (or **State's**) **evidence,** an accomplice in a felony who on an implied promise of pardon, if he fully and fairly discloses the truth, testifies against his fellows in crime.

**Kleptomania,** insanity in the form of an irresistible propensity to steal.

**Knight,** the lowest kind of dignity; *knight bachelor* is the ordinary form and the oldest, but ranks below the knights of special orders; *e.g.*, the Bath. **Knight's fee,** "that which goeth to the livelihood of a knight;" land worth £20 per annum. **Knight-service,** a feudal military tenure (*q.v.*) of the most honorable kind. Various forms of it were escuage, castleward, and grand serjeantry.

## L.

**Laches,** negligence, or unreasonable delay in pursuing a legal remedy, whereby a person forfeits his right. See *Acquiescence.*

**Lacuna** (*a ditch*), a blank in writing.

**Lada,** purgation; acquittal. (2) A form of tenant's service. (2) An inferior court of justice. (4) A water-course.

**Lady Day,** 25th of March; one of the usual quarter days.

**Laesae majestatis; Crimen,** high treason.

**Lagan,** or **Ligan.** See *Jetsam.*

**Lambeth degrees,** those conferred by the Archbishop of Canterbury. He can confer all the degrees that are taken at the universities, though without many of the privileges carried by the latter.

**Lammas Day,** 1st of August. See *Candlemas.* **Lammas lands,** those over which there is a right of pasturage by persons other than the owners from about Lammas, or reaping time, until sowing time.

**Land,** in its restricted sense, means soil; but legally it includes every thing on the soil, buildings, water, etc.

**Landlord,** he of whom lands or tenements are held by a tenant at a rent.

**Landmark,** a monument set up, in order to define the boundaries between adjoining estates.

**Lapse,** to glide or slip away; to cease. If a legatee or devisee die before a testator, the legacy or devise is said to *lapse*, and sinks, as a rule, into the residue. A benefice lapses, if the patron does not present a clerk within six calendar months of its becoming void.

**Larceny,** the unlawful taking and carrying away of things personal, without color of right, with intent to deprive the rightful owner of the same. *Simple* larceny is that which is unaccompanied with aggravating circumstances. *Compound* larceny is that which is committed under circumstances which aggravate the crime. Larceny is commonly distinguished as *grand* or *petty*, according as the value of the thing taken exceeds or falls short of a sum fixed by statute. See *Robbery*, *Embezzlement*.

**Last heir,** he to whom lands come by escheat for want of lawful heirs; that is, in some cases the lord of whom the lands were held, but in others the sovereign or state.

**Last resort.** A court from which there is no appeal is called the court of last resort.

**Latent,** hidden. See *Ambiguity*.

**Latitat** (*he lies hid*), in England, a writ of summons in personal actions at the Queen's Bench, founded on a fictitious concealment of himself by the defendant. Abolished by 2 Wm. IV. c. 39. See *Court of King's or Queen's Bench*.

**Law,** an observed uniformity of action or sequence: *e.g.*, "laws of nature." (2) A rule of action to which men are obliged to conform. The statutes are called the *written* law, as opposed to the unwritten law founded on precedents and custom. See *Jus*. (3) The principles and procedure of the common law as distinguished from those of equity

**Law burrows, Letters of** (Sc.), correspond to the English "security to keep the peace." *Contravention of law burrows* is any act whereby the undertaking to keep the peace is violated.

**Lawful,** legal; that which is sanctioned or permitted by law.

**Law merchant,** the general body of commercial usages which have become an established part of the law of the land,

and which relate chiefly to the transactions of merchants, mariners, and those engaged in trade.

**Laws of Oleron,** a maritime code said to have been drawn up by Richard I., or his mother, Eleanor, at the Isle of Oleron, on which the maritime law is largely founded.

**Lay,** or **Layman,** one of the people; one not belonging to a particular profession; especially opposed to *clerical.* **Lay corporations,** bodies politic composed of lay persons for lay purposes. They are either (1) civil, created for temporal purposes; or (2) eleemosynary, for charitable purposes. **Lay fee,** a fee held by ordinary feudal tenure as distinguished from the ecclesiastical tenure of *frankalmoign* (*q.v.*). **Lay impropriators,** lay persons to whose use ecclesiastical benefices have been appropriated. **Lay days** (otherwise *laying* or *lie days*), those allowed by a charter-party for a ship to *lie* and load or unload. See *Demurrage.*

**Le roy, le vent,** or **S'avisera,** *fr.*, the king assents, or the king will consider; the form of the royal assent or dissent to public bills passed by parliament.

**Leading,** going before; guiding. **Leading a use,** an expression applied to a deed made before a fine and recovery, specifying to whose use the fine shall inure. **Leading case,** one that has been so often followed as to establish definitely a principle of law. **Leading question,** a question which suggests to a witness the answer which is to make. It may only be asked in cross-examination.

**Leap Year.** See *Bissextile.*

**Lease,** sometimes also called *Demise* (*demissio*), is a conveyance of property for life, or years, or at will, by one who has a greater interest in the property. The person conveying is called the landlord, or *lessor;* the property remaining in him after conveyance is his *reversion;* the person to whom the conveyance is made is the tenant, or *lessee.* The consideration is usually the payment of a rent. The operative words used to be, "demise, lease, and to farm let." Until the lessee accepts the term by entry, he has only an *interesse termini* (*q.v.*), or interest in the term. In general, leases must be by deed, except leases at will, or for a term not exceeding three years. A lease is generally drawn in duplicate, one part being kept by the lessee, the other part by the lessor. See *Rent; Underlease.*

**Lease and release,** a mode of conveyance, formerly much used in England, operating under the Statute of Uses, which was superseded in 1841 by a simple release, and in 1845 by a grant under 8 and 9 Vict. c. 106. A lease for a year was made by way of bargain and sale, which, under the Statute of Uses, gave seisin without entry or enrollment, and then the vendor released his reversion to the purchaser by ordinary deed of grant.

**Leasehold,** land held under a lease.

**Leasing,** or **Lesing,** gleaning. (2) Lying, slandering (Sc.).

**Leave and license,** a defense to an action in trespass, setting up the consent of the plaintiff to the trespass complained of.

**Leet, Court.** See *Court Leet.*

**Legacy,** a gift of personalty by will, which, arising as it does from the mere bounty of the testator, is postponed to the claims of creditors. A legacy may be (*a*) *simple, i.e.*, of a specified thing, or part, of a testator's estate, as opposed to (*b*) *general*, which comes out of any part of his assets; (*c*) *demonstrative*, which is a general legacy directed to be paid out of a specified fund. (*a*) is *adeemed, i.e.*, revoked, by the donor parting with the specific thing during his lifetime; (*c*) is not, as in this case it comes out of the general estate, and has this further advantage, that it is not subject to abatement, as are general legacies, if the assets are insufficient. Where a testator has bequeathed more than one legacy to the same person, the question arises whether he intended the second to be *cumulative, i.e.*, in addition to the first, or only *substitutional.* A legacy is said to *lapse* when the legatee dies before the testator, and, in consequence, it never vests.

**Legal,** according, or relating, to law. It is opposed, (1) to illegal, (2) to equitable. **Legal tender,** the gold and silver coin and treasury notes, which are by statute declared to be good and sufficient for the payment of debts, public and private.

**Legalize,** to make lawful.

**Legatee,** one who has a legacy left to him.

**Legislature,** that body of men in the state which has the power of making laws. It usually consists of two branches—the upper house, or Senate, and the lower, or House of Representatives. The Senate is usually a much smaller body, and each senator represents a much larger district or constituency than a representative.

**Legitim, Legitime,** or **Bairn's part of gear,** (Sc.), the legal share (one-half or one-third, according to circumstances) of the father's free movable property, due on his death to his children. By Scotch law, a father can only dispose of part of his personal estate by will (one-third, if he leaves a widow and children); this is called *dead man's part* (*q.v.*).

**Legitimacy,** the condition of those born of parents lawfully married.

**Legitimation,** the act of giving the character of legitimate children to those born out of wedlock, as by the subsequent marriage of the parents and acknowledgment of such children, or by legal proceedings.

**Leonina societas,** *l.*, a partnership in which one gets the *lion's* share.

**Lesion,** (Sc.), the degree of injury or duress sustained by a minor, or person of weak capacity, necessary to entitle him to *reduce* or avoid a deed, which he has been improperly induced to sign.

**Lessee, Lessor.** See *Lease.*

**Let,** hindrance; obstruction. (2) To lease; to grant the use of a thing for compensation.

**Letter,** a written message, or request; a written instrument, or commission, sent to or issued to another, making a demand, granting a privilege, or conferring an authority. **Letter of advice,** one containing information, generally of some act done by the writer. **Letter of attorney.** See *Power of attorney.* **Letter of credit,** one written by a banker or correspondent to another person, requesting him to give the bearer credit (with or without a limit as to amount). If it be not addressed to any particular person or persons, it is called an *open* letter. **Letter of license,** an agreement between a debtor and his creditors, whereby they allow him to carry on his business for a time free from arrest. **Letters of marque,** commissions granted, usually in time of war, to private individuals, authorizing them to fit out vessels for the purpose of capturing the goods or subjects of a hostile nation, by way of reprisal for wrong done. By such letters, the prizes are granted to the captors. See *Reprisal; Privateering.* **Letter-missive.** When a peer was made a defendant in the court of chancery, the lord chancellor sent a letter-missive to him, to request his appearance, together with a copy of the bill, petition, and order. **Letters patent,** an instrument issued by the government to the *patentee*, granting or confirming a right in the latter to the exclusive possession and enjoyment of land, or of a new invention or discovery. **Letters of request,** a mode by which an ecclesiastical suit may be commenced in the arches or superior court, without having it first tried in the consistory, provincial, or inferior court. **Letters of safe-conduct,** a passport, or protection granted by a government to a subject of a hostile power, exempting him from seizure. Our ambassadors abroad now give passports or licenses for the same purposes. **Letters testamentary,** an instrument issued out of the proper court empowering the person named in a will as executor to administer upon the estate of the testator. See *Administration; Cachet; Close rolls.*

**Levant et couchant** (*rising and lying down*), cattle that have been so long on the ground of another, that they have lain down and risen to feed, supposed to be a day and a night.

**Levari facias,** a writ of execution, by which the sheriff is directed to collect a judgment debt by sale of the debtor's chattels, and out of the rents and profits of his lands. See *Sequestrari facias.*

**Levitical degrees,** degrees of kindred within which persons are prohibited to marry. They are set forth in the eighteenth chapter of Leviticus.

**Levy,** to raise money or men.

**Lex,** *l.*, a law; the law; sometimes used as synonymous with *jus* right. **Lex communis,** the common law. **Lex contractus,** the law of the contract. **Lex domicilii,** the law of the country where a person has his domicile (*q.v.*). **Lex fori,** the law of the country where an action is brought. This regulates the forms of procedure and the nature of the remedy to be obtained. **Lex loci,** the law of the place where a contract is made, *contractus*; or thing is done, *actus;* tort is committed, *delicti;* or where the thing, *e.g.*, real estate, is situated, *rei sitae.* This generally governs in suits relating to such contracts, transactions, torts, and real estate. **Lex mercatoria,** the mercantile law, or general body of established usages in commercial matters. **Lex non scripta,** the unwritten law (*q.v.*). **Lex ordinandi,** the same as *Lex fori* (*q.v.*). **Lex sacramentalis,** purgation by oath. **Lex scripta,** the written or statute law. **Lex talionis,** the law of retaliation. **Lex terrae,** the law of the land; the process of law.

**Ley,** (*fr. loi*), law. (2) The oath with compurgators. (3) A meadow. **Ley gager,** a wager of law. (2) One who commences a lawsuit.

**Leze-majesty** (*laesae majestatis crimen*), an offense against sovereign power; treason.

**Liability,** the condition of being subject to an obligation, either (*a*) actual and ascertained, or (*b*) potential and unascertained.

**Libel,** defamatory writing; any published matter that tends (*a*) to degrade a man in the eyes of his neighbors or render him ridiculous, or to injure his property or business; (*b*) to produce evil consequences to society, as being, *e.g.*, blasphemous, seditious, or immoral. It may be "published" by writing, effigy, picture, or the like. Both the author and the publisher are liable to be sued. See *Justification.* (2) In ecclesiastical courts, and in admiralty, the plaintiff's written statement of his case. (3) In Scotch courts, (*a*) the plaintiff's pleadings; (*b*) an indictment.

**Libellant,** the party who files a *libel* in an ecclesiastical or admiralty case against another, who is called the *libellee.*

**Libellus,** *l.*, a little book. **Libellus conventionis,** or **Conventionalis,** the statement of a plaintiff's claim; a bill (*q.v.*). **Libellus famosus,** a libel: a defamatory writing, sign, or picture.

**Liber,** *l.*, book; a principal subdivision of a literary work. **Liber assisarum,** the book of assizes or pleas of the crown, being part five of the "year-books" (*q.v.*). **Liber feudorum,** a code of the feudal law compiled by direction of the Emperor Frederick Barbarossa. **Liber judicialis of Alfred,** his dome-book (*q.v*). (2) Free. **Liber homo,** (Rom.), a freeman, as distinguished from *libertinus*, a freedman. **Liber et legalis homo,** a free and lawful man; one qualified to be a juryman. **Libera batella** (*free boat*), a right of fishing. **Liberam legem amittere** (*to lose one's free law*). The sentence by which conspirators were in ancient time deprived of all their legal rights. **Liberum maritagium,** frank-marriage (*q.v.*). **Liberum servitium,** free service, or such as is becoming to a freeman and soldier. **Liberum tenementum,** frank (or free) tenant. This was formerly a usual plea of a defendant in action of trespass, alleging a general freehold title. Now obsolete.

**Liberate,** a writ to the sheriff to deliver to the cognisee, or creditor, possession of lands and goods of the debtor, which had been extended on forfeiture of his recognizance. See *Merchant staple.* Obsolete. (2) A writ to a jailer to deliver a prisoner that had put in bail for his appearance.

**Liberty,** the state of freedom. (2) An authority to do something which would otherwise be wrongful. (3) A franchise (*q.v.*) (4) The place where a franchise is exercised. See *Non omittas.* (5) Or *liberties*, a privileged district exempt from the sheriff's jurisdiction.

**License,** a permission or authority to do something which would otherwise be inoperative, wrongful, or illegal. It may be either written, or verbal; but all licenses under statutes are written.

**Licentia,** *l.*, leave; a license. **Licentia concordandi,** leave to make the matter up; a formal step in levying a fine (*q.v.*). **Licentia loquendi,** leave to imparl. **Licentia transfretandi,** a writ or warrant directed to the keeper of a seaport, commanding him to let the persons therein named pass over sea.

**Licentiate,** one who has license to practice any art or faculty.

**Licentiousness,** the doing what one pleases without regard to the rights of others; dissoluteness.

**Lidford,** or **Lydford law.** See *Jedburgh justice; Lynch law.*

**Liege,** or **Ligius,** one bound; used of lord and tenant, in feudal tenures. (2) Full, pure, or perfect. **Liege poustie,** a state of sound health, which gave a person lawful power in Scotland to dispose of his heritable property.

**Lien,** a right in one man (1) to *retain* that which is in his possession belonging to another, until certain demands of the person in possession are satisfied; or (2) to *charge* property in another's possession with payment of a debt, etc., *e g.*, a vendor's lien (*q.v*). It may be either (*a*) *particular*, arising out of some charge or claim connected with the identical thing; or (*b*) *general*, in respect of all dealings of a similar nature between the parties. It may be (i) by agreement between the parties, express or implied (*conventional*); or (ii) by operation of law, owing to the special relation between them, as in the case of a solicitor and client. See *Maritime lien.*

**Lieu,** (*fr.*), place. *In lieu of*, in the place or stead of.

**Life annuity,** an annual payment during the continuance of any given life or lives. **Life-estate,** a freehold not of inheritance. It is either—(1) *Conventional*, or expressly created by the act of the parties: (*a*) for one's own life; or (*b*) the life of another—*pur auter vie.* Or (2) *Legal*, which is either (*a*) tenancy-in-tail after possibility of issue extinct; (*b*) curtesy; or (*c*) dower. **Life-land,** or **Life-hold,** land held on a lease for lives. **Life-rent,** (Sc.), a rent received for a term of life. The owner of the property (*real* or *personal*), subject to the life-renter, is called the *fiar*, and the reversion the *fee.* The legal life rents are *terce* (dower) and *curtesy.*

**Ligan,** wreck consisting of goods sunk in the sea, but tied to a buoy, so that they may be found again. See *Jetsam.*

**Ligeance,** allegiance (*q.v.*).

**Light,** that force of nature, by the action of which upon the organs of sight, things are made visible. The direct, reflected, or diffused rays of the sun. (2) The medium through which light is admitted, as a window, a pane of glass. See *Ancient lights.*

**Lignagium,** a right of cutting fuel in woods.

**Ligula,** a copy or transcript of a court-roll or deed.

**Limitation,** a restriction; a thing which limits or restrains. (2) A certain period fixed by statute within which an action must be brought after the cause of action accrues, or the claimant will lose his right to enforce it by law. For particular limitations, the statutes of the several states must be consulted. (3) A clause in a conveyance, will, etc., which declares how long the estate limited, or given thereby, shall continue; *e.g.*, "heirs," "heirs of the body," etc., are words of limitation defining the nature of the estate conveyed.

**Limited,** restricted; circumscribed; not full. **Limited administration,** administration (*q.v.*) of the effects of a testator, or intestate, which is limited either as to time or as to the assets to be administered. **Limited liability.** A company is *limited* or *unlimited*, according as the liability of its share-holders is restricted to the amount they severally hold or guarantee in the capital of the company, or is not. **Limited owner,** a tenant for life, in tail, or by the curtesy, or other person not having a fee-simple in his absolute disposition. **Limited partnership,** a firm in which one or more of the partners are, on compliance with the provisions of statutes regulating such partnerships, relieved from liability beyond the amount of the capital contributed by them.

**Lineal,** in a direct line. See *Kindred.* **Lineal warranty,** a warranty by the ancestor from whom the title did or might come to the heir.

**Liquidated,** fixed; ascertained; *e.g.*, *damages*, the exact amount of which must be paid, or may be collected, upon a default or breach of contract. The term is frequently used in contradistinction to *penalty* (*q.v.*).

**Liquidation,** ascertaining and fixing the value of things, or the amount of damages, before uncertain (2) Paying, settling and discharging an indebtedness or liability. (3) Winding up the business of an insolvent, or company.

**Lis,** *l.*, an action, or dispute. **Lis mota,** a controversy begun. **Post litem motam,** after the dispute has arisen. **Lis pendens,** a pending suit.

**Literal,** written; adhering to the letter.

**Litigant,** one engaged in a law-suit, or *litigation.*

**Litis aestimatio,** *l.*, the measure of damages. **Litis contestatio,** *l.* See *Contestatio litis.*

**Livery,** delivery; formal transfer, or investiture. (2) A writ which lay for the heir, ward of the crown, to obtain possession of his lands, on coming of age. (3) The distinguishing dress delivered to the servants of a lord, or the members of a particular guild, on their entering the service, or joining the company. **Livery of seisin,** the formal transfer of the possession of lands or tenements before land "lay in grant." See *Feoffment; Grant.* It was of two kinds: (*a*) *in deed*, when feoffer and feoffee both went on the premises to be conveyed and the former delivered to the latter a turf, twig, or key, as symbolical of the whole; (*b*) *in law*, when made in view of the land.

**Living.** See *Benefice; Memory.*

**Loan,** a bailment of an article for consumption or use, to be returned in kind, or to be redelivered, without reward. Also, extended to the act of lending money on interest. (2) The thing or money lent.

**Local,** pertaining to a particular place or district. **Local actions,** those which must be brought in the county or district where the subject-matter lies, or the cause of action arose, as distinguished from *transitory* (*q.v.*). **Local allegiance,** such as is due from an alien or stranger born, so long as he continues within the sovereign's dominions. **Local courts,** tribunals of a limited and special jurisdiction, as the borough and county courts. **Local statutes,** those whose operation is limited to a particular place, as distinguished from *general* statutes.

**Locatio,** *l.*, (Rom.), letting for hire. See *Hiring.* **Locatio custodiae,** a deposit for safekeeping, for a reward. **Locatio mercium vehendarum,** the carriage of goods for hire. **Locatio operis,** the hiring of labor and services. **Locatio operis faciendi,** the bailment of things on which work is to be done. **Locatio rei,** the hiring of a thing.

**Location,** the Scotch term for *locatio* (*q.v.*). (2) The act of selecting and designating lands or mining claims, which a person is authorized by law to enter and possess.

**Locative calls,** references to physical objects in entries or deeds, by which the boundaries of the tract claimed or conveyed may be ascertained, and the land be identified.

**Locus,** *l.*, a place. **Locus contractus,** the place of the contract, *i.e.*, the place where it is made. **Locus delicti,** the place where the tort or injury was committed. **Locus in quo,** the place in which. **Locus poenitentiae,** a place of repentance, *i. e.*, opportunity for withdrawing from an intended contract or act, or an impending liability, before one is bound; *e.g.*, by the act or acceptance of the other party. **Locus rei sitae,** the place where the thing is situated. **Locus sigilli,** the place of the seal. **Locum tenens,** one holding the position; a deputy.

**Lodger,** one who occupies rooms in a house, the general control over which remains in the landlord.

**Lopwood,** a right to lop wood for fuel on waste land of a manor.

**Lord,** in feudal tenure, one of whom land is held by a tenant. His right to services, etc., is called his *seigniory* or *lordship.* See *Homage; Manor.* (2) A title of dignity applied to peers of the realm, *lords temporal;* archbishops and bishops entitled to seats in the House of Lords, *lords spiritual*; presiding judges of the court, *lord chancellor*, *lord chief justice*, etc.; and high officers of state, in Great Britain. **Lords of appeal,** those members of the House of Lords who sit and hear appeals; they include the chancellor, the lords of appeal in ordinary, or "law-lords," and peers who have held high judicial office. **Lords justices of appeal,** the judges appointed as members of the court of appeal.

**Lord's Day,** Sunday; the first day in the week. **Lord Paramount,** the crown, of whom all land is in theory held. See *Sovereign*.

**Loss,** in insurance, the destruction of, or damage to, the insured subject by the perils insured against. The death of the person insured under a *life* policy; or, injury, fatal or otherwise, suffered by one insured under an *accident* policy. A loss may be *total* where the whole subject-matter is destroyed or so injured as to be valueless; or *partial*, not amounting to a total loss. In *marine insurance*, a loss not actually total, may be constructively so, where the subject-matter is so nearly destroyed, or so situated that the cost of raising and repairing the vessel would be so great as to justify the owner in abandoning her to the underwriters, and claiming as for a total loss. See *Abandonment*; *Insurance*.

**Lost papers,** such as have been so mislaid that they can not be found after diligent search. Secondary evidence of the contents of such papers is generally admissible.

**Lost or not lost,** words used in a maritime policy which enable the insured to recover, even if the subject of the insurance be lost at the time of making the policy.

**Low-water mark,** that part of the shore to which the water recedes when the tide is lowest.

**Lucid interval,** a period of sanity intervening between two attacks of insanity. An act done during a lucid interval is as valid, and entails the same responsibilities, as the act of a sane person.

**Lucri causa,** *l.*, for the sake of gain; a term descriptive of the felonious intent with which property is taken.

**Lunatic,** a person who (1) has intermittent attacks of insanity, or suffers from delusions; (2) who is found by inquisition (*q.v.*) incapable of managing himself or his affairs; (3) who is confined in an asylum under proper certificates.

**Lying by,** acquiescence (*q.v.*).

**Lynch law,** a form of summary trial and punishment of real or suspected criminals, by persons having no proper judicial authority.

## M.

**Magister,** *l.*, a master; ruler. **Magister navis,** master of a ship; he to whom the entire control of a vessel is committed.

**Magistrate,** a person charged with executive functions. (2) Inferior judicial officers, having summary jurisdiction in criminal offenses, and a limited jurisdiction in civil causes; *e.g.*, police judges and justices of the peace.

**Magna Charta,** *l.*, the Great Charter of English liberties, so called. It was based substantially upon the Saxon common law, and contains the solemn restitution of the ancient liberties of the realm, exacted by the barons from King John, in the year 1214, and was subsequently confirmed by over thirty different statutes, of which those of 9 Henry III. and 25 Edward I. are the most important. It provided *inter alia* against abuses of the royal prerogative, and for the proper administration of justice.

**Maills and duties,** (Sc.), rents of an estate.

**Maim.** See *Mayhem*.

**Mainour, Manour,** or **Meinour,** a thing stolen, which is found in the hand (*in manu*) of the thief who took it.

**Mainovre,** a trespass committed by hand.

**Mainpernable,** that which may be held to bail.

**Mainpernors,** persons to whom a man is delivered out of prison, on their becoming bound to produce him whenever required.

**Mainprise,** the *taking in hand* of a person by *mainpernors*, who undertake to produce him again when required; an old term for bail (*q.v.*).

**Mainsworn,** forsworn.

**Maintainor,** or **Bearer,** one who, without interest in the subject of an action, and not being retained as counsel or attorney, maliciously, or, at least, officiously, interferes and assists with money, or otherwise, to carry it on.

**Maintenance,** the supply of necessaries to those who are incompetent to provide for themselves. (2) Finding money, or otherwise assisting to carry on an action in which one has no lawful interest. See *Champerty; Embracery*.

**Majority,** full age. At common law, a minor comes of age on the day preceding the twenty-first anniversary of his birth. See *Age*. (2) The greater number.

**Maker,** the person who signs a promissory note; by so doing, he engages to pay it according to its tenor.

**Mal,** a prefix, meaning bad; wrong; fraudulent.

**Mala,** *l.*, bad; wrong; fraudulent. **Mala fides,** bad faith, the opposite to *bona fides.* **Mala in se,** acts which are wrong in themselves, whether prohibited by human laws or not, as distinguished from *mala prohibita.* **Mala praxis,** malpractice; bad or unskillful treatment by a physician, or other professional person, resulting in an injury to the person who employs him. **Mala prohibita,** acts which are prohibited by human laws, but not necessarily *mala in se*, or wrong in themselves.

**Malefactor,** a wrong-doer; one convicted of crime.

**Malfeasance,** the commission of an unlawful act.

**Malice,** hatred; ill will; a formed design of doing an unlawful act, whether another may be prejudiced by it or not. If the known and necessary consequence of the act done is injury to another the law implies malice; but *express* malice, *i.e.*, actual ill feeling toward the person injured, may also be proved to exist.

**Malicious,** implying malice; wrongful; wanton; without just cause. **Malicious arrest, imprisonment, prosecution, etc.,** proceedings taken and carried on without probable cause. **Malicious injuries,** such as are inflicted on person or property wantonly and without just cause; *e.g.*, arson, destruction of property, etc.

**Malingerer,** one who feigns illness, or protracts disease or the effects of a wound, to escape military duty, or to excite charity.

**Malitia praecogitata,** *l.*, malice aforethought. See *Malice.*

**Malo grato,** *l.*, in spite; unwillingly.

**Malum.** See *Mala.*

**Malversation,** misbehavior in an office, employment, or commission; as breach of trust, or extortion.

**Manager,** a person appointed to have charge of the business of another, or of a corporation. (2) A person appointed by the House of Representatives to prosecute an impeachment before the Senate.

**Mandamus** (*we command*), a prerogative writ of a remedial nature, addressed to a person, sole or corporate, and not to the sheriff, as are ordinary writs, requiring the person to whom it is addressed to do some act therein specified, which is generally one connected with his duty as a public official, or as a corporation exercising public franchises. The writ may be *alternative, i.e.*, granted on *ex parte* affidavits, and requiring the person to do the thing or show cause why he should not be compelled to do it; or *peremptory, i.e.*, after final hearing, when there is nothing for the defendant to do but to obey.

**Mandant,** the principal in the contract of mandate.

**Mandatary,** he to whom a mandate or charge is given. (2) He that obtains a benefice by *mandamus.*

**Mandate,** a judicial command. (2) A charge or commission. (3) A bailment (*q.v.*) of goods without reward (*mandatum*), to have something done to them; not merely for safe-custody.

**Mania,** an insane delusion. An inclination to act in some things contrary to the dictates of reason, sound judgment, or good morals. A person may be afflicted with a mania on certain subjects, or in certain directions, and be in all other respects mentally sound.

**Manifest,** a document signed by the master of a ship, setting forth *inter alia* the description and destination of the goods shipped by him.

**Mannopus,** goods taken in the hands of a thief.

**Manor,** an estate in fee granted by the crown, prior to the statute of *Quia Emptores* (*q.v.*), 1290, to a person called the lord. The lands of a manor are (*a*) *demesne* (*terrae dominicales,* belonging to the lord), part of which was usually granted by the lord to copyholders or customary freeholders, and a certain part held by villeins at the will of the lord; (*b*) the *lord's wastes,* over which his tenants usually had rights of common given to them. A manor, as a rule, has various franchises (*q.v.*) appendant to it; *e.g.*, the right to waifs and strays, and the right to hold a court baron (*q.v.*).

**Mansion-house,** the residence of the lord of a manor. (2) The chief dwelling-house on an estate.

**Manslaughter,** the unlawful killing of another, without malice express or implied. See *Malice.* It is either (*a*) voluntary, upon a sudden heat, or under strong provocation; (*b*) involuntary, *i.e.*, without intending the death of the person, upon the commission of some other unlawful act.

**Mansum,** or **Manse,** a dwelling-house, especially of a clergyman.

**Manu forti,** *l.*, with a strong hand; a term formerly used in pleading, in cases of forcible entry.

**Manufacture,** to make by hand, directly or through the instrumentality of machinery. (2) An article produced by the work of man's hand, or by machinery. In the patent law the term is restricted to such articles as are thus made, excluding machines and compositions of matter.

**Manumission,** (Rom.), the act of giving freedom to slaves.

**March,** a boundary. **The Marches,** the borders between England and Wales, and between England and Scotland.

**Marchet,** a fine anciently paid by a tenant to his lord, on the marriage of a daughter of the tenant.

**Marine,** belonging or relating to the sea. **Marine contract,** one relating to business done upon the sea, or connected with vessels which sail thereon. **Marine insurance,** a contract of indemnity against losses by perils of the sea to ships, cargoes, freights, or any of them. **Marine interest,** compensation paid for the use of money on *bottomry* or *respondentia* (*q.v.*); usually large in proportion to the risk assumed. **Marine league,** a measure of distance equal to the twentieth part of a degree of latitude.

**Maritagium,** marriage. (2) The right to dispose of an heiress; or, anciently, the daughter of a tenant, in marriage. (3) A marriage portion.

**Marital,** pertaining to marriage, as marital rights, marital duties. See *Jus mariti.*

**Maritime.** See *Marine.* **Maritime law,** the law relating to harbors, ships, and seamen. See *Laws of Olerôn.* **Maritime lien,** a lien, (*q.v.*) (*a*) on a ship, for wages, repairs, supplies furnished, etc.; (*b*) on goods transported in ships, for freight.

**Market,** a public place for buying and selling at appointed times. The term includes *fairs* (*q.v.*). (2) The demand for a particular article. **Market overt,** open market. In the city of London every shop where goods are exposed for sale is *market overt,* and on every day except Sunday; but in other places only the market place and the market day are within the rule as to market overt, which is this, that goods so sold, whatever defect there may be in the vendor's title, *e.g.*, though stolen, become the absolute property of a *bona fide* purchaser. The rule as to purchases in market overt has no binding force in many of the United States.

**Marksman,** a person who can not write, and therefore makes his mark (X) only in executing instruments, another writing his name each side of such mark.

**Marriage,** the status of a man and woman who have engaged in due form of law to live together, and to discharge toward each other the duties of husband and wife. (2) The solemnity by which they are united. The consent of both parties is essential to its validity. The age of consent, and therefore of legal capacity for marrying, is, at common law, fourteen in males, twelve in females. The validity of a marriage is determined by the *lex loci contractus* (*q v.*). **Marriage articles,** an agreement in order to marriage, and preliminary to a settlement, by which it is intended that it should be duly carried out; (2) a marriage settlement (*q.v.*). **Marriage brocage,** a consideration paid for contriving a marriage, and illegal as contrary to public policy. **Marriage portion.** See *Dowry*. **Marriage settlement,** (*a*) *ante-nuptial*, an arrangement made before marriage, and in consideration of it, whereby, as a rule, a jointure is secured to the wife, and portions to children, in the event of the husband's death, and ulterior limitations are made of the settled property in the event of no children taking under it; (*b*) *post-nuptial*, or after marriage, which lacks the consideration of marriage, and is therefore voluntary.

**Marshal,** an officer of the United States, whose duty it is to execute the process of the United States courts. His duties are similar to those of a sheriff.

**Marshaling of assets,** an equitable proceeding which depends upon the principle that a person having two funds out of which to satisfy his claims when another can resort to one of them only, should be compelled to satisfy his claim, if he can, out of that fund to which the other can not resort, thus enabling the latter to secure more complete satisfaction.

**Marshalsea,** a prison belonging to the king's bench. **Marshalsea, Court of the,** was originally held before the steward and marshal of the royal household, and had jurisdiction in causes of debt, or tort, which arose within twelve miles of the sovereign's residence. Abolished, 1849.

**Martial law,** that rule of action which is imposed by the military power in time of war, and within the scope of military operations and occupation.

**Martinmas,** the 11th of November. See *Candlemas*.

**Master,** one who has authority and control over another who is in duty bound to render obedience; *e.g.*, an apprentice, employee, or a scholar at school. (2) The commander, or first officer, of a merchant ship. (3) An officer of a court of chancery appointed to assist the court, especially in the matters of taking and reporting testimony, examining and stating accounts, computing damages, and executing the decrees of the court. **Master of the rolls,** a judge of the Chancery Division, ranking next to the lord chancellor. His original duties, which he still retains, were not judicial, but consisted of keeping the rolls and grants which pass the great seal, and the records. By the Judicature Act, 1881, s. 2, he sits in the Court of Appeal only. He is the only judge who may sit in the House of Commons.

**Mater familias,** *l.*, the mother of a family.

**Material,** important; substantial; capable of properly influencing the result of a trial.

**Matrimonial causes,** include suits for divorce, judicial separation, nullity of marriage, restitution of conjugal rights, and for jactitation of marriage. See those titles. Jurisdiction in such cases formerly belonged to the ecclesiastical courts, but by the Judicature Act, 1872, it was taken from those courts and conferred upon the Probate, Divorce and Admiralty Division of the High Court of Justice.

**Matron**, a mother. See *Jury of Matrons.*

**Maturity,** ripeness; full development; of a *bill*, the time when it becomes due. See *Bill of exchange.*

**Maxim,** an axiom; a general or leading principle. For some of the most important, see *Appendix B.*

**Mayhem,** at common law, the deprivation of a member proper for defense in fight, as an arm, leg, eye, or fore-tooth, or of those parts, the loss of which abates a man's courage; but not a jaw-tooth, ear, or nose, because they were supposed to be of no use in fighting. Modern statutes commonly make no distinction between one member and another with regard to the offense of cutting or wounding.

**Mayor,** the chief magistrate of a city or municipal borough. **Mayor's Court of London,** an inferior court having jurisdiction in civil cases where the whole cause of action arises within the city of London, and also in actions not claiming more than £50, if part of the cause of action so arises, or if the defendant carried on business in the city within six months of action brought. The judge of the court is the *recorder*, and in his absence, the *common sergeant.*

**Measure of damage,** the test which determines the amount of damages to be given.

**Medical jurisprudence,** otherwise called forensic medicine; the science which applies the principles and practice of medicine to the solution of doubtful questions in cases arising in courts of law.

**Mediate,** indirect; intervening. **Mediate powers,** those powers which are incident to primary powers authorizing the agent to act through others. **Mediate testimony,** secondary evidence.

**Medietatis linguae,** *l.*, of the half tongue; a term applied to a jury composed one half of men who speak English and one-half of men who speak a foreign language.

**Meliorations,** (Sc.), improvements.

**Melius inquirendum,** *l.*, a writ that lay for a second inquiry, where partial dealing was suspected, or the former inquest was incomplete on the face of it.

**Memorandum,** an informal record of some fact or agreement. In a policy of marine insurance, a clause limiting the liability of the insurer.

**Memorial,** a petition or representation made by one or more individuals to a legislative body or chief executive.

**Memory, Time of legal.** By Statute of Westminster the First, 3 Edw. I., A.D. 1276, this was limited to the reign of Richard I., July 6, 1189. See *Prescription; Limitation.*

**Men of straw,** men who used in former days to ply about the courts of law for the purpose of giving suborned evidence, and who, from their manner of making known their occupation (*i.e.*, by a straw in one of their shoes), were recognized by the name of *straw-shoes.* (2) A worthless person, one without means.

**Mensa,** *l.*, patrimony; goods; necessaries. **Mensa et thoro,** from bed and board; a species of divorce, or judicial separation of husband and wife.

**Mental reservation,** a silent exception to the general words of a promise or agreement, not expressed, either on account of a general understanding on the subject, or for the purpose of evading liability thereunder.

**Mercantile law,** that which deals with matters affecting trade; *e.g.*, bills of exchange, marine insurance, and the like.

**Merger,** an absorption, by operation of law, of a lesser in a greater right or estate, consequent upon their union in the same person. It takes place independently of the will of the party. For instance, if a man have an estate for years in land, and acquire the fee in the same land by purchase or descent, the term of years is merged in the fee, and no longer exists. See *Extinguishment.*

**Meritorious consideration,** one founded upon some moral obligation, such as natural love and affection; sometimes called *good,* as opposed to *valuable.*

**Merits, Judgment upon,** is one rendered, after a hearing of the case upon the pleadings and evidence, upon the justice of the cause, and not upon technical grounds only.

**Mesne,** middle; immediate; *e.g.*, lord, one between the superior lord and the tenant. **Mesne process,** all those writs which intervene in the progress of a suit or action between its beginning and end, as distinguished from primary and final process. See *Arrest; Capias.* **Mesne profits,** those derived from land, whilst the possession of it has been improperly withheld.

**Messuage,** a dwelling-house, with out-buildings, garden, and the curtilage (*q.v.*).

**Metes and bounds,** the boundary lines of land, with courses, distances, terminal points, and angles.

**Michaelmas term,** in England, one of the four terms of court, beginning on the 2d of November, in each year.

**Middle-man,** an agent between two parties.

**Mileage,** compensation allowed by law to witnesses, sheriffs, members of Congress, and public officers generally, for their trouble and expenses in traveling on public business.

**Military,** pertaining to the army, or the duties, etc., of soldiers. **Military law,** a system of regulations, for the government of persons in military service; distinguished from *martial law,* which affects all persons within the scope of military operations or occupation, whether they are in the service or not. **Military tenures.** See *Knight-service; Cornage,* etc. **Military testament,** a nuncupative will, that is, one made by word of mouth, by which a soldier may dispose of his goods, pay, and other personal chattels, without the forms and solemnities which the law requires in other cases.

**Mineral,** in its widest sense, includes any substance, being part of the earth, which can be got from underneath its surface, for the purpose of profit, whether (*a*) by *mines,* or underground workings, or (*b*) by *quarries,* or open workings.

**Ministerial,** belonging to a minister or subordinate, who is bound to follow instructions; opposed to judicial or discretionary.

**Minority,** the state of being under age, *i.e.,* under twenty-one. See *Infant.* (2) The smaller number.

**Minutes,** notes or records of a transaction, meeting, etc. (2) A memorandum of what takes place in court, made by authority of, and signed by the court, from which the final record is afterward made up.

**Misadventure,** an accident, by which an injury occurs to one, or is inflicted upon another.

**Misappropriation,** the act of fraudulently misapplying funds or property intrusted to one, as in the case of a director, servant, or agent.

**Misbehavior,** improper or unlawful conduct; misconduct.

**Miscarriage,** a failure of justice. (2) Abortion (*q.v.*).

**Misdemeanor,** any crime or indictable offense not amounting to felony.

**Misdirection,** an error in law made by a judge in charging a jury.

**Mise,** expenses; costs. (2) The issue of the obsolete writ of right.

**Misericordia,** an arbitrary amerciament or punishment.

**Misfeasance,** a wrongful act. (2) The improper performance of some lawful act. (3) Negligence.

**Misjoinder,** the improper union of parties or causes of action in one suit at law or in equity. The making of wrong persons plaintiffs or defendants in an action.

**Misnomer,** the giving the wrong name to a person in contracts, wills, or judicial proceedings.

**Misprision,** (1) *of treason,* is the offense of not giving information concerning an act of high treason of which one is aware; (2) *of felony,* to conceal, or aid in concealing, a felony; (3) *positive,* maladministration, embezzlement of public money, wrongful interference with the course of justice, etc.

**Misrepresentation,** a false statement. When made with reference to a material fact, by one party to a contract, to induce another, who is ignorant of the truth, and is actually misled by it, to enter into it, it is ground for the rescission of the contract, whether the party making the statement knew it was false or not. When made willfully, by a party knowing or having reason to believe that it is false, and with the intent to deceive another to his prejudice, it constitutes good ground for an action to recover damages for any injuries that the latter may suffer from acting upon it.

**Mistake,** error; a fault in judgment or conduct; an act done or omitted, by reason of ignorance of law or facts, which a party would not have committed if he had rightly understood the law or facts. Mistakes of *law* do not furnish an excuse for wrongful acts, or a ground of relief from the consequences of acts done in ignorance of the law. Acts done, or contracts made in ignorance of, or under a false impression as to, material *facts,* may sometimes be relieved against.

**Mistrial,** an erroneous trial.

**Misuser,** abuse of any liberty or benefit, which works a forfeiture of it.

**Mitigation,** abatement of damages or of punishment. Circumstances which do not amount to a justification or excuse for an act may properly be considered in mitigation of the punishment, or of the damages which a person injured by the act might otherwise recover.

**Mitter,** *fr.*, to put, to send, or to pass. **Mitter a large,** to put or set at large. **Mitter le droit,** to pass a right. See *Release.* **Mitter l'estate,** to pass the estate.

**Mittimus** (*we send*), a writ for removing and transferring records from one court to another. (2) A precept or command in writing, directed to the keeper of a prison, for the receiving and safe keeping of an offender

**Mixed,** blended; confused; united; compound; not pure or simple. **Mixed action,** one partaking of the nature of both a real and personal action, as where possession is demanded of real property and damages for its unjust detention. See *Ejectment; Mesne profits.* **Mixed contract,** (Rom.), one in which one of the parties confers a benefit on the other, and requires of the latter something of less value than what he has given; as a legacy charged with something of less value than the legacy itself. **Mixed larceny,** otherwise called compound or complicated larceny that which is combined with circumcumstances of aggravation, or violence to the person, or taking from the house. **Mixed personalty,** such personal property as is connected with or relates to realty: *e.g.*, terms of years, real estate directed to be converted into money etc. **Mixed property,** that kind of property which is not altogether real or personal, but a compound of both; *e.g.*, emblements, fixtures, heirlooms, title deeds to an estate, etc. **Mixed questions of law and fact,** cases in which a jury find the particular facts, and the court decides upon the legal result of those facts by the aid of established rules of law.

**Modo et forma,** *l.*, (*in the manner and form mentioned*), a phrase formerly used in pleading, meaning that an allegation must be shown true in every detail, not merely in its general effect.

**Modus,** *l.*, manner; means; way. The manner in which an estate should be held; a qualification of the estate. **Modus decimandi,** a particular *manner* or custom of tithing arising from immemorial usage, and differing from the ordinary payment of one-tenth.

**Moiety,** a half. (2) Any equal share; *e.g.*, a third.

**Molestation,** the offense of annoying a person for the purpose of controlling his actions. (2) (Sc.), An action for disturbing one in the possession of land.

**Molliter manus imposuit,** *l.*, (*he laid hands gently on him*), a defense in an action of battery, that the defendant used only the necessary force, and for a justifiable reason: *e.g.*, the ejection of a trespasser from one's house, the prevention of a crime, etc.

**Money,** gold and silver coins—the common and authorized medium of exchange in a civilized nation. The term is held to include, for many purposes, bank notes, checks, promissory notes, and other instruments for the payment of money only. **Money counts,** the common counts in an action of assumpsit; so called, because they are founded on an alleged promise to pay *money* in consideration of a precedent indebtedness. They are *indebitatus assumpsit, quantum meruit, quantum valebant,* and the account stated, money had and received, money lent, money paid, etc.

**Monition,** in admiralty practice, an order of a court to a person *monished,* to do something. (2) An order to a clergyman to abstain from practices contrary to ecclesiastical law (3) *For process,* in ecclesiastical appeals, an order to the court below to transmit an official copy of the proceedings to the appeal court.

**Monomania,** insanity only upon a single subject, and with a single delusion of the mind.

**Monopoly,** an exclusive privilege of buying, selling, making, working, or using a particular thing, granted by the sovereign power in the state. A limited monopoly in books, publications, and patented articles, is allowed by the laws of the United States. (2) The absolute and exclusive control by a person, or combination of persons, of the sale of a particular commodity.

**Monster,** a child which has not "the shape of mankind." It can not inherit land. Mere deformity does not constitute a monster.

**Monstrans de droit,** *fr.,* (*manifestation* or *proof of right*), a method of obtaining restitution from the crown of either real or personal property, where the title of the crown appears from facts set forth upon record. The judgment against the crown is caused *ouster le main,* or *amoveas manus.*

**Month,** *lunar,* the time which the moon takes to complete its changes; being twenty-eight days. (2) *Solar,* that period in which the sun passes through one of the twelve signs of the zodiac. (3) *Calendar,* one of the twelve months of the year by which we reckon time; consisting of an unequal number of days. The word "month," by the common law, signifies, in matters temporal, a lunar; in matters ecclesiastical, a calendar month. In statutes and in commercial dealings, it means a calendar month.

**Monuments,** permanent landmarks established for the purpose of indicating boundaries. They may be natural, as rivers, streams, marked trees, etc., or artificial, as stones or posts set in the ground.

**Moot,** a meeting, especially for the purpose of arguing points of law by way of exercise. This used once to be done by the students of the Inns of Court before the benchers, and the custom has of late been revived at Gray's Inn. **Moot-case,** or **moot-point,** a point or case unsettled and disputable, such as properly affords a topic of disputation. **Moot-court,** a pretended court, usually held in connection with law schools, where moot-cases are argued and decided. **Moot-hills,** hills of meeting, on which the Britons held their great courts.

**Moral certainty,** that degree of probability which would induce a man to act in the ordinary affairs of life as if the thing probable were actually certain. That degree of certainty which leaves room for no reasonable doubt.

**Moratur in lege,** *l.*, "he demurs" because the party does not proceed to plead, or raise any point of fact, but rests or *abides upon* the *law* of the case. See *Demur*

**More or less,** words in a conveyance implying that the quantity of land is uncertain, and not warranted, and that no right of either party shall be affected by any ascertained excess or deficiency. In an executory contract, such words will only excuse a comparatively small deficiency in the quantity of an estate.

**Morganatic marriage,** the lawful and inseparable conjunction of a man of a noble, and especially *royal* birth, with a woman of inferior station, upon condition that neither the wife nor her children shall partake of the titles, arms, or dignity of the husband, or succeed to his inheritance, but be contented with a certain allowance assigned to them by the morganatic contract.

**Mort d'ancestre.** See *Assize.*

**Mortgage** (*a dead pledge*), a conveyance of property, real or personal, to a person called the *mortgagee*, to secure the performance of some act, such as the payment of money by the *mortgagor*, and to become void upon the performance of such act. At common law such conveyances became absolute upon failure to perform the condition; but, in equity, the mortgagor was permitted to redeem upon payment of the sum intended to be secured, with interest. The manner in which this equity of redemption may be barred is regulated by statutes in England and the several states of our Union. A *legal* mortgage is one created by the conveyance or assignment of the property mortgaged to the mortgagee. An *equitable* mortgage is one in which the mortgagor does not actually convey the property, but does some act by which he manifests his intention to bind the same as a security. Mortgages are sometimes denominated *legal* or *equitable*, as the estate conveyed is legal or equitable. See *Foreclosure; Equity of redemption; Welsh mortgage.*

**Mortis causa.** See *Donatio.*

**Mortmain,** (Sc., *mortification*), such a state of ownership of land as makes it inalienable (whence it is said to be in a *dead hand*). This arises when land becomes the property of a corporation, which has a continuous existence. To prevent this, *Statutes of Mortmain* have been passed in England, and many of the United States, restricting or prohibiting the gift of lands in perpetuity to religious and charitable corporations. See *Perpetuity.*

**Mortuary,** a place where dead bodies are kept previous to interment. (2) A gift left by a man at his death to his parish church, for the recompense of his personal tithes and offerings not duly paid in his lifetime. (3) An ecclesiastical heriot.

**Mote,** a meeting or assemblage. See *Gemot; Moot.*

**Motion,** an application to a court by the parties or their counsel, in order to obtain some rule or order, either in the progress of a cause, or summarily, as in the case of a motion for a writ of *habeas corpus.* A motion may be made either *ex parte,* or on notice to the other side, and when based on matter of fact not found in the record, must be supported by an affidavit that such facts are true.

**Movables,** goods; furniture; chattels personal; things which may be carried from place to place, as distinguished from real estate, and other things which can not.

**Mulct,** a fine of money, or a penalty.

**Mulier puisne.** See *Bastard eigné.*

**Mulierty,** lawful issue.

**Multifariousness,** in equity pleading, the demand in one bill of complaint of several distinct and independent causes of action. It was formerly ground for a demurrer, but greater latitude is now commonly allowed. See *Joinder*

**Multipartite,** divided into several parts

**Multiplepoinding,** (Sc.), the same as *Interpleader* (*q.v.*).

**Multiplicity,** the improper bringing of more than one action for what might be determined in a single action.

**Multitude,** an assembly of ten or more persons.

**Multure,** (Sc.), a grist or grinding. (2) The payment due for grinding.

**Municipal,** strictly speaking, that which relates to a city; more generally, that which pertains to the state. **Municipal corporation,** an incorporation of the persons inhabiting a particular district or place, as a county, township, city, village, etc., for political purposes, enabling them to conduct its local government. **Municipal law,** that which pertains to a particular state or nation, as distinguished from international law (*q.v.*).

**Muniments,** writings (title-deeds, charters, etc.), on which rights depend for their support.

**Murder,** the willful killing of any human being, with malice aforethought, either express or implied By the statutes of several states, murder is divided into degrees, depending upon the amount of malice and deliberation exhibited by the murderer, and whether or not it was committed in the perpetration of some other crime, such as arson, rape, burglary, robbery, and the like.

**Murdrum,** in old English law, the secret killing of another. (2) The fine imposed on the district where it was committed.

**Mutatis-mutandis,** means "with the necessary changes in points of detail."

**Mute,** a term used of one who abstains from pleading to an indictment. Formerly, such an one was subjected to the severest treatment, to compel him to plead or answer; but the statutes of England and most of the states now provide that such an one shall be tried as if he had pleaded "not guilty." See *Peine.*

**Mutiny,** the unlawful resistance of a superior officer, on board a ship or in the army; disobedience of orders, accompanied with force, commotion, threats, and other violent disturbances.

**Mutual,** reciprocal; interchanged; common. **Mutual credits,** credits given by each of two persons to the other. **Mutual promises,** promises made simultaneously by two parties to each other, each one of which is the consideration for the other. They will support each other, unless one or the other be void, in which case neither can be enforced. **Mutual testament,** wills made by two persons, each of whom leaves his effects to the other in case he survives.

**Mutuality,** reciprocity of obligation; the state of things in which one person being bound to perform some act for the benefit of another, that other, on his side, is bound to do something for the benefit of the former; (2) *of assent,* is where both persons know clearly what each of them is undertaking to do; (3) *of remedy,* is where each can enforce the contract against the other.

**Mutuum,** (Rom.), a loan whereby the absolute property in the thing lent passes to the borrower (it being for consumption), and he is bound to restore, not the same thing, but an equivalent in things of the same kind. See *Fungibiles.*

## N.

**Naam, Nam, Namium,** the taking or distraining of movable goods and chattels.

**Naked,** incomplete; not clothed with power. A *naked contract* (*nudum pactum*) is one made without consideration, and therefore void. A *naked authority* is one given without any right in the agent, and wholly for the benefit of the principal.

**Name,** one or more words used to designate a particular individual. Names are either *christian, i.e.,* first names commonly given at baptism, or *surnames,* or patronymics, *i.e.,* names derived from one's parents or ancestors—the family name. See *Alias; Cognomen; Idem sonans.*

**Narratio,** *l.,* a count; a declaration.

**Nationality,** the political status acquired by belonging to a nation or state. It arises by birth, or naturalization, and determines the *allegiance* of a person. The term is in frequent use, also, with regard to ships. Their nationality depends upon that of their owners, and is indicated by the flag they carry.

**Natural,** according to nature; not artificial, exceptional, or violent. **Natural allegiance,** that perpetual obedience which is due from all natural-born subjects to their sovereign, as distinguished from *local* allegiance, which is only temporary. **Natural-born citizens,** those that are born within the jurisdiction of a national government; *i.e.,* in its territorial limits, or those born of citizens temporarily residing abroad. **Natural child,** the child of one's body, not necessarily illegitimate. The word is, however, popularly used as equivalent to bastard. **Natural law,** the law of nature; the dictate of right reason, in contradistinction to positive or statute law. **Natural love and affection,** words used in conveyancing, to express a meritorious consideration, being that love which one has for his kindred. See *Consideration* **Natural person,** a term used in opposition to an *artificial* person or corporation, which has a legal though not an actual unity. **Natural presumption,** a presumption of fact, which derives its force from observation and experience.

**Naturalization,** investing aliens with the privileges and obligations of native subjects.

**Navigable,** capable of being navigated. A river, estuary, etc., is so called when the public have there a right of navigation, *i.e.,* to use it as a highway for shipping, etc.

**Ne,** *l.* and *fr.,* not; lest; that not. **Ne admittas** (*do not admit*), a writ directed to the bishop where a *quare impedit* is depending, to prevent him admitting any one during the progress of the suit. **Ne disturba pas,** the general issue in *quare impedit* (*q.v.*), whereby the defendant simply alleged that "he did not obstruct." **Ne exeat regno,** or **republica,** a high prerogative writ, issuing out of a court of chancery, to prevent a defendant debtor from going away and evading the jurisdiction. **Ne injuste vexes,** a writ, abolished 1833, forbidding a landlord to make excessive or unlawful distress. **Ne re-**

**cipiatur,** a caveat entered by a defendant to prevent a plaintiff, who had entered his cause too late, from having it tried at that sittings. **Ne unques,** never:—*accouple in loyal matrimonie* (*never lawfully married*), a plea in action for dower:—*administrator* or *executor*, a denial that defendant was personal representative of the deceased:—*seisie que dower*, called the "general issue in dower."

**Neat cattle,** oxen and heifers.

**Necessaries,** a relative term, implying not merely such things as are required to sustain life, but also those which are suitable to the rank and position of the person concerned. An infant may make a binding contract for necessaries. A married woman has an implied authority to pledge her husband's credit for such things as are necessary to keep herself and her household in a manner suitable to his condition.

**Necessity,** pressing need; overruling power; compulsion; irresistible force. An act done through necessity, and without will or intention, is one for which the agent is not held responsible.

**Negative pregnant,** an evasive denial, which implies or carries with it an affirmative; a denial in form, which is not a denial in substance.

**Negligence,** want of care. There are three degrees of negligence: (1) ordinary, which is the want of ordinary diligence; (2) slight; and (3) gross; which answer to the *levis*, *levissima*, and *crassa* of the Roman law. The distinction is important in contracts of bailment; for if a thing be deposited with a bailee for hire, he is only liable for (1); if for his own benefit alone, he is liable even for (2); if for the bailee's sole benefit, he is liable only for (3). As to the effects of negligence in asserting a right, see *Laches*. *Contributory* negligence is where a person has, by his own want of care, contributed to bring about a loss or accident, and can not, therefore, recover damages against the defendant.

**Negotiable instruments,** those the right of action upon which is, by exception from the rule formerly existing, freely assignable from one to another, such as bills of exchange and promissory notes. They also form an exception, permitted for the convenience of commerce, to the general rule that a man can not give a better title than he has himself; inasmuch as the *bona fide* holder of a negotiable instrument has a good title, even though he took it from a person who stole it.

**Negotiate,** to transfer a negotiable instrument for value; to treat with another in respect to a purchase or sale, or a proposed agreement.

**Negotiorum gestor,** (Rom.), a person who spontaneously,

and without the knowledge or consent of the owner, intermeddles with property, with the object of benefitting the owner.

**Neife,** a man or woman born in villenage.

**Nemine contradicente,** *l.*, (*no one contradicting*), the phrase to signify the unanimous consent of the members of a deliberative body to a vote or resolution; it is analogous to the term *nemine dissentiente*, used in the English House of Peers.

**Nephew,** the son of a brother or sister.

**Nepos; neptis,** (Rom.), a grandson; a granddaughter.

**Never indebted,** a plea to an action of *indebitatus assumpsit*, by which the defendant denies the existence of the contract or facts on which the plaintiff relied.

**New assignment,** a restatement of his cause of action by the plaintiff, with more particularity and certainty, when, owing to vagueness or generality in his first declaration, the answer of the defendant does not sufficiently meet the issue.

**New for old,** a term used in insurance to designate the deduction made in cases of partial loss for the increased value of the new materials substituted for the old in making repairs, usually one-third of the cost after deducting the value of the old materials used in reconstruction.

**New matter,** statements of fact not previously alleged by either party to a suit, in his pleadings.

**New style,** the modern system of computing time by the Gregorian year, formulated in 1582 by Gregory XIII., introduced into great Britain A. D. 1752, the 3d of September of that year being reckoned as the 14th. Previously, the 25th of March was the civil and legal New Year's day. The Russians and Greeks still use the old style, or Julian year.

**New trial,** a re-hearing of a cause, before another jury, granted by the court, on motion of the party dissatisfied with the result of a previous trial, upon a proper showing that substantial justice and equity require it. The usual grounds for a new trial are errors of the court in rulings on the trial or in charging the jury, misconduct of the jury or witnesses, newly discovered evidence which the party seeking a new trial could not with reasonable diligence have discovered and produced at the trial, surprise which prevents the party or his counsel from adequately presenting his case, and irregularities of any sort which render it probable that an impartial trial has not been had.

**Next friend,** one who, without having been regularly appointed guardian, brings suit and acts for an infant, feme covert, or other person not *sui juris*. The next friend is usually a relation, and is responsible for the propriety of the proceedings, and, *prima facie*, for costs.

**Next of kin.** See *Kin.*

**Nexum** (Rom.), the transfer of ownership of a thing (*res mancipi*), absolutely, or by way of mortgage.

**Niece,** the daughter of a brother or sister.

**Nient** (*law, fr.*), nothing. **Nient comprise,** not included; an exception taken to a petition because the thing prayed for was not *contained* in the deed, or proceeding, upon which the petition was founded. **Nient culpable,** not guilty; a plea to any criminal charge or allegation of tort. **Nient dedire,** to say nothing; to suffer judgment by default. **Nient le fait,** the same as *non est factum;* a plea that the instrument declared on is not defendant's deed.

**Night,** the time of darkness between sunset and sunrise.

**Nihil,** or **Nil,** *l.*, nothing. **Nihil capiat per breve,** or **billam,** that he take nothing by his writ, or bill; the old form of judgment against the plaintiff. **Nil debet,** he owes nothing; the general issue in debt on a simple contract. **Nihil dicit,** he says nothing; the old form of judgment by default. **Nihil habet,** he has nothing; a return made by the sheriff, when he has not been able to find the defendant, or to take any thing on his writ. **Nil habuit in tenementis,** he has no interest in the tenements; a plea denying the lessor's title, formerly pleaded in an action of debt, brought by a lessor against lessee for years, or at will, where there was neither a deed between them, nor occupation by the lessee; for otherwise the lessee would have been estopped.

**Nimious,** (Sc.), excessive; unjustifiable.

**Nisi,** *l.*, unless. A decree, rule, or order of the court is said to be made *nisi* when it is not to be of force *unless* the party against whom it is made fails within a certain time to show *cause* against it, *i.e.*, a good reason why it should not be made. **Nisi prius,** unless before; important words in the writ directing the sheriff to summon jurors for the trial of causes pending in the superior courts of law at Westminster, in England, which have come to be applied, both in England and the United States, to the trial of civil causes before a single judge, with a jury. See *Courts of assize and nisi prius.* **Nisi prius record,** was an instrument in the nature of a commission to the judges at *nisi prius* for the trial of a cause, delivered to the officer of the court in which the cause was to be tried, and containing the particulars of the claim and defense, and, subsequently the *postea* (*q.v.*) and judgment.

**Nobile officium,** *l.*, the equitable jurisdiction of the Court of Session, in Scotland.

**Nolens volens,** *l.*, whether willing or unwilling.

**Nolle prosequi,** *l.*, to be unwilling to prosecute; an entry made on the record, by which the plaintiff or prosecutor declares that he will proceed no further.

**Nominal,** existing in name only; unimportant. **Nominal damages,** a trifling sum awarded, where a breach of duty or an infraction of plaintiff's right is shown, but no substantial injury is proved to have been sustained. **Nominal partner,** one who has not any actual interest in the trade or business, or its profits, but, by allowing his name to be used, holds himself out to the world as apparently having an interest therein. **Nominal plaintiff,** one whose name is used in prosecuting an action, but who has no real interest in the matter in controversy, having assigned his right to another, for whom the suit is brought.

**Nominate contracts,** such as were distinguished by particular names, the use of which determines the rights of all the parties to the contract, and the particular action to be brought for its breach.

**Nominatim,** by name; expressed one by one.

**Nomination,** the act of mentioning by name; presenting the name of a candidate for an office or appointment. See *Presentation.*

**Non,** *l.*, not. **Non-access,** the technical term for the non-existence of sexual intercourse between husband and wife. Access is presumed during wedlock, and the mother's evidence to rebut this presumption is not admissible. **Non-age,** not of full age; infancy. **Non assumpsit** (*he did not promise*), a plea by way of traverse in the obsolete action of assumpsit (*q.v.*). **Non assumpsit infra sex annos** (*he did not promise within six years*). This was the form of pleading the statute of limitations (*q.v.*) in the action of assumpsit (*q.v.*). **Non cepit** (*he took not*), a plea in the action of replevin. **Non-claim,** the omission or neglect to assert a right. See *Claim.* **Non compos mentis,** one not of sound mind; a lunatic, idiot, or drunken person. **Non concessit** (*he did not grant*), a plea by which the defendant denies that the plaintiff has received any such grant, *e.g.*, letters patent, as he claims. Only a stranger to a deed could set up such a plea, the parties to it being estopped. **Non constat,** it is not certain; it does not follow. **Non culpabilis,** not guilty. **Non damnificatus** (*not injured*), a plea in an action of debt on an indemnity bond. **Non decimando, De,** a custom or prescription to be exempt from paying tithes. It can only be set up by spiritual persons, or those claiming under them. **Non demisit** (*he did not demise*), a plea in actions for recovery of rent. **Non detinet** (*he does not detain*), a plea in detinue (*q.v.*). **Non est factum,** a plea denying that the deed on which plaintiff sued was the defendant's deed. **Non est inventus,** a sheriff's return to a writ, when the defendant is not to be found in his bailiwick. **Non-feasance,** an offense of omission. **Non fecit** (*he did not make it*), a plea to an action on a promissory note. **Non impedivit** (*he has not impeded*), the general issue in *quare impedit.* **Non infregit conventionem** (*he has not broken the covenant*), a plea in an action of covenant, denying the breach alleged on the part of the defendant. **Non-issuable pleas,** those upon which a decision would not determine the action upon the merits; *e.g.*, a plea in abatement. **Non-joinder,** the omission to make a person party to an action who should have been joined. **Non-juror,** one who refuses to take the oath of allegiance. **Non liquet** (*it does not appear clear*), a form of verdict. **Non obstante** (*notwithstanding*), a clause importing a license from the crown. So far as this would go to set the prerogative above the laws, the right of the crown is denied by the bill of rights (*q.v.*). **Non obstante veredicto, Judgment,** a party may move that judgment may be entered for him, *notwithstanding the adverse verdict* of the jury. **Non omittas,** the clause "that you omit not by reason of any liberty in your bailiwick," which is usually inserted in all processes addressed to sheriffs, so as to authorize them to enter the liberty in execution of the process. **Non prosequitur,** *he* (the plaintiff), *does not pursue* his action. This differs from a *nolle prosequi* (*q.v.*), being the result of action taken by the *defendant*, upon the plaintiff's failing to take the proper step at the proper time. The defendant entered a *non pros.* and signed final judgment; when the plaintiff was said to be *non prossed.* **Non-residence,** not living in the place where suit is brought; a common ground for proceedings in attachment. (2) In ecclesiastical law, the absence of incumbents from their benefices. (3) A company is said to be *non-resident* when its principal place of business is in another state or district. **Non sequitur** (*it does not follow*), a fallacious conclusion. **Nonsuit,** a judgment against the plaintiff, when he fails to prove his case, or neglects to appear at the trial. **Non sum informatus** (*I am not instructed*), the formal answer of the defendant's attorney (see *Warrant of attorney*), whereby he suffered judgment by default to be entered up against the defendant. **Non tenuit,** was a plea in bar to an action for arrears of rent, denying that the plaintiff *held* as he alleged. **Non tenure,** a plea in a real action, by which the defendant denied that he held the land, or part of the land, mentioned in plaintiff's declaration. **Non user,** a ceasing to exercise. A right which can be acquired by user may be lost by non-user. (2) Neglect of official duty, which causes forfeiture of the office.

**North Britain,** Scotland.

**Not found,** words indorsed on a bill of indictment by a grand jury, when they have not sufficient evidence to find a true bill. See *Ignoramus*.

**Not guilty,** in criminal proceedings, is a general denial of the accusation, and puts the prosecutor to the proof of every material fact alleged. It was also the general issue in actions of trespass, trover, and other actions founded on tort. (2) The verdict of acquittal.

**Not proven,** a verdict allowed to be given in criminal trials in Scotland.

**Notary** or **Notary public,** an officer who takes notes of any thing which may concern the public. While their duties and powers vary somewhat in the different states, they are commonly authorized to administer oaths, to take affidavits, acknowledgments and depositions, to protest notes and bills of exchange for non-payment, to draw up marine protests, etc.

**Note,** a memorandum To *note* a dishonored bill is for a notary to initial it, giving the date and the reason assigned for its not being paid. *Note of hand* see *Promissory note. Notes* are made by a judge of the evidence at a trial.

**Notice,** the information given to a person of some act done, or about to be done; knowledge. Notice may be *actual*, when knowledge is brought home to the party to be affected by it; or *constructive*, when certain acts are done in accordance with law, from which, on grounds of public policy, the party interested is presumed to have knowledge. It may be written, or oral, but written notice is preferable as avoiding all dispute as to its terms. **Notice, averment of,** in pleading, the statement that notice has been duly given. **Notice of dishonor,** the notice given to a drawer or indorser of a bill of exchange, or the indorsers of a promissory note, that the bill has not been accepted, or that an accepted bill, or note, has not been paid at maturity. Demand of payment at the proper time and prompt notice of dishonor are necessary to fix the liability of the drawer of a bill and prior indorsers on a bill or note. **Notice of protest,** the notice of dishonor given by a notary public, when he has made demand and protested a bill for non-acceptance or non-payment. **Notice to produce.** If any party to an action have in his possession any document which would be evidence for the other party if produced, the latter may give him notice to produce it at the trial, and, in default of production, may give secondary evidence of it. See also *Inspection; Production.* **Notice to quit,** a request from a landlord to his tenant to vacate the premises leased and give possession to the landlord at a time therein specified. It should be in writing, giving a sufficient description of the premises occupied, and should be served the required length of time before the tenant is desired to move out. When the tenancy was from year to year, six months notice was required at common law, but the matter of notice is regulated largely by custom and the statutes of the several states.

**Noting bills of exchange,** see *Note.*

**Notorious,** well known; such matters as do not require to be proved.

**Notour bankrupt** (Sc.), one who has been adjudged bankrupt.

**Novation,** the substitution of a new obligation for an old one which is thereby extinguished, *e.g.*, the acceptance of a note of a third party in payment of the original promisor's obligation, or the note of an individual in lieu of that of a firm.

**Novel disseisin,** the name of an old remedy for a fresh or recent disseisin. See *assize.*

**Novellae Constitutiones,** that part of the *Corpus Juris Civilis* (*q.v.*), which was published after the code was completed (A.D. 535—A.D 565).

**Noxal action,** (Rom.), an action for damage done by irrational animals.

**Nudum pactum,** *l.*, a *bare* contract, *i.e.*, one not under seal, and made without any consideration (*q.v.*), upon which no action will lie.

**Nul,** *fr.*, no, or none. **Nul tiel agard,** or **record;** no such award, or record; a plea to an action on an arbitration bond, or judgment, when the defendant denies that there was any lawful award or judgment rendered. **Nul tort,** a plea to a real action that the defendant did no wrong; a species of general issue. **Nul waste,** the general issue in an action of waste

**Nuisance,** something noxious, or offensive. Any thing not authorized by law which worketh hurt, inconvenience, or damage. It may be (*a*) *private*, as where one so uses his property as to damage another's, or disturb his quiet enjoyment of it; (*b*) *public*, or *common*, where the whole community is annoyed or inconvenienced by the offensive acts, as where one obstructs a highway, or carries on a trade that fills the air with noxious and offensive fumes.

**Nullus, nulla,** *l.*, no, or none. **Nulla bona** (*no goods*), a return made by a sheriff to a *fi. fa.*, or other writ commanding him to seize the goods of a person, when he finds no property to distrain upon **Nullius filius** (*a son of nobody*), a bastard.

**Nullity of marriage,** that state of facts with regard to a marriage which renders it void or voidable at the will of one of the parties from the beginning. Thus fraud, or duress, in bringing about the marriage, physical impotence existing in one of the parties, at the time of the marriage and incurable, and the prior subsisting marriage of one of the parties, are grounds for declaring a marriage a nullity In general a suit for nullity is prosecuted in the same court and governed by the same rules of procedure as a suit for divorce.

**Nunc pro tunc,** *l.*, a proceeding taken, judgment declared, etc., *now for then.* Where a proceeding, etc., has been delayed by the action of the court, or any like ground, the court may allow it to be dated as if it had taken place or been delivered on the earlier date.

**Nuncupative will,** one made by word-of-mouth before witnesses, and afterward reduced to writing.

**Nundinatio** (Rom.), trafficking at fairs (*nundinae*).

**Nunquam indebitatus,** *l.* See *Never indebted.*

**Nuper obit,** *l.*, (*he lately died*), an obsolete writ by one coparcener against another for recovery of land, on the death of their common ancestor.

**Nuptial,** pertaining to, or constituting, marriage.

**Nurture,** the care and education of children. The father generally has this right and duty, until the child is fourteen years of age, and is termed the guardian by nurture. In case of his death, or under special circumstances unfitting him to discharge the duties of guardian, the mother becomes the guardian by nurture.

## O.

**Oath,** a solemn affirmation, declaration, or promise made under a sense of responsibility to God for the truth of what is stated, or the faithful performance of what is undertaken. Formerly none but those who believed in a God who would punish the guilty and who took the oath were permitted to testify in a case; but by statute various forms of affirmation or solemn declaration are commonly allowed in lieu of oaths where the latter is not binding on the conscience of the individual, or the witness has conscientious scruples against making oath. Oaths are *judicial, i.e.*, made in the course of judicial proceedings, or *extra-judicial, i.e.*, voluntary or outside of judicial proceedings; *evidentiary*, relating to past facts; or *promissory*, relating to the future performance of acts or duties, *e.g.*, those of a judge, director, or other official. **Oath of calumny** (Rom. and Sc.), one taken by a party that he has a good cause of action and is not actuated by a spirit of malice or chicane. **Oath decisory** (Rom.), one which one of the parties to an action might ask to have tendered to the other when he has not affirmative evidence enough to substantiate his claim or defense, and wishes the case to be decided by what the other will say under oath. **Oath in litem,** one which a party, who under the common law was not a competent witness in his own behalf, might make when the other party had already been shown to be guilty of fraud and suppression of evidence so that no other evidence of the amount of damages could be had. **Oath purgatory,** one made by a party who is in contempt of court to facts which tend to excuse his default. **Oath suppletory** (Rom. and Eccl.), one which the judge may require from either party to a cause to enable him to decide a case in which half-proof has already been taken.

**Obiter dictum,** *l.*, (*a saying by the way*), an opinion of a judge, not necessary to the judgment given of record, and consequently of less authority.

**Objection,** a resistance on legal grounds, *e.g.*, to the admissibility of evidence.

**Oblation,** a tender of payment from a debtor to a creditor. (2) A customary offering to the clergy.

**Obligation,** that which binds a person; usually, to do or abstain from doing a certain act. A *perfect*, as distinguished from an imperfect, obligation is one which can be enforced by the law. (2) A bond. (3) The operative part of a bond.

**Obligor,** he who is bound by an obligation to an *obligee*.

**Obreption** (Sc.), the obtaining a gift of escheat by a false suggestion.

**Obscene,** indecent; tending to corrupt or deprave.

**Obvention,** revenue accruing from a thing; *e.g.*, an industry, or a spiritual living. See *Oblation*.

**Occupation,** actual possession, use, and enjoyment of land or houses. (2) Taking temporary possession of an enemy's country. (3) A trade, or business, which occupies a man's time or attention.

**Occupancy,** taking possession of those things which before did not belong to any body.

**Occupant,** one who has the actual use or possession of a thing; as a house, a room, a pew, etc.

**Of course,** that which may be done in legal proceedings

without asking leave of court, or which the court will grant, on application, without further inquiry.

**Offense,** an open violation of law; a crime or misdemeanor.

**Offer,** a proposition to do a thing which becomes an obligation, or contract, if unconditionally accepted by the person to whom it is made before it is withdrawn.

**Off-going crop.** See *Away-going.*

**Office,** a position or appointment entailing certain rights and duties. (2) The room or place in which an officer transacts public business, and keeps the papers, records, etc., committed to his care. **Office-copy,** a transcript of a record or proceedings filed in any office established by law, under the seal of such office. **Office-found,** the finding by a jury in an inquest of office (*q.v.*), of a fact which entitles the crown to possession.

**Official,** pertaining to a public charge or office (2) One who is attendant on a judge or magistrate. **Official use,** an active use, or trust, imposing a duty

**Officina justitiae,** *l.*, the workshop or business place of justice; a term formerly applied to chancery, in English law, because all writs issued from it, under the great seal, returnable into the courts of common law

**Officious** (of a word or phrase), having a meaning, as opposed to "meaningless." (2) Uncalled for. (3) *Will* (Rom.), one by which a testator leaves his property to his family, according to his *moral obligation.*

**Old style,** (O. S). See *New style.*

**Oleron, Laws of,** a maritime code, compiled during the 12th century, on which almost all subsequent ones are founded.

**Olograph,** an instrument entirely written by the party whose name is signed to it. See *Testament; Will.*

**Omission,** the neglect to perform what the law requires.

**Onerari non debet,** *l.*, (*he ought not to be burdened*), an old plea in an action of debt.

**Onerous,** burdensome; importing a valuable consideration, as opposed to *gratuitous.* A gift, lease, contract, etc., is said to be onerous when the liabilities it entails outweigh the benefits.

**Onerous cause,** (Sc.), a good and legal consideration.

**Onus probandi,** *l.*, the burden of proof (*q.v.*).

**Open,** *to commence, e.g., an account, or the trial of a case.* The right to open a case rests with him who has the affirmative of the issue, or against whom judgment must be rendered if no proof is offered. (2) To make public; as sealed depositions, verdicts, orders, etc (3) To vacate, or subject to re-examination; as judgments and rules of court, biddings, an account stated, etc. **Open account,** a running or unsettled account. **Open court,** as opposed to *chambers*, court held in a *public* place, to which all persons who conduct themselves properly have free access. **Open policy,** one in which the value of the subject insured is left to be ascertained, in case of loss.

**Operation of law,** a term applied to the manner in which a person acquires rights without any act of his own; as the heir's right to real estate left by a person who dies intestate.

**Operative,** a workman; one employed to perform labor for another, chiefly mechanical. **Operative part,** those clauses in a conveyance or other instrument which carry out the main object; especially the clause which contains the words of grant, etc.

**Opinion,** an inference, conclusion, or surmise, formed or entertained by a witness, as opposed to facts directly witnessed or perceived by him. As a rule, a man's opinions are not competent testimony in a case. See, however. *Expert.* (2) A judge's statement of the reasons for the judgment which the court pronounces. (3) An attorney's statement, usually in writing, of what the law is, in his judgment, as to a particular question, or state of facts, or proposed line of conduct, about which a client asks his advice.

**Oppression,** the abuse of his authority by a public officer, wantonly, or for private purposes. See *Extortion.*

**Option,** a power or right to choose, *e.g.*, whether one will buy or not, at or within a certain time, called an *option of purchase.*

**Optional writ,** one so called because it was in the alternative, commanding the defendant to do the thing required, or to show cause to the contrary.

**Oral,** delivered by word of mouth; verbal. See *Parol.* All pleadings were oral until the reign of Edward III.

**Orator,** or **Oratrix** (*one who prays*), a petitioner; plaintiff.

**Ordeal,** a method of criminal trial used by the Saxons, founded on superstition, and long abolished. It was of four kinds, by combat, by fire, by hot water, and by cold water. It was supposed that God would interfere and protect the innocent from the effects of the ordinary laws of nature.

**Order,** a mandate or direction by an individual, or by a judicial authority. A bill or cheque is said to be *drawn to order* when it authorizes the payee to transfer, by indorsement, the right to receive payment of it. *Orders* of a court of law, as distinguished from *judgments*, are (*q.v.*) directions made in summary or interlocutory proceedings.

**Ordinance,** a law; statute; decree. The term is generally applied to the laws of a municipal corporation. (2) In England, an act of Parliament which has not the sanction of all the three estates of the realm; *e.g.*, one passed during the Commonwealth.

**Ordinary,** a judge, especially a bishop, who has jurisdiction in his own right, and not by way of deputy within his province or diocese.

**Ordination,** the conferring of Holy Orders.

**Ore tenus,** *l.*, (*by word of mouth*). A demurrer *ore tenus* was an objection advanced for the first time on the argument of the demurrer, and not stated therein as a ground for demurring.

**Original,** first; primary as opposed to secondary; not derived from any other source, or authority, as original jurisdiction. (2) An authentic instrument, as distinguished from a copy. **Original bill,** the bill filed on the commencement of a suit in equity. **Original conveyance,** one by which a particular estate is created. **Original entry,** the first entry made by a merchant, or other person, in his account book, charging another with merchandise sold, or labor performed. **Original writ,** the mode of beginning all actions at common law. See *Writ.*

**Orphan,** a minor who has lost both his, or her, parents. The term is sometimes applied to an infant who has lost but one. **Orphan's Court,** a court in some of the states which has jurisdiction over the persons and estates of orphans.

**Ostensible,** apparent, or pretended. See *Nominal.* **Ostensible partner,** one whose name appears in a firm name, and is held liable as a partner, whether he is so or not.

**Ostium Ecclesiae.** See *Dower.*

**Oust; ouster,** to dispossess; dispossession. **Ouster le main,** *l. fr.*, to take out of the hand; a writ whereby an heir of lands held of the crown obtained possession of it, on attaining his majority. (2) See *Monstrans de droit.*

**Outer barrister,** see *Utter.*

**Outlawry,** the being put out of the protection of the law for wilfully avoiding the execution of the process of the courts. It was formally abolished by 42 & 43 Vict. c. 59, in civil proceedings, but specially retained in criminal proceedings. An outlaw is *civiliter mortuus,* and has, therefore, no rights of property, or other rights recognized by law. Outlawry is almost unknown in the United States.

**Outstanding,** *legal estate,* one vested in some person other than the one beneficially entitled to the property in question. (2) See *Term.*

**Over,** above; beyond. A gift or limitation *over* means, in conveyancing, one which is to come into existence on the determination of a preceding estate. **Overdraw,** to draw bills or checks upon a person, or bank, for a greater amount than one has on deposit, or is entitled to draw. **Overdue,** the condition of a note, or bill, after the time of payment has passed, without its being paid. If such an instrument is assigned or transferred the holder takes it subject to all the equities between the orignal parties and prior holders. **Overman,** (Sc.), an umpire chosen by arbitrators. **Overplus,** what is left beyond a certain amount; surplus. **Overrule,** to set aside the authority of a former decision.

**Owing,** unpaid; as a debt, whether due or not.

**Owner,** he who has the possession and control over a thing with the right to use it or dispose of it as he sees fit. The term is properly applied only to one who has *absolute* ownership, as distinguished from *special* ownership, or the right to possess and enjoy, which a bailee may have.

**Oyer** (*Law fr.*), to hear. **Oyer** of a deed, was the reading of it aloud in order that defendant might be made aware of its contents. **Oyer and terminer,** a commission directed to the judges and other gentlemen of the county to which it is issued, by virtue whereof they have power to *hear and determine* treasons, and all manner of felonies and trespasses. See *Assizes.*

**Oyez** (*hear ye,* usually pronounced *oh! yes!*), the introduction to any proclamation or advertisement made by public criers.

## P.

**Pactum,** (Rom.), an agreement. **Pactum constitutae pecuniae,** (Rom.), an agreement by a person to pay his creditor. **Pactum de quota litis,** (Rom.), an agreement by which a creditor promised to pay a portion of a debt difficult to recover, to a person who undertook to recover it.

**Pais,** or **pays,** *fr.*, the country. Matter *in pais* is matter of fact, as distinguished from matter of record. Estoppel in pais is an estoppel by words spoken or acts done, as distinguished from an estoppel by deed or record. *Trial per pais,* is a trial by the country, *i.e.*, a jury.

**Pandects,** the name of an abridgment or compilation of the civil law, made by Tribonian and others by order of the Emperor Justinian, which was promulgated A. D. 533.

**Panel** (a little part or page), the sheriff's list of persons summoned to act as jurors at a particular sittings, or for the trial of a particular action. (2) (Sc.), the person accused in a criminal court.

**Paper,** in legal phraseology, means a document, pleading, or exhibit. **Paper-book,** a book or paper containing an abstract of all the facts and pleadings necessary to the full understanding of a case. **Paper money,** the promissory notes of the government, which pass as money. **Paper office** (in the palace of Whitehall), an ancient office where all the public writings, matters of state and council, and generally all the papers and dispatches that pass through the offices of the Secretaries of State are deposited. (2) An office or room in the Court of Qneen's Bench, where the records belonging to that court were deposited.

**Par,** equal; bills of exchange, notes, stocks, and the like, are said to be *at par* when they will sell for their full value; *above*, or *below*, par when they will sell for more, or less, than their face value.

**Parage,** equality of blood or dignity: co-heirs are said to hold by parage.

**Paramount,** superior. *Lord Paramount*, is one of whom land is held by another, called the *mesne lord*, of whom again it is held by a third, called *tenant paravail*. The sovereign is universal lord paramount.

**Paraphernalia,** the personal ornaments of a married woman. They may unlike her separate property be disposed of by the husband during his life; not, however, by his will.

**Paravail.** See *Paramount.*

**Parcel,** a part or portion of land.

**Parcenary,** the tenure of lands by parceners or co-heirs. See *Coparcenary.*

**Parco fracto, De,** a writ for breaking pound (*q.v.*).

**Pardon,** the remission by the chief executive of a punishment, which a person convicted of crime has been sentenced to undergo.

**Parens patriae,** *l.*, father of his country. In England, the sovereign (*q.v.*).

**Parenticide,** one who murders a parent.

**Parents,** the lawful father and mother of a child. It is their duty to provide for their children while they are unable to provide for themselves, and it is their right to exact obedience and to receive their earnings until they are of age.

**Pares,** a person's peers or equals.

**Pari,** *l.*, (abl. of *par*), in, or with, equal. **Pari delicto,** in equal fault; guilty to the same extent. **Pari materia,** in the same matter; on the same subject. **Pari passu** (*with equal step*), equally; without preference.

**Parish,** the district committed to the charge of a parson, vicar, or other minister. (2) In Louisiana, a civil division; corresponding to the county in other states. **Parish officers,** church-wardens, overseers, and constables.

**Park,** in England, a place where wild animals of chase are kept, differing from a chase in being inclosed. In the United States, the term is applied to any public grounds kept for purposes of adornment and popular resort.

**Parliament,** the legislative branch of the government of Great Britain, consisting of the sovereigns and the three estates of the realm, viz., the lords spiritual, the lords temporal, and the commons. See *Houses.*

**Parol,** by word of mouth; not under seal. Pleadings when made *viva voce* were called the *parol;* and to pray that "the parol might demur," was to ask that the pleadings might be stayed until a certain date. See *Evidence.*

**Parricide,** or **patricide,** one who kills his father.

**Pars rationabilis,** *l.,* (*reasonable part*), that part of a man's goods which the law formerly gave to his wife and children at his death.

**Parson,** the minister of a parish, who has the care of souls, and, in England, full possession of all the rights of a parochial church.

**Part,** a share; less than the whole; *e.g., part payment, part performance,* etc. **Part owners,** those who own a thing together, or in common; *e.g.,* a vessel.

**Particeps criminis,** *l.,* a partner in crime.

**Particular average.** See *Average.* **Particular estate,** that interest which is granted or carved out of a larger estate, which then becomes an expectancy either in reversion or remainder (*q.v.*). See *Executory.* **Particular lien,** a right of detaining a chattel from the owner, until a certain claim upon it be satisfied. See *Lien.*

**Particularity,** in pleadings, is the allegation of details.

**Particulars.** See *Bill of particulars.*

**Partition,** the act of dividing. Where land belongs to two or more joint tenants, tenants in common, co-parceners, or the like, each of them is entitled to have partition made so that he may hold his share in severalty and have it distinguished from the rest. This may be effected either voluntarily by deeds of partition, if the parties are *sui juris,* or compulsorily by an action in the proper court.

**Partnership,** is the result of a contract whereby two or more persons agree to combine property or labor, or both, for the purpose of a common undertaking and the acquisition of a common profit. A partnership *prima facie* determines by the death or bankruptcy of any of the partners; but both this and other general rules applicable theretc are generally modified by *articles of partnership, i.e.,* an agreement entered into by the partners at the outset of their undertaking. A *partnership* *at will* is one, the duration of which is not fixed; it may be dissolved at any time by any partner. See *Dormant; Nominal;* and *Ostensible partners.*

**Part-owners,** or **Quasi-partners,** are joint owners, tenants in common, or co-parceners, who have a distinct, although an undivided interest in the property. None of them can dispose of the whole property or act for the others in relation thereto, as partners properly so called can do, but each can only deal with his individual interest; this, however, unlike a partner, he can do without the consent of the others.

**Party,** a person who takes part in a legal transaction, *e.g.*, an agreement or deed, or in a legal proceeding. Parties to an instrument are distinguished as being of the first part, second part, and so on: parties to a suit, as parties plaintiff, or parties defendant. **Party wall,** a wall erected on the line between two adjoining lots, belonging to different owners, for the use of both.

**Pass,** in sales and conveyancing, to transfer or to become transferred. (2) To decide upon or allow *e.g.*, an account, by the proper officer.

**Passage,** a right of way over water. Hence, a voyage, or the money paid for the transportation of a person over the sea.

**Passenger,** one who has taken a place in a public conveyance for the purpose of being transported from one place to another; or one who is so transported.

**Passive,** inactive; suffered, or permitted. **Passive debt,** a debt upon which no interest is payable, as distinguished from an *active* debt. **Passive trust,** a trust as to which the trustee has no active duty to perform. See *Bare trustee.* **Passive use,** a permissive use (*q.v.*).

**Passport,** a license for safe passage from one place to another. (2) A document furnished to persons traveling abroad, certifying their citizenship and designed to protect them from injury to their persons, property or liberty.

**Pasture,** the right of grazing cattle. (2) Land employed for grazing purposes.

**Patent,** a grant of some privilege, property, or authority, made by the government or sovereign of a country to one or more individuals. The term is applied chiefly to the title-deeds by which the government, state or national, conveys its lands and to *letters-patent*, granting to original inventors the exclusive right for seventeen years to manufacture, sell and use the inventions described therein. **Patent office,** a bureau of the Interior Department at Washington to which all applications for letters-patent must be made, and from which they issue when the office is satisfied of the novelty and utility of the invention. **Patent rolls,** registers in which letters-patent are recorded.

**Paterfamilias** (Rom.), one who is *sui juris* and the head of a family.

**Patria potestas** (Rom.), the power of a *paterfamilias* over his family.

**Patricide.** See *Parricide.*

**Patrimony,** an hereditary estate or right.

**Patron,** of a living, the owner of the advowson (*q.v.*).

**Pauper,** a person receiving poor-law relief.

**Pawn,** a bailment of goods by a debtor to his creditor, to be kept till the debt is discharged. It differs from a mortgage in that it passes only a special property in the thing pledged, and the right of the pledgee, as a rule, ceases if he has not possession of the pledge. **Pawnbroker,** one whose business it is to lend money on pledge.

**Payable,** that which ought to be paid, generally speaking, at once.

**Payee,** one to whom a promissory note, cheque, or bill of exchange is made payable.

**Payment,** the satisfaction of a debt, or obligation to pay money. It may be made in money, or any thing which is unconditionally accepted by the payee as a substitute therefor. A receipt is *prima facie,* but not conclusive, evidence of payment. *Part payment* makes it unnecessary within the statute of frauds to make a note in writing of a sale of goods; it also revives a debt so as to bar the operation of the statute of limitations. **Payment into court,** the deposit with the proper officer of a court of a sum of money, made by a party to a suit, (*a*) when he can not safely pay it to either of several persons claiming it, and desires them to interplead, and have the court determine which shall receive it; (*b*) when he desires to relieve himself from the responsibility of administering a fund in his hands as trustee for others; (*c*) when he admits the plaintiff's claim to the extent only of the amount paid in and disputes the rest. The general effect of such payment into court is to relieve the party paying from all liability for costs, unless a judgment is rendered against him for a larger amount than the sum so paid in.

**Peace,** public order; freedom from war, violence, or public disturbance. **Peace, bill of,** a former remedy against unnecessary litigation, adopted where a right had to be enforced by or against a number of persons. The courts of equity interfered in such a case by injunction to quiet the possession of the applicant. **Peace, Commission of the,** in England, a special commission under the great seal, appointing justices of the peace. It is one of the authorities by virtue of which the judges sit upon circuit. See *Justice of the Peace.*

**Peculiar,** in England, a particular parish or church that has jurisdiction within itself, and is exempt from that of the ordinary. **Peculiars, Court of,** a branch of, and annexed to, the Court of Arches.

**Pecuniary,** relating to money. **Pecuniary causes,** in the ecclesiastical courts, such as were brought to recover money damages for withholding ecclesiastical dues, or doing or neglecting some act connected with the Church. **Pecuniary legacy,** a testamentary gift of money

**Pedigree,** lineage, genealogy See *Hearsay.*

**Peer,** an equal. It is a maxim of English law that a man should be tried by his peers or equals. (2) A member of the House of Lords.

**Peine forte et dure,** *fr.*, the ancient method of forcing an accused person to plead, by putting him to the torture.

**Pelfe** or **Pelfre,** booty; ill-gotten gains. (2) The personal effects of a felon.

**Penal,** pertaining to or respecting punishment. **Penal action,** an action for statutory penalty **Penal bill,** the old name for a bond with a condition to do a certain act, or in default thereof pay a certain sum of money by way of penalty. **Penal irritancy** (Sc.), forfeiture by way of penalty **Penal laws** or **statutes,** those laws which prohibit an act, and impose a penalty for the commission of it.

**Penalty,** a sum of money reserved on an agreement, to be paid in case of the non-performance of such agreement, the legal operation of which is, not to create a forfeiture of that entire sum, but only to cover the actual damages occasioned by the breach of contract, *e.g.*, where the payment of a small sum is secured by an undertaking to pay a much larger sum in case of default, as in the case of a bond. See *Liquidated.* (2) A sum of money payable as compensation, or by way of punishment. See *Penal laws.*

**Penance,** an ecclesiastical punishment which affects the body of the penitent, inflicted by an ecclesiastical court for some spiritual offense.

**Pendente lite,** *l.*, while the suit is pending. See *Administration; Alimony.*

**Pension,** a stated allowance granted by the government to an individual, or his representatives, for services performed by him for the country.

**Pepper corn,** the berry or fruit of the pepper plant. Hence, any thing of insignificant value.

**Per,** *l.*, by; through; during. To come in, or to have

title, in the *per* was to claim as heir or assign *through* the person last entitled to an estate. **Per annum,** by the year. **Per auter vie,** during the life of another. **Per capita,** by the head, *i.e.*, by the number of individuals; opposed to *per stirpes*, by the number of families. See *Representation.* **Per contra,** on the other hand. **Per curiam,** by the court. **Per diem,** by the day. **Per fas et nefas,** by right or by wrong. **Per formam doni,** by the form of the gift, which regulates descent. **Per fraudem,** through fraud. **Per incuriam,** through want of care. **Per infortunium,** by misadventure. **Per minas,** by threats. **Per my et per tout,** by half and by whole. See *Joint.* **Per pais, Trial,** trial by the country, *i e.*, by jury. **Per quae Servitia** (*by which service*), a real action by the grantee on a fine of a manor or seigniory to compel the tenants to attorn to him. Abolished, 1833. **Per quod** (*whereby*), words introducing the allegation of special damages; *e.g.*, *per quod consortium,* or *servitium, amisit* (he lost the benefit of her society or services), in actions by a husband or master for injury to his wife, or seduction (*q.v.*) of his servant or daughter. **Per se,** by itself; alone. **Per stirpes,** see *Per capita.* **Per totam curiam,** by the full court. **Per verba de praesenti,—futuro,** by words of the present, *i.e.*, a declaration—future, *i.e.*, a promise; distinctions in the forms of marriage under Scotch law.

**Perambulation,** a walking of boundaries, performed by the sheriff, in pursuance of a writ, to settle disputed lines between adjoining land owners.

**Perception,** the taking possession of, as crops by harvesting, or money by counting it out and accepting it in payment of a debt.

**Perduellion,** treason.

**Perdurable,** lasting long, or for ever.

**Peremptory,** absolute; final admitting of no excuse for non-performance; *e.g.*, an order; mandamus. See *Challenge.*

**Perfect,** complete; used of contracts and obligations to distinguish those which can be enforced by law from *imperfect* ones which can not, and of trusts, to denote those which have been executed.

**Performance,** the act of doing something; especially something required by a contract or condition, which relieves one from all further liability thereunder. Performance, or part performance, of a parol contract will prevent the party receiving it from avoiding the contract, under the statute of frauds because it is not reduced to writing.

**Peril,** danger; risk; that which threatens or causes a loss, *e.g.*, of the subject of insurance. **Perils of the Sea,** an expression used in bills of lading to denote causes of loss or injury for which carriers will not hold themselves liable, and in policies of marine insurance to cover those risks for which the insurer is liable.

**Perjury,** a false statement under oath, or affirmation, willfully made in regard to a material matter, in judicial proceedings.

**Permissive,** suffered, or allowed; as **Permissive use,** one resorted to prior to the statute of uses, to evade the law of mortmain, forfeiture, and the like; and **Permissive waste,** the neglect to repair.

**Pernancy,** receipts of rents and profits; the person receiving was called a *pernor*.

**Perpetual injunction,** an injunction which finally disposes of the matter in dispute, and is indefinite in point of time.

**Perpetuating testimony,** the act of reducing to writing the testimony of a witness, to be used in a suit thereafter to be commenced, when by reason of age, or infirmity, or his going abroad, the testimony is likely to be lost. This is generally provided for by the statutes of the several states.

**Perpetuity,** is the tying-up or disposing of property so that it never becomes at the absolute disposal of any person or number of persons. This is contrary to public policy, hence the *rule against perpetuities*, generally adopted, which forbids any executory interest to come into being later than a life or lives in being and 21 years after allowing for gestation where it exists. Estates tail are an apparent exception. See also *Mortmain*.

**Person** or **Persona,** any body capable of having and becoming subject to rights; a human being, also called *natural* person. (2) An *artificial* person, or corporation (*q.v.*). **Persona designata,** *l.*, one described as an individual, as distinguished from one described merely as a member of a class.

**Personal,** appertaining to a person, or to the person. **Personal action,** one brought to recover personal property, or for damages for the breach of a contract, or injuries to person or property, as distinguished from *real actions* (*q.v.*). **Personal chattels,** things movable which may be attached to the person and carried about with him from one place to another; as distinguished from *chattels real* or interests in land. **Personal contract,** a contract relating to personal property. **Personal property,** the right or interest which a man has in things movable, or in any estate less than a freehold. The latter is termed an *impure*, or mixed, personalty **Personal representatives,** the executors, or administrators, of a deceased person. **Personal rights,** the rights of personal security, comprising those of life, limb, reputation, and liberty.

**Personation,** the offense of pretending to be another person, whether real or fictitious.

**Persuasion,** influencing another by request, entreaty, or representation When carried to such an extent as to deprive the person influenced of freedom of will, it is a ground for setting aside a will made in pursuance thereof

**Pertinent,** tending to prove or disprove the allegations of the parties.

**Petit.** See *Cape; Jury; Petty.*

**Petition,** a supplication made by an inferior to a superior, and especially to one having jurisdiction. The right to petition the government for a redress of grievances is secured to the people by the constitution of the United States. The written statement of the plaintiff's case in an action is commonly called a petition. **Petition of right,** in England, one of the methods of obtaining possession or restitution, from the crown, of either real or personal property. (2) The statute 3 Car. I c. 1, a parliamentary declaration of the liberties of the people, assented to by Charles I. in the beginning of his reign. Its chief provisions were the denial of any right in the crown to tax or to imprison arbitrarily.

**Petitory,** that which demands, or petitions. **Petitory action,** one in which the *title* to property is litigated, as distinguished from a *possessory* action, in which possession is sought. (2) In Scotland, an action in which damages are sought.

**Petty,** small; trifling; of little importance. **Petty-bag Office,** an office formerly belonging to the common-law jurisdiction of the court of chancery, and now transferred to the high court; so called, because the writs issued out of it and the returns were kept in a little sack or bag In it are transacted matters relating to solicitors, and out of it issue all original writs and certain commissions. **Petty constables,** inferior officers in every town and parish, subordinate to the high constable of the hundred. **Petty jury.** See *Jury.* **Petty larceny.** See *Larceny.* **Petty sergeantry,** is holding lands of the crown by the service of annually rendering some warlike weapon or implement. **Petty sessions,** sittings of one or two justices of the peace, who are empowered by statute to try in a summary way, and without jury, certain minor offenses **Petty treason,** treason of a domestic nature, as if a servant killed his master, or a wife her husband. In the United States, and, since 9 Geo. IV c. 31, in England, this is known and treated only as murder.

**Pew,** a seat in a church separated from others by a suitable inclosure, and with room for standing and kneeling conveniently. The owner is generally regarded as having an interest in the real property; but he can not maintain trespass, nor prevent the church authorities from tearing down and rebuilding.

**Picketing,** is the offense of posting persons outside a manufactory, or place of business, for the purpose of molesting or intimidating workmen engaged there.

**Pignus,** *l.*, a pledge, or pawn; the contract of pledge.

**Pillory,** a wooden frame with movable boards and holes, through which the head and hands of a criminal were put, to punish him. This mode of punishment has been generally abolished.

**Pilotage,** the compensation given a pilot for conducting a vessel into, or out of, port. (2) The office or employment of a pilot.

**Pin-money,** a yearly allowance, settled on a woman before marriage, to defray her personal expenses.

**Piracy,** the commission on the sea of such acts of robbery and violence as would amount on land to felony See *Capture.* (2) Infringement of copyright.

**Piscary,** the right of fishing in the waters of another.

**Placita Communia,** *l.*, the common pleas, *i.e.*, civil actions between man and man, as distinguished from *placita coronae*, or pleas of the crown, criminal actions in which the king is plaintiff. (2) The court where they were tried. (3) Penalties.

**Plaint,** the statement in writing of a cause of action, with which all actions in a county court begin, and upon which a summons is issued.

**Plaintiff,** one who brings an action.

**Plea,** the formal answer of a defendant to the plaintiff's declaration in an action. Pleas were (*a*) *dilatory*, *i.e.*, either to the jurisdiction, or in suspension of the action, or in abatement, by showing some formal defect in the indictment; (*b*) *peremptory*, *i.e.*, in bar of the action; *e.g.*, the pleas of not guilty and *autrefois acquit* (2) Any pleading in the ecclesiastical courts (3) A legal proceeding; hence (*a*) *pleas of the crown*, criminal prosecutions; (*b*) *common pleas*, civil causes.

**Plead,** to answer the opponent's plea in an action. (2) To make a plea, *e.g.*, of not guilty. (3) To argue a cause in court.

**Pleader,** one who draws pleadings.

**Pleadings,** the alternate and opposing statements of the parties to an action from the declaration, petition, or bill of complaint, until issue is joined. The regular common law pleadings were the *Declaration*, or *Count*, the *Plea*, *Replication*, *Rejoinder*, *Surrejoinder*, *Rebutter*, and *Surrebutter*. By the civil codes of procedure adopted in many of the states, the regular pleadings are now limited to the *Petition*, *Answer*, and *Reply*. In equity, the regular pleadings are the *Bill of Complaint*, *Plea*, or *Answer*, and *Replication*. Demurrers and motions are employed in both equity and common law practice, but are not regarded as belonging to pleadings in the strict sense of the term. If a party makes default in pleading, the statements made in the previous pleading of the opposite party are taken as admitted.

**Pledge,** a pawn, or thing delivered to another as security for payment of a debt, or performance of an obligation. (2) The transaction by which the pawn is given and the money obtained.

**Plena probatio** (Rom.), full proof, *i.e.*, by two witnesses.

**Plenarty,** a term signifying that a benefice is "full," *i.e.*, not vacant.

**Plenary,** full, conclusive. **Plenary suits,** are those in which the proceedings must be full and formal, as opposed to *summary*, in which the proceedings are brief and informal.

**Plene administravit,** *l.*, (*he has fully administered*), the defense of an executor or administrator when sued for a debt of his testator which he has no assets to satisfy; if he has assets, but insufficient, he pleads *plene administravit praeter*, *i.e.*, *except* what he specifies.

**Plight,** to pledge, as one's faith, or troth; not applied to goods and chattels. (2) The state or condition of a thing, as a will, or an estate.

**Plough-bote,** see *Bote; Estovers.*

**Plough-land,** see *Hide.*

**Plurality,** a greater number. A plurality of votes is a larger number of votes cast for one candidate than any other has received. It may be less than a majority, which is more than half of all votes cast.

**Pluries** (*often*), a writ that issues in the third instance, after the first and the *alias* have been ineffectual.

**Poaching,** unlawfully taking or destroying game.

**Pocket-Sheriff,** one appointed by the sole authority of the crown, not being one of the three nominated by the judges in the exchequer.

**Poinding,** (Sc.), the taking of goods, etc., in execution, or by way of distress. (2) The detention of cattle found trespassing. See *Pound.*

**Policy,** of a statute, is its object or intention; this is sometimes distinguished from the letter of it. (2) The instrument by which insurance is effected on the life, or property of an individual. **Public policy,** general interest.

**Poll,** the head, whence *poll-tax,* a capitation tax; to poll a jury, *i.e.*, to question them one by one as to their verdict; to poll, *i.e.*, to take votes, etc. (2) See *Deed-poll.*

**Pollicitatio,** (Rom.), a promise before it is accepted.

**Polyandry,** the state of a woman who has several husbands.

**Polygamy,** plurality of wives or husbands.

**Pone,** an obsolete writ to remove suits from an inferior court into the superior courts at Westminster. **Pone per vadium,** a writ to force a defendant to appear for trial, by exacting sureties from him. Obsolete.

**Pontage,** duty paid for crossing, or for repair of, a bridge.

**Popular action,** one brought by one of the public to recover some penalty given by statute to any one who chooses to sue for it. See *Qui tam.*

**Porrecting,** producing for examination, or taxation, as porrecting a bill of costs, by a proctor.

**Port,** a harbor, or place for taking in or discharging cargo, and especially one where customs are levied.

**Portion,** that part of a person's estate which is given or left to a child. It usually takes the form of a sum of money given to younger children on attaining twenty-one or marrying. See *Hotchpot; Satisfaction.* There are two ways of raising portions, one by sale or mortgage, the other by perception of profits.

**Positive,** actual; express; absolute; not doubtful; direct, as opposed to negative, *e.g.*, evidence. (2) Laid down; made by men; *e.g.*, *positive* law, as opposed to *natural* law.

**Posse,** a possibility. A thing is said to be *in posse* when it may possibly exist; *in esse* when it actually exists. **Posse comitatus,** the "power of a county," which includes all able-bodied men therein, above the age of fifteen, who may be called on by the sheriff to assist him in preserving the peace.

**Possessio** (Rom.), detention, which by means of *usucapio* (length of possession) became actual ownership. **Possessio fratris,** possession by a brother, or one in such privity with a person as to make it equivalent to his own possession.

**Possession,** the state of owning, or having a thing in one's own power or control with the intention of exercising ownership. It may be (*a*) *actual;* (*b*) *constructive,* or *in law,* *i.e.*, without actual personal occupation; (*c*) *apparent*, as where land descends to the heir of a disseisor; (*d*) *naked*, *i.e.*, without color of right. Possession must be adverse, *i.e*, inconsistent with the rights of the true owner, in order that a title may be gained by the person in possession, under the statute of limitations. Possession of stolen goods raises a presumption of larceny, against the holder. Possession may be without enjoyment, *e.g.*, that of a bailee. The maxim, "Possession is nine-tenths of the law," means that every claimant can only succeed by the strength of his own title, and therefore the weakness of his opponent's title avails him nothing if the latter is in possession. (2) Seisin (*q.v.*). (3) Occupation, *e.g.*, by a lessee. (4) The thing possessed. **Possession money**, a sheriff's officer's fee for keeping possession of property under a writ of execution. See *Poundage*.

**Possessory actions**, those relating to, or arising out of, the possession of land.

**Possibility**, a future event which may or may not happen. (2) An interest depending on the occurrence of an uncertain event.

**Post**, after; occurring in a book, it refers to a later page or line. *Action*, or *Writ of Entry, in the post*, a writ given by the statute of Marlbridge, 52 Hen. III. c. 30, in cases where the number of alienations or descents between the defendant and the original disseisor exceeded two. Abolished, 1883. **Post date**, to date an instrument as of a day later than the one on which it was made. **Post diem**, after the day. **Post-disseisin**, a writ for him who having recovered lands by *novel disseisin*, was again dispossessed by the former disseisor. **Post-entry**, a subsequent or additional entry of goods at a custom house to make up the original entry to the proper total. **Post-liminium**, after the threshhold or boundary; the restoration to its former owner of the right to property taken by an enemy, when immediately recaptured and brought back within the jurisdiction of the country from which it was taken. **Post litem motam.** See *Lis.* **Post-mortem** (*after death*), as a *post-mortem* examination. **Post-natus** (*born after*), the second son. (2) One born in Scotland after the accession of James I., and therefore not an alien in England. (3) One born after the separation of England and the United States. **Post notes**, bank notes payable at a distant period and not on demand. **Post-nuptial settlement**, one made after marriage (*q.v.*). **Post-obit bond**, a bond, conditioned to be void on the payment by the obligor of a sum of money, upon the death of another person from whom the obligor expects to inherit something. **Post-office,** an office for the receipt and delivery of mail.

**Postage,** the money charged by law for carrying letters, papers, etc., by mail.

**Postea,** was formerly a statement of the proceedings in a common law action, indorsed by the judge, before whom the trial was had, on the *nisi prius* record.

**Posterity,** all the descendants of a person in a direct line.

**Posthumous child,** a child born after its father's death; or taken out of the body of a dead mother.

**Postman,** a senior barrister in the old Court of Exchequer who had a right of precedence in motions. See *Tub-man.*

**Post master,** a government officer who keeps a post office, sells postage stamps and attends to the receipt, forwarding and delivery of letters, etc., passing through the mails issues and pays money orders, postal notes, etc. **Post master General,** the chief officer of the post office department of the United States. He is a member of the cabinet.

**Postremo-geniture,** the custom of Borough English (*q.v.*).

**Postulatio** (Rom.), the first act in a criminal proceeding.

**Potwallers,** or **Potwallopers** (*wallop*, to boil), persons who cooked their own food, *i.e.*, householders who, in some boroughs, were given a vote on this qualification.

**Pound,** an inclosure in which stray cattle, or those taken damage feasant, or as distress, are placed; it may be *overt, i.e.*, open to the sky, or *covert.* (2) A place where goods distrained are kept; if they are liable to damage from exposure, they must be placed in a pound covert. **Pound-breach,** breaking open a pound to take cattle; it is an indictable offense.

**Poundage,** the amount allowed the sheriff or other officer as commissions on the money made by virtue of an execution. It is regulated by the statutes of the several states.

**Pourparty,** to divide the lands which fall to parceners.

**Pourpresture,** any thing done to the nuisance or hurt of the queen's demesnes, or of a highway, etc., by inclosure or building. It is more usually called a common or public nuisance, but was originally an invasion of the rights of the crown.

**Poursuivant,** a king's messenger; those employed in martial causes were called *poursuivants-at-arms.* The four poursuivants in the herald's office are called *Rouge Croix, Blue Mantle, Rouge Dragon,* and *Portcullis.*

**Power,** an authority to act which one person gives to another. It may authorize the donee to do something on his own behalf, or to act for the donor either generally or in a particular matter. A power is said to be *naked* when the donee has no interest in the subject-matter; *coupled with an interest* when the donee has an interest in the subject-matter. The former may be revoked at the will of the donor; the latter, not without the consent of the donee. Powers may be conferred by written instruments called *powers of attorney*, which are revoked by the death of the donor, except where coupled with an interest, by deed, or by will. **Power of appointment,** an authority conferred by deed or will, to make a gift or distribution of property, or to dispose of an interest in real estate. It may be (*a*) *appendant*, *i.e.*, appurtenant, to be exercised out of the estate limited to the donee; (*b*) *in gross*, *i.e.*, to create an estate which will take effect upon the expiration of his own estate; (*c*) *collateral*, *i.e.*, with reference to an estate in which the donee takes no interest; (*d*) *general*, when the donee is at liberty to appoint to whom he pleases; (*e*) *special*, when he is restricted to a particular class, or particular individuals or objects.

**Practice,** that part of the law which regulates the conduct of legal proceedings. (2) The conduct of legal proceedings in the courts through all their various stages. **Practice court.** See *Bail court.*

**Praecipe** (*command*), a slip of paper upon which the particulars of a writ which a person wishes to have issued are written; it is lodged in the office out of which the required writ is to be issued. **Praecipe quod reddat,** an original writ, now abolished, commanding the defendant to do a certain thing, or show cause to the contrary. **Praecipe, tenant to the,** the person to whom a tenant in tail, seeking to bar the entail by a recovery with double voucher, granted a freehold estate in the lands in question. See *Recovery.*

**Praedial,** that which arises immediately from the ground, as grain, hay, fruit, herbs and the like. See *Tithes.*

**Praedium,** (Rom.), an estate; lands in the provinces. *Praedia volantia*, heavy articles of furniture which ranked as immovables. *Praedium dominans*, an estate to which a servitude is due; the ruling estate, as opposed to *praedium serviens.*

**Praemunire,** to forewarn; a word used in the writ to summon a person guilty of submitting to or maintaining the authority of a foreign power (notably that of the pope), in England, contrary to the so-called statutes of *praemunire*, of which that of 16 Ric. II. c. 5, was the chief. (2) The offense of maintaining papal authority in England. The punishment was forfeiture of property, and to be put out of the protection of the crown; but it is now obsolete.

**Praepositura,** (Sc.), the intrusting of a wife with authority to transact certain business on behalf of her husband, and to bind him by her contracts. A wife is impliedly *praeposita negotiis* for the purpose of managing her husband's household affairs.

**Praepositus,** an officer of a hundred. (2) The person from whom descent is to be traced.

**Prayer,** that part of a bill which asks for relief. It may be *general* asking for any relief the court is authorized to grant; or *special*, asking for a particular form of relief.

**Preamble,** introduction; preface. (2) The introduction of a legislative resolution or act, which sets forth its intent and the mischiefs to be remedied.

**Prebend,** a stipend granted to a prebendary in a cathedral church, in consideration of his officiating therein.

**Precarium,** (Rom.), a form of permissive use or occupancy, the duration of which depended on the owner's will. It was an *innominate contract.*

**Precatory words,** in a will, such as "desire," "hope," "trust," create an implied trust, unless the trust is one which the court is unable to enforce.

**Precedence,** the right to go before another.

**Precedent condition,** one which delays the vesting or enlargement of an estate, or right, until a specified event has happened.

**Precedents,** previous decisions of the court, which should always be followed in similar cases by courts of co-ordinate authority. (2) Forms of procedure which have been sanctioned by the courts or long usage, and are therefore to be followed.

**Precept,** a command given by a person in authority, or public officer to another, as by a judge to a sheriff, or by a bishop to an archdeacon. See *Induction.*

**Precinct,** a constable's district. (2) A minor political division of a city or town.

**Precognition** (Sc.), the heads or "proof" of the preliminary examination out of court of a witness.

**Pre-contract,** a prior contract to marry. This was formerly a canonical impediment to a marriage with any other person.

**Predecessor,** one who precedes another; the correlative to *successor*, as ancestor is to heir.

**Pre-emption,** the right to purchase property before or in preference to any other person; given by statute to settlers on the public lands. (2) In international law it is the right to buy at a fair price in time of war any materials, not being contraband of war (see *Confiscation*), entering the ports of the country exercising the right, and which would otherwise fall into the hands of the enemy.

**Preference,** any attempt by a person unable to pay his

debts, as they become due to favor one creditor at the expense of the others.

**Preferred stock,** that part of the capital stock of a company which, under its by-laws, has superiority as to payment of dividends up to a fixed amount, over the common stock.

**Pregnancy,** the state of a woman who is with child. See *Jury of Matrons; Ventre.*

**Prejudice,** a forejudgment, or bias, which interferes with a man's impartiality and sense of justice. Propositions for compromise and communications between opposing parties are often made "*without prejudice,*" so that if the negotiation fails, nothing that has passed in the course of it can be taken advantage of by the other party, or brought as evidence against the person making the offer

**Preliminary,** something which precedes, as *preliminaries of a treaty, i.e.,* the first sketch of a treaty which both parties are desirous to conclude. **Preliminary proof,** the sworn statement of a party, or his principal witnesses, as to the time and manner of a loss; usually required by insurance companies as a prerequisite to a demand for payment of the loss.

**Premeditation,** a design, or intention formed to commit a crime, or do an act, before it is done.

**Premises,** that which has been already stated. (2) Property already described in an instrument. (3) Houses or lands. (4) That part of a deed which precedes the *habendum.*

**Premium,** the consideration paid for the issuance or renewal of a policy of insurance. **Premium note,** a note given in whole or part payment of the premium due on a policy of insurance. **Premium pudicitiae,** the consideration which a man promises to pay for illicit cohabitation with a woman.

**Prender** or **Prendre,** see *Profit.*

**Prepense,** aforethought. See *Malice.*

**Prerogative,** the exceptional powers and privileges of the crown (*q.v.*); or of any high office. **Prerogative court,** an ecclesiastical court of each of the English archbishops, the appeal from which is to the privy council. The testamentary jurisdiction was transferred to the probate court in 1857. **Prerogative writs,** are those the issue of which is discretionary with the court, as opposed to *Writs of right,* so called. They are the writs of *procedendo, mandamus, prohibition, quo warranto, habeas corpus,* and *certiorari;* and are only granted on proper cause shown.

**Prescribe,** to lay down. *e.g.*, rules. (2) To claim by prescription.

**Prescription** (*Usucapio,* Rom.), the gaining of a right or title by lapse of time. It is either (*a*) *negative,* so called because the title given thereby arose originally from the real owner being barred of his remedy to recover the land in question; or (*b*) *positive*, which unlike (*a*), relates to incorporeal hereditaments, and originated at common law from immemorial, or long, usage only; it being presumed that there had originally been a grant which had in the interval been lost. Positive prescription only arises if the hereditaments have been enjoyed peaceably, without interruption, openly, and as of right (*nec vi, nec clam, nec precario*). The period of prescription was originally "time out of mind;" but is generally limited now to the time beyond which a man is prevented by the statutes of limitation from recovering his rights.

**Presentation,** of a bill of exchange, cheque, or note (also called *presentment*), is to tender it for acceptance, or payment, as the case may be. (2) Of a clergyman, is to offer him to the bishop for institution to a benefice. This is done by the owner of the advowson.

**Presentment,** the report by a grand jury of an offense brought to their notice; an inquisition of office.

**Presents, These,** is the term by which a deed refers to itself.

**President,** the title of the chief executive of the United States. (2) The presiding officer of a corporation, society, or deliberative body.

**Presumption,** a conclusion, or inference, of law, or fact drawn from the proved existence of some other fact. Presumptions may be either (*a*) *juris et de jure* (of law and by the principles of law), such as the presumption of incapacity in a minor to act, which are conclusive and irrebuttable; (*b*) *juris* (of law), which may be disproved, or "rebutted," by evidence; or (*c*) *judicis*, or *facti, i.e.*, presumptions of fact, drawn by a judge from the evidence.

**Presumptive,** that which may be inferred or presumed. A *presumptive title* is one which arises out of, or is presumed from, mere possession without claim of right.

**Pretensed,** pretended, or claimed; *e.g.*, right, or title.

**Preterition,** or **Praeteritio** (Rom.), the entire omission of a child's name in the father's will, which rendered it null; disherison (*exheredatio*) being allowed, but not preterition.

**Pretium affectionis,** *l.*, an imaginary, or "fancy," value set on a thing by one peculiarly desirous of possessing it.

**Prevarication,** collusion between an informer and a defendant, in order to a feigned prosecution. (2) Equivocation; deceitfully seeming to undertake a thing, with the purpose of defeating, or destroying, it. (3) Malversation, or misconduct, in a public office.

**Price,** the money consideration given for the purchase of a thing.

**Prima facie,** *l.*, at first view; on the first aspect. *Prima facie* evidence, presumptions, etc., are such as will prevail, if not rebutted, or disproved.

**Primae impressionis,** *l.* See *First impression.*

**Primage,** a customary duty paid by a merchant, or consignee, to the master and sailors of a ship or vessel.

**Primary,** first, or principal. **Primary evidence,** the best evidence of which the case in its nature is susceptible; original, as opposed to secondary, or derivative; used especially of documents.

**Primate,** an Archbishop (*q.v.*).

**Primer election,** first choice, used with reference to partitions. **Primer fine,** one paid formerly on suing out the writ of *praecipe.* **Primer seisin,** the right of the crown in feudal times to receive of the heir of a tenant *in capite,* who died seized of a king's fee, one, or a half, year's profits of the land.

**Primogeniture,** the right of the eldest born to succeed to the inheritance, to the exclusion of younger children. This rule of the feudal law has never prevailed in the United States, and, even in England, has given way to local customs to some extent. See *Gavelkind, Borough-English.*

**Principal,** the leading, or most important; the original; one from whom an *agent* derives his authority; one who is first responsible, and for whose fulfillment of an obligation a *surety* becomes bound; the chief, or actual, perpetrator of a crime, as distinguished from the *accessory,* who may assist him; the important part of an estate, as distinguished from *incidents,* or *accessories*; a sum of money loaned, as distinguished from the *interest* paid for its use.

**Principle,** a first truth, or proposition so clear that it is almost universally received. *Principles* are *recognized,* but not *established* by courts of law. (2) That which constitutes the essence of a matter, such as a new discovery, or invention.

**Priority,** a preference, or earlier right, used chiefly to denote the rights of creditors and lien-holders to be paid out of the assets of an insolvent estate in the order of securing their liens.

**Prisoner,** one held in confinement against his will, usually to answer for some crime with which he is charged, or as a punishment for crime of which he has been convicted. When unlawfully confined he may secure his release by writ of *habeas corpus* (*q.v.*).

**Private,** affecting, or belonging to, individuals, as distinct from the public generally; *e.g.*, private acts, private nuisances, etc

**Privateer,** a vessel owned by one, or more, private individuals, armed and equipped at his, or their, expense, for the purpose of carrying on maritime war under the authority of one of the belligerents. Privateering was abolished among European nations by the Declaration of Paris 1856.

**Privies,** persons who have an interest in a thing because of their peculiar relations to another. Thus, an heir is privy in blood to the ancestor; an executor, or administrator, privy in representation to the deceased; the lessee privy in estate to the lessor; a person having an interest derived from a contract to which he is not a party, is privy to one of the parties, etc.

**Privilege,** an exceptional right, or exemption. It is either (*a*) *personal*, attached to a person, or office; or (*b*) attached to a thing, sometimes called *real*. The exemption of embassadors and members of congress from arrest while going to, returning from, or attending to the discharge of their public duties, is an example of the first. (2) *Privileged communications*, or statements, *e.g.*, between counsel and client, are (*a*) those which a witness can not be compelled to disclose; (*b*) those which can not be made the ground of an action for defamation, or libel. (3) *Privileged debts* are those which an executor may pay in preference to all others, such as funeral expenses and servants' wages. **Privilege, writ of,** a process to enforce a privilege.

**Privilegium,** a law relating to, or directed against, a private person. (2) A privilege. (3) Property *propter privilegium*, a privilege of hunting and killing animals *ferae naturae*, to the exclusion of other persons.

**Privity,** participation in knowledge, or interest. Persons who so participate are called *privies* (*q.v.*) Privity in deed, *i.e.*, by consent of the parties, is opposed to privity in law, as in the cases of lord by escheat, and of tenant by curtesy.

**Privy Council,** the chief council of the crown, its members being nominated by the sovereign without patent, or grant. **Privy purse,** the income set apart for the private use of the sovereign. **Privy seal,** is one affixed to charters, patents, etc., signed by the sovereign, as an authority to the lord chancellor to affix the great seal (*q.v.*); and also to some documents of less consequence which do not pass the great seal. The *privy signet* is used by the sovereign on private letters, and on grants which pass his hand by bill signed.

**Prize,** a vessel, or goods, captured at sea from a public enemy in time of war, and which after condemnation becomes the property of the captors. **Prize court,** the tribunal which adjudicates upon cases of maritime captures made in time of war, and other matters connected with international law. In the United States the courts of admiralty discharge the duties of prize courts.

**Pro,** *l.*, for; as; on account of; according to. **Pro bono publico,** for the public, or general, good. **Pro confesso,** as confessed; a decree taken when the defendant in a suit fails to appear or make answer. **Pro falso clamore suo,** a nominal amercement of a plaintiff *for his false claim*, which used to be inserted in a judgment for the defendant. **Pro forma,** as a matter of form. **Pro hac vice,** for this occasion. **Pro indiviso** (*as undivided*), said of the possession of lands by joint or co-owners before partition. **Pro interesse suo,** according to his interest. **Pro rata (parte),** in proportion. **Pro re nata,** as the thing occurred; or, to meet the emergency. **Pro tanto,** for so much; to that extent. **Pro tempore,** for the time being.

**Probate,** the proof before an officer authorized by law that an instrument, offered as the last will and testament of a deceased person, is his last will and testament. When proved to the satisfaction of the officer, it is received, filed and recorded, and is then said to be admitted to probate. **Probate Court,** the name given in many states to the court which has jurisdiction in the matter of proving wills, appointing executors and administrators, and supervising the administration of estates. See *Surrogate.* **The Probate, Divorce, and Admiralty Division,** of the High Court, in England, exercises the jurisdiction formerly belonging to the Court of Probate, the Court for Divorce and Matrimonial Causes, and the High Court of Admiralty (*q.v.*). It consists of two judges, one of whom is called the president, and registrars.

**Probationer,** one who is upon trial.

**Procedendo** (scil, *ad judicium*), a prerogative writ addressed by a superior to an inferior court directing the latter to proceed forthwith to deliver judgment. (2) One remitting to an inferior court an action which has been removed on insufficient grounds to the superior court by *habeas corpus, certiorari,* or any like writ. These writs originally issued from the common law side of the court of chancery, which is now part of the high court.

**Procedure,** the mode in which the successive steps in a litigation are taken See *Practice*

**Process,** the means whereby a court enforces obedience to its orders. Process is termed (*a*) *original,* when it is founded on the original writ and intended to compel the appearance of the defendant; (*b*) *mesne*, when issued pending suit to secure the attendance of jurors, witnesses, etc.; and (*c*) *final*, when issued to enforce execution of a judgment. (2) In patent law, the art, or method, by which any particular result is produced, as the smelting of ores, the vulcanizing of india rubber, etc.

**Prochein,** next. **Prochein ami,** next friend (*q.v.*).

**Proclamation,** a public announcement made by authority of a chief executive, as the President, governor of a state, or mayor of a city. (2) The declaration of the cryer, made by authority of the court, of what is about to be done.

**Proctor,** a manager of another person's affairs. In the ecclesiastical and admiralty courts the proctors discharged duties similar to those of a solicitor; they no longer exist as a distinct body.

**Procuration,** agency; the act by which one person authorizes and *procures* another to act in his place; a letter of attorney. (2) Money which parish priests pay yearly to the bishop, or archdeacon, *ratione visitationis*. (3) A fee, or commission, taken by scriveners on effecting a loan.

**Procurator,** a proctor (*q.v.*); one who acts for another by virtue of a procuration. **Procurator Fiscal,** the public prosecutor in Scotland, who also takes the place of the coroner.

**Producent** (Eccl.), the person calling a witness.

**Profert,** *l.*, (*he produces*). A declaration on the record that a party alleging a deed in his pleadings produces it in court. In ancient times it was actually produced when the pleading was orally delivered, or filed; but in modern practice the formal declaration is treated as giving the court constructive possession of the instrument.

**Professional privilege,** that of a barrister, or solicitor, in communicating with clients. See *Privilege*.

**Proffer,** to offer, present, or propose.

**Profit,** gain; income of money, or land, in which latter sense it is generally used in the plural. Profits are said to *lie in prender* when they consist of a right in the lord to take something, and to lie *in render* when the tenant is bound to offer to pay them, as in the case of rent. By *gross profits* is frequently meant the difference between the price at which goods are sold and that paid on their purchase. By *net profits* is understood the real profit, or gain, ascertained by deducting from gross profits all expenses of handling, storing, selling, and delivery.

**Prohibition, Writ of,** which was formerly called *Inhibition*, issues out of a superior court to prevent an inferior court from taking cognizance of, or determining any matter out of, its jurisdiction.

**Prolicide,** the destruction of human offspring; it includes foeticide and infanticide.

**Prolixity,** a long and unnecessary statement of facts in a pleading or affidavit.

**Promise,** an engagement by a *promisor* to a *promisee* for the performance, or non-performance, of a particular thing. See *Consideration*

**Promissory note,** or **note of hand,** an unconditional promise in writing, made by one person to another, signed by the maker, engaging to pay on demand, or at a fixed, or determinable future time, a sum certain in money to, or to the order of, such other, or to bearer

**Promoter,** a common informer (obsolete). (2) The prosecutor of an ecclesiastical suit. (3) One who forms a company; he is usually the owner of a property. patent, etc., which he wishes the company to buy from him; he is in a fiduciary position toward the company when formed.

**Proof,** the establishing of the truth of an allegation by evidence (*q.v.*). (2) The evidence itself. The person alleging the affirmative generally has the necessity thrown on him of proving it; this is called the *onus probandi,* or burden of proof. To *shift* the *onus* is to adduce sufficient evidence to raise a presumption in one's favor, until rebutted by the opponent. (3) The affidavits made to support any claim, or statement of facts, which is doubted, or disputed, or of which a person acting in a representative capacity requires evidence under oath.

**Proper,** that which is one's own. (2) Genuine; suitable; correct.

**Property,** the right of ownership; this may be (*a*) *general,* or absolute; or (*b*) *special,* or qualified, as in the case of animals *ferae nuturae* (*q.v.*), or of a bailee for a special purpose. (2) The thing owned. In this sense it is (*a*) real or (*b*) personal. See those titles.

**Propinquity,** relationship; near kindred.

**Proposal,** a formal offer to do something.

**Propositus** (*the person proposed*), the person from whom a descent is to be traced. See *Praepositus.*

**Propria persona,** see *In Propria Persona.*

**Proprietary,** or **Proprietor,** one who has property in a thing; an owner. **Proprietary chapel,** one belonging to a private person.

**Proprietate probandi,** *l.*, a writ to a sheriff to try by inquest to whom certain property belonged previous to distress.

**Proprio vigore,** *l.*, by its own force.

**Propter,** *l.*, for; *on account of.* **Propter affectum,** on account of some bias, or affection. **Propter defectum,** on account of some defect, or incapacity. **Propter delictum,** on account of crime. All of these terms are used to denote grounds for challenging a jury, or jurors.

**Prorogation,** a putting off to another time, or postponement. The prorogation of Parliament never extends over 80 days, but it may be renewed from time to time by proclamation.

**Prosecutor,** one who brings an action against another in the name of the government. A *public prosecutor* is an officer appointed, or elected, to conduct all prosecutions in behalf of the government. A *private prosecutor* is one who, not holding office, prefers an accusation against another.

**Prospectus,** a document issued with a view to the formation of a company, setting forth the objects of the proposed undertaking, and inviting persons to subscribe for shares.

**Prostitute,** a woman who indiscriminately consorts with men for hire. Prostitution is generally regarded as a crime, and made punishable by law, and the keeper of a house for the purpose may be indicted for maintaining a common nuisance.

**Protector of the settlement,** the person without whose consent a tenant in tail can only cut off the entail so as to bar his own issue, not the remaindermen. He is either appointed by the settlor, or is the person entitled to the first estate for life, or for years; instituted by the Fines and Recoveries Act, 3 & 4 Wm. IV., c. 74. See *Base Fee.*

**Protest,** a solemn declaration of opinion, generally of dissent. (2) An express reservation whereby a person protects himself against the effects of any admission that might be implied from his act. Hence *appearance under protest*, which is made where a party intends to object to the jurisdiction, which he should do forthwith by motion to dismiss the action on that ground. (3) *Protest of a bill* is a declaration written by a notary (*q.v.*) upon a bill of exchange that he has demanded acceptance, or payment, of it and been refused, with the reasons (if any) for such refusal. It is only necessary in case of a foreign bill (*q.v.*). See *Acceptance; Dishonor.* (4) A document drawn up (or *extended*) by the master of a ship and formally attested, stating the circumstances under which damage has happened to the ship, or her cargo.

**Protestando, protestation,** a form of pleading, abolished in 1834, whereby a person protected himself against an admission, made by him in that form, being used against him in that, or another, action.

**Prothonotaries,** first, or principal, notaries; officers in the courts of exchequer and common pleas, who were superseded by the masters in 1837.

**Protocol,** the original draft, or record; especially of proceedings in an ecclesiastical cause. (2) (International law.) A record of preliminary negotiations.

**Province,** the district over which the jurisdiction of an archbishop extends. Hence *Provincial Courts*, the ecclesiastical courts of the two archbishops. (2) A territorial division, or colony, of a country. (3) Duty; power; responsibility; thus it is the province of the court to judge of the law, that of the jury to decide the facts.

**Provisional,** made, or existing, for a time, or until something further is done, as provisional orders, appointments, etc.

**Proviso,** (*it being provided*), a condition, or stipulation; *e.g.*, a proviso for redemption. See *Mortgage; Redemption.*

**Proxy,** a person appointed by another to represent him, usually at a meeting, *e.g*,, of a company, or of creditors. (2) The writing by which the appointment is made. (3) An annual payment by clergy to the bishop, etc., on visitation.

**Puberty,** the age of fourteen in males and twelve in females, at which they are deemed physically fit for and legally capable of contracting marriage.

**Public,** the whole body politic; or all of the citizens of a state or community. (2) That which affects, or is open or related to, all, as distinguished from private.

**Publication,** a making public. (2) Of a *libel*, bringing it to the knowledge, or notice, of a third person. (3) Of a *will;* its acknowledgment by the testator, in the presence of witnesses, as his last will.

**Publici juris,** *l.*, (*of public right*), a thing is said so to be when it is common property.

**Puffer,** (Sc., *white bonnet*), one who attends an auction by arrangement with the vendor for the purpose of bidding, and thereby raising the price. The employment of a puffer is a fraud upon the purchaser and renders the sale invalid at his option.

**Puis darrein continuance,** *fr.*, a plea introducing matter which has arisen or come, to the knowledge of the pleader, *since the last adjournment*, or after defendant had delivered his plea.

**Puisne,** (*L. fr.*), (*later born*). See *Mulier*. (2) Later in date, *e.g.*, an incumbrance. (3) Lower in rank, *e.g.*, justices of the Queen's Bench Division other than the Lord Chief Justice.

**Pur,** (*L. fr.*), by; for; during. **Pur, or per, autre vie.** See *Autre vie.*

**Purchaser,** one who acquires by buying. (2) One who acquires land otherwise than by descent.

**Purge,** to clear one's self of a criminal charge. (2) See *Contempt.*

**Purlieu,** land formerly added to an ancient forest by unlawful encroachment, and disafforested by the *Charta de Foresta.*

**Purparty,** a share. To make purparty is to divide and sever lands held in common by parceners.

**Purpresture.** See *Pourpresture.*

**Purview,** the body of a statute as distinguished from the preamble; the general scope, or object, of a statute.

**Putative,** supposed; reputed.

## Q.

**Qua,** in the character of; in virtue of being.

**Quacumque via (data),** *l.*, whichever way it is taken.

**Quadrennium utile,** *l.*, (Sc.), the term of four years allowed to a minor after attaining majority, during which he may bring an action to "reduce," or avoid, any deed granted to his prejudice during minority.

**Quae est eadem,** *l.*, (*which is the same*), a form of plea in actions of trespass and the like, traversing the time and place named in the declaration.

**Quaere,** *l.*, inquire; meaning that the question, or proposition, to which the word is appended is a doubtful one.

**Quaestus** (Rom.), that estate which a man has by acquisition, or purchase, in contradistinction to *haereditas*, which he has by descent.

**Quakers,** members of a religious society, more correctly denominated *Friends.* Their principles forbade them to bear arms, or to make oath. Affirmations were allowed in lieu of oaths chiefly on their account.

**Qualification,** that which makes a man fit, or eligible, for an office or position, or to exercise a franchise, such as voting. (2) A limitation; diminution.

**Qualified,** limited. See *Base fee; Property.* **Qualified indorsement,** one *sans recours, i.e.*, giving no right to resort to the indorser for payment.

**Quality,** the nature of an estate (*q.v.*), as regards the time of its commencement, or the certainty of its duration. (2) The state or condition of persons, or goods.

**Quamdiu se bene gesseret,** *l.*, as long as he shall conduct himself properly; *i.e.*, during good behavior.

**Quando acciderint,** *l.*, a judgment against an executor, or administrator, to be levied *when* assets come into his hands.

**Quantity,** that which is ascertained by weighing or measuring. (2) The duration of an estate (*q.v.*), or degree of an interest.

**Quantum,** *l.*, how much; as much as. **Quantum damnificatus,** an issue formerly sent out of chancery to be tried at common law, *how much* the plaintiff *was damaged.* **Quantum meruit** (*as much as he has earned*), a form of action brought by one party to a contract against the other, not founded on the contract itself, but on an implied promise to pay for so much as the party suing has done. If one party refuses to perform his part, the other may rescind and sue on a *quantum meruit.* **Quantum valebant** (*as much as they were worth*). Where goods have been supplied and no price mentioned (as by an innkeeper to a guest), or where they are not supplied as ordered, and are yet not returned, the person supplying them is said to sue on a *quantum valebant.*

**Quarantine,** in England, the period of forty days during which a widow is entitled to remain in her husband's dwelling house after his death. (2) Forty perches of land. (3) The period during which persons coming from a ship, or country, where an infectious disease is known to prevail, are isolated, or not allowed to land.

**Quare,** *l.*, wherefore; why. **Quare clausum fregit,** see *Trespass.* **Quare ejecit infra terminum** (*why ejected within the term*), a writ against one who ejected another during the currency of a term created by the former. **Quare impedit** (*why he obstructs*), an action which lies to recover a right of presentation to which another has asserted a claim, or to oblige a bishop to admit the person presented, or to establish title to an advowson. **Quare obstruxit** (*why he obstructed*), a writ which lay for one obstructed in his right to pass over defendant's land.

**Quarter-days,** Lady-day, March 25th; Midsummer-day, June 24th; Michaelmas-day, September 29th; and Christmas-day, December 25th.

**Quarter-sessions, General,** in England, a court of record held once every quarter by two, or more, justices of the peace, for the finding of indictments by the grand jury, the trial of such minor offenses as the court has jurisdiction over, and the hearing of appeals from petty and special sessions in such matters as rating and licensing.

**Quash,** to annul or discharge, *e.g.*, an indictment, a conviction, or order.

**Quasi,** *l.*, as if; almost. **Quasi contract,** one which arises without express agreement between the parties; an implied contract. **Quasi-delict, offense,** or **tort,** the wrong for which a person is responsible, though it is not committed by himself; *e.g.*, a master is liable for any thing done by a servant in the course of his employment. **Quasi-deposit,** a species of bailment resulting from the finding or accidental possession of another's property. **Quasi-entail,** is where an estate *pur autre vie* is limited to a man and the heirs of his body. **Quasi-personalty,** things which are personalty in the eye of the law, though appertaining to things real; *e.g.*, emblements, fixtures, or chattels-real. **Quasi-possession,** enjoyment of a right, as opposed to possession of a thing. **Quasi-realty,** things which in contemplation of law, appertain to, and pass as, realty, though in themselves they are personalty; *e.g.*, heir-looms and title deeds, etc. **Quasi-trustee,** a person who reaps a benefit from a breach of trust, and so becomes answerable to the *cestui que trust.*

**Que estate,** *l.*, (*whose estate*), a term employed by a person claiming a right by prescription because enjoyed by those *whose estate* he holds.

**Queen's counsel,** barristers who, on account of superior standing, or ability, are appointed counsel to the crown and called within the bar. They take precedence of the junior bar. A queen's counsel may only be employed against the crown (*e.g.*, in defending a prisoner) by special license, but this is not refused unless the crown desires to retain him.

**Querela,** *l.*, complaint; an action. See *Audita querela; Duplex querela.*

**Querens,** or **querent,** a plaintiff; complainant.

**Question,** an interrogatory. (2) An issue to be decided by a court of law. It may be (*a*) *of law*, or (*b*) *of fact.*

**Qui tam,** *l.*, (*who as well*), a "popular" action on a penal statute, which is partly at the suit of the queen, or state, and partly at that of an informer. See *Common Informer.*

**Quia,** *l.*, (*because*). **Quia emptores** (*because purchasers*), the Statute 18 Edw. I. c. 1, also called of Westminster the Third, which began with those words. It was passed to prevent subinfeudation, by enacting that upon any future alienation of land the feoffee should hold the same direct of the chief lord and not of his feoffor. In the opinion of some, it first created the right of alienation as against the lord of the fee. See *Manor.* **Quia timet** (*because he fears*), a bill which was filed to protect property from apprehended future injury.

**Quid pro quo,** *l.*, (*something for something*), a consideration.

**Quiet enjoyment,** the name of a covenant in a lease by

which the lessor warrants that the lessee shall not be disturbed in his possession. It does not amount to a warranty of title.

**Quietus,** freed, or acquitted. The word used in the exchequer to signify the discharge given to an accountant to the crown; *e.g.*, a sheriff.

**Quint-exact,** or **Quinto exactus,** a person called or summoned to appear *for the fifth* and last *time* before he was declared an outlaw.

**Quit-claim,** to release a claim, or right of action.

**Quit-rent** (*quietus reditus*), or *fee farm rent*, one payable by a tenant to the lord of the manor, and so called because it was originally a payment in lieu of services.

**Quittance,** an acquittance, or release.

**Quo animo,** *l.*, (*with what mind*), the intent. **Quo jure,** a writ which lay to force a claimant to right of common to show his title. **Quo minus,** a writ (abolished, 1832) whereby the Court of Exchequer obtained jurisdiction in personal actions; the plaintiff alleging that in consequence of the injury done him by the defendant, he was *less able* to pay a debt due by him to the crown. This could only be true of an accountant to the crown; but by a fiction the allegation was allowed in all personal actions in that court. **Quo warranto** (*by what authority*), a writ, or proceeding, by which the government inquires into the right of a person, or corporation, to hold an office, or exercise a franchise, which was never lawfully held, or which has been forfeited by neglect or abuse.

**Quoad,** as far as. **Quoad hoc,** as to this. **Quoad ultra,** as to the rest.

**Quod,** *l.*, that. **Quod computet,** an interlocutory judgment, or decree, *that* the defendant *account*. **Quod ei deforceat,** a writ (abolished, 1833) for him who had lost possession by default of appearance in a possessory action. **Quod permittat,** a writ (abolished, 1833) against a person who built a house on his own ground so as to be a nuisance. **Quod recuperet** (*that he do recover the debt, or damages*), a final judgment for a plaintiff in a personal action.

**Quorum,** the minimum number, *e.g.*, of directors or legislators, necessary to be present in order to constitute a formal meeting capable of transacting business.

**Quot,** one twentieth part of the movable estate of a person dying in Scotland, anciently due to the bishop of the diocese.

**Quousque,** *l.*, (*until*), temporary. Used as a word of limitation in old conveyances, and in the old writ of *capias ad satisfaciendum.*

# R.

**Rack-rent,** rent calculated on the footing that no fine, or premium, shall be taken; hence, one which is very high, representing nearly the full annual value of the property.

**Rape,** a division of a county. (2) The act of having carnal knowledge of a woman by force and against her will.

**Rasure,** see *Erasure.*

**Rate,** a public valuation or assessment of a man's estate for purposes of taxation. (2) *Rate of exchange,* the price at which a bill drawn in one country upon a person resident in another may be sold in the latter.

**Ratification,** the act of adopting, or confirming, a thing done, or contract made, by another, without authority, or by the person himself, at a time when he was legally incompetent. See *Infant.*

**Ratio decidendi,** *l.,* the *reason for the decision,* in a cause, or matter

**Rationabili parte,** *l.,* an old writ of right for lands, etc.

**Rationes,** the pleadings in a suit.

**Ravished,** the technical term used in an indictment for rape.

**Ravishment,** the taking away of a wife from her husband, or a ward from his guardian.

**Real,** appertaining to land, as opposed to *personal.* See *Chattels.* **Real action,** one brought for the specific recovery of lands, tenements, and hereditaments. **Real contract,** a contract respecting real property. **Real covenant,** a covenant, or obligation, in a conveyance of real estate, by which the grantor binds himself and his heirs to do, or to refrain from doing, something with reference to the estate conveyed. **Real estate, Real property,** or **Realty,** landed property, including all estates and interests in lands which are held for life (*not* for years, however many), or for some greater estate, and whether such lands be of freehold, or copyhold, tenure. **Real right** (Sc.), a right of property in a thing (*jus in re*), entitling the owner to an action for possession, as opposed to a right against a person, or personal right. **Real things,** things substantial, and immovable, and the rights and profits annexed to, or issuing out of, them. **Real warrandice** (Sc.), an infeoffment of one tenant given in security of another.

**Re-attachment,** a second attachment of one who has been already attached and dismissed.

**Rebate,** discount; deduction from a payment, in consideration of its being made before it falls due.

**Rebut,** to disprove; answer. See *Presumption.* (2) To repel, or bar, a claim.

**Rebutter,** the answer of a defendant to a plaintiff's surrejoinder. See *Pleadings.*

**Rebutting evidence,** that which is given by one party in a cause, to explain, or disprove, evidence produced by the other party

**Recaption,** or reprisal, a remedy open to one who has been deprived of his goods, wife, child, or servant, by another; he may *re-take* them provided he do so without a breach of the peace, and not in a riotous manner.

**Recapture,** the recovery by force of property captured by the enemy. See *Postliminium.*

**Receipt,** an acknowledgment in writing of having received a sum of money, or other article. While it is presumptive evidence that the person signing it has received the money or articles described therein, it is not conclusive; and the party may show, if such was the fact, that it was obtained by fraud, or through mistake.

**Receiver,** a person appointed, usually by an order of court, to receive the rents and profits of property, where it is desirable that these should come into the hands of a responsible and impartial person; *e.g.*, in actions for dissolution of partnership, in foreclosure of railroad mortgages, etc. He is, when appointed by the court, its officer, and is required, as a rule, to give security, for the due performance of his duties, and is responsible for good faith and reasonable diligence. **Receiver of stolen goods,** one who receives any goods knowing them to have been feloniously stolen, extorted, etc.

**Recession,** a re-grant.

**Reciprocal contract,** one by which the parties enter into mutual engagements, such as partnership, sale, etc.

**Reciprocity,** mutuality (*q.v.*); a term specially applied to treaty dealings between states.

**Recital,** the rehearsal, or making mention, in an instrument of something which has been done before. Recitals lead up to and explain the operative part, and are either *introductory* or *narrative.* Recitals in a deed are binding upon the party making them, and his privies.

**Reclaim,** to demand again; to claim anew, or repossess something which has been temporarily yielded to another. (2) To put waste or wild lands, or lands injured by incursions of rivers or the sea, in a cultivated and fruitful condition.

**Reclaimed animals,** those that are made tame by art, industry, or education, whereby a qualified property may be acquired in them. See *Animals.*

**Recognisance,** an obligation, or acknowledgment, of a debt enrolled in a court of law, with a condition to be void on the performance of a thing stipulated; *e.g.*, to appear before the proper court to answer charges, to keep the peace, or to pay the debt, interest and costs that the plaintiff may recover.

**Recognition,** an acknowledgment, express or implied, that an act done for one by another was done by authority of the former.

**Recognitors,** the jury impaneled in an assize of novel disseisin, etc.

**Reconventio** (Rom.), a counter-claim or cross action.

**Reconversion,** is the return, in contemplation of law, of property, which has been constructively converted, to its original condition. See *Conversion*.

**Reconveyance,** takes place where a mortgagee, on being paid off, conveys the mortgaged property back to the mortgagor.

**Record,** a written memorial, enrolled as an authentic testimony of the acts of the legislature, or of a court. (2) The copy of a deed, or other instrument relating to real estate made and preserved in a public office for the information of others dealing with reference to such real estate. **Record, courts of,** those in which a full and final record is made of all judicial acts and proceedings in suits brought in them. **Record, debts of,** those which appear to be due by the evidence of a court of record; such as judgments. **Record, trial by.** If a record be asserted on one side to exist, and the opposite party deny its existence, this is an issue of *nul tiel* record; and the court awards a trial by inspection of the record. Upon this, the party affirming its existence is bound to produce it in court on a given day; failing to do so, judgment is given for his adversary.

**Recordari facias loquelam,** *l.*, an original writ, in the nature of a *certiorari*, issuing out of chancery, addressed to a sheriff to remove a cause depending in an inferior court not of record to a superior court. Obsolete.

**Recorder,** the name of a county officer who has charge of the records of deeds and instruments relating to real estate, and other legal instruments required by law to be recorded. (2) A judicial officer of some cities, *e.g.*, the city of London, having the power and authority of a judge, whose duty it is to assist the mayor and other magistrates in legal matters.

**Recoupment,** the right of the defendant to set up a claim for damages against the plaintiff in the same action, because of his violation of some obligation growing out of the contract on which he sues, or for some failure of consideration.

**Recourse,** the right to look back to the payee, or previous indorser, of a note for the amount thereof, in case it is not paid by the maker. See *Indorsement.*

**Recovery,** the obtaining a thing by judgment or trial. It may be *true* (see, *e.g., Ejectment; Real action*) or *feigned.* Of the latter class were the fictitious actions called *common* and *double recovery,* resorted to, in fraud of the Statute *De donis,* for the purpose, *inter alia,* of barring estates tail.

**Rectification,** the correction of an instrument so as to make it express the true intention of the parties. See *Mistake.* (2) The ascertainment of boundaries.

**Recto, Breve de,** writ of right. See *Writ.*

**Rectus in curia,** *l.,* one against whom no accusation is made. (2) An outlaw who has reversed his outlawry.

**Recuperatores,** (Rom.), judges to whom the praetor referred a question of law.

**Recusants,** (Eng.), persons who absented themselves from their parish church, and refused to conform to the established religion.

**Reddendo singula singulis,** *l.,* (*by applying each term to its correlative*). This is a rule of construction; as in the sentence, "If any one shall draw, or load, a sword or gun."

**Reddendum,** the clause in a lease reserving rent. It usually begins with the words, "yielding and paying."

**Re-demise,** a re-granting of land demised or leased.

**Redemption,** literally a buying back; the paying off a loan, upon which a conveyance of real estate by mortgage, as security, becomes void and will not take effect as a deed. See *Equity of redemption.*

**Red-handed,** with the marks of crime fresh on him.

**Redhibitio,** (Rom.), an action allowed to a buyer, by which to annul the sale of some movable, and oblige the seller to take it back again, on the ground of deceit, etc.

**Reditus albi** (*white rents*), rents paid in silver. **Reditus nigri** (*black rents*), rents paid in grain, or base money. (2) Black-mail.

**Reductio ad absurdum,** *l.,* the method of disproving an argument by showing that it leads to an absurd consequence.

**Reduction,** (Sc.), an action for the purpose of *reducing,* or setting aside as null and void, some deed, will, etc. **Reduction—improbation,** (Sc.), an action for reduction where fraud, or forgery, is alleged. **Reduction into possession,** is the act of converting a chose in action into a chose in possession, *e.g.,* by obtaining pay.

**Re-entry,** the act of resuming possession of lands, or tenements, in pursuance of a right reserved by the owner on parting with the possession. Leases usually contain a clause providing that the lessor may terminate the lease, and re-enter on non-payment of rent, or breach of any of the covenants by the lessee.

**Reeve,** an officer of justice appointed to execute process, make arrests, keep the peace, etc. There were several kinds of reeves, as the shire-reeve, or sheriff, the tithing-reeve, and the borough-reeve.

**Re-examination,** a second examination; one that follows and relates to the cross-examination.

**Re-exchange,** the difference in the value of a bill (including damages), caused by its being dishonored in a foreign country in which it is payable; this depends on the rate of exchange between the two countries.

**Re-extent,** a second extent for the same debt.

**Referee,** one to whom any thing is referred for arbitration, inquiry and report, or trial.

**Reference,** the submission of a matter in question to a referee (*q.v.*); this may be either by consent, or by order of reference. (2) The proceedings before a referee. (3) *Reference in case of need.* The drawer, or indorser, of a bill of exchange may add the name of a person to whom it may be presented *in case of need*, *i,e.*, if dishonored by any person liable to pay it.

**Reform,** of an instrument. See *Rectification.*

**Regalia,** the royal rights of a sovereign, viz., power of judicature, of life and death, of war and peace, ownership of masterless goods (see *Waifs; Wreck*), assessments and minting of money.

**Regardant,** *fr.*, vigilant. **Villein regardant,** one attached to a manor to perform the base services. (2) Appendant.

**Regicide,** the killing of a king, or queen. (2) One who kills a king or queen.

**Regio assensu,** *l.*, a writ whereby the sovereign gives his assent to the election of a bishop.

**Register,** a book in which facts of a public, or quasi public, character, such as marriages, births, or deaths, are recorded by public authority.

**Registrar,** or **Registrary,** an officer whose business is to keep a public register. (2) A functionary in several of the courts, whose duties, generally speaking, resemble those of a master or chief clerk (*q. v.*). **Registrar-General,** an officer in England to whom the general superintendence of the whole system of registration of births, deaths, and marriages is intrusted.

**Re-grant,** a second grant of real estate, which, after having been previously granted, had come back into the hands of the former owner, by escheat, etc.

**Regrate,** see *Engross.*

**Regress,** a going back; re-entry.

**Regular clergy,** or **Regulars,** monks who live by the *rules* of their respective societies.

**Re-hearing,** a second trial of a cause after judgment has been pronounced. A second consideration and hearing of argument in a court of appeal, or error, when the court is in doubt as to the correctness of the decision rendered.

**Re-insurance,** insurance effected by an underwriter in another company to protect himself against some, or all, of the risks he has assumed by the original insurance.

**Re-issuable notes,** bank notes, or those which may be re-issued after payment.

**Rejoinder,** see *Pleadings.*

**Relation,** a carrying back. When an act is done, or an order, or adjudication made at one time, and it operates upon the subject matter as if done at an earlier date, it is said to do so by relation. Thus, a deed delivered to a third party in escrow, and by him to the grantee upon the performance by the latter of some condition, is said to relate back to the time of the first delivery. So letters of administration relate back to the death of the intestate. (2) See *Relator.* (3) See *Kin.*

**Relator,** the person who furnishes the information on which an information (*q.v.*), or a proceeding in *quo warranto,* is based. Such proceedings are usually in the name of the attorney-general *ex relatione* of the relator.

**Release,** the giving up, or surrender of a claim or right of action. It may be to the person against whom the claim exists, or the right may be enforced, which operates as a discharge of the claim, or extinguishment of the right; or, as in the case of release of an interest in real estate, it may be to another who has some interest already in the real estate, when it operates as a conveyance. See *Lease* and *Release.*

**Releasee,** he to whom a release is made by a *releasor.*

**Relegation,** temporary exile, or banishment, which does not produce civil death. See *Abjuration.*

**Relevancy,** is the degree of connection between a fact tendered in evidence and the issue to be proved. An irrelevant fact is one which has no applicability to the issue joined, and is therefore inadmissible in evidence.

**Relicta confessione,** *l.,* a confession of judgment by *cognovit actionem,* after a plea has been put in and withdrawn.

**Relief,** legal remedy for wrongs. (2) A payment which

the tenant made to the lord on coming into possession of, or taking up (*relevare*), an estate. (3) See *Forfeiture*.

**Relinquishment,** a forsaking, or abandonment of, a count in a declaration, or the whole, or part, of one's claim.

**Relocation** (Sc.), a renewal of a lease; *tacit relocation* is permitting a tenant to hold over without any new agreement.

**Rem, action in,** see *Action*. By proceedings *in rem* the property in relation to which the claim is made, or the proceeds of such property in court, can be made available to answer the claim, and be proceeded against. **Rem, judgment in,** a judgment which gives to the successful party possession of some definite thing.

**Remainder,** that expectant portion or residue of interest in lands, or tenements which, on the creation of a particular estate, is at the same time limited over to another, who is to enjoy it after the determination of such particular estate. A *contingent* remainder is one which is limited to take effect on an event, or condition, which may not happen, or be performed. A *vested* remainder is one by which a present interest passes to the party, but the right of possession is postponed until after the determination of the particular estate. See *Perpetuity*.

**Remainder-man,** a person entitled to a remainder.

**Remand,** to re-commit a person to prison. (2) To send back a cause to the same court out of which it came, for trial, or some further action on it there.

**Remanet,** the name given to a cause, the trial of which has been postponed from one sitting to another.

**Remedy,** the legal means to recover a right, or redress a wrong.

**Remission,** a release of a debt, or fine. (2) Pardon of an offense, or crime.

**Remit,** see *Remand; Remission*.

**Remitter.** Where he who has a title to lands, but is out of possession, obtains possession under some other, and, of course, defective title, he is remitted by operation of law to his ancient and better title; and is held to be *in* by virtue thereof.

**Remittitur damnum** (*the damage is remitted*), an entry on the record by a plaintiff, who either is given by the jury greater damages than he has declared for, or is willing to give up some part, that he releases such excess, or portion.

**Remoteness,** distance; want of connection between a wrong and the resulting injury sufficiently close to entitle the party injured to claim compensation from the wrong-doer.

**Render,** see *Profit*.

**Renewal,** a change of something new for something old.

(2) An extension of the term of a lease, or the time of payment of a note.

**Renounce,** to give up a right. An executor who declines to prove his testator's will is said to "renounce probate."

**Rent,** a periodical payment (usually made in money, but which may be in kind, or in service), due by a tenant of land, or other corporeal hereditament, to his landlord. Payment of it operates as an acknowledgment of tenure. At common law, three kinds of rent were recognized: *rent-service*, so called because some corporeal service was, in theory at least, to be performed as an incident to the tenure; *rent-charge*, rent reserved with a clause authorizing its collection by distress; and *rent-seck*, which was collectible only by an action at law, in case of non-payment. These distinctions have long since been abolished by statute in England, and most of the states. A *pepper-corn-rent* is one purely nominal, and stipulated for merely as an acknowledgment of tenure. See *Ground-rent; Fee-farm-rent; Quit-rent; Rack-rent.*

**Repatriation,** recovery of the rights of a natural born subject by one who has expatriated himself, or become a statutory alien.

**Repeal,** to annul, or set aside, a law by a legislative act. Repeals may be *express*, *i.e.*, declared by direct language in the new act, or *implied*, *i.e.*, when the new law contains provisions contrary to, or irreconcilable with, those of the former law. By the common law, when a statute repeals another, and the repealing statute is itself repealed, the former statute is revived, but in many of the states this rule has been abolished.

**Repleader** (*to plead again*). Motion for a repleader used to be made where the pleadings failed to raise a definite issue.

**Replegiare,** *l.*, see *Replevin.*

**Replevin,** a form of action which lies to recover possession of specific chattels which have been taken from the plaintiff unlawfully. It may be brought by a general owner, who has the right to immediate possession, or by one who has a special property and possession at the time the goods are taken.

**Replication,** the plaintiff's answer to the defendant's plea or answer

**Reports,** collections of cases judicially argued and determined. See *Appendix A.*

**Representation,** a statement made by either of the parties to a contract (*e.g.*, of insurance), to induce the other to enter into it. See *Misrepresentation.* (2) The legal standing of one who acts for, or in place of, another, or succeeds to his rights and duties; *e.g.*, an agent, executor, devisee, or heir, who is said to *represent* respectively, the principal, testator, or ancestor.

**Representative,** one who represents, or acts for, another; usually applied to one who is elected as a member of congress, or of some legislative body, from a particular district.

**Reprieve,** to suspend the execution of a sentence for a time.

**Reprisal,** the taking one thing in satisfaction for another. *Reprisals* are resorted to between nation and nation, when no other means of obtaining redress is open. Reprisals may be made by embargo (*q.v.*), or by the issuing of *Letters of Marque* (*q.v.*)

**Republication,** a second execution of a will, or a new ratification of it, as by a codicil, after cancellation or revocation.

**Repugnant,** that which is contrary to, or inconsistent with, something else. In a deed the first, in a will the second, of two inconsistent gifts, etc., prevails. A repugnant condition is void.

**Reputation,** the opinion generally entertained of a man's character, or condition, by those who know him, or his family. See *Hearsay; Libel.*

**Request,** a demand, or notice of a desire on the part of one of the parties to a contract that the other shall perform his part.

**Requisition,** a formal demand for something which one has a right to receive by virtue of a contract, or of some office. (2) The demand made by the governor of one state on the governor of another for the return of a fugitive from justice.

**Res,** *l.*, a thing, or things. **Res communes,** things which can not be appropriated to the exclusive use of an individual, as light, air, running water, etc. **Res gestae,** all the *things done,* including words spoken, in the course of a transaction. **Res integra,** a subject, or point, not yet decided. **Res judicata,** a point already judicially decided; it is conclusive until the judgment is reversed. **Res mancipi,** (Rom.), things which could be sold. **Res nullius,** a thing which has no owner.

**Re-sale,** a second sale of the same thing by the same person.

**Rescission,** the rescinding, or putting an end to, a contract by the parties, or one of them, *e.g.*, on the ground of fraud.

**Rescissory action,** (Sc.), one to rescind, or annul, a deed, or contract.

**Rescue,** or **Rescous,** the act of forcibly taking out of the hand of the law a person, or thing; *e.g.*, a prisoner, or distress.

**Reservation,** in a grant, the withholding of something, or stipulation for the return to the grantor of something, (*e.g.* rent), out of the thing granted.

**Reset of theft,** (Sc.) receiving of stolen goods.

**Resiance,** residence.

**Residence,** place of abode, or of carrying on business. It is of importance with reference to the law of domicile (*q.v.*), and to the founding of the court's jurisdiction.

**Residuary,** relating to the residue, or that which is left after certain portions, or interests, are disposed of. **Residuary clause,** that clause of a will which disposes of all the property remaining after previous bequests and devises are satisfied. The person who takes surplus real estate under such a clause is called a *residuary devisee;* and one who takes the surplus of the personal estate is called a *residuary legatee.*

**Resignation,** the act of declining to serve longer in an office, and renouncing its rights and privileges.

**Resolution,** the expression of opinion by a legislative, or popular, assembly. (2) The annulling of a contract by consent of the parties, or by the decision of a competent tribunal.

**Resolutive clause,** (Sc.), one in a deed annulling it on the commission of any specified acts.

**Resort, Court of last,** one from which there is no appeal.

**Respite,** a temporary suspension of the execution of a sentence. (2) The grant of additional time, by creditors to a debtor, within which to pay his debts.

**Respondeat ouster**, *l.*, (*let him answer* or *plead, over*), a form of judgment given where a defendant, or criminal, failed in substantiating a dilatory plea, so that the case had to be gone into on the merits.

**Respondent,** the party who makes answer to a bill in chancery. (2) One who is security for another; a *fide jussor* (*q.v.*).

**Respondentia,** a loan of money on maritime interest on goods laden on a vessel, with the understanding that if the goods are lost the money shall not be repaid. It differs from bottomry (*q.v.*), in being an hypothecation of the cargo only.

**Responsa prudentum,** *l.*, the opinions and decisions of learned lawyers, which formed part of the Roman laws.

**Rest.** See *Account.*

**Restitutio in integrum,** *l.*, the rescinding of a contract, or transaction, on the ground of fraud, etc., so as to *restore* the parties *to their original position.*

**Restitution,** a restoring of property or a right to one who has been deprived of it. *Writ of restitution,* the means by which a successful appellant may recover any thing which he has been deprived of under the prior judgment. **Restitution of con-**

**jugal rights.** In England, whenever a husband, or wife, is found guilty of the injury of *substraction;* that is, of living separate from the other, without any sufficient reason, the court will compel the respondent to resume cohabitation, on petition brought by the other party for restitution of conjugal rights. **Restitution of minors,** (Sc.), the restoring them to rights lost by deeds executed during their minority.

**Restraining order,** an injunction. **Restraining statute,** one which narrows and restricts the operation of the common law.

**Restraint of marriage.** On grounds of public policy, conditions attached to a gift to a person who has never been married, in *general* restraint of marriage, are void. This does not apply to conditions against second marriage, or marriage with a particular person. **Restraint of trade.** Contracts prohibiting a person from carrying on a particular trade are void, unless limited either as to time or area.

**Restrictive indorsement,** one prohibiting, or limiting, the further negotiation of a bill of exchange, cheques, etc.

**Resulting trust,** or **use,** one that arises from the operation or construction of equity, where the legal estate is transferred, and no trust or use is expressly declared, nor any consideration, or evidence of intent, appears to direct the trust or use, which then *results* or comes back to the original grantor.

**Retainer,** the engagement of a solicitor by a client, or of counsel by a solicitor, to give his professional services either *generally,* or in some particular proceeding. (2) The document containing such engagement. (3) *Retainer by an executor,* or administrator, is his right to pay his own debt out of the assets of his testator in priority to all other debts of equal degree.

**Retorno habendo,** *l.,* a writ to compel a party to return property to the party to whom it is adjudged to belong, in an action of replevin.

**Retorsion,** retaliation by one sovereign state against another.

**Retract,** to withdraw, *e.g.,* a damaging statement, or a proposition, before it has been accepted.

**Retraxit,** an obsolete proceeding analogous to a *nolle prosequi (q.v.),* except that it barred any future action.

**Return,** a report by an officer of the manner in which he has executed a writ. **Return-day,** the day named in the writ, or fixed by law, when the officer must report his action thereunder.

**Reus,** *l.,* (Rom.), a party to a suit.

**Reverse,** to set aside a judgment, on appeal or proceedings in error.

**Reversion,** that portion left of an estate after a grant of a particular portion of it has been made to another person by the owner or *reversioner; e.g.*, on the creation of a term of years out of a fee there is a right of *reverter* in the grantor, so that the fee *returns* to him on the determination of the term.

**Reversionary interest,** that which is to be enjoyed at a future time, after the determination of an intermediate estate. **Reversionary lease,** one to take effect *in futuro.* (2) A second lease to commence after the expiration of a former lease.

**Reverter.** See *Reversion.*

**Review,** a second examination of a matter, or hearing of a suit. See *Bill of review.*

**Revive,** to resuscitate a right of action, *e.g.*, for a debt barred by the statute of limitations, by acknowledging it; or for a matrimonial offense once condoned, by committing another. (2) To restore to its original force a judgment, which has become dormant owing to lapse of time, change of parties, etc.

**Revocation,** the recalling, or withdrawing, of a grant, *e.g.*, of a gift by will, an agency, etc. See *Power of attorney.* (2) The making void of a deed, will, or other instrument. A will may be revoked (*a*) by another will; (*b*) by burning or other act done with the intention of revoking, (*c*) by the disposition of the property during the testator's lifetime; (*d*) by marriage.

**Rien,** *fr.*, nothing. **Rien en arrere,** a plea that there is nothing remaining due in an action for rent, or an action of replevin to recover goods distrained. **Rien passe per le fait,** nothing passed by the deed; a plea used, where the execution of a deed can not be denied, to test its validity.

**Right,** a well founded claim; the correlative of obligation. It may be (*a*) personal, or public; (*b*) primary, or secondary; (*c*) *in rem* or *in personam*; (*d*) *absolute* as that of an owner, or *qualified* as that of an agent, or bailee. See *Jus.* **Right of Action,** a claim which one may enforce by suit. It was formerly opposed to a *right of entry*, which may be either *original*, or reserved by deed, *e.g.*, by a lease, for breach of covenant. **Right to begin.** The person on whom lies the affirmative of the issue has in general the right to begin, *i.e.*, to be the first to address the court.

**Riot,** a tumultuous disturbance of the peace by three, or more, persons assembled of their own authority

**Riparian owner,** one who has rights to, or connected with, the banks of a river.

**Risk,** the danger insured against; in a life policy, death;

in a fire policy, fire; in a marine policy, perils of the sea. See *Insurance.*

**Robbery,** is theft from the person accompanied by violence, or threats, putting in fear

**Roe, Richard,** the fictitious defendant in ejectment (*q.v.*)

**Rolling stock,** the engines and cars of a railway company employed in the transportation of passengers and goods.

**Rolls,** a record entered on a long strip of parchment which can be rolled up; hence, any records of a court, or office. **Rolls Court.** See *Master of the rolls.*

**Root,** in a figurative sense, used to signify the person from whom one or more others are descended. See *Purchaser; Title.*

**Roup** (Sc.), auction.

**Rout,** is a lesser form of a riot (*q.v.*).

**Royal fish,** whale and sturgeon; so called because they belong to the king of England when washed ashore, or caught near the coast.

**Royalty,** payment to a patentee, author, composer, etc., for the right to make, sell, or use patented articles, books, plays, music, etc. (2) Payment to the owner of mines, etc., varying according to the amount actually gotten.

**Rule,** an order made by a court, or other competent authority. (2) A general principle well recognized and established. **Rules of court,** may be either *general,* regulating practice in the court, or *special,* applying to a particular individual or case, of which it has jurisdiction. An award of arbitrators is said to be made a *Rule of court* when, in pursuance of statutes passed for that purpose, steps are taken to give it the force and effect of a judgment.

**Run,** to pass by; to take effect. The statute of limitations is said to run against a claim when the time has passed by within which it can be enforced by an action at law **Run with the land,** see *Covenant.*

## S.

**Sacrilege,** breaking into, or out of, a church, accompanied by the commission of a felony therein.

**Said,** a term used to designate with certainty the person *before mentioned* in a deed, contract, or pleading.

**Sale,** a transfer of the absolute, or general, property in a thing for a price in money. See *Bargain; Bill of sale.* **Sale note,** see *Bought and sold notes.*

**Salic,** or **Salique law,** an ancient law of the kingdom of France, in virtue of which males only can reign.

**Salvage,** compensation made to those (called *salvors*) by whose skill and exertions ships, or goods, are saved from imminent peril. **Salvage loss,** in marine insurance, the loss sustained by the necessary sale of goods at a port short of the port of destination, in consequence of perils by the sea. It is treated as total, and the amount realized from the sale of the goods is credited on the amount payable under the policy.

**Sample,** a small quantity of any substance, or merchandise, exhibited as a fair specimen of the whole. When a sale is made by sample, the bulk must correspond substantially with the sample, or the buyer may refuse to accept it, or, in some states and under certain circumstances, may accept and use it and recover damages for the inferiority of the article furnished.

**Sanction,** of a law, is the power of enforcing it, or inflicting a penalty for its violation. (2) Consent.

**Sans,** *fr.*, without. **Sans nombre,** without number; used with reference to a right to pasture animals on a common when the number is not definitely fixed. **Sans recours,** without recourse. See *Indorsement.*

**Satisfaction,** compensation for an injury. (2) Payment of money owing. *Entry of satisfaction* is made when a judgment has been satisfied by payment or execution, or the money has been paid for which a mortgage was given as security. The latter is usually made on the margin of the record of the mortgage.

**Scandal,** a libelous statement or action. (2) In pleading, matter which is indecent, charges which are irrelevant, and the like. All such, the court has power to strike out.

**Scandalum magnatum,** *l.*, words spoken in derogation of a peer, or judge, or other great officer of the realm. They formerly constituted a special offense.

**Scienter** (*knowingly; willfully*), an allegation in the pleading that the defendant, etc., did the thing in question willfully.

**Scilicet,** you may understand; to wit; that is to say. A word introducing an explanatory sentence in a pleading, or something which needs to be supplied in order to a full understanding of a phrase.

**Scintilla juris et tituli,** *l.*, (*a spark, or fragment, of law and title*), a legal fiction formerly resorted to for the purpose of enabling feoffees to uses, to support contingent and shifting uses when they come into existence.

**Scire facias** (*cause to know*), a judicial writ, founded upon some record, and requiring the person against whom it is brought to show cause why the party bringing it should not have advantage of such record, or why the record should not be annulled and vacated. It is deemed an action, and the defendant can plead to it; but in some cases it is an original writ, in others it is rather a writ of execution. See *Patent.* **Scire feci,** the sheriff's return on a *scire facias,* that he has given notice to the party against whom it was issued.

**Scrip certificate,** or **scrip,** is an acknowledgment by a company that the holder of the scrip is entitled to a specified number of shares, etc., therein.

**Script,** the original or principal document; as distinguished from a duplicate or copy.

**Scrivener,** one who draws contracts, or places money out at interest, for his clients, receiving a commission.

**Scroll,** a mark made with a pen, intended to take the place of a seal.

**Scutage,** escuage (*q.v.*)

**Seal,** an impression upon wax, paper, or other substance capable of being impressed in order to authenticate the document to which it is attached. (2) The metal die, or other instrument, with which the impression is made. See *Scroll.*

**Search,** an examination of a man's house, premises, or person, for the purpose of discovering proof of his guilt in relation to some crime, or misdemeanor, of which he is accused. It can properly be made only by an officer duly authorized by a *search-warrant* issued by a justice, or other competent authority, specifying the place where search is to be made, and in as particular terms as the case will admit of the things to be looked for. **Search, Right of,** is that which men-of-war have in time of war, in order to ascertain whether the ship searched, or her cargo, is liable to seizure. See *Contraband.*

**Seaworthiness,** the sufficiency of a vessel in materials, construction, equipment, officers, men and outfit, for the voyage, or service, in which it is employed. It is an implied condition of all policies of marine insurance, unless otherwise expressly stipulated, that the vessel shall be seaworthy.

**Seck,** see *Rent.*

**Second deliverance,** a second writ which was allowed to a plaintiff in replevin (*q.v.*) who was non-suited; practically obsolete. See *Non-suit.*

**Secret trust,** a gift by a testator upon a trust not committed to writing.

**Secta,** (*followers*) the witnesses of a plaintiff whom he produced in court immediately on making his declaration under the ancient form of proceeding. Hence the word *suit,* applied to an action.

**Section,** a division of an act, or book, less than a chapter, and greater than a clause. (2) A sub-division of a township (*q.v.*) under United States survey, one mile square, and containing six hundred and forty acres.

**Security,** that which renders certain the performance of a contract, as the personal obligation of another, or the pledge, or mortgage of property belonging to the obligor. (2) A surety, or guarantor.

**Secus,** *l.*, (*otherwise*), to the contrary effect.

**Sedition,** the raising of commotions and disturbances in the state, and stirring up ill-will against the lawful authorities.

**Seduction,** the offense of a man in inducing a woman to have unlawful sexual intercourse with him.

**Seignory,** the relation of a feudal lord to his tenants. (2) A manor (*q.v.*), or lordship.

**Seisin,** feudal possession, as distinct from mere possession, or occupation. A person was "seized in deed" when actual possession was taken; "seized in law," *e.g.*, by descent, before taking possession. The doctrine of seisin is no longer of importance.

**Seizure,** the act of taking possession of property for a violation of a public law, or by virtue of an execution.

**Self-defense,** the protection of one's person and property from injury. A man may defend himself when attacked, repel force by force, and even commit homicide in resisting an attempted felony, such as murder, rape, robbery, burglary, and the like.

**Semble,** *fr.*, (*it seems*), used in reports to show that a point is not decided directly, but may be inferred.

**Semper paratus,** *l.*, a plea that the defendant has been *always ready* to perform what is demanded of him.

**Senate,** the name of the less numerous of the two bodies constituting the Congress of the United States, or the legislature of one of the states. A member of this body is called a *senator*.

**Senatus consultum,** *l.*, a decision of the Roman Senate, which had the force of law.

**Senility,** extreme age, or its effects on the mind.

**Sentence,** judgment in an ecclesiastical, or criminal, proceeding.

**Separate estate,** is property belonging to a married woman for her separate use, independently of her husband and his debts.

**Separation,** the living apart of husband and wife, in pursuance of a mutual agreement. The agreement is set aside by subsequent cohabitation. An agreement for *future* separation is invalid. See *Judicial*.

**Sequestration,** a prerogative process in the nature of a

continuing execution, addressed to certain commissioners, empowering them to take the rents and personal estate of a person in contempt for disobedience of a decree, or order, and to keep the same until the defendant clear his contempt.

**Sergeants-at-arms,** officers appointed by legislative bodies to carry out their orders. **Sergeants-at-law,** or **of the coif,** barristers of superior degree, in England, who formerly (till 1846) enjoyed a monopoly of audience in the Court of Common Pleas.

**Sergeanty,** service due the crown for lands held of it. See *Grand; Petty.*

**Seriatim,** *l.*, severally and in order.

**Service,** the duty which a tenant owes his lord by reason of his estate. *Free* service was opposed to *base*, or *villien*, service, the former consisting (*e.g.*) in payment of rent, the latter (*e.g.*) in plowing the lord's land. With the exception of rents, few services now remain except in manors (*q.v.*), and in respect of copyhold land. See *Feud.* (2) The relationship of servant to master. (3) The formal mode of bringing a judicial proceeding to the notice of the person affected by it.

**Servient tenement.** See *Easement.*

**Sessions,** sittings of courts, legislative bodies, etc., for the transaction of business. See *County; Petty; Special; Quarter.*

**Set.** A drawer frequently gives to the payee several parts, called a *set*, of the same bill (*q.v.*) of exchange, any one of which being paid, the others are void. This is to obviate possible inconveniences from loss, or miscarriage.

**Set-off,** a cross or counter-claim. A counter-claim had originally to be made by cross-action, in which the defendant in the first action was plaintiff; but by 2 Geo. II. c. 22, which has been generally adopted in the United States, it was allowed to raise a set-off as a defense in certain cases of mutual debts, which did not include a claim founded in damages, or in the nature of a penalty.

**Settled land,** land limited *by way of succession* to a person other than the one for the time being entitled to the beneficial enjoyment thereof, who is called a limited (*q.v.*) owner.

**Settlement,** a deed, will, or other instrument whereby land is *settled* (see *Settled land*). The principal kinds of settlements are (*a*) marriage, or ante-nuptial, (*b*) post-nuptial, and (*c*) family settlements, also called re-settlements. (*a*) is founded on the consideration (*q.v.*) of the marriage, and is binding on the settlor; but (*b*) is voluntary, and may be avoided by the settlor by selling, or mortgaging, the settled property. (2) A mutual accounting, by which the parties come to an agreement as to what is due from one to the other; payment in full. (3)

Residence in a place under such circumstances as to entitle one to public support, or relief in case of becoming a pauper. See *Act of Settlement.*

**Sever,** to divide. A joint tenancy is *severed* when one joint tenant conveys his share to a stranger. (2) To remove growing crops, fixtures, etc. (3) Defendants are said to sever in their defenses when they plead independently.

**Several,** distinct; separate; as opposed to joint (*q.v.*). Thus, a *several covenant* is one by two or more separately, each binding himself for the whole.

**Severalty.** Persons are said to hold lands, or tenements, in severalty who are sole owners of ascertained shares therein.

**Share,** a portion of any thing; in a company, a certain portion of the capital entitling the *shareholder* to a proportionate part of the surplus profits, otherwise called a dividend. A fully paid share is one on which the whole nominal amount has been "called up" or paid.

**Shelley's case, Rule in.** When a person takes an estate of freehold by any gift, or conveyance, and in the same instrument an estate is limited, either mediately or immediately, to his heirs, or the heirs of his body, the word *heirs* is treated as a word of limitation and not of purchase, so that he takes a fee-simple, or an estate tail, as the case may be. In many states the rule in Shelley's case has been abrogated by statute.

**Sheriff,** (*shire-reeve*), the chief executive officer of a county. It is his duty to keep the peace, make arrests, execute the processes of the courts, and perform such other duties as may be prescribed by law. Formerly he had a judicial authority in the *Sheriff's tourn* (or court), and the county court, and this still survives in Scotland.

**Shifting use.** See *Use.*

**Ship's husband,** a person appointed by the owners of a ship to manage on shore all matters connected with the employment thereof, such as repairs and affreightment. He is the general agent of the owners in relation to the ship, and usually, though not necessarily, a part owner. **Ship's papers,** documents required to prove the ownership of a ship and her cargo. They include her certificate of registry charter party, passport, and bill of health.

**Shire,** a geographical division of the country, like our county. **Shire-gemot,** the Saxon county court. **Shire-reeve,** a sheriff.

**Sign-manual,** the signature of the sovereign; any one's name written by himself.

**Signature,** the name, or mark, (see *Marksman*) of a person subscribed (or printed) by himself, or by his direction.

**Similiter,** *l.*, (*in like manner*), a term used to designate the joinder of issue, by the parties to a suit.

**Simony,** (Eccl. law), the offense of buying, or selling, holy orders, or an ecclesiastical benefice.

**Simple,** plain; unconditional; not under seal, nor of record; not combined with any thing else. See *Contract; Debt; Larceny.* **Simple trust,** a vesting of property in one person for the use of another, the nature of the trust not being further declared by the settlor.

**Sine,** *l.*, without. **Sine die,** without day, *i.e.*, indefinitely. **Sine prole,** without issue.

**Sinecure,** a rectory *without care of souls.* (2) An office which has revenue without any employment.

**Sister,** a woman who has the same father and mother with another, or has one of them only. In the latter case, she is called a half-sister.

**Skilled witnesses,** witnesses who are allowed to give evidence on matters of opinion and abstract fact. See *Expert.*

**Slander,** the malicious defamation of a person in his reputation, profession, or business, by words. To impute a criminal offense, or misconduct in business, is a slander actionable without proof of special damage; but in any case proof of special damage arising from the false and malicious statements of another is a sufficient ground of action. Slander of title is only actionable on such proof being given. See *Malice; Libel.*

**Smart-money,** damages awarded beyond the actual damage, in cases of gross misconduct on the part of the defendant, by way of punishment and example.

**Smuggling,** the offense of importing, or exporting, prohibited articles, or of defrauding the revenue by importing, or exporting, goods without paying duty on them.

**Soc,** jurisdiction. (2) Privilege. (3) A shire or territory.

**Socage,** tenure by any certain, or determinate, service. It was (*a*) *free*, or (*b*) *villein socage*, according as the service (*q.v.*) was free or base. All forms of socage, except *common socage*, which is the modern freehold tenure, were abolished by 12 Car. II. c. 24. A tenant in socage was called a *soc-man* or *socager.*

**Sodomy,** carnal copulation between human beings, or between man and an animal, contrary to nature.

**Solatium** (Sc.), extra damages allowed in certain actions in addition to the actual loss suffered, as *consolation* for wounded feelings.

**Sole,** single. See *Feme; Corporation.*

**Solicitor,** a person employed to conduct legal proceedings, or to advise on legal questions. **Solicitor-general,** a law officer of the crown, in England, ranking next to the attorney-general (*q.v.*) He is usually a member of the House of Commons.

**Solvit ad diem,** *l.*, was a plea in an action of debt, that the money was *paid at the day* appointed.

**Son assault demesne,** *fr.*, (*his own assault*), the plea of self-defense in an action of assault.

**Sound in damages.** An action is said to, when it is brought for the recovery of unascertained damages

. **Sovereign, The,** is the person in whom the supreme executive power of the state is vested.

**Speaking demurrer,** one which alleges new matter in addition to that contained in the pleading demurred to.

**Special,** that which relates to a particular act, thing, or person; opposed to general. **Special agent,** one whose authority is confined to a particular or individual instance. **Special constable,** one appointed for a particular occasion. **Special damages,** those awarded for any peculiar injury sustained by the party complaining, beyond the general damages presumed by law. **Special demurrer,** one which points out with particularity the objection to the sufficiency of the pleading demurred to. **Special deposit,** the placing of a particular thing in the custody of another, which is to be returned in specie. **Special examiner,** one appointed by the parties with leave of the court. **Special issue,** one which denies some particular material allegation, and thus, in effect, denies the right of action, though not traversing the whole declaration. **Special partner,** one whose liability is limited to the amount contributed by him to the business of the firm, and who has not the powers of a general partner. **Special pleaders,** in England, members of an inn of court, usually not called to the bar, who devote themselves mainly to the drawing of pleadings, and to attending at judges' chambers. **Special pleading,** the science of pleading. (2) The allegation of new matter to avoid the effect of the previous allegations of the other party, as distinguished from a direct denial of them. **Special property,** that right in property as distinguished from general ownership, which entitles one to retain its possession for a particular time or purpose. **Special sessions,** sittings of two or more justices for the transaction of particular business confided to them, such as issuing licenses, making appointments, etc. **Special tail,** where an estate-tail is limited to the children of two given parents, as to A. and the heirs of his body by B. **Special trust,** one by the terms of which the trustee is required to do a thing particularly pointed out. **Special verdict,** a finding by the jury of particular facts in a case, usually in answer to questions submitted, leaving to the court the application of the law to the facts thus found.

**Specialty,** a writing sealed and delivered, containing some agreement, usually for the payment of money.

**Specific legacy,** the bequest of a particular thing, or of things particularly separated or described. **Specific performance,** the actual carrying out of a contract in the particular manner agreed upon. Courts of equity will compel a specific performance of a contract, in many cases, where damages (the usual remedy at law) would not adequately compensate for its non-performance; *e.g.*, in the case of contracts concerning land, or for the sale of a specific, or unique, chattel.

**Specificatio** (Rom.), was a form of *accession* (*q.v.*), by which he, who by his labor converted the material of another into a new product, became owner of the product; he was, however, liable to compensate the owner.

**Specification,** a detailed description of the nature and subject-matter of his invention, or discovery, furnished by the inventor on his application for letters patent, and embodied in them when granted to him. (2) A more detailed statement of the charges preferred against an officer charged with a military offense.

**Sponsor** (Rom.), a surety who, being a Roman citizen, bound himself by the word *spondeo*. His heirs were not bound. The *fidejussor* (*q.v.*), was of later introduction. See *Fidepromissor*.

**Spoliation,** the mutilation, or destruction, of a thing, as the erasure, or alteration, of a writing. (2) A waste of church property by an incumbent. (3) A suit in an ecclesiastical court for the fruits of a living, or to determine which of two claimants is entitled to it.

**Springing use,** see *Use*.

**Spuilzie** (Sc.), taking away movables belonging to another, without his consent or legal authority.

**Spunging-house,** a private house where a debtor was formerly confined for twenty-four hours before being imprisoned.

**Squatter,** one who settles on the lands of others, or public lands, without any legal authority.

**Stakeholder,** one with whom property is deposited pending the settlement of a dispute, the decision of a wager, etc., between two or more others.

**Stale demand,** one which has not been made for so long that it must be taken to be waived.

**Stallage,** the privilege of erecting a stall within a market. (2) The payment due for the same.

**Standing by,** acquiescence (*q.v.*).

**Standing mute.** See *Mute.*

**Stannary,** a tin mine. **Stannary courts,** courts of record in Devonshire and Cornwall, England, for the administration of justice among the miners.

**Star chamber.** See *Camera stellata.*

**Stare decisis,** *l.*, to stand by decided cases. The name of a doctrine giving to precedents the authority of established law; not, however, always regarded.

**Stated account.** See *Account.*

**State's evidence.** See *King's evidence.*

**Status,** the condition of a person in the eye of the law (2) By analogy, a *thing* is said to have a status. **Status quo,** the existing state of things at any given date. To leave in *statu quo*, is to leave unaltered.

**Statute,** a law enacted by the legislative power in a country or state. It may be (*a*) declaratory, *i.e.*, one which does not alter the existing law, as opposed to remedial or amending; (*b*) enabling, *i.e.*, removing restrictions, as opposed to disabling. Statutes may also be either public, or private, the latter including those which have a special application to particular persons or places. The public general statutes are called the *Statutes at Large.* **Statute of Frauds, of Uses, etc.** See *Frauds; Uses, etc.*

**Statutory,** by statute, as opposed to the rules of equity or common law.

**Stay of execution,** delay in issuing an execution, or suspension of the authority to levy one already issued, until a future time; generally allowed in cases of appeal, or proceedings in error, on the filing of a sufficient bond for the satisfaction of the judgment, or decree, if affirmed **Stay of proceedings,** the suspension of an action, peremptorily, where a plaintiff is wholly incapacitated from suing, or ought not to be allowed to plead; or temporarily, *e.g.*, pending appeal, or where there is an action pending elsewhere (*lis alibi pendens*), o determine the same question, or one which should be first determined, or until the plaintiff, if non-resident, shall furnish security for costs.

**Stealing.** See *Larceny.*

**Steelbow goods** (Sc.), corn, cattle, etc., advanced by a landlord to a tenant to enable him to stock his farm, and to be returned in kind on the expiration of the lease.

**Stent** (Sc.), a tax, or duty.

**Stet processus,** *l.*, an order of the court to stay proceedings made, strictly, only by consent of the parties, and entered on the record. See *Stay.*

**Stevedore,** a person whose business it is to undertake the stowage and discharge of cargoes.

**Steward,** of a manor, the lord's deputy who transacts the legal and other business of the manor, keeps the court rolls, etc.

**Stillicidium** (Rom.), the right to have the water which falls on one's house fall on his neighbor's ground.

**Stint,** limit. *Common without stint* is one unlimited as to the number of beasts that may be pastured there, or as to the time of pasturing. See *Sans nombre.* (2) A limited right of pasture.

**Stipendiary estate,** one granted in return for services (*q.v.*).

**Stipulation,** a bargain, proviso, or condition. (2) In admiralty practice, a recognizance in the nature of bail for the appearance of a defendant.

**Stirps,** *l.*, the nob, stem, or stock of a tree. In law, it signifies the person from whom a family is descended. See *Per capita.*

**Stock,** a family. (2) The capital of a merchant, or other person engaged in business, including his merchandise, money, and credits. The goods he keeps for sale. (3) The capital of a corporation, usually divided into equal shares of a fixed nominal value, the ownership of which is evidenced by certificates. **Stock-broker,** one who buys and sells stocks, shares, etc., as the agent for others. **Stock certificate,** a certificate of title to stock in a corporation. **Stock exchange,** an association of stock brokers and jobbers, governed by rules and regulations made by themselves. (2) The building where the business of the exchange is carried on. **Stock-jobber,** one who deals in stocks, shares, etc., on his own account.

**Stoppage in transitu.** An unpaid vendor may, in case of the vendee's insolvency, stop the goods sold *in transitu*, *i.e.*, before they reach their destination (*terminus ad quem*), or, in the case of warehoused goods, before delivery is complete, provided he has not given the purchaser documents sufficient to pass the property in the goods, which documents the latter has parted with to a third person *bona fide*.

**Stowage,** storage; money paid for housing goods. (2) The method of lading a ship.

**Stranding,** the running of a ship on shore accidentally, or voluntarily. When accidental, or done voluntarily to avoid a worse fate, the loss is one within the terms of an ordinary policy of marine insurance.

**Stranger,** one who is not a party to a deed, proceeding, etc.

**Strictissimi juris,** *l.*, (*of the most strict law*), *i.e.*, to be most strictly applied.

**Strike,** an organized refusal of workmen to work.

**Struck jury,** a special jury obtained usually by striking from a list of forty-eight names furnished by the court, or a proper officer thereof, on the application of one of the parties, twelve names by the attorneys on each side of a case, leaving sixteen, who are then summoned to try the case. If all appear, and are not otherwise excused, or challenged for cause, the number is reduced to twelve by the exercise of two peremptory challenges on each side, when the jury is complete.

**Style,** an appellation, title, or official name. (2) See *New style.*

**Sub,** *l.*, under. **Sub-agent,** an under agent; one employed by an agent to perform some, or all, of the business relating to the agency. **Sub-contract,** a contract made by a contractor with a third person to perform a part, or all, of the work he has undertaken. **Sub-infeudation,** the act by which an inferior lord carved out an estate from that held by him of a superior, and granted it to another, who held directly of him. See *Quia emptores.* **Sub-lease,** an under-lease (*q.v.*). **Sub modo,** under condition, or restriction. **Sub potestate,** under the power, or protection, of another. **Sub sigillo,** under seal. **Sub silentio,** in silence. **Sub-tenant,** one who rents from a tenant.

**Subject-matter,** the cause; the thing in dispute.

**Submission,** a putting under; a yielding. (2) The agreement by which parties agree to refer matters in dispute between them to a referee, or arbitrators, for decision.

**Subornation,** the offense of procuring another to commit a crime, *e.g.*, perjury.

**Subpoena,** a writ commanding attendance in a court under a penalty. See *Citation; Writ of summons.* The *Subpoena ad testificandum* is personally served upon a witness to compel him to attend and give evidence. (2) The *Subpoena duces tecum* is personally served upon a person who has in his possession any book, instrument, etc., the production of which in evidence is desired, commanding him to *bring it with him*, and produce it at the trial.

**Subreption,** the obtaining a gift from the crown by concealing what is true.

**Snbrogation,** substitution of one person for another, the person substituted acquiring the other's rights in respect to a debt, or claim, which he has paid.

**Subscribe,** to *write* one's name *under; i.e.*, to attest, or authenticate, a writing, deed, etc., by one's signature. (2) To agree in writing to take and pay for something, *e.g.*, shares of stock in an incorporated company, or to furnish a certain sum of money for a particular purpose.

**Subsequent,** following after. *A condition subsequent* is one which, if not performed, defeats, or diverts, a right, or estate, already existing or vested. See *Condition precedent.*

**Subsidy,** in English law, a tax, or tribute, granted by parliament to the king for the urgent occasions of the kingdom. Generally, governmental aid in establishing, or carrying on, private enterprises which are assumed to be of great public importance, such as railroads, or steamship lines, which can not, in the nature of things, be self supporting.

**Substitute,** one placed under, or in place of, another to transact the business for which he was appointed. See *Substitution.*

**Substitution** (Rom.), a conditional appointment of an heir. (2) In Scotch law, the enumeration of a series of heirs described in technical language. They are called *substitutes.* See *Institution.*

**Subtraction,** the neglect, or refusal, to perform a duty or service, or to pay rent, tithes, or the like.

**Succession,** the act of following, or coming into, the rights of another, used particularly of the right of the heir to the possession and beneficial interest in the estate of a deceased ancestor; also of the mode of acquiring the rights of one set of persons, constituting a corporation, by another set, on becoming members.

**Successor,** the technical word in the case of a corporation, answering to "heirs, executors, or administrators," in the case of a person proper. (2) See last title.

**Sucken,** (Sc.), the lands *astricted* to a mill, the tenants of which are bound to grind their corn there. See *Multure.*

**Sue,** to bring a civil action.

**Suffragan.** See *Bishop.*

**Suffrage,** vote; elective franchise. (2) Aid.

**Suggestio falsi.** See *Misrepresentation.*

**Sui juris** (*of his own right*). A person who is neither a minor nor insane, nor subject to any other disability, is said to be *sui juris, i.e.,* able to deal with his property.

**Suicide,** one who kills himself. See *Felo de se.*

**Suit,** a civil action.

**Summary,** short; speedy; as opposed to plenary or regular. *Summary jurisdiction* is the power of a court to give judgment, or to make an order forthwith without further preliminaries, such as committing for trial.

**Summing up,** the argument made by counsel at the close

of the evidence. (2) The concise review of the evidence made by a judge in charging the jury.

**Summons,** a writ commanding the sheriff to notify a party therein named to appear in court on, or before, a specified date, and answer the complaint in an action commenced against him.

**Sumptuary laws,** those in restraint of luxury and excessive expenditure.

**Superior** (Sc.), the grantor of a feudal right. See *Lord; Dominant.*

**Supersedeas,** a writ by which proceedings are stayed.

**Superstitious uses,** lands, money etc., given or left for religious purposes not recognized by law, *e. g.*, for saying prayers for the souls of the dead; as opposed to charitable uses.

**Supplemental bill,** an addition to an original bill in equity, in order to supply some defect in its original frame and structure, or to allege facts which have occurred since the filing of the original bill.

**Suppletory oath,** the oath of a litigant party in the spiritual and civil law courts.

**Suppliant,** the party preferring a petition of right.

**Supplicavit,** a mandatory writ directing justices to require security to keep the peace from a person named. Disused.

**Support,** to argue in favor of, or maintain, *e. g.*, a proposition, rule, or order. (2) The right of support to land, or a building, is the right not to have it let down by the act of an adjoining, or, as in the case of mines, an underlying owner.

**Suppressio veri,** *l.*, a willful concealment of material facts.

**Supra** (*above*). This word occurring by itself in a book, etc., refers the reader to a previous part, like *ante.* **Supra protest,** after protest. See *Acceptance.*

**Supreme Court of Judicature,** in England, was substituted by the Judicature Acts, 1873 and 1875 (as modified by the Appellate Jurisdiction Acts, 1876), for the superior courts of law and equity previously existing. It consists of (*a*) the High Court of Justice, and (*b*) the Court of Appeal. See those titles.

**Surcharge,** to put more cattle upon a common than one has a right to do. (2) To prove that items have been omitted from an account which ought to be allowed and credited to the party *surcharging.* To *surcharge and falsify* is to rectify an account by inserting credits and striking out charges which have been wrongfully omitted, or inserted, to the detriment of the party seeking relief.

**Surety,** one who makes himself responsible for the due fulfillment of another's obligation, in case the latter, who is called the *principal,* fails himself to fulfill it.

**Surname,** a name added to the christian name. In modern times, the family name.

**Surplusage,** in pleading, the allegation of unnecessary matter, which is forbidden, and may be struck out by the court.

**Surprise,** the act by which a party to a contract, or a suit, is taken unaware, and, through no fault of his own, put in a position which will be injurious to his interests. Equity will sometimes relieve parties from the obligation of contracts which they were surprised into making, and courts frequently grant new trials on the ground of surprise.

**Surrebutter; Surrejoinder.** See *Pleading.*

**Surrender,** the yielding up of an estate for life, or years, (especially of a lease) so that it merges in the fee or reversion. It may be by deed, or by operation of law.

**Surrogate** (Eng. law), one appointed by a chancellor, bishop, etc., to act for him. (2) The title of a judical officer in some of the states, *e.g.*, New York, who has jurisdiction in the matter of probating wills, granting letters of administration, etc.

**Survivor,** one of two or more persons who lives longer than the others. When one of two or more joint tenants survives the others he becomes possessed of the whole estate, in England, by virtue of the right of *survivorship*. This right has been abolished by statute, or never recognized, in many states of the Union.

**Suspension,** of an estate, or right, takes place where it is temporarily extinguished, but may afterward revive. (2) Of a clergyman, is where he is deprived of his living, or of the right to officiate, for a time. (3) In Scotch law, is equivalent to a stay of proceedings (*q.v.*).

**Symbolic delivery,** the delivery of something as a representative of another thing, of which actual delivery can not be conveniently made, on account of its bulk or situation.

**Syndic,** an agent, or attorney, of a corporation.

## T.

**Tacit,** silent, implied from silence.

**Tack,** a lease. (2) An addition.

**Tacking.** In English law, a mortgagee who has the legal estate in the property mortgaged, and who makes a subsequent advance to the mortgagor without notice of an intermediate advance, may tack his second to his first mortgage and recover both before the intermediate mortgagee can recover any thing. He is thus said to squeeze out the other mortgagee. This doctrine is inconsistent with the laws of most of the states, which require the recording of mortgages, and give to the record the effect of constructive notice.

**Tail.** An estate tail is a freehold of inheritance, limited to a person and the heirs of his body in general, or some of them in particular.

**Tailzie** (Sc.),an arbitrary line of succession laid down by a proprietor, in substitution for a legal line of succession.

**Take,** to lay hold upon; to carry away; to be entitled to, as a devisee takes under a will.

**Tales,** (*l. talis*), jurors summoned to fill up any vacancies existing in the regular panel. **Tales, de circumstantibus,** such jurors selected from the bystanders.

**Tallagium,** a term formerly employed to denote all kinds of taxes.

**Tangible,** that which may be felt or touched; corporeal.

**Tax,** a sum assessed against and collected from a citizen for the support of the government. An *income tax* is one proportioned to the amount of his income. A *poll tax,* one which is assessed on all individuals alike without reference to the value of his property, or the amount of his income. *Indirect* taxes are those levied on articles manufactured, or imported; *e.g.,* excise and customs; so-called because the tax is not levied on the consumer directly, but is in reality paid by him in the enhanced price of the article. (2) To fix, or adjust; as the amount of the costs to be paid by the losing party.

**Teinds** (Sc.), *decimae,* or tithes. **Teinds court** (Sc.), is a commission for the plantation of churches, and settling of stipends of ministers out of the tithes of the various parishes. The commissioners are the judges of the court of session.

**Teller,** one who keeps tally. Hence, an officer in a bank who receives, or pays out, money; a person appointed to receive or count the votes in a legislative, or deliberative, body.

**Temple,** two inns of court, called *Inner* and *Middle,* anciently the dwelling-place of the Knights-Templars.

**Temporalities,** the revenues and secular possessions of a see.

**Tenancy,** the condition, or estate, of a tenant. (2) The term for which he holds. (3) The land which he holds. **Tenancy in common,** the holding by two, or more, persons of distinct but undivided shares in land and tenements. Upon the death of a tenant in common, his share goes to his representative, and not, as in a joint tenancy (*q.v.*), to the survivors.

**Tenant,** one who holds land, usually by service (*q.v.*); a lessee. **Tenant at sufferance,** one who holds over at the end of his term without any contract, express, or implied, that he may do so. **Tenant at will,** one who holds land at the will of the lessor. A tenancy at will may be determined by either party at any time, and the death of either party determines the tenancy The lessee can not transfer his estate. **Tenant for life,** one who has the right to property for his own or another's life. **Tenant for years,** one who holds for a term; a lessee. **Tenant from year to year** one whose tenancy can only be determined at the end of a complete year, or number of years, from the commencement of his holding, and upon due notice given, in ordinary cases six months. A lease at an annual rent, under which no certain term is fixed, creates not a tenancy at will, but one from year to year. **Tenant in fee; tail,** etc. See *Fee; Tail,* etc. **Tenant-right,** a custom entitling an outgoing tenant of a farm to compensation for unexhausted improvements. (2) In Ireland, a custom either insuring a permanence of tenure without liability to any other increase of rent than may be sanctioned by local custom, or entitling a tenant to receive purchase-money from an incoming tenant, for what may be called the goodwill of his farm.

**Tender,** an offer. The offer to deliver money, or specific personal property in pursuance of a contract, and in such a way as to leave nothing further to be done to fulfill his obligation by the party tendering. See *Legal tender.*

**Tenement,** every thing that may be *holden,* provided it be of a permanent nature, whether it be corporeal or incorporeal. (2) A house. See *Easement.*

**Tenendum** (*to be held*), that clause in a deed (*q.v*) wherein the tenure of the land is stated, how and of whom it is to be held.

**Tenor,** the purport and effect of a document, as opposed to its actual words. (2) It is sometimes opposed to "effect," to signify a correct copy

**Tenterden's Act, Lord,** 9 Geo. IV. c. 14, adopted substantially in most of the states, supplements the statute of frauds, and requires the following *inter alia* to be in writing: (*a*) acknowledgments of debts that are statute barred; (*b*) representations as to a person's character or solvency, made in order to obtain him credit, etc.; (*c*) executory contracts for the sale of goods.

**Tenths,** a tribute of a tenth of the annual value of an ecclesiastical benefice, according to the valuation made in Henry VIII.'s reign, formerly paid to the pope and afterward to the king, as head of the church.

**Tenure,** the mode of holding property or office. Tenure of land was formerly *allodial,* or *feudal,* the latter being held of a superior, the former not. All land, in England, is now in theory held of the crown, mediately or immediately. Lay tenures were divided into (*a*) frank tenements or freehold, and (*b*) villenage; (*a*) into (i.) military tenures (as to which see

*Knight service; Grand sergeantry,* and *Cornage*) and (ii.) free socage (see *Burgage; Gavelkind*). Ecclesiastical tenures, which were not abolished by 12 Car II. c. 24, with the other feudal tenures, are frank almoign (*q.v.*) and tenure by divine service, *e.g.*, to sing so many masses, for neglect of which the lord can distrain at once. Most of these forms of tenure are unknown in the United States, and are fast becoming obsolete in England.

**Terce** (Sc.), dower. See *Life-rent.*

**Term,** a word, or expression; a condition; *e.g.*, the *terms* of a contract. (2) An end or limit, hence a period of time limited for the payment of a note, the performance of a contract, or the enjoyment of an estate. (3) The period of time during which a court holds a session.

**Terminus,** *l.*, a limit, or boundary, either of space or time. **Terminus a quo,** the starting point. **Terminus ad quem,** the destination.

**Terre** (or **ter**) **tenant,** one who holds, or has the seisin of, land.

**Terrier,** a register or survey of land.

**Territorial waters,** are those within three miles from the coast of a country; by international law they are held to be within the jurisdiction of that country.

**Territory,** a portion of country subjected to a particular jurisdiction, municipal, judicial, or military. (2) A division of land belonging to the United States and not within the boundaries of any particular state, and governed by United States officers.

**Testament,** is properly a will, or disposition of *personal* property. The word is, however, used generally as equivalent to "will" (*q.v.*).

**Testamentary,** relating to a will, *e.g.*, capacity, disposition, etc. (2) Given or appointed by will, *e.g.*, a testamentary gift, guardian, etc. **Testamentary causes,** proceedings relating to wills and administration of decedents' estates.

**Testate,** the condition of one who dies having made a will.

**Testator, testatrix,** one who makes a will.

**Testatum,** the witnessing part of a deed (*q.v.*) or other formal instrument. It follows the recitals, where there are any, and introduces the operative part of the instrument by the words, "*Now this indenture witnesseth,*" or the like. **Testatum writ,** one issued into a county other than that in which the venue was laid, a return of *non est inventus*, or *nulla bona* having been made to the prior writ issued into the latter county.

**Teste,** the witnessing part of a writ, warrant, etc., indicating by whose authority it is issued.

**Testimonium clause,** the attesting clause in a will.

**Testimony,** statements made by a witness under oath or affirmation.

**Text book,** a legal treatise which lays down principles, or collects decisions on any branch of the law

**Theft,** larceny (*q.v.*).

**Third party,** one who is a stranger to a contract, or proceeding, not being plaintiff, or defendant.

**Thirlage** (Sc.), a tenure or servitude by which a tenant was bound to carry his corn to a certain mill to be ground, the payment, which was in kind, being called a multure.

**Thirty-nine articles.** See *Articles of Faith, or Religion.*

**Thread.** See *Filum aquae.*

**Tick,** credit.

**Ticket of leave,** a license to be at large, granted to a convict for good behavior, and recallable for misconduct.

**Tide-waters,** all arms of the sea, bays, coves, and rivers in which the water, whether salt or not, rises and falls with the tide.

**Tigni immittendi** (scil. **Jus,** Rom.), the right of inserting a beam or timber from the wall of one house into that of a neighboring house, in order that it may rest on and be supported by the latter.

**Timber,** is properly only oak, ash, elm, and trees used for building. It is realty until severed, when it becomes personal estate. See *Waste.*

**Time,** the measure of duration, as days, months, years, etc. (2) The particular hour, day, etc., when an act is done, or a crime committed. See *Essence*; *Memory.*

**Tipstaff,** an officer of a court, whose duty it is to arrest persons guilty of contempt, and to take charge of prisoners.

**Tithes,** were originally the tenth part of the yearly profits of (*a*) lands, (*b*) the stock upon lands, and (*c*) the personal industry of the cultivator; the first being called *praedial,* the second *mixed.* and the third *personal* tithes. They were formerly paid in kind, being due by the inhabitants of a parish for the maintenance of the parish church, and were called *rectorial* (or great tithes), and *vicarial* (smaller or lesser tithes), according as they were payable to the rector (lay or spiritual), or to the vicar. Since 1836 a rent charge, varying with the price of corn has in most cases been substituted for payment in kind.

**Tithing,** a local division formerly containing ten families, forming part of a hundred (*q.v.*).

**Title,** the distinguishing name of an act, book, etc. A general head comprising particulars, as of a book or an action. (2) An appellation of honor or dignity. (3) A claim of right. Title, in this sense, may be *original*, as in the case of an inventor's title to a patent, or *derivative*, where the owner takes from a predecessor. A *marketable* title to land is one which the courts will force on an unwilling purchaser. A *bad* title is one which gives the holder no legal estate. A *doubtful* title is one which may not be bad, yet not so free from doubt as that a court of equity will force a purchaser to take it. The usual *covenants* of title given by vendors and mortgagors are (*a*) for right to convey, (*b*) for quiet enjoyment, (*c*) for freedom from incumbrances, and (*d*) for further assurance when called on. By the existing laws of England, and many of the states, these covenants are implied in every conveyance, and need not be inserted. **Title deeds,** the muniments, or evidences, of ownership to land.

**To wit,** to know; that is to say; namely.

**Tocher,** (Sc.), dowry; marriage portion.

**Toft,** a place where a house has formerly stood.

**Toll,** a payment for passage over a road, ferry, etc., or for grinding at a mill. (2) To bar, or take away, *e.g.*, a writ of entry.

**Tonnage,** the carrying capacity of a ship or vessel. (2) A tax or duty paid on such capacity. (3) A duty formerly charged on wine, assessed by the *tun*.

**Tontine,** a system of granting life-annuities with benefit of survivorship among the annuitants.

**Tort,** injury or wrong. **Tortfeasor,** a wrongdoer; a trespasser. **Tortious,** wrongful, or by wrong.

**Torture,** the infliction of bodily pain to extort a confession from supposed criminals, and information as to their associates in crime; last used in 1640, in England, and never used in the United States.

**Totidem verbis,** *l.*, in so many words.

**Toties quoties,** *l.*, as often as occasion shall arise.

**Tout temps prist et encore est** (*A. fr.*), a defendant's plea in an action for breach of contract, that he *always has been, and still is ready*, to fulfill it.

**Town,** a civil division less than a county; a small collection of houses, or a village. A **township,** *i.e.*, a division of the public lands of the United States into tracts of six miles square, containing thirty-six sections (*q.v.*), of six hundred and forty acres each.

**Trade-mark,** a distinctive mark, signature, or device affixed to an article, or to the wrapper, etc., in or with which it is sold, to show that it is manufactured, grown, or selected by a special person or persons. In a plain case of infringement courts of equity will enjoin the wrong-doer from using the imitation trade-mark. The test of infringement is whether the defendant used the mark, name, etc., which is alleged to constitute the infringement, with the object of palming off his goods as those of the plaintiff.

**Trader,** one who buys and sells goods and chattels with the purpose of making a profit. A farmer gardener etc., who merely sells what he has raised, is not regarded as a trader.

**Trade-union,** an association of workmen in any trade. It usually has for one of its chief objects the protection of their interests as against their employers, *e.g.*, by organizing strikes for raising wages.

**Transcript,** a copy, especially an official copy.

**Transfer,** to pass from one to another; to convey.

**Transhipment,** the act of taking a cargo out of one ship, and loading it on another.

**Transire,** (Eng. law), a warrant or certificate that the ship has paid customs dues, and may therefore sail. This constitutes her *clearance.*

**Transitory actions,** those the venue of which could be laid in any county. In general, the statutes of the several states require that all actions shall be brought in the county where the defendants, or some of them, or the subject-matter of the action may be found.

**Transitus.** See *Stoppage.*

**Transportation,** the punishment of sending a criminal beyond seas, or into exile.

**Traverse,** in pleading, is the denial of some matter of fact alleged. A traverse is either *general,* denying generally and *in toto* all that was alleged in the last pleading of the adverse party, or *special,* pursuing the exact words of that portion of the pleading which it is intended to deny

**Treason,** or *leze-majesty,* an offense against the duty of allegiance. In England, it includes offenses against the person of the sovereign or other high officials, intimidation of parliament, etc. In the United States, it consists only in levying war against the government, or in giving aid and comfort to the enemy. A person can be convicted of treason only on the testimony of two witnesses to the same overt act, or confession in open court.

**Treasure-trove,** money, plate, bullion, etc., found hidden in the earth, or any private place, the owner of which is unknown. In England, it belongs to the crown. Under the civil law, it belonged one-half to the finder, and one-half to the person on whose property it was found. If the owner was the finder, it all belonged to him.

**Treasurer of the United States,** an officer whose duty it is to receive and keep the moneys of the United States; to disburse them only on warrants drawn by the Secretary of the Treasury, and countersigned by the proper officer; to take receipts, and to keep and render accurate accounts to the comptroller. Assistant treasurers are appointed to receive and disburse public moneys in each of the principal cities.

**Treaty,** a negotiation preliminary to an agreement. (2) A compact between nations. On the part of the United States it may be made by the President, by and with the consent of the senate, two thirds of those present concurring.

**Trespass,** any transgression of the law, less than treason, felony, or misprision of either. It is especially used of *trespass quare clausum fregit*, *i.e.*, entry on another's close (*q.v.*), or land without lawful authority. *Trespass on the case* or *case* is a general name for torts which had no special writ or remedy prior to 13 Edw. I., c. 24, and for which by that statute new writs were, when necessary, to be framed on the lines of those already existing. See *Actiones nominatae; Breve.*

**Trespasser,** one who commits a trespass. A *trespasser ab initio*, is one who, having lawfully entered, does something he is not entitled to do; his trespass, or wrong, then "relates back," and he is a trespasser *from the beginning.*

**Trial,** the examination of a cause, civil or criminal, by a competent tribunal; the decision of the issues of law or fact in an action. It may be by a judge or judges, with or without a jury (*q.v.*). See *New Trial, Bar, Referee.*

**Trinity term,** one of the four terms or sittings of English courts, beginning on the 22d of May.

**Trinoda necessitas,** *l.*, (*the threefold necessity*), three taxes to which all lands were formerly liable, viz.: bridge-bote, burg-(fortress) bote, and fyrd (military contribution).

**Triors,** or **triers,** persons chosen by the court to decide on challenges (*q.v.*) to a jury.

**Tripartite,** divided into three parts: a deed or contract to which there are three distinct parties.

**Trover,** or *trover and conversion*, was a special form of *trespass* (*q.v.*) *on the case*, based on the *finding* (actual or fictitious) by the defendant of goods lost by the plaintiff. The necessity for a fictitious allegation of the finding was abolished in England, by the C. L. P. Act, 1852, s. 49.

**True bill,** the indorsement which the grand jury (*q.v.*) makes upon a bill of indictment when, having heard the evidence, they are satisfied that there is a *prima facie* case against the accused. See *Ignoramus*

**Trust,** a right of property held by one person, called the *trustee*, for the benefit of another, called the beneficiary, or *cestui que trust*. Trusts are divided into *active*, where the trustee has some duty to perform, so that the legal estate must remain in him or a successor, or the trust be defeated; *passive*, where the trustee simply holds the title in trust for the cestui que trust, and has no duties to perform; *express*, where it is created by express terms in a deed, will, or other instrument; *implied*, including *precatory*, *constructive*, and *resulting* trusts, where a court of equity will presume, from the nature of the transaction, the relations of the parties, and the requirements of good faith, that a trust was intended, though no express words be employed to create it.

**Tubman,** a barrister in a Court of Exchequer, who had privileges of seat and pre-audience next to the postman (*q.v.*).

**Turpis causa,** a base or immoral consideration, on which no action can be founded.

**Tutor,** (Sc.), a guardian (*q.v.*), of an infant under the age of puberty. A tutor frequently has charge of both the person and property of the pupil; a curator only of the property.

## U.

**Uberrima fides,** *l.*, (*utmost good faith*). Contracts made between persons in a particular relationship of confidence, as guardian and ward, or attorney and client, require the fullest information to be given beforehand by the person in whom the confidence is reposed to the person confiding, and perfect fairness in dealing, or the court will refuse to enforce the contract on behalf of the former.

**Udal right,** (Sc.), a right to land by undisturbed possession, not founded on charter or feoffment.

**Ultimus haeres,** *l.*, the ultimate heir; in England, the sovereign.

**Ultra vires,** *l.*, (*beyond their powers*). A company, or corporation, is said to act *ultra vires*, when it exceeds the authority imparted to it by its charter, articles of association, etc.

**Ultroneous witness,** (Sc.), one who gives voluntary evidence

**Umpire,** one who decides a question in dispute; a referee, and especially one who is chosen by arbitrators to determine finally a point on which they are unable to agree.

**Uncertainty,** vagueness, indefiniteness. A gift by will

is *void for uncertainty*, if it is impossible to ascertain the testator's intention with regard to it. Uncertainty in pleading is not permitted, lest it should mislead, or embarrass, the opposite party.

**Uncore** (or **Encore**) **prist,** *L. fr.*, always ready. See *Tout.*

**Unde nil habet,** *l.*, the form of a writ providing a remedy for a widow to whom no dower had been assigned within the period limited by law.

**Under-lease,** or **Sub-lease,** a grant by a lessee to another of a part of his whole interest under the original lease, reserving to himself a reversion. The lessee is then called an *under* (or *sub*) *lessor*, and his assign an *under* (or *sub*) *lessee.* An under-lease for the whole term, not reserving any part to the lessee, is an assignment (*q.v.*). A lessee continues liable to his lessor on the covenants contained in the lease, whether he assigns, or underleases; a sub-lessee is not liable to the original lessor; an assignee of a lease is. **Undertaking,** a promise; especially one formally given in the course of a legal proceeding, which may be enforced by attachment, or otherwise. **Under-tenant,** one who holds by under-lease (*q.v.*). **Underwriter,** an insurer of ships, so called from his writing his name under the policy of insurance (*q.v.*).

**Undue influence,** any improper pressure by which a party is induced to benefit the party pressing. Against such, the courts will relieve.

**Uniformity.** See *Act of uniformity.*

**Unilateral contract** (Rom.). When the party to whom an engagement is made makes no express agreement on his part, the contract is called unilateral (*one-sided*), even in cases where the law attaches certain obligations to his acceptance of the engagement. A loan for use is of this kind.

**Union,** a popular term for the United States of America.

**United States of America,** the states and territories, bounded on the north by Canada, the great lakes and British America, and on the south by Mexico and the Gulf of Mexico, and extending from the Atlantic to the Pacific Ocean, united under one national government, having a national constitution adopted in 1787, and amended from time to time since. At present there are 38 states and 10 territories, including Alaska.

**Unity,** oneness; agreement in particulars. Joint tenants are said to have **Unity of interest,** as none of them has a greater interest in the subject of tenancy than the others have. See *Joint tenancy.* **Unity of possession,** the possession by one person of several different estates, or rights in the same land; as where land subject to an easement, rent, or charge, comes into the hands of the person entitled to the easement, or where a lessee of lands afterwards buys the fee simple, etc.; by this unity of possession the lesser right is extinguished. See *Merger*. **Unity of title,** is where an estate comes to two or more persons by the same title. See *Joint-tenancy*.

**Universal,** relating to the whole, or all. **Universal agent,** one who is appointed to do all acts which his principal can do, and which he has the power to delegate. **Universal legacy,** a bequest of the whole of the testator's property to one or more persons. **Universal partnership,** one in which the partners agree to hold all their property in common. **Universal representation,** (Sc.), the doctrine by which the heir is held to represent the ancestor as to all things, and hence to be responsible for his debts.

**Unlawful,** contrary to law. **Unlawful assembly,** a generic term comprehending riot, affray, etc. See those titles.

**Unliquidated,** not ascertained See *Damages*.

**Uno flatu,** *l.*, (*with one breath*), at the same moment.

**Unsound mind,** a generic term, including lunacy and idiocy.

**Upper Bench,** the style of the Queen's Bench during the protectorate of Cromwell.

**Upset price,** that at which property sold by auction is put up, or under which it can not be sold.

**Ure,** custom. (2) Effect; operation. See *Enure*.

**Usage,** practice long continued. The habit, mode, or uniform course of dealing in a particular trade.

**Usance,** the time at which a bill of exchange drawn in one country on another country is usually made payable.

**Use.** Before the *Statute of Uses* a use was in its nature equitable, being a right enforced by the court of chancery to the beneficial ownership of an estate, the possession of which was vested in confidence in another, called the *feoffee to uses*, the beneficiary being the *cestui que use*. The effect of this separation of the legal and beneficial ownership being to enable secret transfers of land to be made, and also the rights of the crown and of the lord to forfeiture, escheat, and the like to be evaded, the *Statute of Uses* (27 Hen. VIII., c. 10) was passed, enacting (in effect) that where any person was *seised* to the use, confidence, or trust of another, the latter should take a legal estate co-extensive with the equitable one which he would have had prior to the statute. The statute does not apply to leaseholds or copyholds; nor does it *execute* (*i.e.*, operate on) a second use, otherwise called a *use upon a use*, or upon a use or trust which has active duties attached to it, called an *active* use. *Common law uses* are those last mentioned, which were unaffected by the statute. A *springing* use is one which is to come into operation at a future date. A *shifting* use, one which shifts from one person to another on the happening of a certain event, or non-performance of a condition. The word "trust," is now used instead of "use," where he who has the possession for the benefit of another, has also an active duty to perform in respect to the subject-matter. See *Trust; Grant; Feoffee.* (2) Enjoyment; application to one's service. **Use and occupation.** An action may be brought by the owner of real property against a person using or occupying it, on an *implied* agreement to pay for his use and occupation.

**User,** use; enjoyment.

**Uses, Statute of.** See *Use.*

**Usucapio,** (Rom.), title by prescription (*q.v.*).

**Usufruct,** (Rom.), the right to the beneficial ownership of a thing, the proprietorship of which is in another.

**Usufructuary,** he who enjoys the usufruct.

**Usurpation,** a taking and holding of a thing without right. (2) Presenting to an advowson without title.

**Usury,** originally interest charged for the use of money; now, illegal interest only. **Usury laws,** those fixing the rate of interest which may be charged, and prescribing penalties for taking interest in excess of the lawful rate.

**Uterine,** born of the same mother.

**Uti possidetis** (*as you possess*), (Rom.), an interdict, or special edict, of the praetor declaring the ownership of real estate to be in the person then in possession.

**Utlary,** outlawry (*q.v.*).

**Utter,** to offer; to publish; to attempt to pass off a forged document or counterfeit coin as genuine.

**Utter** or **Outer barristers,** all such counsel as are not either queen's counsel or sergeants-at-law.

## V.

**Vacant,** empty; not occupied. A *vacant succession* is an inheritance, the heir to which is unknown.

**Vacantia bona,** (Rom.), things without an owner; the goods of one dying without successors.

**Vacate,** to cancel, annul, or render of no effect. (2) To move out of, *e.g.,* a house.

**Vacation,** the period of time between the end of one term of court and the beginning of another.

**Vadium mortuum,** *l.,* a dead-pledge or mortgage.

**Vagabond** or **Vagrant,** a wanderer; an idle fellow; one who, being able to maintain himself by lawful labor, either refuses to work, or resorts to unlawful practices, such as begging or fortune-telling, to gain a living.

**Valeat quantum,** *l.*, let it avail what it may.

**Valid,** good; effectual; of binding force.

**Valuable.** See *Consideration.*

**Value,** the utility or worth of an object. A *holder for value* is one who has given a valuable consideration for that which he holds. **Value received,** a phrase generally inserted in a note or bill of exchange, though unnecessary, to denote that a consideration has been given for it.

**Valued.** A *valued policy* is one in which the value of the thing insured is settled at the time of making the insurance, and is inserted in the policy, as distinguished from an *open* policy, in which tho value is left to be afterwards ascertained.

**Valuer,** a person who appraises property.

**Variance,** a disagreement between successive pleadings by the same party, or the statements in the pleadings and the evidence adduced in proof thereof.

**Vassal,** one bound to render feudal service to a lord.

**Vavasour; vidame,** one who, holding of a superior lord, has others holding under him; a mesne lord.

**Vendee,** one to whom any thing is sold.

**Venditioni exponas,** *l.*, that you expose for sale; a writ directing a sheriff to sell goods which he has taken under a *fieri facias* (*q.v.*).

**Vendor,** one who sells any thing. A *vendor's lien* is the right which he has, while his purchase-money, or any part of it, is unpaid, to charge the land sold with payment thereof, even after he has conveyed or delivered possession of it to the purchaser; provided only that he has not waived his lien by accepting security for the purchase-money or the like. In many states, the lien is not valid unless expressly reserved in the deed.

**Venire facias** (*make to come*), a writ to the sheriff to summon a jury. **Venire facias ad respondendum,** a writ of summons to answer an indictment for misdemeanor. **Venire facias de novo,** a second writ to summon another jury for a new trial.

**Venter** or **Ventre,** the womb. A person *in ventre* is one conceived, but not yet born. See *Gestation.* The writ *de ventre inspiciendo* was an original process issuing out of chancery, on the petition of the person next entitled to land, to *examine* whether the woman, from whom an heir might be born who would exclude the petitioner, was really *enciente*, and so to guard against supposititious births. See *Jury of Matrons.*

**Venue,** or **Visne,** the neighborhood; the county in which an act is done, or a cause of action arises, and from which the jury is taken for the trial of the case. A *change of venue* is the sending of a case to be tried before the jury of another county, when circumstances render it impossible to have an impartial trial in the county where the cause of action arose.

**Verbal,** made by word of mouth, oral (*q.v.*)

**Verdict,** the decision of a jury reported to the court, on the matters submitted to them on the trial of a cause. It may be *general, i. e.*, for plaintiff, fixing the amount to be recovered, or for defendant without more or *special*, the latter giving the facts found, and leaving the conclusion of law to the court.

**Verge,** a rod. Hence in some copyhold estates *tenants by the verge*, who where admitted by delivery of a rod.

**Verification,** the averment in a pleading that the party making it is ready to verify, or establish, the truth of the facts alleged. (2) The affidavit of the party pleading, his agent, or attorney, that the allegations of the pleading are true, required by the statutes of many states.

**Versus,** *l.*, against.

**Vert,** or **Verd,** the right (*a*) of cutting green wood; (*b*) of pasturage.

**Vested,** established; which ought to be maintained. A right, or estate, is said to be vested in a person when he becomes entitled to it. It may be *vested in possession*, when he has a right of present enjoyment, or *vested in interest*, when he has a present fixed right of future enjoyment; *i.e.*, a right to an estate, the possession of which is postponed to a fixed time, or the happening of a certain event.

**Vesture,** pasturage.

**Vetera statuta,** *l.*, the ancient statutes commencing with *Magna Charta*, and ending with those of Edward II.

**Veto,** *l.*, (*I forbid*), the refusal of an executive officer, whose assent is necessary to the validity of an act passed by a legislative body, to concur therein. The veto power is given to the President of the United States and the governors of many of the states.

**Vexata quaestio,** *l.*, an undetermined point, which has been often discussed.

**Vexatious,** annoying; harassing· oppressive. **Vexatious suit,** one brought without probable cause, for purposes of annoyance, or oppression.

**Vi et armis,** *l.*, with force and arms; words inserted in a declaration of trespass.

**Via,** (Rom.), a right of way (*q.v.*).

**Viability,** a capability of living after birth; extra-uterine life.

**Vice,** in the place of; instead of. **Vice-Chancellor,** a judge of the court of chancery, originally appointed to relieve the lord chancellor of part of his judicial duties. The first was created in 1813. **Vice-comes,** *l.*, the sheriff. **Vice-President,** the second officer in point of rank in the United States. He is elected at the same time, and for the same term, as the president. He is president of the senate, but has no vote, unless they be equally divided. In case of the removal from office, death, resignation, or inability of the president, the duties of his office devolve on the vice-president.

**Vice versa,** *l.*, on the contrary.

**Vicinage,** neighborhood; proximity.

**Vicountiel,** that which belongs to the sheriff or *vice-comes.*

**Vide** (*see*), a word of reference. *Vide ante*, or *supra*, refers to a previous passage; *vide post*, or *infra*, to a subsequent one.

**Videlicet** (*to wit*), a word formerly used in pleading to precede the specification of particulars which need not be proved exactly as laid.

**Viduity,** widowhood.

**View,** an inspection of property in controversy, or of a place where a crime has been committed, by the jury, or certain persons called *viewers*, under an order of court.

**Vill,** a manor, village or town.

**Villain,** or **villein,** a man of base or servile condition, though not actually a slave. *Villeins regardant* were those annexed to and passing with a manor, as opposed to *villeins in gross.* who were annexed to the person of the lord. See *Service; Socage.*

**Villenage,** base tenure (*q.v.*). See *Villain.*

**Vinculo Matrimonii,** *l.*, from the bond of matrimony. See *Divorce.*

**Vindicatio** (Rom.), an action for land.

**Vindictive damages,** those given by way of punishing the offender, over and above the actual loss suffered.

**Violation,** an act contrary to another's right, committed with force. (2) A rape.

**Violence,** force used against law, private rights, or public liberty; an assault, or intimidation by a display of force.

**Violent profits** (Sc.), those due from a tenant who forcibly retains possession after he should have given it up.

**Vis,** *l.*, force. **Vis impressa,** direct force; original force. **Vis major,** irresistible force; inevitable accident.

**Visitor,** one who periodically inspects the management of a public or charitable institution.

**Visne.** See *Venue.*

**Vitiation** (Sc.), material alteration in an instrument.

**Viva voce,** *l.*, by word of mouth. See *Evidence.*

**Vivary,** a park, warren, fishery.

**Vivisection,** the dissecting of living animals for scientific purposes.

**Vocatio in jus,** (Rom.), a citation to trial.

**Void,** of no force, or effect; absolutely null.

**Voidable,** of imperfect obligation, so that it may be legally annulled, or, on the other hand, cured or confirmed, at the option of one of the parties; *e.g.*, the contract of an infant with an adult.

**Voir dire** (*veritatem dicere*), a preliminary examination of a witness as to his competency *to speak the truth.* See *Initialia.*

**Voluntary,** acting without compulsion; done by design. (2) When applied to a gift, promise, or conveyance, it means that it is made either without, or for only a *good,* consideration (*q.v.*). **Voluntary waste,** that which is the result of the deliberate act of the tenant of property, as where he pulls down a wall, or cuts timber; opposed to permissive waste (*q.v.*)

**Volunteer,** one who receives a gift, promise, or conveyance, without giving a valuable consideration therefor. (2) One who offers his services to his country in time of war.

**Vouch,** to call to warranty. In the old practice of recoveries (*q.v.*), the person against whom the action for the land was brought, *vouched* him who had warranted the title, *i.e.*, called on him to defend it. The former was called the *voucher*, the latter the *vouchee.* In the fictitious proceeding, called common recovery, the crier of the court was the person ultimately vouched, and was called the *common vouchee.* See *Imparl.* (2) To rely on; to quote.

**Voucher,** a document which evidences a transaction; a receipt. (2) See *Vouch.*

## W.

**Wadset,** (Sc.), a kind of mortgage. The lender is called the *wadsetter*, and the borrower the *reversor.*

**Wager,** a bet; a test; a mutual promise by two persons to each other that the one shall in a certain event pay the other a certain sum of money. **Wager of battle.** See *Battel.* **Wager of law.** See *Compurgator.* **Wager policy,** one made when the insured has no interest in the subject of insurance.

**Wages,** the agreed compensation paid by a master to a servant for work done.

**Waif,** goods found, but claimed by nobody (*bona vacantia*). (2) Goods stolen, but *waived* (*waviata*), or thrown away by the thief in his flight; by the English common law they belonged to the king.

**Waive,** to forego, to decline to take advantage of, *e. g.*, a legal right, or an omission or irregularity of another person. By *waiver*, a legal right is lost. But mere lying by is not waiver; there must be a positive act. (2) See *Waif.* (3) To make a woman an outlaw.

**Wales, Prince of,** the eldest son of the reigning English sovereign, his wife being called the *Princess of Wales.*

**Wapentake,** a hundred; the hundred court.

**Ward,** an infant who is under guardianship (*q.v.*). A *ward of court* is an infant under the protection of the Court of Chancery. (2) See *Watch.* (3) A division of a city, borough, or parish for election purposes.

**Warden,** a guardian or keeper. (2) See *Cinque ports.*

**Wardship,** the condition of a ward.

**Warehouse,** a place for receiving and storing goods and merchandise for hire. The *warehouseman* is bound to use ordinary diligence in preserving such goods. **Warehouse receipt,** one given on the receipt of goods in a warehouse, by the terms of which the warehouseman agrees to deliver the goods to the person depositing them, or his assignees. The assignment of such a receipt, and its presentation to and acknowledgment by the warehouseman, operates as a delivery of the goods described.

**Warrandice** (Sc.), warranty.

**Warrant,** an authority. (2) A precept under hand and seal to some officer to arrest an offender. (3) A writ of summons. (4) See *Dock.* **Warrant of attorney,** a written authority addressed to a solicitor of the court in which it is intended that a judgment shall be entered up, authorizing him to appear on behalf of the person giving the authority and to confess judgment. The instrument is usually given to secure payment of a debt, and is defeasible on payment by a certain day.

**Warrantia chartae,** *l.*, a real action in cases where a person was enfeoffed with warranty, and was not able to vouch the warrantor. Abolished in 1833.

**Warranty,** a guarantee concerning goods or land, given to a purchaser by the vendor. **Warranty of goods,** is as a rule, an undertaking that they are of a certain quality. **Warranty of land,** that the title is good. Warranty may be expressed or implied, the latter being a limitation of the maxim *caveat emptor* in certain cases, as where goods are ordered to be be made for a particular purpose. **Voucher to**

**warranty,** the former practice in real actions of calling the warrantor into court to defend a suit brought against his tenant, or vendee, for the recovery of land in his possession.

**Warren,** a place privileged by prescription, or by grant from the crown, for the keeping of wild beasts or fowls. See *Game.*

**Waste,** any spoil or destruction in houses, gardens, trees, etc., to the prejudice of the inheritance. It is either (*a*) *permissive*, consisting in mere neglect or omission to do what is necessary to prevent injury; or (*b*) *voluntary* (*q.v.*). Sometimes a tenant, by the terms of the instrument creating his estate holds his lands *without impeachment of waste, i.e.*, with a general permission to commit waste of any ordinary character. (2) Uncultivated, or common, ground. See *Manor.*

**Watch,** was the name for a body of constables, or police officers, on duty by night; *ward*, being chiefly applied to those on duty by day.

**Water-bailiff,** an officer in seaport towns whose duty it is to search ships. **Water-course,** a stream, artificial or natural. (2) A right to the flow of water over one's own land, or to discharge water on to one's neighbor's land. **Water-gavel,** a rent paid for fishing in, or for other benefit received from, some river or other water.

**Waveson,** flotsam (*q.v.*)

**Way,** a passage. (2) A right of passage. It may be (*a*) a foot-way (*iter*); (*b*) a horse and footway (*actus*); or (*c*) a cartway (*via* or *aditus*). Ways are either public or private; those which are public being usually called highways. A private right of way may be founded on grant, license, or prescription, being either an easement or customary right. A *way of necessity* is one which arises by operation of law, where a person grants to another a piece of land which can only be reached by crossing land of the grantor's.

**Way-bill,** a document containing the names of passengers, or the description of goods, carried in a public conveyance.

**Way-going crops.** See *Away-going.*

**Ways and means,** the style of a committee usually appointed in legislative bodies to determine the manner of raising funds for the use of the government.

**Welsh mortgage,** a conveyance of an estate redeemable at any time by the mortgagor, on payment of the loan; the rents and profits being in the meantime received by the mortgagee in satisfaction of interest, subject to an account. The mortgagee can not foreclose.

**Were,** or **Wergild,** a fine imposed for homicide or grave injury.

**Wharfage,** money paid for landing goods upon, or loading them from, a wharf.

**Wharfinger,** one who owns or keeps a wharf for the purpose of receiving and shipping goods. His duties and liabilities are similar to those of a warehouseman.

**Whereas,** a word which introduces a recital of a fact.

**White rents.** See *Reditus albi.*

**Wife.** See *Husband and wife; Equity to a settlement.*

**Wild animals.** See *Animals.*

**Wild's case, rule in.** A devise to B and his children or issue, B having no issue at the time of the devise, gives him an estate-tail; but if he have issue at the time, B and his children take as joint tenants, or as tenants in common, according to the other words of the will.

**Will,** the final declaration of the disposition which a man desires to have made of his property after death. It is revocable during the testator's lifetime. It must as a rule be in writing (see *Execution; Nuncupative*), but not in any particular form. Infants under the age of discretion and lunatics have no testamentary capacity. The capacity of infants who have attained years of discretion and married women to make wills is variously defined by the statutes of the several states.

**Willful,** intentional; deliberate. Mortgagees and others in possession of securities, land, etc., are liable for losses caused by their willful default.

**Winding-up,** the process of calling in and distributing the assets of a company which is bankrupt, or unable or unwilling to carry on its business any longer It is the only legal way of terminating the existence of a company. (2) The word is also applied in a similar way to partnerships, and sometimes to what is more properly called the *administration* (*q.v.*) of a deceased person's estate.

**Window.** See *Light.*

**Withdrawal, of juror,** when a jury can not agree upon a verdict, or the parties desire, or the court advises, that the trial should proceed no further, a juror is often withdrawn by consent of the litigants, so as to put an end to the proceedings.

**Withernam.** See *Capias.*

**Without day,** indefinitely. A defendant was formerly said to go without day when he was successful, the action not being adjourned to any future date.

**Without prejudice.** See *Prejudice.*

**Without recourse** (*sans recours*). See *Indorsement.*

**Witness,** one who sees an act performed, *e.g.*, the execution of a deed. (2) One who gives evidence in a cause. The attendance of a witness on the trial of a cause in court is secured by the issuing of a subpœna (*q.v.*). See *Privilege; Attest; Oath; Perjury.*

**Woolsack,** the seat of the lord chancellor in the house of lords.

**Wounding.** See *Mayhem; Battery.*

**Wreck,** any portion of a wrecked or lost ship, or her cargo, which is recovered, either on shore, or at sea; thus including flotsam, jetsam, and ligan (see those titles). Wreck originally belonged to the crown, and has in many cases been the subject of grant to individuals.

**Writ,** a judicial process, by which a person is summoned to appear. (2) A legal instrument to enforce obedience to the orders and sentences of the courts. It is issued by authority of a court, or other competent tribunal, and directed to the sheriff, or other officer, authorized by law to execute the same. He must return it with a brief statement of what he has done in pursuance of it, to the court, or officer, authorizing its issue. Writs are either (*a*) *prerogative,* when the granting of them is in the discretion of the court, as in the case of *habeas corpus;* or (*b*) of right, when the applicant is entitled as of course. The latter class includes *original* writs, by which an action used formerly to be commenced (see now *Writ of Summons*), and *judicial* writs, under which head almost all writs at present existing fall, such as writs of summons, writs in aid (*q.v.*), and writs of execution. (3) An action; *e.g.*, the writs of waste and of partition. **Writ in aid,** one issued after a writ of execution has failed. See *e.g., Assistance; Venditioni.* **Writ of Dower,** a writ of which there were two forms, the writ of right and the writ *unde nil habet* (*q.v.*). **Writ of entry,** was a real action by a person disseised, to recover possession. It was said to be in the *per* where the disseisor's heir, or assign, was in possession; in the *per* and *cui,* where two descents, or alienations, had taken place; in the *post,* where there had been more than two. **Writ of error,** an original writ, directing an inferior court to send the record of proceedings before it to a superior court for review. See *Error; False judgment.* See also *Execution; Formedon; Mainprise; Praecipe; Quare Impedit; Restitution; Waste,* etc.

**Writers to the signet,** also called *clerks to the signet,* persons who perform, in the supreme courts of Scotland, duties analogous to those of a solicitor.

**Wrong,** the infringement of a right.

# Y.

**Year,** the period in which the earth makes one complete revolution around the sun; twelve calendar months; three hundred and sixty-five days. See *Bissextile; New Style.* **Year and day; Year, day, and waste.** See *An jour, et waste.* **Year to year.** See *Tenant from.*

**Year-books,** annual reports, in a regular series of cases, from the time of King Edward II. to Henry VIII., taken by the prothonotaries, or chief scribes of the courts, at the expense of the crown.

**Yeoman,** formerly meant a 40*s.* freeholder not advanced to the legal rank of a gentleman; one who farms his own freehold.

**Yielding and paying,** the first words of the *reddendum* clause in a lease, constituting a covenant to pay rent.

# APPENDIX A.

EXPLANATIONS OF ABBREVIATIONS AND REFERENCES TO REPORTS, COMMONLY FOUND IN LAW BOOKS.*

---

## A.

*A.* Answer; anonymous.
*A. & E.* Adolphus and Ellis, Queen's Bench, Eng., 1834–40.
*A. & E. (N. S.).* Adolphus and Ellis, Queen's Bench, Eng., New Series, 1841–52.
*A. C.* Court of Appeal in Chancery, Eng.
*A. D.* (*Anno Domini.*) In the year of our Lord.
*A. R.* (*Anno Regni.*) In the year of the reign.
*Abb. Adm.* Abbott's Admiralty, U. S. District Court, Southern District of New York, 1847–50.
*Abb. App.* Abbott's New York Court of Appeals Decisions.
*Abb. N. C.* Abbott's New Cases, Practice, New York, from 1876.
*Abb. Pr.* Abbott's Practice Cases, New York Courts, 1854–65.
*Abb. Pr. (N. S.).* Abbott's Practice Cases, New York Courts, New Series, 1866–75.
*Abb. U. S.* Abbott, U. S. Circuit and District Courts, 1865–71.
*Abp* Archbishop.
*Abr.* Abridged; Abridgment.
*Abr. Ca. Eq.* Abridged Cases in Equity, Eng.
*Act.* Acton's Prize Causes, Privy Council, Eng., 1809–11.
*Act Reg.* (*Acta Regia.*) Royal Acts.
*Ad. & E.* See *A. & E.*
*Add.* Addison, Pennsylvania County Courts and Court of Errors, 1791–9.
*Add. E. R.* Addams' Ecclesiastical Reports, Eng., 1822–6.
*Adm.* Admiralty.
*Admr.* Administrator.

---

*When the name of any *court* is mentioned the reference is to the *reports* published by the reporters whose names are mentioned. The dates and numbers of volumes annexed show the period, or the place, in a given series of reports covered by the reports referred to. In both cases the figures are inclusive.

*Admrx.* Administratrix.
*Ae.*, or *Aet.* (*Aetatis.*) Of age, or aged.
*Ag't.* Agent.
*Aik.* Aikens, Vermont Supreme Court, 1825–7.
*Al.* Aleyn, King's Bench, Eng., 1646–8.
*Ala.* Alabama, Supreme Court, from 1840.
*Ala. Sel. Cas.* Alabama Select Cases, Supreme Court, 1861–3.
*Alb. L. J.* Albany Law Journal, Albany, N. Y. from 1870.
*Alc. & N.* Alcock and Napier, King's Bench, Ireland, 1831–3.
*Alc. R. Cas.* Alcock's Registry Cases, Ireland, 1832–7.
*Allen,* Massachusetts Supreme Court, Vols. 83–96.
*Allen* (*N. B.*), New Brunswick Reports, 1861–6.
*Am.* American.
*Am. & E. Ry. Cas.* American and English Railway Cases, Northport, N. Y.. from 1883.
*Am. Cor Cas.* American Corporation Cases, Chicago, from 1868.
*Am. Dec.* American Decisions, Courts of Various States from earliest period.
*Am. L. C.* American Leading Cases, Hare and Wallace.
*Am. L. Rec.* American Law Record, Cincinnati, from 1872.
*Am. L. Reg.* American Law Register. Philadelphia, from 1852.
*Am. L. Rev.* American Law Review. Boston, from 1866.
*Am. L. T.* American Law Times, Washington.
*Am. Rep.* American Reports, Various States, Albany, from 1870.
*Amb.* Ambler. Chancery, Eng. 1737–84.
*And.* Anderson, Common Pleas, Eng., 1558–1605.
*Andr.* Andrews, King's Bench, Eng., 1737–8.
*Ann.* Annaly King's Bench, Eng.
*Anon.* Anonymous, Election Cases, Eng., 1741–74.
*Anst.* Anstruther, Exchequer, Eng., 1792–5.
*Ans.* Answer.
*Anth.* Anthon, New York Supreme Court, Nisi Prius Cases, 1808–51.
*Ap. C.* Appeal Cases, Law Reports.
*Arches,* Court of, Eng.
*Ariz.* Arizona Territory, Supreme Court, from 1866.
*Ark.* Arkansas, Supreme Court, from 1837
*Arkley,* Justiciary Reports, Scotland, 1846–8.
*Arm. M. & O.* Armstrong, Macartney and Oglo, Nisi Prius, Ireland, 1840–2.
*Arn.* Arnold, Common Pleas, Eng. 1838–9.
*Arn. & H.* Arnold and Hodges, Queen's Bench, Eng., 1840–1.
*Ash.* Ashmead, Pennsylvania, Various Courts, 1808–41.

*Ass.* *Liber Assisarum*, Book of Assizes, Queen's Bench, Eng., 327–77.
*At. R.* Atlantic Reporter, St. Paul, from 1886.
*Atk.* Atkyns, Chancery, Eng., 1736–54.
*Atty.* Attorney.
*Atty. Gen.* Attorney General.

## B.

*B.* Baron of the Exchequer; (*Banca*) Bench.
*B. & A.* Barnewall and Alderson, King's Bench, Eng., 1817–22.
*B. & Ad.* Barnewall and Adolphus, King's Bench, Eng., 1830–4.
*B. & B.* Broderip and Bingham, Common Pleas, Eng., 1819–22.
*B. & C.* Barnewall and Creswell, King's Bench, Eng., 1822–30.
*B. & L.* Browning and Lushington, Admiralty, Eng., 1863–5.
*B. & P.* Bosanquet and Puller, Common Pleas, Eng., 1797–1804.
*B. & P. (N. R.).* Bosanquet and Puller, New Reports, Common Pleas, Eng., 1804–7.
*B. & S.* Best and Smith, Queen's Bench, Eng., from 1861.
*B. C.* Bail Court, Eng.
*B. C. C.* Bail Court Cases, Eng., Lowndes and Maxwell, 1850–2.
*B. C. R.* Bail Court Reports, Eng., Saunders and Cole, 1842–8.
*B. R.* (*Bancum Regis*) King's Bench, Eng.
*B. R.* National Bankrupt Register, United States Courts, 1867–79.
*Bail.* Bailey, South Carolina, Superior Courts and Court of Appeals, 1828–32.
*Bail. Eq.* Bailey, South Carolina, Equity Cases, 1830–1.
*Bald.* Baldwin, U. S. Circuit Court, Third Circuit, 1828–33.
*Ball & B.* Ball and Beatty, Chancery, Ireland, 1807–14.
*Ban. & A.* Banning and Arden, Patent Cases, U. S. Courts.
*Bank.* Bankruptcy.
*Bar. & Arn.* Barron and Arnold, Election Cases, Eng., 1843–6.
*Bar. & Aust.* Barron and Austin, Election Cases, Eng., 1842.
*Barb.* Barbour, New York Supreme Court, 1847–73.
*Barb. Ch.* Barbour, New York Chancery Cases, 1845–8.
*Barn.* Barnardiston, King's Bench, Eng., 1726–34.
*Barn. Ch.* Barnardiston, Chancery, Eng., 1740–1.
*Barnes*, Notes of Cases, Common Pleas, Eng., 1732–56.
*Barr*, Pennsylvania Reports, Vols. 1–10.

*Batty*, King's Bench, Ireland, 1825–6.
*Beasl.* Beasley, New Jersey Equity, Vols. 12 and 13.
*Beat.* Beatty, Chancery, Ireland, 1827–9.
*Beav.* Beavan, Roll's Court, Eng., 1838–66.
*Bee*, Admiralty, U. S. District Courts, 1779–1809.
*Bel.* Bellewe, King's Bench, Eng., 1378–1400.
*Bell. App.* Scotch Appeals, House of Lords, 1842–55.
*Bell, C. C.* Crown Cases, Reserved, Eng., 1858–60.
*Bell, Com.* Commentaries on the Laws of Scotland.
*Bell, Dec.* Decisions, Court of Sessions, Scotland, 1794–5.
*Belt*, Supplement to Vesey, Sr., Chancery, Eng.
*Ben.* Benedict, U. S. District Court, Southern Dist. of N. Y., 1865–79.
*Benl.* Benloes, Bendloes, or Benlowes, King's Bench, Eng., 1531–1628.
*Benl. & D.* Benloes and Dalison, Common Pleas, Eng., 1512–79.
*Bert.* Berton, New Brunswick, 1835–9.
*Best & S.* See B. and S.
*Bibb*, Kentucky Court of Appeals, 1808-17.
*Bing.* Bingham, Common Pleas, Eng., 1822–34.
*Bing. N. C.* Bingham, New Cases, Common Pleas, Eng., 1834–40.
*Binn.* Binney, Pennsylvania Supreme Court, 1799–1814.
*Biss.* Bissell, U. S. Circuit Court, Seventh Circuit, 1851–83.
*Bk'cy.* Bankruptcy.
*Bl. Com.* Blackstone, Commentaries on the Laws of England.
*Bl. H.* Henry Blackstone, Common Pleas, Eng., 1788–96.
*Bl. R.* or *Bl. W.* Sir Wm. Blackstone, King's Bench, 1746–79.
*Black*, U. S. Supreme Court, Vols. 66 and 67.
*Black., D. & O.* Blackham, Dundas and Osborne, Nisi Prius, Ireland, 1846–8.
*Blackf.* Blackford, Indiana Supreme Court, 1817–47.
*Bland*, Maryland High Court of Chancery, 1811–32.
*Blatch.* Blatchford, U. S. Circuit Court, Second Circuit, from 1845.
*Blatch. & H.* Blatchford and Howland, U. S. District Court, Southern Dist. of N. Y., 1827–37.
*Blatch. Pr.* Blatchford, Prize Cases, U. S. District Court, Southern Dist. of N. Y., 1861–5.
*Bli.* Bligh, House of Lords, Eng., 1819–21.
*Bli. (N. S.)* Bligh, House of Lords, Eng., New Series, 1827–37.
*Bond*, U. S. Courts, Southern Dist. of Ohio, 1856–71.

*Bosw.* Bosworth, New York City Superior Court, Vols. 14–23.

*Br.* { Brooke, Chancery Eng., 1509–47.
Bruce, Court of Sessions, Scotland, 1714–5. }

*Br. & G.* Brownlow and Gouldesborough, Common Pleas, Eng., 1558–1624.

*Br. N. C.* Brooke, New Cases, King's Bench and Chancery Eng., 1515–58.

*Brac.* Bracton De Legibus Et Consuetudinibus Angliae.

*Bradf.* Bradford, New York Surrogates Courts, 1849–57.

*Bradw.* Bradwell, Illinois Appellate Courts, 1877–86.

*Brayt.* Brayton, Vermont Supreme Court, 1815–19.

*Breese*, Illinois Supreme Court, Vol. 1.

*Brev.* Brevard, South Carolina Constitutional and District Court, 1793–1816.

*Brews.* Brewster, Pennsylvania, various courts, in Chancery, 1856–73.

*Bridg.* Sir J. Bridgman, King's Bench, Eng., 1615–20.

*Bridg. O.* Orlando Bridgman, Common Pleas, Eng., 1660–7.

*Bright.* Brightley Court of Nisi Prius, at Philadelphia and Pennsylvania Supreme Court, 1809–51.

*Bro. C. C.* Brown (William), Chancery Cases, Eng., 1778–94.

*Bro. P. C.* Brown, House of Lords (Parliamentary) Cases, Eng., 1702–78.

*Brock.* Brockenborough, U. S. Circuit Court, 4th Circuit, 1802–36.

*Broun*, Justiciary Cases, Scotland, 1842–5.

*Brown, Adm.* Admiralty, U. S. Courts, Western Districts.

*Brown, N. P.* Nisi Prius Cases, Michigan.

*Browne*, Pennsylvania Common Pleas, 1st Judicial District, 1806–14.

*Bruce*, Court of Sessions, Scotland, 1714–15.

*Brunner*, Collected Cases, U. S. Courts, 1791–1880.

*Buck*, Reports in Bankruptcy, Eng., 1816–20.

*Bulst.* Bulstrode, King's Bench, Eng., 1609–49.

*Bunb.* Bunbury, Exchequer, Eng., 1714–60.

*Burn.* Burnett, Wisconsin Territory, Supreme Court, 1842.

*Burr.* Burrows, King's Bench, Eng. 1756–72.

*Burr. S. C.* Burrows, Settlement Cases, King's Bench, Eng., 1732–76.

*Busb.* Busbee, North Carolina Supreme Court, 1852–3.

*Busb. Eq.* Busbee, North Carolina (Cases in Equity), 1852–3.

*Bush*, Kentucky Court of Appeals, 1866–79.

## C.

*C.* Cases; Chancellor; Chancery; Chapter; Codex (*Juris Civilis*) Justinian; Common; Court.

*C. A.* Court of Appeal.

*C. & J.* Crompton and Jervis, Exchequer, Eng., 1830-2.

*C. & K.* Carrington and Kirwin, Nisi Prius, Eng., 1843-53.

*C. & L. C. C.* Cave and Leigh, Crown Cases, Eng.

*C. & M.* Crompton and Meeson, Exchequer 1832-4.

*C. & P.* Carrington and Payne, Nisi Prius, Eng., 1823-41.

*C. B.* Chief Baron of the Exchequer; Common Bench; Common Bench Reports, Eng., 1845-56.

*C. B. (N. S.)* Common Bench Reports, New Series, Eng., 1856-65.

*C. C.* Chancery Cases; Circuit Court; County Court; Crown (or Criminal) Cases.

*C. C. A.* County Court Appeals.

*C. C. P.* Court of Common Pleas.

*C. C. R.* Crown Cases Reserved.

*C. E.* Canada East.

*C. J.* Chief Justice.

*C. J. B.* Chief Judge in Bankruptcy.

*C. L. Mag.* Criminal Law Magazine and Reporter, Jersey City, N. J., from 1880.

*C. L. P. Act.* Common Law Procedure Act, 1871, Eng.

*C. L. R.* Common Law Reports.

*C. M. & R.* Crompton Meeson, and Roscoe, Exchequer, Eng., 1834-5.

*C. O. D.* Collect on Delivery. A phrase used where no credit is intended

*C. P.* Common Pleas.

*C. P. D.* Common Pleas Division, Law Reports, Eng.

*C. R.* (*Carolus Rex*) King Charles I.

*C. S.* Court of Sessions, Scotland; (*Custos Rotulorum*) Keeper of the Rolls.

*C. S. A.* Confederate States of America.

*C. S. C. R.* Cincinnati Superior Court Reporter, 1870-3.

*C. W.* Canada West.

*Ca.*, or *Cas.* Cases *t.* (*tempore*) F., in time of Finch; *t.* Holt, in time of Holt; *t.* H., in time of Hardwicke; *t.* K., in time of King; *t.* N., in time of Northington; *t.* Talb., in time of Talbot; B. R., or *t.* Wm. III., in time of William III. (12 mod.).

*Ca. Sa.* *Capias Satisfaciendum* (*q.v.*)

*Cai.* Caines, New York Supreme Court, 1803-5.

*Cai. Cas.* Caines' Cases, New York Court of Errors, 1801-5

*Cal.* California, Supreme Court, from 1850.

*Cald.* Caldecott, Settlement Cases and Justice of the Peace, Eng., 1776–81.
*Call,* Virginia Court of Appeals, 1797–1825.
*Calth.* Calthorpe, King's Bench, Eng., 1609–18.
*Cam. & N.* Cameron and Norwood, North Carolina Court of Conference, 1800–4.
*Camp.* Campbell, Nisi Prius, Eng., 1807–16.
*Can.* Canada Supreme Court Reports, from 1876.
*Can. L. J.* Canada Law Journal, 1855–64.
*Can. L. J. (N. S.).* Canada Law Journal, New Series, from 1865.
*Can. L. T.* Canadian Law Times, from 1881.
*Cap.* Chapter, or Title.
*Car. & K.* See C. & K.
*Car. & M.* Carrington and Marshman, Nisi Prius, Eng., 1841–2.
*Car. & P.* See C. & P.
*Car. H. & A.* Carrow, Hamerton, and Allen, Magistrate's Courts, 1844–7.
*Car. L. R.* Carolina Law Repository, North Carolina, 1813–16.
*Carp.* Carpmael, Patent Cases, Eng., 1860.
*Cart.* Carter, Common Pleas, Eng., 1664–88.
*Carth.* Carthew, King's Bench, Eng., 1688–1700.
*Cary,* Chancery, Eng., 1558–1603.
*Cas. B. R.* Cases in King's Bench *t.* Wm. III. (12 mod.).
*Cas. C. L.* Cases in Crown Law.
*Cas. L. & Eq.* Cases in Law and Equity (10 mod.).
*Cas. P.* Cases in Parliament.
*Cas. Pr. C. P.* Cases of Practice, Common Pleas, Eng.
*Cas. Pr. K. B.* Cases of Practice, King's Bench, Eng., 1732–60.
*Casey,* Pennsylvania State Supreme Court, Vols. 25–36.
*Cent. L. J.* Central Law Journal.
*Cf.* (*Confer.*) Compare.
*Ch.* Chancery.
*Ch. Cas.* Chancery Cases, Eng,, 1660–88.
*Ch. Cas. Ch.* Choice Cases in Chancery Eng., 1557–1606.
*Ch. Cas. Sp.* Special Cases in Chancery, Eng., 1669–93.
*Ch. Pre.* Precedents in Chancery Eng., 1689–1723.
*Ch. R.* Reports in Chancery, Eng., 1675–1721.
*Chand.* Chandler, Wisconsin Supreme Court, 1849–51.
*Charlt.* Charlton T. U. P. Georgia Supreme Courts, 1805–10.
*Charlt. R. M.* Charlton R. M., Georgia, 1811–37.
*Chas.* Charles I., Eng.
*Chase's Dec.* Chase's Decisions, U. S. Circuit Court, Fourth Circuit, 1865–9.

*Cheves*, South Carolina Court of Appeals, at Law 1839-40.
*Cheves, Ch., or Eq.* South Carolina Court of Appeals, in Equity, 1839-40.
*Chip D.* D. Chipman, Vermont Supreme Court, 1789-1824.
*Chip. N.* N. Chipman, Vermont Supreme Court, 1789-1791.
*City H. Rec.* City Hall Recorder New York, Criminal, 1816-1821.
*Civ. Pro. Rep.* Civil Procedure Reports, New York, various courts, from 1881.
*Cl. & F.* Clark and Finnelly, House of Lords, Eng., 1831-46.
*Clark, Ch.* New York Court of Chancery, 1839-41.
*Clarke (Ia.)*, Iowa Supreme Court, Vols. 1-8.
*Clay* Clayton, York Assize, Nisi Prius, Eng., 1651.
*Cliff* Clifford, U. S. Circuit Court, 1st Circuit, 1858-78.
*Cliff. & S.* Clifford and Stephens, Referee's Court in Parliament, Eng., 1867-72.
*Co.* Coke, King's Bench and other courts, Eng., 1568-1611.
*Co. Inst.* Coke's Institutes, 1, 2, 3, and 4.
*Co. Lit.* Coke on Littleton.
*Coch.* Cochran, Nova Scotia Law Reports, (N S.) 1859.
*Cock & R.* Cockburne and Rowe, Elaction Cases, Eng., 1833.
*Cod Jur. Civ.* Codex Juris Civilis.
*Code Rep.* The Code Reporter New York, various courts, 1848-51.
*Code R. (N. S.).* Code Reports, New Series, New York, various courts, 1851.
*Col. & C.* Coleman and Caines' Cases, New York Supreme Court, 1794-1805.
*Col. Cas.* Coleman's Cases, New York Supreme Court, 1793-1800.
*Col. C. C.* Collyer's Chancery Cases, 1844-6.
*Cold.* Coldwell, Tennessee Supreme Court, 1860-70.
*Coll.* Colles, Cases in Parliament, House of Lords, Eng., 1697-1713.
*Colo.* Colorado Territory and State Supreme Court, from 1864.
*Com.* Common; Commissioner; Commentaries.
*Comb.* Comberbach, King's Bench, Eng., 1685-99.
*Comst.* Comstock, New York Court of Appeals, Vols. 1-4.
*Comyn*, King's Bench, Eng., 1695-1739.
*Con.* (*Contra.*) Against, on the other hand.
*Con. & L.* Conner and Lawson, Chancery Ireland, 1841-3.
*Cong.* Congress.
*Conn.* Connecticut Supreme Court of Errors, from 1814.
*Cooke*, Tennessee, various courts, 1811-14.

*Cooke & A.* Cooke and Alcock, King's Bench, Ireland, 1833–4.

*Coop. C. C.* Cooper's Chancery Cases, Eng., 1837–8.

*Coop. Ch.* Cooper, Tennessee, Court of Chancery.

*Coop. t. Brough.* Cooper, Cases in time of Lord Brougham, 1833–4.

*Coop. t. Cott.* Cooper, Cases in time of Lord Cottenham, 1846–7.

*Coop. t. Eld.* Cooper, Cases in time of Lord Eldon, 1792–1815.

*Corb. & D.* Corbett and Daniel, Election Cases, Eng., 1819.

*Coup. (Sc.).* Couper, Scotch Justiciary, 1871.

*Cow.* Cowen, New York Supreme Court and Court of Errors, 1823–8.

*Cowp.* Cowper, King's Bench, Eng., 1774–8.

*Cox*, Chancery, Eng., 1783–96.

*Cox C. C.* Cox's Criminal Cases, Eng., 1843–75.

*Coxe*, New Jersey Law, Vol. 1, 1790-5.

*Cr. & Ph.* Craig and Phillips, Chancery, Eng., 1840–1.

*Cr. & St.* Craigie and Stewart, Scotch Appeals, House of Lords, 1726–1821.

*Crabbe*, U. S. District Court, Eastern District of Pennsylvania, 1836–46.

*Cranch*, U. S. Supreme Court, Vols. 5–13.

*Cranch, C. C.* Cranch, U. S. Circuit Court for District of Columbia, 1801–41.

*Craw. & D.* Crawford and Dix, Circuit Cases, Ireland, 1837–46.

*Craw. & D., Ab. C.* Crawford & Dix, Abridged Cases, Ireland, 1837–8.

*Crim. Con.* Criminal Conversation: Adultery.

*Crim. L. Mag.* Criminal Law Magazine, Jersey City, N. J. from 1880.

*Cripps*, Ecclesiastical Courts, Eng., 1846–9.

*Cro.* Croke, Queen's Bench and King's Bench, Eng., 1581–1641 (sometimes refers to Keilwey's Reports, published by Serjeant Croke).

*Ct. of Cl.* U. S. Court of Claims, from 1863.

*Cunn.* Cunningham, King's Bench, Eng., 1733–6.

*Curt.* Curtis, U. S. Circuit Court, 1st Circuit, 1851–6.

*Curt. E. R.* Curteis, Ecclesiastical Reports, Eng., 1834–44.

*Cush.* Cushing, Massachusetts Supreme Court, Vols. 55–66.

*Cushm.* Cushman, Mississippi High Court of Errors and Appeals, Vols. 23–9.

## D.

*D. (Diem).* Day, Dictum, Digest (*Juris Civilis*), District, Division.

*D. & C.* Deacon & Chitty, Bankruptcy, Eng., 1832–5.
*D. & L.* Dowling & Lowndes, various courts, Eng., 1844–8.
*D. & M.* Davison and Merivale, Queen's Bench, Eng., 1843–4.
*D. & R.* Dowling and Ryland, King's Bench, Eng., 1822–8.
*D. & R. (N. P. C.).* Dowling and Ryland, Nisi Prius Cases, Eng., 1822–3.
*D. (N. S.).* Dowling, Common Bench, Eng., New Series, 1841–2.
*D. C.* District Court; District of Columbia.
*D. G.* (*Dei Gratia.*) By the grace of God.
*D. P.* (*Domus Procerum.*) House of Lords.
*D. T.* or *Dak.* Dakotah Territory Supreme Court, from 1861.
*Dal.* Dalison, Common Pleas, Eng., 1486–1580.
*Dall.* Dallas, U. S. Courts and Courts of Pennsylvania, 1754–1806.
*Dalr.* Dalrymple's Decisions, Court of Session, Scotland, 1698–1720.
*Daly*, New York Court of Common Pleas, from 1859.
*Dan.* Daniel, Exchequer, Equity, Eng., 1817–19.
*Dana*, Kentucky Court of Appeals, 1833–40.
*Dan. & Ll.* Danson and Lloyd's Commercial Cases, King's Bench, Eng., 1828–9.
*Dav.* Davey, Common Law Reports, Ireland, 1604–11.
*Daveis*, U. S. District Court, Maine, 1839–49.
*Day*, Connecticut Supreme Court of Errors, 1802–13.
*Dea.* Deane, Admiralty and Ecclesiastical Courts, Eng., 1855–6.
*Dea. & Sw.* Deane and Swabey, Probate and Divorce, Eng.
*Deac.* Deacon, Bankruptcy, Eng., 1836–9.
*Deac. & Chit.* See D. & C.
*Deady*, U. S. District Court, Oregon, 1859–69.
*Dears. & B.* Dearsley and Bell, Crown Cases Reserved, Eng., 1856–8.
*Dears. C. C.* Dearsley Crown Cases, Eng., 1852–6.
*Deas & A.* Deas and Anderson, Court of Session, Scotland, 1829–32.
*Deft.* Defendant.
*De G.* De Gex, Bankruptcy, Eng., 1845–8.
*De G., F. & J.* De Gex, Fisher and Jones, Chancery and Bankruptcy Appeals, 1859–62.
*De G. & J.* De Gex and Jones, Chancery and Bankruptcy Appeals, 1857–9.
*De G., J. & S.* De Gex, Jones and Smith, Chancery and Bankruptcy Appeals, 1862–5.

*De G., M. & G.* De Gex, Macnaghten and Gordon, Chancery and Bankruptcy Appeals, 1851–7.

*De G. & Sm.* De Gex and Smale, Chancery and Bankruptcy Appeals, 1846–52.

*Del.* Delaware Supreme Court, from 1855.

*Del.* Delane Election Cases, Eng., 1836.

*Del. Ch.* Delaware Court of Chancery, 1814–73.

*Dem.* Demarest, Surrogate's Court, N. Y., from 1882. Demise, *i.e.*, on the demise of.

*Den. C. C.* Denison, Crown Cases, Eng., 1844–52.

*Denio,* New York Supreme Court and Court of Errors, 1845–8.

*Dep.* Department; Deputy.

*Desau.* Desaussure, South Carolina Court of Chancery and Court of Appeals, 1784–1816.

*Dev.* Devereux, North Carolina Supreme Court, at law, 1826–34.

*Dev. Eq.* Devereux, North Carolina Supreme Court, in Equity, 1828–34.

*Dev. & B.* Devereux and Battle, North Carolina Supreme Court, at law, 1834–9.

*Dev. & B. Eq.* Devereux and Battle, North Carolina Supreme Court, in Equity, 1834–9.

*Dev. Ct. Cl.* Devereux, U. S. Court of Claims, 1856.

*Dick.* Dickens, Chancery, Eng., 1559–92.

*Dict.* (*Dictum*) a judicial opinion; Dictionary.

*Dict. of Dec.* Dictionary of Decisions Court of Session, Scotland (Morison and others), from beginning to 1822.

*Dill.* Dillon, U. S. Circuit Court, Eighth Circuit, 1871–80.

*Dirl.* Dirleton, Court of Session, Scotland, 1665–77.

*Dis.* Disney, Cincinnati Superior Court, 1854–9.

*Dist.* District.

*Do.* (*Ditto.*) The same.

*Dod.* Dodson, Admiralty, Eng., 1811–22.

*Dom. Proc.* (*Domus Procerum.*) House of Lords, Eng.

*Doug.* Douglas, King's Bench, Eng., 1778–84.

*Doug. E. C.* Douglas, Election Cases, Eng., 1775–6.

*Doug.* (*Mich*). Douglass, Michigan Supreme Court, 1843–7.

*Dow,* House of Lords, Eng., 1812–18.

*Dow & C.* Dow and Clark, House of Lords, Eng., 1827–32.

*Dowl. Pr. C.* Dowling's Practice Cases, various courts, Eng., 1830–42.

*Dra.* Draper, King's Bench, Upper Canada, 1829–31.

*Drew.* Drewry, Chancery, Ireland, 1852–9.

*Drew. & Sm.* Drewry and Smale, Chancery, Ireland, 1859–65.

*Drink.* Drinkwater, Common Pleas, Eng.

*Dru.* Drury, Chancery, Ireland, 1843–4.
*Dru. & Wal.* Drury and Walsh, Chancery, Ireland, 1837–40.
*Dru. & War.* Drury and Warren, Chancery, Ireland, 1841–3.
*Dru. Sel. Cas.* Drury, Select Cases in Chancery, Ireland, 1868–9.
*Dud.* (*Ga.*) Dudley, Georgia Superior Courts, 1830–3.
*Dud.* (*S. C.*) Dudley, South Carolina Court of Appeals, at law, 1837–8.
*Dud. Eq.* Dudley, South Carolina Court of Appeals, in Equity, 1837–8.
*Duer*, New York City Superior Court. Vols. 8–13.
*Dunl. B. & M.* Dunlop, Bell and Murray, Court of Session, Scotland, 1838–62.
*Durie*, Court of Session, Scotland, 1621–42.
*Durn. & E.* Durnford and East, Term Reports, King's Bench, Eng., 1785–1800.
*Dutch.* Dutcher, New Jersey Law Reports, Vols. 25–29.
*Duv.* Duvall, Kentucky Court of Appeals, 1856–6.
*Duv.* (*Can.*). Canada Supreme Court, from 1876.
*Dy.* Dyer, King's Bench, Eng., 1513–82.

## E.

*E.* East; Eastern.
*E. & A.* Ecclesiastical and Admiralty Division, Law Reports.
*E. & Ir. App. Ca.* English and Irish Appeal Cases, House of Lords, Eng., from 1865.
*E. & O. E.* Errors and Omissions Excepted; a phrase used in qualifying a receipt, or statement of account, to cover slight mistakes.
*E.g.* (*Exempli gratia*), for example.
*Eag. & Y.* Eagle & Younge, Tithe Cases, Exchequer, Eng., 1204–1820.
*East*, King's Bench, Eng., 1801–12.
*Ecc. or Eccl.* Ecclesiastical.
*Ec. or Eccl. & Adm.* See E. & A.
*Ed.* Edition; Edward.
*Eden*, Chancery, Eng., 1757–66.
*Edm.* Edmonds' Select Cases, New York Courts.
*Edw.* Edward I. of England.
*Edw. Adm.* Edwards, Admiralty, Eng., 1808–10.
*Edw. Ch.* Edwards, New York Vice Chancellor's and Supreme Court, 1831–50.
*El. & B.* Ellis and Blackburn, Queen's Bench, Eng., 1852–8.
*El. & E.* Ellis and Ellis, Queen's Bench, Eng., 1858–61.

*El., B. & E.* Ellis, Blackburn & Ellis, Queen's Bench, Eng., 1858-60.

*El., B. & S.* Ellis, Best and Smith, Queen's Bench, Eng.

*Elchie,* Faculty Collection, Court of Session, Scotland.

*Eliz.* Queen Elizabeth.

*Eng.* England; English.

*Eq.* Equity; Equity Division, Law Reports and Law Journal.

*Eq. Ca. Abr.* Equity Cases Abridged, Anonymous, Eng., 1732-69.

*Eq. R.* Equity Reports, Eng., 1855-6.

*Er.* Error.

*Esp.* Espinasse, Nisi Prius, Eng., 1793-1810.

*Esq.* Esquire.

*Et al.* (*Et alii, aliae, alios*), and others.

*Etc.* (*Et cetera*), and so forth.

*Et seq.* (*Et sequentes, sequentia*), and the following.

*Ex.* Exchequer; Exchequer Reports by Welsby, Hurlstone and Gordon, Eng., 1847-56.

*Ex. Ch.* Exchequer Chamber.

*Ex. D.* Exchequer Division, High Court of Justice, Eng.

*Exr.* Executor.

*Exrx.* Executrix.

## F.

*F. & F.* Foster and Finlason, Nisi Prius, Eng., 1858-67.

*F. O. B.* Free On Board; a phrase used in contracts of sale indicating that the seller is to deliver the goods on board cars or ship directed to the vendee, who pays freight.

*Fac. Dec.* Faculty Decisions, Court of Session, Scotland, 1752-1848.

*Fairf.* Fairfield, Maine Supreme Court, Vols. 10-12.

*Falc.* Falconer, Court of Session, Scotland, 1681-6.

*Falc. & F.* Falconer and Fitzherbert, Election Cases, 1837-8.

*Far.* Farresley (7 Mod. Rep.)

*Fed. Rep.* Federal Reporter, U. S. Circuit and District Courts, from 1880.

*Ferg.* Ferguson, Scotch Consistory, 1811-17

*Fi. fa.* *Fieri facias* (*q.v.*)

*Finch, H.* Chancery, Eng., 1673-80.

*Finch, T.* Chancery, Eng., 1689-1722.

*Fish.* Fisher's Patent Cases, U. S. Circuit and Supreme Courts.

*Fish. Dig.* Fisher's Digest, all courts, Eng., from 1756.

*Fitz G.* Fitz Gibbon, King's Bench, Eng., 1728-32.

*Fla.* Florida Supreme Court, from 1846.

*Flan. & K.* Flanagan and Kelly, Rolls Court, Ireland, 1840–2.

*Flippin,* U. S. Circuit Court, Sixth Circuit, 1877–80.

*Fo. or Fol.* Folio.

*Fogg,* New Hampshire Supreme Court, Vols. 32–37.

*Fonbl.* Fonblanque, Bankruptcy, Eng., 1849–51.

*Forb.* Forbes, Court of Session, Scotland, 1705–13.

*For.* Forrester, Cases, time of Talbot, Eng., 1734–8.

*Forrest,* Exchequer, Eng., 1800–1.

*Forst.* Forster, Crown Cases, Ireland, 1767.

*Fort.* Fortescue, various courts, Eng., 1704–36.

*Fost.* Foster, Crown Cases, Eng., 1743–61.

*Fost. (N. H.)* Foster, New Hampshire Supreme Court, Vols. 21–31.

*Fount.* Fountainhall, Court of Session, Scotland, 1678–1812.

*Fox & S.* Fox & Smith, King's Bench, Ireland, 1822–4.

*Fras.* Fraser, Election Cases, Eng., 1790–1.

*Freem.* Freeman, King's Bench, Eng., 1670–1704.

*Freem. Ch.* Freeman, Chancery, Eng., 1660–1706.

*Freem. (Miss.) Ch.* Freeman, Mississippi Superior Court of Chancery, 1839–43.

## G.

*G. & D.* Gale and Davison, Exchequer, Eng., 1841–3.

*G. & J.* Glyn and Jameson, Bankruptcy, Eng,, 1821–8.

*Ga.* Georgia Supreme Court, from 1846.

*Ga. Dec.* Georgia Decisions, Superior Courts, 1842–3.

*Gaii, Institutionum Commentarii,* IV.

*Gale,* Exchequer, Eng., 1835–6.

*Gall.* Gallison, U. S. Circuit Court, First Circuit, 1812–15.

*Geo.* King George, England.

*George,* Mississippi Supreme Courts, Vols. 30–39.

*Gibbs,* Michigan Supreme Court, Vols. 2–4.

*Giff.* Giffard, Chancery, Eng., 1857–65.

*Giff. & H.* Giffard and Hemming, Chancery, Eng., 1731–6.

*Gilb.* Gilbert, Chancery and Exchequer, Eng., 1706–25.

*Gilb. Q. B.* Gilbert, Queen's Bench, Eng., 1713–4.

*Gill,* Maryland Court of Appeals, 1843–51.

*Gill & J.* Gill and Johnson, Maryland Court of Appeals, 1829–42.

*Gilm.* Gilmour, Court of Session, Scotland, 1661–5.

*Gilm. (Ill.)* Gilman. Illinois Supreme Court, Vols. 6–10.

*Gilm. (Va.)* Gilmer, Virginia Court of Appeals, 1820–1.

*Gilp.* Gilpin, U. S. District Court, Pennsylvania, 1828–36.

*Glanv.* Glanville Tractatus de Legibus, et Consuetudinibus Regni Angliae.

*Glass.* Glasscock, all courts, Ireland, 1831–2.
*Glyn & J.* See G. & J.
*Godb.* Godbolt, King's Bench, Eng., 1574–1638.
*Godol.* Godolphin, King's Bench, Eng.
*Gosf.* Gosford, Court of Session, Scotland.
*Goulds.* Gouldsborough, King's Bench, 1585–1601.
*Gov.* Governor.
*Gow*, Nisi Prius, Eng., 1818–20.
*Grant Cas.* Grant's Cases, Pennsylvania Supreme Court, 1852–63.
*Grant*, (*U. C.*). Upper Canada Error and Appeal Reports, 1846–66.
*Grant* (*U. C.*) *Ch.* Grant, Chancery, Upper Canada, 1849–82.
*Gratt.* Grattan, Virginia Court of Appeals, 1844–80.
*Gray*, Massachusetts Supreme Court, Vols. 67–82.
*Green*, New Jersey Law Reports, Vols. 13–15.
*Green Ch.* New Jersey Court of Chancery, Vols. 2–4.
*Green, C. E.* New Jersey Chancery Reports, Vols. 16–27.
*Greene*, Iowa Supreme Court, 1847–54.
*Greenl.* Greenleaf, Maine Supreme Court, Vols. 1–9.
*Gwil.* Gwillim, Exchequer, Eng., 1285–1800.

## H.

*H. & C.* Hurlstone and Coltman, Exchequer, Eng., 1862–5.
*H. & G.* Hurlstone and Gordon, Exchequer, Eng, 1854–7.
*H. & H.* Horn and Hurlstone, Exchequer, Eng., 1839.
*H. & N.* Hurlstone and Norman, Exchequer, Eng., 1856–62.
*H. & P.* Hopwood and Philbrick, Election Cases, Eng., 1863–7.
*H. & R.* Harrison and Rutherford, Common Pleas, Eng., 1866–8.
*H. & T.* Hall and Twells, Ld. Chancellor and Appeal, Eng., 1849–50.
*H. Bl.* See *Bl. H.*
*H. L.* House of Lords, Eng.
*H. L. C.* House of Lords Cases, Clark and Finnelly, Eng., 1847–66.
*H. L. R.* House of Lords Reports, New Series, Eng.
*H. R.* House of Representatives.
*Had.* Earl of Haddington, Court of Sessions, Scotland.
*Hagg. Adm.* Haggard, Admiralty, Eng., 1822–32.
*Hagg. Con.* Haggard, Consistory, Eng., 1789–1821.
*Hagg. Eccl.* Haggard, Ecclesiastical, Eng., 1827–32.
*Hailes*, Court of Sessions, Scotland, 1766–91.
*Hall*, New York City Superior Court, 1828–9.

*Halst.* New Jersey Law, Vols. 6–12.
*Halst. Ch.* New Jersey Chancery, Vols. 5–8.
*Ham.* Hammond, Ohio Reports, Vols. 1–9.
*Handy*, Cincinnati Superior Court, 1854–6.
*Har.* (*Del.*) Harrington, Delaware Superior Court, 1832–58.
*Har.* (*Mich.*) Harrington, Michigan Court of Chancery 1838–42.
*Harr.* (*N. J.*) Harrison, New Jersey Law, Vols. 16–19.
*Har. & G.* Harris and Gill, Maryland Court of Appeals, 1826–9.
*Har. & J.* Harris and Johnson, Maryland Court of Appeals, 1800–26.
*Har. & McH.* Harris and McHenry, Maryland Provincial Court and Court of Appeals, 1658–1799.
*Har. & R.* Harrison and Rutherford, Common Pleas, Eng., 1866–8.
*Har. & W.* Harrison and Wollaston, Queen's Bench, Eng., 1835–7.
*Harc.* Harcarse, Court of Sessions, Scotland, 1681–91.
*Hard.* Hardres, Exchequer, Eng., 1655–60.
*Hardin*, Kentucky Court of Appeals, 1805–8.
*Hare*, Chancery, Eng. 1841–53.
*Harp.* Harper, South Carolina Constitutional Court, 1823–4.
*Harp. Eq.* Harper, South Carolina Court of Appeals in Equity, 1824.
*Harris*, Pennsylvania State Supreme Court, Vols. 13–24.
*Hawks*, North Carolina Supreme Court, 1820–6.
*Hayes*, Exchequer Ireland, 1830–2.
*Hayes & J.* Hayes and Jones, Exchequer, Ireland, 1832–4.
*Hayw.* (*N. C.*), Haywood, North Carolina Superior Courts, 1789–1806.
*Hayw.* (*Tenn.*). Haywood, Tennessee Court of Errors and Appeals, 1816–18.
*Head*, Tennessee Supreme Court, 1858–60.
*Heisk.* Heiskell, Tennessee Supreme Court, 1870–3.
*Hem. & M.* Hemming and Miller, Chancery, Eng., 1862–5.
*Hemp.* Hemstead, U. S. Courts, Ninth Circuit, 1820–56.
*Hen. & M.* Hening and Munford, Virginia Court of Appeals, 1806–9.
*Het.* Hetley, Common Pleas, Eng., 1628–31.
*Hill* (*N. Y.*), New York Supreme Court and Court of Appeals, 1841–5.
*Hill* (*S. C.*), South Carolina Court of Appeals, 1833–7.
*Hill* (*S. C.*), *Ch.* South Carolina Court of Appeals in Chancery, 1833–7.

*Hill & D.* Hill and Denio (Lalor's Supplement), New York Supreme Court, etc., 1842-4

*Hilt.* Hilton, New York Court of Common Pleas, 1855-60.

*Hob.* Hobart, King's Bench, Eng., 1613-44.

*Hodges,* Common Pleas, Eng., 1835-7

*Hoff Ch.* Hoffman, New York Assistant Vice-Chancellor's Court, 1839-40

*Hoff L. C.* Hoffman's Land Cases, U. S. District Court, Cal., 1853-8.

*Hog* Hogan, Rolls Court, Ireland, 1816-34.

*Holt,* Nisi Prius, Eng., 1815-7.

*Home,* Court of Session, Scotland, 1735-44.

*Hope,* Court of Session, Scotland.

*Hop & C.* Hopwood and Coltman, Election Cases, Eng., 1868-75

*Hopk.* Hopkins, New York Court of Chancery, 1823-6.

*Houst* Houston, Delaware Supreme Court, etc., 1855-79.

*Houst C C.* Houston, Delaware Criminal Cases, 1856-79.

*How.* Howard, U. S. Supreme Court, Vols. 47-65.

*How. App Cas.* Howard's Court of Appeals Cases, New York, 1847-8.

*How. (Miss.)* Howard, Mississippi Supreme Court, Vols. 2-8.

*How. Pr.* Howard, Practice Cases, New York Courts, 1844-84.

*How. Pr. (N. S.)* Howard, Practice Cases, New York Courts, New Series, from 1884.

*Hud. & B.* Hudson and Brooke, Irish Common Law Reports, 1837-8.

*Hugh.* Hughes, U. S. Circuit Court, Fourth Circuit, 1792-1883.

*Hughes,* Kentucky Court of Appeals, 1785-1801.

*Hume,* Court of Session, Scotland, 1781-1822.

*Humph.* Humphreys, Tennessee Supreme Court, 1839-51.

*Hun,* New York Supreme Court, from 1874.

*Hut.* Hutton, Common Pleas, Eng., 1612-39.

## I.

*I. E.* (*id est*) That is.

*I. O U* I owe you; a term applied to a written admission of indebtedness.

*Ia.* Iowa Supreme Court, from 1855.

*Ib.*, or *Ibid* (*Ibidem.*) In the same place, volume, or case.

*Id.* (*Idem.*) The same.

*Id. T.* Idaho Territory Supreme Court, from 1866.

*Ill.* Illinois Supreme Court, from 1819.

*Ill. App.* Illinois Appellate Court, from 1877.
*Ind.* Indiana Supreme Court, from 1848.
*Ind. T* Indian Territory.
*Ins. L. J.* Insurance Law Journal, St. Louis, from 1871.
*Inst.* Institutes; Coke's, or Justinian's; (*Instante*), the present month
*Int. Rev Rec.* Internal Revenue Record.
*Ir* Ireland; Irish.
*Ir. C. L. R.* Irish Common Law Reports, 1849–66.
*Ir. Ch.* Irish Chancery Reports, 1850–66
*Ir. Eq.* Irish Equity Reports, 1838–51.
*Ir. J.* Irish Jurist, 1849–66.
*Ir. L.* Irish Law, 1838–50.
*Ir. L. R.* Irish Law Recorder, 1827–38.
*Ir. L. T.* Irish Law Times, from 1867.
*Ir. R. (C. L.).* Irish Reports, Common Law, 1867–78.
*Ir. R. (Eq.).* Irish Reports, Equity, 1867–78.
*Ired.* Iredell, North Carolina Supreme Court at Law, 1840–52.
*Ired. Eq.* Iredell, North Carolina Supreme Court, in Equity, 1840–52.
*Irv.* Irvine's Justiciary Cases, Scotland, 1852–67.

## J.

*J.* Judge; Justice; King James.
*J. & W.* Jacob and Walker, Chancery, Eng., 1819–21.
*J. P.* Justice of the Peace.
*J. R.* (*Jacobus Rex.*) King James.
*Jac.* (*Jacobus.*) or Jas. King James.
*James*, Nova Scotia Law Reports, 1853–5.
*Jebb & B.* Jebb and Bourke, King's Bench, Ireland, 1841–2.
*Jebb C. C.* Jebb's Crown Cases, Reserved, Ireland, 1822–40.
*Jebb & S.* Jebb and Symes, King's Bench, Ireland, 1838–41.
*Jeff.* Jefferson, Virginia General Court, 1730–1840.
*Jenk.* Jenkins, Exchequer, Eng., 1620–3.
*Johns.* Johnson, Chancery, Eng., 1859.
*Johns. & H.* Johnston and Hemming, Chancery, Eng., 1860–2.
*Johns.* Johnson, New York Supreme Court, etc., 1806–23.
*Johns. Cas.* Johnson's Cases, New York Supreme Court, etc., 1799–1803.
*Johns. Ch.* Johnson, New York Court of Chancery, 1814–23.
*Jones (N. C.)*, North Carolina Supreme Court, at Law, 1853–62.
*Jones (N. C.) Eq.* North Carolina Supreme Court, in Equity, 1853–63.

*Jones* (*Ir.*). Exchequer, Ireland, 1834–8.
*Jones & C.* Jones and Carey, Exchequer, Ireland, 1838–9.
*Jones & L.* Jones and Latouche, Chancery, Ireland, 1844–6.
*Jones & S.* Jones and Spencer, New York City Superior Court, from 1871, Vols. 33–41.
*Jones T.* King's Bench, Eng., 1670–85.
*Jones, W.* King's Bench, Eng., 1620–51.
*Jr.* (*Junior.*) The Younger.
*Jur.* The Jurist, Reports all courts, Eng., 1837–54.
*Jur.* (*N. S.*). The Jurist, New Series, all courts, Eng., 1855–66.
*Jur. Sc.* The Scottish Jurist, Court of Session, 1829–73.
*Just.* Justinian's Institutes.
*Just. Cas.* Justiciary Cases, Scotland, from 1885.

## K.

*K.* King.
*K. & G.* Keane and Grant, Common Pleas, Eng., 1854–62.
*K. B.* Court of King's Bench.
*K. C. R.* Reports in time of King, Chancellor, 1724–34.
*Kames*, Court of Session, Scotland, 1716–68.
*Kames R. D.* Kames' Remarkable Decisions, Court of Session, Scotland, 1716–52.
*Kames S. D.* Kames' Select Decisions, Court of Session, Scotland, 1752–68.
*Kan.* Kansas, Supreme Court, from 1862.
*Kay.* Chancery, Eng., (V. C. Wood) 1853–4.
*Kay & J.* Kay and Johnson, Chancery, Eng., (V. C. Wood) 1854–8.
*Keb.* Keble, King's Bench, Eng., 1661–79.
*Keen*, Roll's Court, Eng., 1836–9.
*Kel.* Sir John Kelynge, King's Bench, Eng., 1673–1706.
*Kel.* 1, 2. Wm. Kelynge's Reports, two parts, King's Bench, Eng., 1730–4.
*Keilw.* Keilwey, King's Bench, Eng., 1496–1530.
*Kelly*, Georgia Supreme Court Reports.
*Ken.* Kenyon, Notes of Cases, King's Bench, Eng., 1753–9.
*Kent*, Commentaries on American Law.
*Kern.* Kernan, New York Court of Appeals, Vols. 11–14.
*Kerr*, New Brunswick.
*Keyes*, New York Court of Appeals, 1863–8.
*Kilk.* Kilkerran, Court of Sessions, Scotland, 1738–52.
*Kirby*, Connecticut Superior Court, 1785–88.
*Kn.* Knapp, Privy Council, Eng., 1829–36.
*Kn. & O.* Knapp and Ombler, Election Cases, Eng., 1834–5.
*Ky.* Kentucky, Court of Appeals, cited thus from Vol. 79, 1880.

*Ky. Dec.* Kentucky Decisions, Sneed, 1801–5.

*Ky. L. R* Kentucky Law Reporter, Frankfort, Ky., from 1880.

## L.

*L. & C. C. C.* Leigh and Cave, Crown Cases Reserved, Eng., 1861–5.

*L. & M.* Lowndes and Maxwell, Bail Court, Eng., 1850–2.

*L. C.* Lord Chancellor; Lower Canada.

*L. C. Adm* Lower Canada Admiralty Courts, 1873–84.

*L. C. Jur.* Lower Canada Jurist.

*L. C. L. J.* Lower Canada Law Journal, 1865–8.

*L. C. R.* Lower Canada Reports.

*L. J.* Lord Justice; Law Journal, Eng., 1823–31.

*L. J. (N. S.).* Law Journal (New Series), Eng., from 1832. Reports of all the Courts, designated as follows: *Adm.*, Admiralty; *Bank.*, Bankruptcy; *Ch.*, Chancery; *C. P* Common Pleas; *Ex.*, Exchequer; *M. C.*, Magistrate's Cases; *Mat. Cas.*, Divorce and Matrimonial Cases: *P. C.*, Privy Council; *P.*, or *Prob.*, Probate; *Q. B.*, Queen's Bench.

*L. L. D.* Doctor of Laws.

*L. M. & P.* Lowndes, Maxwell, and Pollock, Bail Court, Eng., 1850–1.

*L. Mag.* The Law Magazine, London, Eng., 1828–56.

*L. Mag. & R.* The Law Magazine and Review London, Eng., from 1856.

*L. Q. R.* Law Quarterly Review London, from 1885.

*L. R.* Law Reports, all courts, Eng., from 1865. Divisions designated as follows: *Adm.*, Admiralty; *App. Cas.*, House of Lords and Privy Council; *C. C.*, Crown Cases Reserved; *C. P.*, Common Pleas; *Ch.*, Chancery; *D.*, Divorce and Matrimonial; *Eq.*, Master of the Rolls and Vice-Chancellor's; *Exch.*, Exchequer; *H. L. Cas.*, House of Lords Appeals; *P.*, or *Prob.*, Probate; *P. C.*, Privy Council Appeals; *Q. B.* Queen's Bench.

*L. R. (Ir.)* Law Reports, Ireland, from 1878.

*L. Rev.*, Law Review.

*L. S.* (*Locus Sigilli.*) The place for the seal.

*L. T.* The Law Times, all courts, Eng., 1843–59.

*L. T. (N. S.)* The Law Times, (New Series) all courts, Eng., from 1859. Divisions designated as in Law Reports.

*La.* Louisiana Supreme Court, 1830–41.

*La. Ann* Louisiana Annual, Supreme Court, from 1846.

*Lane*, Exchequer, Eng. 1605–12.

*Lang. & T.* Langfield and Townsend, Exchequer Ireland, 1841–2.

*Lans.* Lansing, New York Supreme Court, 1869–73.

*Latch*, King's Bench, Eng., 1625-8.
*Law Rec.* Law Recorder all courts, Ireland, 1827-38.
*Law Rep.* Law Repository, North Carolina Supreme Court, 1811-16.
*Ld.* Lord.
*Leach C. C.* Leach, Crown Cases, Eng., 1730-88.
*Lee.* Ecclesiastical Courts, Eng., 1752-8.
*Lee & H.* Lee's Reports in time of Hardwicke, King's Bench, Eng., 1783-8.
*Leg. Chr.* Legal Chronicle, Pottsville, Pa., from 1872.
*Leg. Gaz.* Legal Gazette, Philadelphia, various courts, 1869-72.
*Leg. Int.* Legal Intelligencer.
*Leg. N.* Legal News, Montreal, from 1878.
*Leg. Obs.* Legal Observer, Eng., 1830-57.
*Leigh*, Virginia Court of Appeals and General Court, 1829-41.
*Leon.* Leonard, King's Bench, Eng., 1582-1615.
*Lev.* Levinz, King's Bench, Eng., 1660-96.
*Lew. C. C.* Lewin's Crown Cases, Eng., 1822-38.
*Ley*, King's Bench, Eng., 1608-29.
*Lib. Ass.* (*Liber Assissarum*). Book of Assizes, King's Bench, 1327-77. Year Book pt. 5.
*Lit.* Littleton, Common Pleas and Exchequer, Eng., 1626-32.
*Litt.* Littell, Kentucky Court of Appeals, 1822-4.
*Litt. Sel. Cas.* Littell's Select Cases, Kentucky Court of Appeals, 1795-1821.
*Ll. & G.* Lloyd and Goold, Chancery Ireland, 1834-9.
*Ll. & W.* Lloyd and Welsby Queen's Bench, Eng., 1829-30.
*Lock. R. C.* Lockwood's Reversed Cases, New York Court of Errors, 1799-1847.
*Lofft*, King's Bench, Eng., 1772-4.
*Longf. & T.* Longfield and Townsend, Exchequer, Ireland, 1841-2.
*Low.* Lowell, U. S. Circuit Court, District of Massachusetts, 1865-71.
*Lud.* Luder, Election Cases, Eng., 1784-7.
*Lum.* Lumley's Poor Law Cases, various courts, Eng., 1834-42.
*Lush.* Lushington, Admiralty, Eng., 1860-3.
*Lutw.* Lutwyche, Common Pleas, Eng. 1682-1704.
*Lutw. R. C.* Lutwyche, Registration Cases, Eng., 1843-53.

## M.

*M. & G.* Manning and Granger, Common Pleas, Eng., 1840–5.
*M. & M.* Moody and Malkin, Nisi Prius, Eng., 1826–30.
*M. & P.* Moore and Payne, Common Pleas, Eng., 1827–31.
*M. & R.* Manning and Ryland, King's Bench, Eng., 1827–9.
*M. & Rob.* Moody and Robinson, Nisi Prius, Eng., 1830-44.
*M. & S.* Maule and Selwyn, King's Bench, Eng., 1813–6.
*M. & Scott,* Moore and Scott, Common Pleas, Eng., 1831–4.
*M. & W.* Meeson and Welsby, Exchequer, Eng., 1836–47.
*M. C.* Member of Congress; Master Commissioner; Magistrates' Cases.
*M. C. C.* Moody's Crown Cases, Eng., 1824–44.
*M. P.* Member of Parliament, Eng.
*M. R.* Master of the Rolls, Eng.
*Mac. & G.* Macnaghten and Gordon, Chancery, Eng., 1849–51.
*Mac. P. C.* Macrory's Patent Cases, 1852–3.
*Mac F.* Mac Farlane, Jury Courts, Scotland, 1838–9.
*Mack.* Mackey, District of Columbia, from 1880.
*Macl. and R.* MacLean and Robinson, Scotch Appeals, House of Lords, 1839.
*Macph.* Macpherson and others, Court of Session, Scotland, 1862–73.
*Macq.* Macqueen, Scotch Appeals, House of Lords, 1851–65.
*Madd.* Maddock, Chancery, Eng., 1815–22.
*Madd. & G.* Maddock and Geldart, Chancery, Eng., 1821.
*Man.* Manitoba Reports, from 1875.
*Mar.* Marine, Maritime.
*Mar. L. C.* Maritime Law Cases, Admiralty, Eng., 1860-75.
*March,* King's Bench, Eng., 1639–43.
*Marr.* Marriott, Admiralty, Eng., 1776–9.
*Marsh.* Marshall, Common Pleas, Eng., 1813–6.
*Marsh. A. K.* Marshall, A. K., Kentucky Court of Appeals, 1817–21.
*Marsh. J. J.* Marshall, J. J., Kentucky Court of Appeals, 1829–32.
*Marsh. Dec.* Chief Justice Marshall's Decisions, by Brockenbrough, 1802–36.
*Mart. (La.).* Martin, Louisiana Supreme Court, 1809–30.
*Mart. (N. C.).* Martin, various courts, North Carolina, 1789–96.
*Mart. & Y.* Martin and Yerger, Tennessee Supreme Court, 1827–28.
*Mas.* Mason, U. S. Circuit Court, First Circuit, 1816–30.

*Mass.* Massachusetts Supreme Court, from 1804.
*Mat.* Matrimonial and Divorce Division, Eng.
*McAll.* McAllister, U. S. District Court, California, 1855–9.
*McArth.* McArthur, District of Columbia, Supreme Court, 1873–9.
*McCa.* McCahon, U. S. Courts, Kansas, 1858–68.
*McCl.* McCleland, Exchequer, Eng., 1824.
*McCl. & Yo.* McCleland and Younge, Exchequer, Eng., 1824–5.
*McCord,* South Carolina Constitutional Court and Court of Appeals, 1821–8.
*McCord Ch.* South Carolina Court of Appeals, in Chancery, 1825–7.
*McCra.* McCrary, U. S. Circuit Court, Eighth Circuit, 1880–3.
*McLean,* United States Circuit Court, Seventh Circuit, 1829–55.
*McMull.* McMullan, South Carolina Court of Appeals, in Equity, 1835–42.
*McMull. Eq.* McMullan, South Carolina Court of Appeals, in Equity, 1840–2.
*Md.* Maryland, Court of Appeals, from 1851.
*Md. Ch.* Maryland High Court of Chancery, from 1847.
*Me.* Maine Supreme Court, from 1829.
*Meigs,* Tennessee Supreme Court, 1838–9.
*Mem.* Memorandum; Memoranda.
*Mer.* Merivale, Chancery, Eng., 1815–7.
*Met.* Metcalf, Massachusetts Supreme Court, Vols. 42–54.
*Met. (Ky.)* Metcalfe, Kentucky Court of Appeals, 1858–63.
*Mich.* Michigan Supreme Court, from 1847.
*Miles,* Philadelphia District Court, 1835–41.
*Mills,* South Carolina Constitutional Court, 1817–8.
*Milw.* Milward, Ecclesiastical, Ireland, 1819–43.
*Minn.* Minnesota Supreme Court, from 1851.
*Minor,* Alabama Supreme Court, 1820–6.
*Miss.* Mississippi High Court of Errors and Appeals, 1818–69. Mississippi Supreme Court, from 1870. (All in one series.)
*Mo.* Missouri Supreme Court, from 1821.
*Mo. Ap.* St. Louis Court of Appeals, from 1876.
*Mod.* Modern Cases, King's Bench, Eng., 1669–1701.
*Mod. C. L. & Eq.* Modern Cases in Law and Equity. (8 & 9 Mod. Rep.)
*Mol.* Molloy, Chancery, Ireland, 1807–31.
*Mon.* Monroe, T. B., Kentucky Court of Appeals, 1824–8.

*Mon., B.* Monroe, B., Kentucky Court of Appeals, 1840–57.
*Mont.* Montagu, Bankruptcy, Eng., 1830–2.
*Mont. & A.* Montagu and Ayrton, Bankruptcy, Eng., 1833–8.
*Mont. & B.* Montagu and Bligh, Bankruptcy, Eng., 1832–3.
*Mont. & Ch.* Montagu and Chitty, Bankruptcy, Eng., 1838–9.
*Mont. D. & D.* Montagu, Deacon, and De Gex, Bankruptcy, Eng., 1840–4.
*Mont. & Mac.* Montagu and MacArthur Bankruptcy, Eng., 1828–30.
*Mont. T.* Montana Territory, Supreme Court, from 1868.
*Moore, J.* B. Moore, Common Pleas, Eng., 1817–27.
*Moore, Sir F.* Queen's Bench, Eng., 1512–1621.
*Moore Ind. Ap.* Moore's Indian Appeals, Privy Council, 1836–73.
*Moore P. C. C.* Moore's Privy Council Cases, 1836–52.
*Moore P. C. C. (N. S.)* Moore's Privy Council Cases (New Series), 1852–73.
*Morr.* Morris, Iowa Supreme Court, 1839–46.
*Mos.* Moseley, Chancery, Eng., 1726–30.
*Mss.* Manuscript.
*Munf.* Munford, Virginia Court of Appeals, 1810–20.
*Mur. & H.* Murphy and Hurlstone, Exchequer, Eng., 1837.
*Murph.* Murphey, North Carolina Supreme Court, 1804–19.
*Murr.* Murray, Jury Courts, Scotland, 1815–30.
*Myl. & C.* Mylne and Craig, Chancery, Eng., 1835–41.
*Myl. & K.* Mylne and Keene, Chancery, Eng., 1832–5.

## N.

*N. A.* North America.
*N. & M.* Neville and Manning, King's Bench, Eng., 1832–6.
*N. & P.* Neville and Perry, Queen's Bench, Eng., 1836–8.
*N. B.* (*Note bene*), note well; New Brunswick Reports from 1 Allen, 1861.
*N. B. R.* National Bankruptcy Register, 1867–79.
*N. Benl.* New Benloe, King's Bench, Eng., 1509–1625.
*N. C.* North Carolina Supreme Court, from 1789.
*N. C. T. R.* North Carolina Term Reports, 1816–18.
*N. E. Rep.* The North-eastern Reporter, St. Paul, from 1885.
*N. F.* New Foundland.
*N. H.* New Hampshire Superior Court, from 1816.
*N. H. & C.* Nichol, Hare and Carrow, English Railway Cases, 1835–55.

*N. J.* New Jersey Supreme Court and Court of Errors and Appeals.

*N. J. L.* New Jersey Law Reports (last named court) from 1830.

*N. J. Eq.* New Jersey Court of Chancery and Supreme Court, from 1795.

*N. M.* New Mexico.

*N. P.* Nisi Prius.

*N. R.* New Reports (Bosanquet & Puller), Common Pleas, Eng., 1804–1807.

*N. R.* New Reports, all courts, Eng., 1862–5.

*N. S.* New Style; New Series; Nova Scotia Law Reports from 1853.

*N. S. Dec.* Nova Scotia Decisions, Supreme Court, 1866–75.

*N. W. Rep.* The North-western Reporter. St. Paul, from 1879.

*N. Y.* New York Court of Appeals, from 1847

*N. Y. C. Rep.* New York Code Reporter 1848–51.

*N. Y. Leg. Obs.* New York Legal Observer

*N. Y. Sup.* New York City Superior Court, from 1828.

*N. Y. Supr.* New York Supreme Court (Lansing & Hun), from 1869.

*Neb.* Nebraska Supreme Court, from 1870.

*Nels.* Nelson, Chancery, Eng., 1625–92.

*Nem. Con.* *Nemine Contradicente* (*q.v.*)

*Nev.* Nevada Supreme Court, from 1865.

*New Sess. Cas.* Carrow, Hamerton and Allen, New Session Cases, all courts, Eng., 1844–7.

*Newb. Adm.* Newberry U. S. District Courts in Admiralty, 1842–57.

*Nolan*, King's Bench, Settlement Cases, Eng.

*Non Obst. Ver.* (*Non obstante veredicto*), notwithstanding the verdict.

*Non Pros.* (*Non Prosequitur*). He will not prosecute.

*Non Seq.* (*Non Sequitur*). It does not follow.

*North.* Northington, Chancery, (by Eden), Eng., 1757–66.

*Nott & H.* Nott and Huntington, U. S. Court of Claims, from 1863.

*Nott & McC.* Nott and McCord, South Carolina Constitutional Court, 1817–20.

*Noy*, King's Bench, Eng. (time of Elizabeth, James and Charles.)

## O.

*O. Benl.* Old Benloe, Common Pleas, Eng., 1486–1580.

*O. C. C.* Ohio Circuit Court Reports, from 1885.

*O. G.* Official Gazette, U. S. Patent Office, from 1872.
*O. R.* Ohio Supreme Court Reports, 1821–51.
*O. S.* Ohio State, Supreme Court Reports, from 1852; Old Style.
*Olc. Adm.* Olcott, Admiralty, U. S. District Court, Southern Dist. of New York, 1843–7.
*Old.* Oldright, Nova Scotia Law Reports, 1860–6.
*O'M. & H.* O'Malley and Hardcastle, Election Cases, 1869–75.
*Ont.* Ontario Appeal Reports from 1876.
*Or.* Oregon Supreme Court, from 1853.
*Otto,* U. S. Supreme Court, Vols 91–107.
*Over.* Overton, Tennessee, various courts, 1791–1817.
*Owen,* King's Bench, Eng., 1556–1615.
*Oxley,* Young's Admiralty Decisions, Canada, 1865–80.

## P.

*P.* Probate Division, Law Reports, Eng.; Parliament; Pleas; Page.
*P. & D.* Perry and Davison, Queen's Bench, Eng., 1838–41.
*P. & K.* Perry and Knapp, Election Cases, Eng., 1833.
*P. C.* Privy Council, Law Reports, Eng.; Pleas of the Crown.
*P. M.* (*Post Meridiem.*) Afternoon; Postmaster.
*P. W.*, or *Wms.* Peere Williams, Chancery, Eng., 1695–1735.
*Pa.* Pennsylvania Supreme Court, 1829–32.
*Pa. L. J.* Pennsylvania Law Journal, 1842–8.
*Pa. St.* Pennsylvania State, Supreme Court, from 1845.
*Pac. L. R.* Pacific Law Reporter, St. Paul, from 1883.
*Paige,* New York Court of Chancery, 1828–45.
*Paine,* U. S. Circuit Court, Second Circuit, 1810–40.
*Palm.* Palmer, King's Bench, Eng., 1619–29.
*Park.* Parker, Exchequer, Eng., 1743–66.
*Park. C. C.* Parker Criminal Cases, various courts of New York, 1839–68.
*Pars. Eq. Cas.* Parsons' Equity Cases, First Judicial District, Pennsylvania, 1850.
*Pat. App.* Paton, Scotch Appeals, House of Lords, Eng., 1753–1821. (2) Paterson, Scotch Appeals, House of Lords, 1851–73.
*Pat. & H.* Patton, Jr., and Heath, Virginia Special Court of Appeals, 1855–6.
*Peake,* Nisi Prius, Eng., 1790–1812.
*Peake Add. Cas.* Peake's Additional Cases, Nisi Prius, Eng., 1795–1812.
*Peck,* Tennessee Supreme Court, 1822–4.

*Peck (Ill.)*, Illinois Supreme Court, Vols. 11–30.
*Peckw.* Peckwell, Election Cases, Eng., 1796–1806.
*Pen.* Pennington, New Jersey Laws, Vols. 2 and 3.
*Pen. & W.* Penrose and Watts, Pennsylvania Supreme Court, 1829–32.
*Pet.* Peters, U. S. Supreme Court, Vols. 26–41.
*Pet. Adm.* Peters' Admiralty Decisions, U. S. District Court, Eastern District of Pennsylvania, 1780–1807.
*Pet. C. C.* Peters, U. S. Circuit Court, 1803–18.
*Phil.* Phillips, Chancery, Eng., 1841–9.
*Phila.* Reports of various courts in Philadelphia, from 1850.
*Phil. (N. C.).* Phillips, North Carolina Supreme Court, at Law, 1866–8.
*Phil. (N. C.) Eq.* Phillips, North Carolina Supreme Court, in Equity, 1866–8.
*Phillim.* Phillimore, Ecclesiastical Courts, Eng., 1809–21.
*Pick.* Pickering, Massachusetts Supreme Court, Vols. 18–41.
*Pig. & R.* Piggott and Rodwell, Election Cases, Eng., 1843–5.
*Pike*, Arkansas Supreme Court, Vols. 1–5.
*Pinn.* Pinney, Wisconsin Supreme Court, 1839–52.
*Pitts.* Various courts, Pittsburgh, Pa., 1853–73.
*Pitts. L. J.* Pittsburgh Legal Journal, 1853.
*Pl.* (*Placita*) Pleas.
*Plow.* Plowden, King's Bench, Eng., 1548–78.
*Pol.* Pollexfen, King's Bench, Eng., 1669–83.
*Poph.* Popham, King's Bench, Eng. (Elizabeth, James, and Charles).
*Port.* Porter, Alabama Supreme Court, 1834–9.
*Pow. R. D.* Power, Rodwell and Dew, Election Cases, Eng., 1848–56.
*Pp.* Pages.
*Pr. Ed.* Prince Edward's Island Reports, 1850–82.
*Pres.* President.
*Price*, Exchequer, Eng., 1814–24.
*Pro.*, or *Prob.* Probate Division, Law Reports, Eng., from 1865.
*Pro Tem.* (*Pro Tempore*) For the time being.
*Prox.* (*Proximo*) The coming month.
*Pub. Doc.* Public Documents.
*Pugs.* Pugsley, New Brunswick.
*Pyke*, Quebec, King's Bench, 1809–10.

## Q.

*Q.* (*Quaere*) Question; Queen.
*Q. B.* Queen's Bench.

*Q. B. (N. S.)* Adolphus and Ellis, Queen's Bench, New Series, 1841-52.

*Q. B. Div.* Queen's Bench Division, Law Reports, Eng., from 1865.

*Q. C.* Queen's Counsel, or Council.

*Q. L. J.* Quarterly Law Journal, Richmond, Va., 1856-9.

*Q. L. R.* Quebec Law Reports, from 1874.

*Quin.* Quincy, Massachusetts, various courts, 1764-71.

*Q. V.* (*Quod vide*) Which see.

## R.

*R.* Roll's Court. See *Master of the Rolls.*

*R. & M.* Ryan and Moody, Nisi Prius, Eng., 1823-6.

*R. & R. C. C.* Russell and Ryan's Crown Cases, Eng., 1799-1823.

*R. I.* Rhode Island Supreme Court, from 1828.

*R. S.* Revised Statutes.

*Railw. Cas.* Railway Cases, Eng., by Nicholl, Hare, Oliver, Beavan, etc., all courts, 1835-54.

*Rand.* Randolph, Virginia Court of Appeals, 1821-8.

*Rawle,* Pennsylvania Supreme Court, 1828-35.

*Raym.* Lord Raymond, King's Bench, Eng., 1694-1732.

*Raym., T.* T. Raymond, King's Bench, Eng., 1660-84.

*Redf.* Redfield, New York Surrogate's Court, 1857-82.

*Redf. & B.* Redfield and Bigelow Leading Cases.

*Rep.* Reports; Coke's Reports (*q.v.*); The Reporter, Boston, from 1876.

*Rep. Ch.* Reports in Chancery, Eng., 1625-1713.

*Rev. Leg.* Revue Legale, Montreal, from 1869.

*Rice,* South Carolina Court of Appeals and Errors, at Law, 1838-9.

*Rice, Ch.* South Carolina Court of Appeals and Errors, in Equity, 1838-9.

*Rich.* Richardson, South Carolina Court of Appeals and Errors, at Law, 1844-68.

*Rich. Cas.* Richardson Cases, South Carolina Court of Appeals and Errors, 1831-2.

*Rich. Eq.* Richardson, South Carolina Court of Appeals and Errors, in Equity, 1844-68.

*Ridg. App.* Ridgway's Irish Appeals, House of Lords, Eng., 1784-96.

*Ridg. L. & S.* Ridgway, Lapps & Schoale, Ireland, 1793-5.

*Ridg., t. Hard.* Ridgway, King's Bench, Eng., in time of Hardwicke, 1733-45.

*Riley,* South Carolina Court of Appeals, etc., at Law, 1836-7.

*Riley Ch.* South Carolina Court of Appeals, etc., in Equity, 1836–7.
*Robertson,* Scotch Appeals, House of Lords, Eng., 1707–27.
*Rob.* Robinson, House of Lords, Eng., 1840–1.
*Rob. Adm.* Dr. W. Robinson, Admiralty, Eng., 1838–52.
*Rob. Eccl.* Dr. Robertson, Ecclesiastical Courts, Eng., 1844-55.
*Rob. (La.)* Robinson, Louisiana Supreme Court, 1841–9.
*Rob. (N. Y.)* Robertson, New York City Superior Court, Vols. 24–30.
*Rob. (Va.)* Robinson, Virginia General Court and Court of Appeals, 1842–4.
*Rolle,* King's Bench, Eng., 1614–25.
*Rom.* Rome; Roman.
*Root,* Connecticut Supreme Court, 1789–98.
*Rose,* Bankruptcy, Eng., 1810–16.
*Russ.* Russell, Chancery, Eng., 1823–9.
*Russ. & M.* Russell and Mylne, Chancery, Eng., 1829–31.
*Ry. Cas.* See Railw. Cas.

## S.

*S.* Section; Series.
*S. & D.* Shaw and Dunlop, Court of Session, Scotland, 1800–62.
*S. & S.* Simon and Stuart, Chancery, Eng., 1822–6.
*S. & Sm.* Searle and Smith, Probate and Divorce, Eng.
*S. & T.* Swabey and Tristram, Probate and Divorce, Eng.
*S. C.* Same Case; Supreme Court; South Carolina Reports, from 1868.
*S. C. R.* Supreme Court Reporter, St. Paul, from
*S. E. R.* South-eastern Reporter, St. Paul, from 1887.
*S. Rep.* Southern Reporter, St. Paul, from 1887.
*S. P.* Same point, or principle.
*S. L. T.* Southern Law Times, Chattanooga, Tenn., from 1885.
*S. W. R.* South-western Reporter, St. Paul, from 1886.
*Salk.* Salkeld, King's Bench, Eng., 1689–1712.
*Sandf.* Sandford, New York City Superior Court, Vols. 3–7.
*Sandf. Ch.* Sandford, New York Court of Chancery, 1843–7.
*Saund.* Saunders, King's Bench, Eng., 1666–73.
*Saund. & Co.* Saunders and Cole, Bail Court, Eng., 1842–8.
*Saus. & Sc.* Sausse and Sculley, Chancery, Ireland, 1837–40.
*Sav.* Savile, Common Pleas, Eng., 1579–94.
*Saw.* Sawyer, U. S. Circuit Court, Ninth Circuit, from 1870.
*Sax. Ch.* Saxton, New Jersey Court of Chancery, 1830–2.
*Say.* Sayer, King's Bench, Eng., 1751–6.
*Sc.* (*Scilicet.*) Understand; to wit; Scotch.

*Sc. Jur.* The Scottish Jurist, Court of Sessions, 1829–73.
*Sc. L. R.* Scottish Law Reporter, from 1865.
*Scam.* Scammon, Illinois Supreme Court, Vols. 2–5.
*Scan. Mag.* (*Scandalum Magnatum*) Slander, or Libel, of persons in high authority.
*Sch.* (*Scholium*) A note.
*Sch. & L.* Schoales and Lefroy, Chancery Ireland, 1802–9.
*Sco.* Scott, Common Pleas, Eng., 1834–40.
*Sco. (N. R.).* Scott's New Reports, Common Pleas, Eng., 1840–5.
*Scot.* Scotland.
*Sel. Cas.* Select Cases; Cases published anonymously under this title, Chancery, Eng., 1724–33.
*Seld.* Selden, New York Court of Appeals, Vols. 5–10.
*Sem.* (*Semble*) It seems.
*Sen.* Senate; Senator.
*Seq.* (*Sequitur*) It follows. (*Sequentes, Sequentia*) The following.
*Serg. & R.* Sergeant and Rawle, Pennsylvania Supreme Court, 1814–28.
*Ses. Cas.* Sessions Cases, King's Bench, Eng., 1844–57.
*Ses. Cas. Sc.* Court of Session Cases, Scotland, from 1821.
*Shaw,* Court of Sessions, Scotland, 1821–38.
*Shaw App.* Shaw's Scotch Appeals, House of Lords, 1821–4.
*Shaw & D.* Shaw and Dunlop, Court of Session, Scotland.
*Shaw & McL.* Shaw and Maclean, Scotch Appeals, House of Lords, 1835–8.
*Shaw, Just.* Justiciary Cases, Scotland, 1819–31, and from 1848–52.
*Shaw, T.* Court of Teinds, Scotland, 1821–31.
*Show.* Shower King's Bench, Eng., 1679–94.
*Show. P. C.* Shower's Parliamentary Cases, Eng., 1740.
*Sid.* Siderfin, King's Bench and Exchequer, Eng., 1657–70.
*Sim.* Simon, Chancery Eng. 1826–52.
*Sim. (N. S.)* Simon, Chancery, Eng., New Series, 1850–2.
*Sim. & St.* Simon and Stuart, Chancery, Eng., 1822–6.
*Skin.* Skinner, King's Bench, Eng., 1681–97.
*Sm. & G.* Smale and Gifford, Chancery, Eng., 1852–7
*Sm. & M.* Smede and Marshall, Mississippi High Court of Errors and Appeals, 1843–50.
*Sm. & M. (Ch.)* Smede and Marshall, Mississippi Superior Court of Chancery, 1840–53.
*Smith,* King's Bench, Eng., 1803–6.
*Smith & B.* Smith and Batty, King's Bench, Ireland, 1824–5.
*Smith, E. D.* New York Common Pleas, 1850–8.
*Smith (Ind.)* Indiana Supreme Court, 1848–9.

*Smith L. C.* Smith's Leading Cases (Hare and Wallace.)
*Smith (Pa.)*, Pennsylvania State Supreme Court, Vols. 51–81.*
*Smythe*, Common Pleas and Exchequer, Ireland, 1839–40.
*Sneed (Ky.)*, Printed Decisions Kentucky Court of Appeals, 1801–5.
*Sneed (Tenn.)*, Tennessee Supreme Court, 1853–8.
*South.* Southard, New Jersey Law, Vols. 4 and 5.
*South. L. R.* Southern Law Review.
*Spears*, South Carolina Court of Appeals, etc., at Law, 1842–4.
*Spears Eq.* South Carolina Court of Appeals, etc., in Equity, 1842–4.
*Spenc.* Spencer, New Jersey Law, Vol. 20.
*Spinks*, Admiralty, Eng., 1855–9.
*Spot.* Spottiswoode, Court of Session, Scotland.
*Sprague*, Admiralty Decisions, U. S. District Court, Massachusetts, 1841–64.
*S. S.* (*Scilicet.*) To wit.
*St. Tr.* State Trials, Eng., 1163–1820.
*Stair*, Court of Session, Scotland, 1661–81.
*Stark.* Starkie, Nisi Prius, Eng., 1814–22.
*Stat.* Statute; Statutes.
*Stew.* Stewart, Alabama Supreme Court, 1827–31.
*Stew. & P.* Stewart and Porter, Alabama Supreme Court, 1831–4.
*Stew. Adm.* Stewart, Vice-Admiralty Reports, Nova Scotia, 1803–13.
*Stockt.* Stockton, New Jersey Equity, Vols. 9–11.
*Story*, U. S. Circuit Court, First Circuit, 1829–45.
*Stra.* Strange, King's Bench, Eng., 1716–47.
*Strobh.* Strobhart, South Carolina Court of Appeals, etc., at law, 1843–50.
*Strobh. Eq.* Strobhart, South Carolina Court of Appeals, etc., in equity, 1846–50.
*Stu.* Stuart, King's Bench, Lower Canada, 1800–35.
*Stu., M. & P.* Stuart, Milne and Peddie, Court of Session, Scotland, 1851–3.
*Stu. Adm.* Stuart, Vice-Admiralty Reports, Lower Canada, 1836–74.
*Sty.* Style, King's Bench, Eng., 1645–55.
*Sumn.* Sumner, U. S. Circuit Court, First Circuit 1829–39.
*Sup.* Superior; Supreme.
*Supra*, Above; Before.
*Swa. Adm.* Swabey Admiralty, Eng., 1858–9.
*Swa. & Tr.* Swabey and Tristram, Probate and Divorce, Eng., 1858–66.
*Swan*, Tennessee Supreme Court, 1851–3.

*Swans.* Swanston, Chancery, Eng., 1818–19.
*Sweeney*, New York City Superior Court, Vols. 31 and 32.
*Swin.* Swinton, Justiciary Court, Scotland, 1835–41.
*Syme*, Justiciary Court, Scotland, 1826–9.

## T

*T.* Territory; Term.
*T. & M.* Temple and Mew Criminal Appeal, Eng., 1848–51.
*T. R.* Term Reports (Durnford and East), King's Bench, Eng., 1785–1800.
*Tam.* Tamlyn, Rolls Court, Eng., 1829–30.
*Taney*, U S. Circuit Court, Fourth Circuit, 1836–61.
*Tapp.* Tappan, Ohio Common Pleas, Fifth Circuit, 1816–19.
*Taunt.* Taunton, Common Pleas, Eng., 1807–19.
*Tayl.* (*N. C.*) Taylor, North Carolina Superior Courts, 1799–1802.
*Tayl.* (*U. C.*) Taylor, King's Bench, Upper Canada, 1823–7
*Tenn.* Tennessee Supreme Court.
*Tenn. Ch.* Tennessee Chancery Reports, from 1872.
*Tex.* Texas Supreme Court, from 1846.
*Tex. App.* Texas Appellate Courts, from 1876.
*Thach.* Thacher, Criminal Cases, Boston Municipal Court, 1823–43.
*Thomp. & C.* Thompson and Cook, New York Supreme Court.
*Thoms.* Thomson, Nova Scotia Decisions, 1834–51.
*Tinw.* Tinwald, Court of Session, Scotland.
*Toth.* Tothill, Chancery Eng., 1509–47
*Tread.* Treadway, South Carolina Constitutional Court, 1810–16.
*Tuck.* Tucker New York Surrogate's Court, 1864–9.
*Tuck. S. C.* Tucker's Select Cases, New Foundland.
*Tud. L. C.* Tudor's Leading Cases.
*Turn. & R.* Turner and Russell, Chancery Eng., 1822–4.
*Tyler*, Vermont Supreme Court, 1800–3.
*Tyng*, Massachusetts Supreme Court, Vols. 11–17
*Tyr.* Tyrwhitt, Exchequer Eng., 1830–5.
*Tyr. & G.* Tyrwhitt and Granger, Exchequer Eng., 1835–6.

## U.

*U. C.* Upper Canada; Queen's Bench Reports, from 1843; Common Pleas Reports, from 1850.
*U. C. J.* Upper Canada Jurist, 1844–8.

*U. C. L. J.* Upper Canada Law Journal.
*U. S.* United States Supreme Court Reports.
*U. S. C. C.* United States Circuit Court.
*U. S. D. C.* United States District Court.
*U. S. R. S.* United States Revised Statutes.
*U. T.* Utah Territory Supreme Court from 1855.
*Ult.* or *Ulto.* (*ultimo*). The last month preceding.

## V.

*V.* (*Versus*) against. (*Vide*) See.
*V. C.* Vice Chancellor.
*V. P.* Vice President.
*Va.* Virginia Supreme Court of Appeals, cited thus from Vol. 75, 1881.
*Va. Cas.* Virginia Cases, General Court, 1789–1826.
*Va. L. J.* Virginia Law Journal.
*Van Ness*, Prize Cases, U. S. District Court, New York, 1814.
*Vaugh.* Vaughan, Common Pleas, Eng., 1666–73.
*Vent.* Ventris, King's Bench, Eng., 1668–92.
*Vern.* Vernon, Chancery, Eng., 1681–1719.
*Vern. & S.* Vernon and Scriven, King's Bench, Ireland, 1786–8.
*Ves.* Vesey, Chancery, Eng., 1747–55.
*Ves. Jr.* Vesey, Jr., Chancery, Eng., 1789–1817.
*Ves. & B.* Vesey and Beames, Chancery, Eng., 1812–4.
*Ves. Sr.* See *Ves.*
*Vid.* (*Vide*) See (*Videlicet*), to-wit; that is to say.
*Vin. Abr.* Viner's Abridgment, English Law,
*Viz.* (*Videlicet*) To-wit; Namely; You may see.
*Vroom*, New Jersey Law, Vols. 30–49.
*Vt.* Vermont Supreme Court, from 1826.

## W.

*W. & S.* Wilson and Shaw, Scotch Appeals, House of Lords, 1825–34.
*W. & T.* White and Tudor's Leading Cases, Equity.
*W. Bl.* Sir Wm. Blackstone, various courts, Eng., 1746–79.
*W. H. & G.* Welsby, Hurlstone, and Gordon, Exchequer, 1847–54.
*W. L. B.* Weekly Law Bulletin, Cincinnati, from 1879.
*W. L. J.* Western Law Journal, Cincinnati, 1843–53.
*W. L. M.* Western Law Monthly, Cleveland, O., 1859–63.
*W. N.* Weekly Notes, all courts, Eng., from 1866.

*W. N. Cas.* Weekly Notes of Cases, all courts, Pennsylvania, from 1875.
*W. P. C.* Wollaston's Practice Cases, all courts, Eng.
*W. R.* Weekly Reporter, all courts, Eng.
*W. Va.* West Virginia Supreme Court of Appeals, from 1863.
*W. W. & D.* Willmore, Wollaston, and Davison, Queen's Bench, Eng., 1837.
*W. W. & H.* Willmore, Wollaston, and Hodge's, Queen's Bench, Eng., 1838–9.
*Wal.* Wallace, U S. Supreme Court, Vols. 68–90.
*Wal. C. C.* Wallace, U. S. Circuit Court, Third Circuit, 1801.
*Wal., Jr.* Wallace, Jr., U. S. Circuit Court, Third Circuit, 1842–62.
*Walk. Ch.* Walker, Michigan Court of Chancery, 1842–5.
*Wallis,* Chancery, Ireland, 1766–91.
*Ware,* U. S. District Court, Maine, 1822–6.
*Wash.* Washington, U. S. Circuit Court, Third Circuit, 1803–27.
*Wash. L. R.* Washington Law Reporter.
*Wash. T.* Washington Territory Supreme Court, from 1854.
*Wash. (Va.)* Washington, Virginia Court of Appeals, 1790–6.
*Watts,* Pennsylvania Supreme Court, 1832–40.
*Watts & S.* Watts and Sergeant, Pennsylvania Supreme Court, 1841–5.
*Web. P. C.* Webster's Patent Cases.
*Welsh,* Registry Cases, Ireland, 1832–40.
*Wend.* Wendell, New York Supreme Court and Court of Errors, 1828–41.
*West,* House of Lords, Eng., 1839–41.
*West & H.* West's Reports, time of Hardwicke, Chancery, 1736–9.
*West Jur.* The Western Jurist, Des Moines, Ia.
*Whart.* Wharton, Pennsylvania Supreme Court, 1835–41.
*Wheat.* Wheaton, U. S. Supreme Court, Vols. 6–25.
*Wheel. C. C.* Wheeler's Criminal Cases, New York Courts, 1796–1824.
*White,* Justiciary Cases, Scotland, 1855–8.
*Wight.* Wightwick, Exchequer, Eng., 1810–11.
*Willes,* various courts, Eng., 1737–58.
*Wilm.* Wilmot's Notes and Opinions, King's Bench, Eng., 1757–70.
*Wils.* Wilson, King's Bench and Common Pleas, Eng., 1742–74.
*Wils. & S.* Wilson and Shaw, Scotch Appeals, House of Lords, 1825–34.
*Wils. Ch.* Wilson, Chancery, Eng., 1818–9.

*Wils. Ex.* Wilson, Exchequer, Eng., 1817.
*Wils. Sup. Ct.* Wilson, Superior Court of Marion County, Indiana, 1871–4.
*Winch*, Common Pleas, Eng., 1622–5.
*Winst.* Winston, North Carolina Supreme Court, at Law, 1863–4.
*Winst. Eq.* Winston, North Carolina Supreme Court, in Equity, 1863–4.
*Wis.* Wisconsin Supreme Court, from 1853.
*Wms.* Peere Williams, Chancery, Eng., 1695–1735.
*Wolf. & B.* Wolferstan and Bristow, Election Cases, Eng., 1859–65.
*Wolf. & D.* Wolfertsan and Dews, Election Cases, Eng., 1856–8.
*Wood. & M.* Woodbury and Minot, U. S. Circuit Court, First Circuit, 1845–7.
*Woods*, U. S. Circuit Court, Fifth Circuit, 1870–81.
*Woolw.* Woolworth, U. S. Circuit Court, Eighth Circuit, 1863–9.
*Wright*, Ohio Supreme Court, 1831–4.
*Wright (Pa.)*, Pennsylvania State Supreme Court, Vols. 37–50.
*Wyo.* Wyoming Territory Supreme Court, from 1870.
*Wythe*, Virginia High Court of Chancery, 1788–99.

## Y.

*Y. & C.* Younge and Collier, Exchequer, Eng., 1834–40.
*Y. & C. N. C. C.* Younge and Collier, New Chancery Cases, Eng., 1841–3.
*Y. & J.* Younge and Jervis, Exchequer, Eng., 1826–30.
*Y. B.* Year Books, King's Bench, Eng., 1307–1537.
*Yates*, Select Cases, New York Courts, 1811.
*Yeates*, Pennsylvania, various courts, 1791–1808.
*Yel.* Yelverton, King's Bench, Eng., 1603–13.
*Yerg.* Yerger, Tennessee Supreme Court, 1832–7.
*Young*, Vice-Admiralty Reports, Canada, 1865–80.
*Younge*, Exchequer, Equity, Eng., 1830–2.

## Z.

*Zab.* Zabriskie, New Jersey Law, Vols. 21–24.

# APPENDIX B.

## Latin and French Maxims of the Law, Translated and Explained.

---

*A coelo usque ad centrum:* from the heavens to the center of the earth; descriptive of the vertical extent of an owner's right in land.

*A communi observantia non est recedendum:* common usage (or observance) should not be departed from.

*A jure suo cadunt:* they fall from, or lose their right.

*A l'impossible nul n'est tenu:* no one is bound to do an impossible thing.

*A non posse ad non esse sequitur argumentum necessarie negative; licet non affirmative:* from impossibility to non-existence the argument follows necessarily; but existence can not be argued from possibility.

*A piratis et latronibus capta dominium non mutant:* the ownership of things taken by pirates and thieves does not change.

*A tempore cujus contrarii memoria non existit:* from a time of which memory to the contrary does not exist.

*A verbis legis non est recedendum:* from the words of the law there must be no departure; *i.e.*, statutes must be strictly construed.

*Ab assuetis non fit injuria*: from that which has grown customary no legal wrong can arise See *Acquiescence.*

*Abbreviationem ille numerus et sensus accipiendus est, ut concessio non sit inanis:* in abbreviations, the number and sense is to be so interpreted, that the grant be not made void.

*Abundans cautela non nocet:* extreme care does no mischief.

*Accessio cedit principali:* the accessary, or thing annnexed to, goes with the principal.

*Accessorium non ducit* (or *trahit*) *sed sequitur suum principale:* that which is the accessory, or incident, does not lead, or carry, but follows, or goes with, its principal.

*Accessorius sequitur naturam sui principalis:* an accessory follows the nature of his principal, and therefore can not be guilty of a higher crime.

*Accusare nemo se debet:* no one is bound to accuse himself.

*Accusator post rationabile tempus non est audiendus, nisi se bene de omissione excusaverit:* an accuser ought not to be heard after a reasonable time, unless he has made a good excuse for his delay.

*Acta exteriora, indicant interiora secreta:* outward acts show the inward intent.

*Actio non datur non damnificato:* no action is given to one who is not injured.

*Actio personalis moritur cum persona:* a personal action dies with the person. The rule has been greatly modified by the statutes of Great Britain and the various states.

*Actio poenalis in haeredem non datur, nisi forte ex damno locupletior haeres factus sit:* a penal action is not given against an heir, unless such heir is benefited by the wrong.

*Actori incumbit onus probandi:* the burden of proof lies on a plaintiff.

*Actore non probante reus absolvitur:* when the plaintiff does not prove his case the defendant is acquitted.

*Actor sequitur forum rei:* a plaintiff follows the court of the (*reus*) defendant; *i.e.*, he must bring his action in that court which has jurisdiction over the defendant.

*Actus curiae* (or *legis*) *nemini facit injuriam:* the act of the court does wrong to no one.

*Actus Dei neminem gravabit* (or *nemini nocet*): the act of God prejudices no one.

*Actus me invito factus, non est meus actus:* an act done by me against my will is not my act. Thus the law presumes coercion by a prince over his subject, and by a husband (in general) over his wife.

*Actus non facit reum, nisi mens sit rea:* an act does not make a man guilty, unless he be so in intention.

*Ad ea quae frequentius accidunt jura adaptantur:* the laws are adapted to those cases which most frequently arise.

*Ad proximum antecedens fiat relatio, nisi impediatur sententia:* the relative should be referred to the next, or last, antecedent, unless the sense forbid.

*Ad questiones facti non respondent judices; ad questiones legis non respondent juratores:* in trial by jury the judges do not decide questions of fact, nor the jury questions of law.

*Aedificare in tuo proprio solo non licet quod alteri noceat:* it is not lawful to build on your own land what may injure another.

*Aedificatum solo, solo cedit:* that which is built upon the land goes with the land.

*Aequitas est quasi aequalitas:* equity is as it were equality.

*Aequitas factum habet quod fieri oportuit:* equity considers that to have been done which ought to have been done.

*Aequitas nunquam contravenit leges:* equity never contravenes the laws.

*Aequitas sequitur legem:* equity follows law. See *Equity.*

*Aestimatio praeteriti delicti ex post facto nunquam crescit:* the estimation of a crime committed is never increased by what happens afterward

*Affectus punitur licet non sequatur ectus:* the intention is punished, although the consequence do not follow.

*Affinis mei affinis non est mihi affinis:* one related by marriage to one related to me by marriage has no affinity to me.

*Affirmanti, non neganti, incumbit probatio:* the proof lies upon him who affirms, not upon him who denies.

*Agentes et consentientes pari poena plectentur:* acting and consenting parties are liable to the same punishment.

*Alienatio licet prohibeatur, consensu tamen omnium in quorum favorum prohibita est potest fieri:* though alienation be forbidden, yet it may be made with the consent of all in whose favor the prohibition is made.

*Alienatio rei praefertur juri accrescendi:* alienation is favored (by the law) rather than accumulation. See *Perpetuity.*

*Alii per alium non acquiritur obligatio:* one man can not incur a liability through another. [Unless the latter is his agent duly authorized.]

*Aliquid conceditur ne injuria remanerit impunita quod alias non concederetur:* something is conceded, which otherwise would not be, lest an injury remain unredressed.

*Aliquis non debet esse judex in propria causa quia non potest esse judex et pars* one ought not to be a judge in his own case, for it is not possible for one to be both judge and suitor.

*Aliud est celare, aliud tacere:* it is one thing to conceal; another, to be silent.

*Aliud simulatum, aliud actum:* one thing is pretended, another thing done. See, *e.g., Fraud on a power.*

*Allegans contraria non est audiendus:* a person making contradictory allegations is not to be listened to.

*Allegans suam turpitudinem non est audiendus:* a person alleging his own infamy is not to be listened to.

*Allegari non debuit quod probatum non relevat:* that which, if proved, would not be relevant, ought not to be alleged.

*Ambigua responsio contra proferentem est accipienda:* an ambiguous answer is to be taken against him who makes it.

*Ambiguis casibus semper praesumitur pro rege:* in doubtful cases the presumption is always in favor of the crown.

*Ambiguitas verborum latens verificatione suppletur; nam quod ex facto oritur ambiguum verificatione facti tollitur:* latent ambiguity may be supplied by evidence; for an ambiguity which arises from an extrinsic fact may be removed by proof of the fact

*Ambiguitas verborum patens nulla verificatione excluditur:* an ambiguity patent can not be removed by proof.

*Ambiguum pactum contra venditorem interpretandum est:* an ambiguou contract ought to be construed against the seller.

*Ambiguum placitum interpretari debet contra proferentem:* an ambiguous plea ought to be interpreted against the pleader.

*Animus ad se omne jus ducit:* intention attracts all law to itself In many inportant actions the law holds their efficacy to depend on he intention with which they are proved to have been performed, *e.g.*, in the matter of change of domicile, the intention of permanently abiding in the new residence (*animus manendi*), or of returning to the old one (*animus revertendi*) is essential.

*Animus hominis est anima scripti:* a man's purpose is the spirit of his writing.

*Apices juris non sunt jura:* the niceties of the law are not the law

*Aqua cedit solo:* water passes with the soil. In the eye of the law water is land covered with water; the ownership of water, therefore, goes with that of the soil beneath. Where a river divides properties belonging to different persons, the center, or *medium filum*, of the stream is taken to be the boundary line.

*Aqua cedit et debet currere:* water flows, and ought to flow, *i.e.*, there is no property in running water, merely a right to use it; and this right may only so be exercised as not to interfere with the use of the water by other persons similarly entitled.

*Argumentum ab inconvenienti plurimum valet in lege:* an argument drawn from inconvenience is very forcible in law, *i.e.*, when the case is a doubtful one, and the construction of the statute, or instrument involved, is not clear.

*Arma in armatos sumere jura sinunt:* the laws permit the taking up of arms against armed persons.

*Assignatus utitur jure auctoris:* an assignee enjoys the rights of his assignor.

*Benigne faciendae sunt interpretationes, propter simplicitatem laicorum, ut res magis valeat quam pereat; et verba intentioni, non è contra, debent inservire;* in construing written instruments some latitude of interpretation must be allowed on account of the want of technical knowledge in the general public, so that the instrument may rather be upheld than come to nought; and words ought to subserve the intention, not the reverse.

*Benignior sententia, in verbis generalibus seu dubiis est praeferenda*: the more liberal meaning of general, or doubtful, words is to be preferred.

*Bis dat qui cito dat*: he gives double who gives promptly.

*Bona fides exigit ut quod convenit fiat*: good faith requires that what is agreed upon should be done.

*Bona fides non patitur, ut bis idem exigatur*: good faith does not suffer that payment should be twice exacted for the same thing.

*Boni judicis est ampliare jurisdictionem*: it is the duty of a good judge to enlarge his jurisdiction; *i.e.*, to amplify the remedies of the law and apply its rules to the advancement of substantial justice.

*Boni judicis est causas litium dirimere et interest reipublicae ut sit finis litium*: it is the duty of a good judge to prevent litigation; and it is for the benefit of the state that there should be an end of lawsuits.

*Bonus judex secundum aequum et bonum judicat, et aequitatem stricto juri praefert*: a good judge decides according to equity and right, and prefers equity to strict law.

*Casus omissus et oblivioni datus dispositioni communis juris relinquitur*: a case omitted and forgotten [in framing a law] is left to the disposal of the common law.

*Causa proxima, non remota spectatur*: the immediate, not the remote, cause is to be regarded.

*Caveat emptor; qui ignorare non debuit quod jus alienum emit*: let the buyer beware; who ought not to be ignorant that he is buying another's rights.

*Certum est quod certum reddi potest*: that is certain which can be rendered certain.

*Cessante causa, cessat effectus*: the cause ceasing, the effect ceases.

*Cessante ratione legis, cessat ipsa lex*: the reason of the law ceasing, the law itself ceases.

*Chirographum apud debitorem repertum praesumitur solutum*: a bond found with the debtor is presumed to be paid.

*Circuitus est evitandus*: circuity is to be avoided.

*Clausula generalis de residuo non ea complectitur quae non ejusdem sint generis cum iis quae speciatim dicta fuerunt*: a general clause concerning the residue does not comprehend those things which are not of the same kind with those which have been specially expressed.

*Clausula quae abrogationem excludit ab initio non valet:* a clause [in a law] which precludes its repeal is invalid from the beginning.

*Clausulae inconsuetae semper inducunt suspicionem:* unusual clauses always excite suspicion.

*Cogitationis poenam nemo patitur:* no one suffers punishment for his thoughts.

*Commodum ex injuria sua nemo habere debet:* no person ought to derive benefit from his own wrong.

*Communis error facit jus:* a common error makes (or becomes) law.

*Concessio versus concedentem latam interpretationem habere debet:* a grant ought to have a liberal interpretation (or be strictly construed) against the grantor.

*Conditio illicita habetur pro non adjicta:* an unlawful condition is held as not annexed.

*Conditio praecedens adimpleri debet priusquam sequatur effectus:* a condition precedent must be fulfilled before the effect can follow.

*Conditiones quaelibet odiosae; maxime autem contra matrimonium et commercium:* any conditions are odious; but especially those against marriage and commerce.

*Confessio facta in judicio omni probatione major est:* a confession made in court is of greater effect than any proof.

*Confirmare nemo potest priusquam jus ei acciderit:* no one can confirm before the right accrues to him.

*Confirmatio omnes supplet defectus, licet id quod actum est ab initio non valuit:* confirmation supplies all defects though that which was done was not valid at the beginning.

*Confirmat usum qui tollit abusum:* he confirms a use who checks an abuse.

*Consensus facit legem:* consent makes the law; *i.e.*, the agreement of the parties is the law between them.

*Consensus, non concubitus, facit matrimonium:* consent, not cohabitation, constitutes marriage.

*Consensus tollit errorem:* consent removes or obviates mistake.

*Consentientes et agentes pari poena plectantur:* those consenting and those perpetrating are liable to equal punishment.

*Consentire videtur qui tacet:* silence gives consent.

*Constructio legis non facit injuriam:* the construction of the law does (*i.e.*, should be made to do) no injury

*Consuetudo est optimus interpres legum:* custom is the best expounder of the laws.

*Consuetudo ex certa causa rationabili usitata privat communem legem:* a custom founded on a certain and reasonable ground supersedes the common law.

*Consuetudo loci est observanda:* the custom of the place is to be observed.

*Contemporanea expositio est optima et fortissima in lege:* a contemporaneous interpretation is the best and most authoritative in the eye of the law.

*Contra non valentem agere nulla currit praescriptio:* no prescription runs against a person under disability. This maxim is only true within certain limits fixed by the Statutes of Limitation.

*Contractus ex turpi causa vel contra bonos mores, nullus:* a contract arising out of a base consideration, or against morality, is null

*Conventio vincit legem:* an agreement prevails against any implication of law.

*Copulatio verborum indicat acceptationem in eodem sensu:* the coupling of words together indicates that they are to be understood in the same sense.

*Cui licet quod majus non debet quod minus est non licere:* he who has authority to do the more important ought not to be prohibited from doing that which is less important.

*Cuicunque aliquis quid concedit, concedere videtur et id, sine quo res ipsa esse non potuit:* whoever grants any thing to another is supposed to grant that also without which the thing itself would be of no use. See *Way of necessity,*

*Cuilibet in arte sua perito est credendum:* every skilled person is to be believed with reference to his own art. See ***Expert.***

*Cujus est commodum ejus debet esse incommodum:* he who has the advantage should also bear the disadvantage.

*Cujus est dare ejus est disponere:* whose it is to give, his it is to regulate the manner of the gift.

*Cujus est divisio alterius est electio:* when one party has the division, the other has the choice.

*Cujus est instituere ejus est abrogare:* he that legislates may also abrogate.

*Cujus est solum ejus est usque ad coelum et ad inferos:* he who owns the surface soil owns also (*prima facie*) up to the sky above it, and the center of the earth beneath it. Under the former would be included buildings; under the latter, minerals.

*Culpa lata dolo aequiparatur:* gross negligence is held equivalent to intentional wrong.

*Culpae poena par esto:* let the punishment be proportioned to the crime.

*Cum confitente sponte mitius est agendum*: one confessing willingly should be dealt with more leniently.

*Cum duo inter se pugnantia repertuntur in testamento ultimum ratum est:* where two things repugnant to each other are found in a will, the last prevails.

*Dans et retinens nihil dat*: giving and retaining [possession] gives nothing.

*De jure judices, de facto juratores, respondent:* the judges answer concerning the law, the jury concerning the facts.

*De minimis non curat lex*: the law takes no account of trifles.

*De non apparentibus et non existentibus eadem est ratio:* concerning things which do not appear, the law is the same as concerning things which do not exist.

*Debet esse finis litium*: there ought to be an end of law suits.

*Debita sequuntur personam debitoris:* debts follow the person of the debtor.

*Debitor non presumitur donare*: a debtor is not presumed to give. "A man must be just before he is generous."

*Delegatus non potest delegare:* a delegate can not delegate; *i.e.*, the person to whom an office, or a duty, is delegated, *e.g.* an attorney, director, or trustee can not lawfully devolve the duty upon another, unless he be expressly authorized to do so.

*Delicatus debitor est odiosus in lege:* a luxurious debtor is odious in the eye of the law.

*Derivativa potestas non potest esse major primitivâ:* the derivative power can not be greater than the primitive.

*Deus solus haeredem facere potest, non homo*: God alone, and not man, can make an heir; *i.e.*, heirship is matter of birth, not of grant.

*Dies dominicus non est juridicus*: Sunday is not a judicial day.

*Dies inceptus pro completo habetur:* a day begun is held as complete.

*Dolosus versatur in generalibus:* he who wishes to deceive uses general, or ambiguous terms.

*Dolus auctoris non nocet successori:* the fraud of a predecessor prejudices not his successor.

*Dolus circuitu non purgatur:* fraud is not purged by circuity.

*Domus sua cuique est tutissimum refugium:* to every one his own house is the safest refuge. "Every man's house is his castle."

*Dona clandestina sunt semper suspiciosa:* clandestine gifts are always suspicious.

*Donatio non praesumitur:* a gift is not presumed.

*Donatio perficitur possessione accipientis:* a gift is perfected by possession of the receiver.

*Dormiunt aliquando leges, nunquam moriuntur*: the laws sometime sleep, never die.

*Duo non possunt in solido unam rem possidere*: two can not possess the whole of one thing in its entirety.

*Ei incumbit probatio, qui dicit, non qui negat*: the proof lies upon him who affirms, not upon him who denies.

*Ejus est periculum cujus est dominium aut commodum*: he who has the dominion or advantage has the risk.

*Ejus nulla culpa est cui parere necesse sit*: he is not in any fault who is bound to obey.

*Electio semel facta non patitur regressum*: election once made can not be recalled; *i.e.*, if made deliberately and with full knowledge of the circumstances. See *Quod semel, etc.*

*Emptor emit quam minimo potest, venditor vendit quam maximo potest*: the buyer buys for as little as possible; the seller sells for as much as possible.

*Ex antecedentibus et consequentibus fit optima interpretatio*: the best interpretation is made from the context.

*Ex diuturnitate temporis omnia praesumuntur rite esse acta*: after a lapse of time every thing is presumed to have been properly done.

*Ex dolo malo non oritur actio*: no right of action can arise out of a fraud.

*Ex nudo pacto non oritur actio*: from a nude contract, (*i.e.*, one not supported by consideration) no right of action can arise.

*Ex turpi causa non oritur actio*: from an immoral cause, (*i.e.*, on a contract founded on an immoral consideration), no right of action can arise.

*Exceptio probat regulam de rebus non exceptis*: an exception proves the rule concerning things not excepted.

*Exempla illustrant non restringunt legem*: examples illustrate, but do not restrain the law.

*Expedit reipublicae ne sua re quis male utetur*: it is for the public good that no one use his property badly.

*Expedit reipublicae ut sit finis litium*: it is for the public good that there be an end of litigation.

*Experientia docet*: experience teaches.

*Expressio eorum quae tacite insunt nihil operatur*: the expression of those things which are tacitly implied has no effect.

*Expressio unius est exclusio alterius*: the mention of one is the exclusion of another; *i.e.*, by particularizing one or more members of a class, or objects of a group, an intention may be indicated to exclude the rest.

*Expressum facit cessare tacitum*: what is expressed makes

what is silent to cease; *i.e.*, where we find an express declaration we should not resort to implication.

*Extra legem positus est civiliter mortuus*: he who is placed out of the law is civilly dead.

*Extra territorium jus dicenti impune non paretur*: one exercising jurisdiction out of his territory can not be obeyed with impunity.

*Facta sunt potentiora verbis:* deeds are more powerful than words.

*Factum a judice quod ad ejus officium non spectat, non ratum est:* an action of a judge which relates not to his office, is of no force.

*Falsa demonstratio non nocet*: false description does not vitiate; *e.g.*, a legacy or devise. See *Nihil facit*, etc.

*Falsa orthographia, sive falsa grammatica, non vitiat concessionem:* bad spelling or bad grammar does not vitiate a grant

*Falsus in uno, falsus in omnibus*: false in one thing, false in all.

*Fatetur facinus qui judicium fugit:* he who flees judgment confesses his guilt.

*Fiat justitia, ruat coelum:* let right be done, though the heavens should fall.

*Fictio legis inique operatur alicui damnum vel injuriam:* a legal fiction does not properly work loss or injury. For instances of legal fictions, see *Ejectment; Seduction; Trover.*

*Fieri non debuit, sed factum valet*: it ought not to have been done, but being done it is binding; *e.g.*, a marriage without proper consents.

*Fractionem diei non recipit lex:* the law does not take notice of a portion of a day. When therefore a thing is to be done upon a certain day, all that day is allowed to do it in. Exceptions to this rule are, however, allowed in cases of necessity, and for the purposes of justice, and in cases of documents registered on the same day priority of registration may be shown by the numbers or the like.

*Fraus est celare fraudem*: it is fraud to conceal fraud.

*Fraus latet in generalibus:* fraud lies hid in general expressions.

*Frustra fit per plura, quod fieri potest per pauciora*: that is needlessly done by many (words) which can be done by less.

*Frustra probatur quod probatum non relevat:* it is useless to prove that which, when proved, is not relevant.

*Furiosi nulla voluntas est:* a madman has no free will; *i.e.*, he is not criminally responsible.

*Furtum non est ubi initium habet detentionis per dominum rei;* there is no theft where the origin of the possession was with the consent of the owner; *i.e.*, where the original possession is lawful, as in the case of a bailee.

*Generalia specialibus non derogant:* general words do not derogate from special.

*Grammatica falsa non vitiat chartam:* false grammar does not vitiate a deed.

*Haereditas nunquam ascendit:* inheritance never ascends. This maxim of the feudal law has been deprived of its force by the statutes of England and the various states regulating descents.

*Haeres legitimus est quem nuptiae demonstrant:* he is the lawful heir whom the marriage proves to be so.

*Id certum est quod certum reddi potest:* that is certain which can be reduced to a certainty.

*Idem est non esse et non apparere:* not to be and not to appear are the same; *i.e.*, in the law of evidence, where he on whom the onus of proving an affirmative fails in such proof, the contrary is presumed, though there be no evidence in support of that presumption.

*Ignorantia facti excusat, ignorantia juris non excusat:* ignorance of the fact excuses; ignorance of the law excuses not; inasmuch as every one is held to be cognisant of it; *quod quisque tenetur scire.*

*Imperitia culpae adnumeratur:* want of skill (in one professing to have it) is accounted a fault.

*Impotentia excusat legem:* impossibility is an excuse at law.

*Impunitas semper ad deteriora invitat:* impunity always invites to worse faults.

*In aequali jure melior est conditio possidentis:* where the rights are equal, the condition of the possessor is best.

*In alternativis electio est debitoris:* in alternatives the debtor has the election.

*In consimili casu, consimile debet esse remedium:* in similar cases the remedy should be similar.

*In contractibus tacite insunt quae sunt moris et consuetudinis:* in contracts matters of custom and general usage are implied.

*In conventionibus contrahentium voluntas potius quam verba spectari placuit:* in agreements, the intention of the parties should be regarded rather than the words actually used.

*In dubio haec legis constructio quam verba ostendunt:* in a doubtful case, the construction which the words point out is the construction given by the law.

*In dubio pars melior est sequenda:* in a doubtful case the gentler course is to be pursued.

*In fictione juris semper aequitas existit:* in legal fictions there is always an inherent equity. See *Fiction.*

*In jure, non remota causa, sed proxima spectatur:* in law, the proximate, and not the remote cause is to be regarded.

*In maleficiis voluntas spectatur non exitus:* in criminal acts the intention is to be regarded, not the result.

*In odium spoliatoris omnia praesumuntur:* all things are presumed against a spoliator; *i. e.,* one who destroys evidence.

*In pari delicto, potior est conditio possidentis* [or *defendentis*]: where both parties are equally in the wrong, the possessor [or defendant], has the better position.

*In propria causa nemo judex sit:* no one should be a judge in his own case.

*In re communi potior est conditio prohibentis:* in a partnership, the partner who forbids a change has the better right; *i.e.,* where the voices are equally divided.

*In societatis contractibus fides exuberet:* the strictest good faith must be observed in partnership transactions.

*In traditionibus chartarum non quod dictum sed quod factum est inspicitur:* in the delivery of deeds, regard must be had, not to what was said at the time, but to what was done. See *Escrow.*

*Inclusio unius est exclusio alterius:* the inclusion of one is the exclusion of another. See *Expressio.*

*Incommodum non solvit argumentum:* inconvenience does not destroy an argument.

*Index animi sermo:* speech is the index of the mind.

*Iniquum est aliquem rei suae esse judicem:* it is unjust for any one to be judge in his own case.

*Injuria non excusat injuriam:* one wrong does not justify another.

*Injuria non praesumitur:* injury is not presumed.

*Intentio imponit nomen operi:* the intention gives the name to the act.

*Interest reipublicae ut sit finis litium:* it is for the interest of the state that there should be an end of litigation. See *Limitation of Actions; Maintenance.*

*Interpretatio talis fienda est ut res magis valeat quam pereat:* such an interpretation is to be adopted, that the thing may rather stand than fall. See *Benigne, etc.*

*Interpretatio talis (in) ambiguis semper fienda est, ut evitetur inconveniens et absurdum:* in doubtful matters, such an interpretation is to be adopted that inconsistency and absurdity may be avoided.

*Invito beneficium non datur:* a benefit can not be forced on one who is unwilling to receive it.

*Judex aequitatem semper spectari debet:* a judge ought always to aim at equity.

*Judicandum est legibus non exemplis:* we should judge by the laws, not precedents

*Judices non tenentur exprimere causam sententiae suae:* judges are not bound to explain the reason of their judgments

*Judicia posteriora sunt in lege fortiora:* the later decisions are the stronger in law.

*Judicis est judicare secundum alleguta et probata:* it is the duty of a judge to decide according to facts alleged and proved.

*Judicis est jus dicere non dare:* it is for a judge to administer, not to make laws

*Judicium a non suo judice datum, nullius est momenti:* a judgment rendered by one not a proper judge is of no weight.

*Jura eodem modo destituuntur quo constituuntur:* laws are abrogated in the same manner in which they are made.

*Juratores sunt judices facti:* jurors are the judges of fact.

*Juri pro se introducto cuique licet renunciare:* every man may renounce the benefit of a stipulation inserted in his favor.

*Jus accrescendi inter mercatores locum non habet, pro beneficio commercii:* the right of survivorship does not exist among merchants, for the benefit of commerce.

*Jus accrescendi praefertur oneribus et ultimae voluntati:* the right of survivorship prevails against any attempt by a joint tenant to incumber or devise his interest.

*Jus ex injuria non oritur:* a right can not arise out of wrongdoing.

*Jus publicum privatorum pactis mutari non potest:* a public right can not be altered by the agreements of private persons.

*Lata culpa dolo aequiparatur:* gross negligence is tantamount to fraud.

*Leges posteriores priores contrarias abrogant:* later laws abrogate prior contrary laws.

*Le salut du peuple, est la supreme loi:* the safety of the people is the supreme law.

*Leges vigilantibus, non dormientibus subveniunt:* the laws aid the vigilant, not those who sleep on their rights.

*Legis interpretatio legis vim obtinet:* the interpretation of law obtains the force of law.

*Lex citius tolerare vult privatum damnum quam publicum malum:* the law will more readily tolerate a private loss than a public evil

*Lex dilationes exhorret:* the law abhors delays.

*Lex judicat de rebus necessarie faciendis quasi re-ipsa factis:* the law judges of things which must necessarily be done, as if actually done

*Lex nil facit frustra; nil jubet frustra:* the law does nothing in vain; commands nothing in vain.

*Lex non cogit ad impossibilia*: the law does not compel impossibilities. See *Impossibility*

*Lex non curat de minimis*: the law cares not about trifles.

*Lex non favet delicatorum votis:* the law favors not the wishes of the dainty. In deciding whether an alleged nuisance should be restrained by injunction, the court considers whether it is such as would materially inconvenience persons of ordinary, not fastidious, habits.

*Lex prospicit non respicit*: the law looks forward, not backward; *i.e.*, statutes are not, as a rule, retrospective.

*Lex respicit aequitatem*: the law pays regard to equity.

*Lex semper dabit remedium:* the law will always furnish a remedy.

*Lex spectat naturae ordinem*: the law has regard to the order and course of nature.

*Linea recta semper praefertur transversali:* the direct line is always preferred to the collateral.

*Locus regit actum.* The place governs the act; that is, the validity of a legal transaction is, by international comity, usually governed by the law of the place where it was concluded.

*Magis de bono quam de malo lex intendit:* the law favors a good (*i.e.*, lawful) rather than a bad construction.

*Majus dignum trahit ad se minus dignum:* the more worthy draws to itself the less worthy.

*Mala grammatica non vitiat chartam*: bad grammar does not vitiate a deed.

*Maledicta expositio quae corrumpit textum*: it is a cursed exposition which corrupts the text.

*Malitia supplet aetatem:* Malice supplies [the want of] age. Between seven and fourteen years of age an infant is presumed to be incapable of a criminal intention, but the contrary may be proved.

*Malus usus est abolendus*: an evil custom should be abolished.

*Melior est conditio defendentis*, or *posidentis*: the condition of the party in possession is the better one; *i.e.*, where the right of the parties is equal. *Possession is nine-tenths of the law.*

*Melius est petere fontes quam sectari rivulos:* it is better to go to the fountain head than to follow streamlets from it. This applies especially to quotations, extracts, and conclusions deduced from leading cases and authorities.

*Mens testatoris in testamentis spectanda est*: in wills the intention of the testator is to be regarded.

*Minatur innocentibus qui parcit nocentibus:* he threatens the innocent who spares the guilty.

*Minime mutanda sunt quae certam habent interpretationem:*

things which have a certain interpretation are to be altered as little as possible. This applies especially to conveyancing terms.

*Misera est servitus ubi jus est vagum aut incertum:* wretched is the slavery where the law is changeable or uncertain.

*Mobilia sequuntur personam:* movables follow the person. In accordance with this maxim, personal assets of an intestate are distributed according to the laws of the country where he is domiciled, not of that where they are situate.

*Modus et conventio vincunt legem:* the form of the agreement and consent overrule the law.

*Multa non vetat lex, quae tamen tacite damnavit:* the law forbids not many things which yet it has silently condemned.

*Multitudo imperitorum perdit curiam:* a multitude of ignorant practitioners destroys a court.

*Necessitas non habet legem:* necessity has no law.

*Necessitas publica major est quam privata:* public necessity is stronger than private.

*Necessitas quod cogit, defendit:* necessity defends what it compels; *e.g.*, acts necessary for self-preservation.

*Necessitas sub lege non continetur, quia quod alias non est licitum necessitas facit licitum:* necessity is not limited by law; since, what otherwise is not lawful, necessity makes lawful.

*Necessitas vincit legem:* necessity overcomes law.

*Ne lites sint immortales dum litantes sunt mortales:* let not law suits last forever, seeing that the litigants are but mortal.

*Nemo agit in seipsum:* no one can implead himself.

*Nemo contra factum suum venire potest:* no one can go against his own deed. See *Estoppel*.

*Nemo dat quod non habet:* no one can give that which he has not; *i.e.*, no one can give a better title to a thing than he possesses himself. But see *Negotiable.*

*Nemo de domo sua extrahi potest:* no one can be dragged out of his own house. Every man's house is his castle.

*Nemo debet bis puniri pro uno delicto:* no one ought to be punished twice for the same offense.

*Nemo debet bis vexari pro una et eadem causa:* no man ought to be twice harassed, *i.e.* sued, for one and the same cause.

*Nemo debet esse judex in propria causa:* no one should be judge in his own cause.

*Nemo debet locupletari aliena jactura:* no one ought to be enriched at another's expense.

*Nemo est haeres viventis:* no one is the heir of a living man; *i.e.*, strictly speaking, the question of heirship only arises on the death of the owner. See *Heir; Haeres.*

*Nemo ex suo delicto meliorem suam conditionem facere potest:* no one can make his condition better by his own tort.

*Nemo patriam exuere nec ligeantiae debitum ejurare possit:* no man can disclaim his native land, nor abjure the bond of allegiance. See *Naturalization.*

*Nemo potest esse simul actor et judex:* no one can be at once suitor and judge. See *Nemo debet esse judex.*

*Nemo potest facere per alium, quod per se non potest:* no one can do through another what he can not do himself.

*Nemo potest mutare consilium suum in alterius injuriam:* no one can change his purpose to the injury of another. See *Estoppel.*

*Nemo potest plus juris ad alium transferre quam ipse habet:* no one can transfer a greater right to another than he himself has. See *Nemo dat, etc.*

*Nemo praesumitur ludere in extremis:* no one is presumed to trifle at the point of death; *i.e.*, an expression in a will is not to be taken as meaningless or absurd if this can be avoided.

*Nemo praesumitur malus:* no one is presumed to be bad.

*Nemo tenetur ad impossibile:* no one is bound to [perform] an impossibility. See *Impossibility.*

*Nemo tenetur edere instrumenta contra se:* no one is obliged to produce instruments which tell against himself. Changed by statute in most states and in England.

*Nemo tenetur seipsum accusare:* no one is bound to criminate himself.

*Nihil facit error nominis cum de corpore vel persona constat:* a mistake in the name does not matter when there is certainty as to the thing or person. See *Falsa demonstratio, etc.*

*Nihil quod est inconveniens est licitum:* nothing that is inconsistent is allowed. *E.g.*, contracts are void which are opposed to public policy.

*Nil consensui tam contrarium est quam vis atque metus:* nothing is so opposed to consent as force and fear. See *Duress.*

*Nimia subtilitas in jure reprobatur:* too much subtlety in law is reprehensible.

*Nimium altercando veritas amittitur:* by too much altercation truth is lost.

*Nomina sunt notae rerum:* names are the marks of things.

*Non accipi debent verba in demonstrationem falsam quae competunt in limitationem veram:* words which admit of a true (*i.e.*, intelligible or consistent) meaning ought not to be received in a false sense.

*Non aliter a significatione verborum recedi oportet quam cum manifestum est aliud sensisse testatorem:* it behoves us not to depart from the literal meaning of words, unless it is evident that the testator intended some other meaning.

*Non debet cui plus licet, quod minus est non licere:* it is not right that he who is allowed to do the greater should not be allowed also to do the lesser. Cf. *Omne majus, etc.*

*Non decipitur qui scit se decipi:* he is not deceived who knows himself to be deceived.

*Non est regula quin fallat:* there is no rule which may not fail; *i.e.*, every rule has its exceptions.

*Non omne damnum inducit injuriam:* not every loss works an injury.

*Non omne quod licet honestum est:* not every thing which the law allows is honorable.

*Non possessori incumbit necessitas probandi possessiones ad se pertinere:* a person in possession is not bound to prove that the possessions belong to him. Cf. *Melior est conditio, etc.*

*Non potest adduci exceptio ejus rei cujus petitur dissolutio:* an objection can not be founded on the same thing the avoidance of which is sought; *i.e.*, one can not impugn the legality of an instrument or proceeding, and at the same time assert that it is binding on the other party.

*Non potest probari quod probatum non relevat:* that may not be proved which, if proved, is immaterial.

*Non potest rex gratiam facere cum injuria et damno aliorum:* the king can not confer a favor on one subject which occasions injury and loss to others.

*Non quod dictum est, sed quod factum est, inspicitur:* regard is to be had, not to what is said, but to what is done.

*Non refert an quis assensum suum praefert verbis, aut rebus ipsis et factis:* it matters not whether a man gives his assent by his words or by his acts and deeds.

*Non refert quid notum sit judici, si notum non sit in forma judicii:* it matters not what is known to the judge, if it be not known in a judicial form; *i.e.*, if he have not judicial cognisance (*q.v.*) of it.

*Non videntur qui errant consentire:* they are not considered to consent who act under a mistake. See *Mistake.*

*Noscitur ex sociis, qui non cognoscitur ex se:* he who can not be known from himself may be known from his associates; so the meaning a word may be ascertained from the context.

*Novatio non praesumitur:* novation is not presumed.

*Nuda pactio obligationem non parit:* a naked promise [*i.e.*, one without a consideration] does not create a [legal] obligation.

*Nulla pactione effici potest ut dolus praestetur:* by no contract can one effect that a fraud shall be maintained.

*Nullum simile est idem nisi quatuor pedibus currit:* no like is identical, unless it run on "all fours."

*Nullum tempus occurrit regi* [or *rei publicae*]: no time can prejudice the king [or commonwealth]. In other words, the Statutes of Limitation do not run against the crown or the state.

*Nullus commodum capere potest de injuria sua propria:* no one can obtain an advantage by his own wrong.

*Nunquam crescit ex post facto praeteriti delicti aestimatio:* the heinousness of a past offense is never increased by what happens afterward.

*Odiosa et inhonesta non sunt in lege praesumenda:* odious and dishonest things are not to be presumed in law.

*Officium nemini debet esse damnosum:* an office ought to be injurious to no one [employed in it].

*Omissio eorum quae tacite insunt nihil operatur:* the omission of those things which are understood without special mention, is of no consequences.

*Omne majus in se continet minus:* the greater contains the less.

*Omne quod solo inaedificatur solo cedit:* every thing which is built upon the soil belongs to the soil.

*Omnes licentiam habent iis, quae pro se introducta sunt, renunciare:* every one has the right to renounce those stipulations which have been introduced for his own benefit.

*Omnia paesumuntur contra spoliatorem:* all things are presumed against a spoliator; *e.g.*, if he wrongfully withholds or destroys evidence in his possession, it will be presumed to be adverse.

*Omnia praesumuntur rite et solenniter esse acta donec probetur in contrarium:* all things are presumed to have been done properly and with due formalities, until it be proved to the contrary.

*Omnis innovatio plus novitate perturbat quam utilitate prodest:* every innovation occasions more harm by its novelty than benefit by its utility.

*Omnis ratihabitio retro-trahitur et mandato priori aequiparatur:* every ratification has a retrospective effect, and is equivalent to a previous request.

*Omnium contributione sarciatur quod pro omnibus datum est:* that which is given for all should be recouped by the contribution of all. A principle of the law of general average (*q.v.*)

*Optimus legum interpres consuetudo:* custom is the best interpreter of the laws.

*Pacta privata juri publico derogare non possunt:* private compacts can not derogate from public right.

*Paribus sententiis reus absolvitur:* where the opinions are equal, *i.e.*, the votes, or judges, are equally divided, judgment is for the defendant.

*Partus sequitur ventrem:* the offspring follows the dam. This maxim applies to the status of slaves and animals.

*Pater est quem nuptiae demonstrant:* he is the father whom the marriage points out.

*Pendente lite nihil innovetur:* during a litigation no change in the position of things, or of the parties, should be made.

*Plus peccat auctor quam actor:* the instigator of a crime offends more than the doer of it.

*Potior est conditio defendentis*, or *possidentis:* the condition of one defending, or possessing, is the better. See *Possession.*

*Praestat cautela quam medela:* caution, or prevention, is better than cure.

*Prior tempore, potior jure:* first in time, strongest in law.

*Privatorum conventio juri publico non derogat:* the agreements of private individuals can not derogate from the rights of the public.

*Privatum commodum publico cedit:* private advantage must yield to public.

*Privilegium non valet contra rempublicam:* a privilege avails not against the interest of the public

*Probandi necessitas incumbit illi qui agit:* the necessity of proving rests upon him who sues.

*Probatis extremis, praesumuntur media:* the extremes being proved, the mean is presumed.

*Quae communi legi derogant stricte interpretantur:* those things which derogate from the common law are to be strictly interpreted.

*Quae contra rationem juris introducta sunt, non debent trahi in consequentiam:* things introduced contrary to the spirit of the law ought not to be drawn into a precedent.

*Quae in curia regis acta sunt rite agi praesumuntur:* what has been done in court is presumed to be rightly done.

*Quae non valeant singula, juncta juvant:* things which may not avail singly, when united are effective

*Quaecunque intra rationem legis inveniuntur, intra legem ipsam esse judicantur:* those things which are within the reason of a law are considered to be within the letter of it.

*Quaelibet concessio fortissime contra donatorem interpretanda est:* every grant is to be construed most strongly against the grantor.

*Quando aliquid mandatur, mandatur et omne per quod pervenitur ad illud:* when any thing is commanded, every thing by which it must be accomplished is commanded.

*Quando aliquid prohibetur ex directo, prohibetur et per*

*obliquum:* when a thing is forbidden to be done directly, it is also forbidden to be done indirectly.

*Quando lex aliquid alicui concedit, concedere videtur et id sine quo res ipsa esse non potest:* when the law gives a man any thing, it gives him also that without which the thing can not exist. See, *e.g.*, *Way of necessity.*

*Quando res non valet ut ago, valeat quantum valere potest:* when any instrument does not operate in the way I intend, let it operate as far as it can.

*Quando verba statuti sunt specialia, ratio autem generalis, generaliter statutum est intelligendum:* when the words of a statute are special, but its object general, it is to be construed as general.

*Qui approbat non reprobat:* he who accepts [in part] can not reject.

*Qui destruit medium, destruit finem:* he who destroys the means, destroys the end.

*Qui facit per alium, facit per se:* he who does a thing through another does it himself; *i.e.*, a principal is liable for the acts of his agent acting within the scope of his authority.

*Qui haeret in litera, haeret in cortice:* he who sticks at the letter sticks in the bark; *i.e.*, does not get at the solid substance of the law.

*Qui in jus dominiumve alterius succedit jure ejus uti debet:* he who succeeds to the right or property of another should also perform his duties; *e.g.*, the heir is subject to the debts of his ancestor to the extent of any property coming to his hands as such.

*Qui in utero est pro jam nato habetur, quoties de ejus commodo quaeritur:* he who is in the womb is held as already born, whenever his benefit is in question. See *Gestation.*

*Qui mandat ipse fecisse videtur:* he who gives the order is taken to be himself the doer. Cf. *Qui facit per alium, etc.*

*Qui non improbat, approbat:* he who does not blame, approves.

*Qui non prohibet quod prohibere potest, assentire videtur:* he who does not forbid what he can forbid, is understood to assent.

*Qui parcit nocentibus, innocentes punit:* he who spares the guilty punishes the innocent.

*Qui per fraudem agit, frustra agit:* what a man does fraudulently, he does in vain: [for the courts will give relief against him.]

*Qui prior est tempore, potior est jure:* he who is first in time, is stronger in law.

*Qui sentit commodum, sentire debet et onus:* he who receives the advantage, ought also to bear the burden.

*Qui tacet, consentire videtur:* he who is silent is understood to consent.

*Qui tardius solvit, minus solvit:* he who pays too late pays too little.

*Qui vult decipi decipiatur:* let him be deceived who wishes to be deceived; *i.e.*, the court will not relieve a person who has been guilty of negligence so gross as to invite deception.

*Quicquid plantatur solo, solo cedit:* whatever is affixed to the soil, passes with a grant of the soil. See *Fixtures.*

*Quicquid solvitur, solvitur secundum modum solventis:* whatever is paid, is paid according to the direction of the payer: *i.e.*, the debtor may state, at the time of payment, which of two, or more, debts he intends to liquidate.

*Quilibet potest renunciare juri pro se introducto:* any one may give up a right introduced for his own benefit.

*Quo ligatur eo dissolvitur:* as an obligation is contracted so it must be dissolved; *e.g.*, a deed by a deed.

*Quod ab initio non valet, in tractu temporis non convalescet:* that which is invalid in its commencement, gains no strength by lapse of time.

*Quod contra legem fit, pro infecto habetur:* what is done contrary to law is considered as not done; *i.e.*, no one can derive lawful advantage from it.

*Quod fieri debet, facile praesumitur:* that which ought to be done is easily presumed.

*Quod fieri non debet, factum valet:* that which ougnt not to be done is [sometimes] valid when done; *e.g.*, a marriage without the proper consents.

*Quod necessitas cogit, excusat:* that which necessity compels she excuses; *i.e.*, a man is not held criminally responsible for actions which he is forced to commit.

*Quod nullius est, est domini regis:* that which is the property of nobody belongs to our lord the king. See *Waifs; Wreck.*

*Quod per me non possum, nec per alium:* what I can not do of myself, I can not do by another; *i.e.*, a person can not delegate a power he does not himself possess.

*Quod pure debetur, praesenti die debetur:* that which is due unconditionally, is due at once.

*Quod semel placuit in electione, amplius displicere non potest:* when election is once made it can not be revoked.

*Quod tacite intelligitur, deesse non videtur:* what is tacitly assumed does not appear to be wanting.

*Quod turpi ex causa promissum est, non valet:* a promise founded on an immoral consideration is not binding

*Quod vanum et inutile est, lex non requirit:* the law requires not what is vain and useless

*Quoties in verbis nulla est ambiguitas, ibi nulla expositio contra verba fienda est:* where there is no ambiguity in the words of an instrument, no interpretation must be given to it contrary to the words; *i.e.*, parol evidence to contradict or vary the clear words of a written instrument is inadmissible.

*Ratihabitio mandato aequiparatur:* ratification is tantamount to a direction

*Res inter alios acta, alteri nocere non debet:* a transaction between other persons should not prejudice one who was not a party to it.

*Res judicata pro veritate accepitur:* a thing adjudged is taken as true

*Res sua nemini servit:* no one can have an easement over his own property See *Easement.*

*Respondeat superior:* let the principal be held responsible.

*Rex non potest peccare:* the king can do no wrong.

*Rex nunquam moritur:* the king never dies; *i.e.*, the crown never falls vacant

*Salus populi* (or *reipublicae*) *suprema lex:* the safety of the commonwealth is the highest law.

*Salus ubi multi consiliarii:* where there are many counsellors there is safety.

*Satius est petere fontes quam sectari rivulos:* it is better to seek the source than to follow the streamlets; *i.e.*, it is better to examine original reports, etc., than to trust to quotations.

*Scire debes cum quo contrahis:* a man ought to know with whom he is contracting.

*Scire et scire debere aequiparantur in lege:* knowledge and the duty of knowing are held for the same, in law; *i.e.*, the law considers a man cognisant of that which he ought to know

*Scribere est agere.* writing is equivalent to doing; *i.e.*, in some crimes, as treason, writing is sufficient proof of intent.

*Semper in dubiis benigniora praeferenda:* in doubtful matters the more liberal construction is to be preferred.

*Semper in obscuris quod minimum est sequimur:* in obscure constructions we go no further than is necessary.

*Semper praesumitur pro matrimonio:* the presumption is always in favor of the validity of a marriage.

*Semper praesumitur pro negante:* the presumption is always in favor of the negative.

*Sic utere tuo ut alienum non laedas:* use your own so as not to injure another.

*Simplex commendatio non obligat:* mere recommendation does bind [like a warranty.]

*Socii mei socius, meus socius non est:* the partner of my partner is not my partner.

*Spoliatus debet ante omnia restitui:* a person who has been robbed ought first of all to have his goods restored.

*Stabit praesumptio donec probetur in contrarium:* a presumption stands until the contrary is proved.

*Stare decisis, et non quieta movere:* adhere to precedents and do not unsettle things established.

*Summum jus, summa injuria:* the strictest administration of the law sometimes works the greatest injustice.

*Suppressio veri, expressio falsi:* suppression of the truth is [equivalent to] a false representation

*Testamentum omne morte consummatur:* every will is perfected by death.

*Testes ponderantur non numerantur:* witnesses are weighed, not numbered; *i.e.*, the mere number of the witnesses brought forward to prove any fact is not so important as their credibility, judgment, etc.

*Traditio loqui facit chartam:* delivery makes a deed speak; *i.e.*, come into operation. See *Escrow*.

*Transit terra cum onere:* the land passes with its incumbrance

*Ubi aliquid conceditur, conceditur et id sine quo res ipsa esse non potest:* when any thing is granted, that also is granted without which it could not exist. See *e.g.*, *Way of necessity*.

*Ubi eadem ratio, ibi eadem lex:* where the same reason exists, there the same law prevails.

*Ubi jus, ibi remedium:* where there is a right there is a remedy.

*Unum est tacere, aliud celare:* it is one thing to be silent, another to conceal; *e.g.*, a vendor, in most cases, is not bound to disclose latent defects to an intending purchaser; but if he by fraudulent device conceal a defect which would otherwise be patent, the contract will be voidable by the purchaser.

*Unumquodque dissolvitur eodem modo quo colligatum est:* every obligation must be dissolved with the same solemnity with which it was created; *e.g.*, an obligation incurred under a deed can only be released by another deed.

*Utile per inutile non vitiatur:* the useful is not vitiated by the useless; *e.g.*, clear words of grant are not affected by words which are superfluous.

*Verba accipienda sunt secundum subjectam materiam:* words are to be understood with reference to the subject-matter.

*Verba aliquid operari debent:* words ought to be interpreted in such a way as to have some operation.

*Verba chartarum fortius accipiuntur contra proferentem:* the words of a grant are to be taken most strongly against the person employing them.

*Verba cum effectu accipienda sunt:* words ought to be used so as to give them their effect.

*Verba generalia restringuntur ad habilitatem rei vel aptitudinem personae:* general words must be narrowed to the nature of the subject, or the capacity of the person; *i.e.*, of the grantor.

*Verba illata, vel relata, inesse videntur:* words implied or referred to are considered to be incorporated.

*Verba intentioni debent inservire:* words ought to be made subervient to the intent.

*Verba ita sunt intelligenda, ut res magis valeat quam pereat:* words are to be so understood that the object may be carried out rather than fail. See *Benigne*, etc.

*Veritas demonstrationis tollit errorem nominis:* correctness of the description removes the error of the name; *e.g.*, in a will, if the identity of a legatee is established, a mere error in his name is unimportant.

*Via trita est tutissima:* the trodden path is the safest.

*Vicarius non habet vicarium:* a substitute can not have a substitute. See *Delegatus*, etc.

*Vigilantibus non dormientibus jura subveniunt:* laws come to the assistance of the vigilant, not of the sleepy. See *Laches*.

*Volenti non fit injuria:* no injury is done, in the eye of the law, where the person injured consents.

*Voluntas in delictis, non exitus spectatur:* in crimes the intention, and not the consequence, is looked to.

*Voluntas reputatur pro facto:* the will is to be taken for the deed.

*Voluntas testatoris est ambulatoria usque ad extremum vitae exitum:* the will of a testator is revocable until the latest moment of life.

*Vox emissa volat; litera scripta manet:* the spoken word flies away; the written one remains.

Made in United States
Cleveland, OH
26 September 2026

44826303R00208